"Only a scholar who has spent decades on the topic could deliver the excellent and nuanced study that Spencer provides here. His wide-ranging discussion of emotions as understood from both ancient philosophical and contemporary psychological and neurological studies illumines the reports of Jesus's emotions in the Gospels—those usually seen as negative as well as those we view as positive. But even beyond this, Spencer demonstrates how studies of emotions can help us overcome the limitations imposed by Enlightenment-bound understandings of the nature of God, of the incarnation, and of our own human nature. This is a welcome introduction to those not familiar with the study of emotion in biblical texts, and it is an advance of the discussion for scholars in the field."

—**Jerry L. Sumney**, Lexington Theological Seminary

"In *Passions of the Christ*, Spencer has done an extremely impressive job of combining erudite New Testament exegesis with his vast knowledge of ancient and contemporary philosophy, theology, and psychological research on emotions. By highlighting the value of giving proper attention to the emotions of Jesus as they are described in the Gospels, Spencer not only enriches his readers' understanding of the passionate Christ but also illuminates often overlooked emphases in each pericope discussed. In short, this book is a highly valuable interdisciplinary approach to the study of the Gospels' portrayals of Jesus."

—**Kathy Barrett Dawson**, East Carolina University

Passions
of the
Christ

*The Emotional Life
of Jesus in the Gospels*

F. SCOTT SPENCER

Baker Academic
a division of Baker Publishing Group
Grand Rapids, Michigan

Published by Baker Academic
a division of Baker Publishing Group
PO Box 6287, Grand Rapids, MI 49516-6287
www.bakeracademic.com

Printed in the United States of America

Library of Congress Cataloging-in-Publication Data
Names: Spencer, F. Scott (Franklin Scott), author.
Title: Passions of the Christ : the emotional life of Jesus in the gospels / F. Scott Spencer.
Description: Grand Rapids, Michigan : Baker Academic, a division of Baker Publishing Group,
    2021. | Includes bibliographical references and index.
Identifiers: LCCN 2020037104 | ISBN 9781540961761 (paperback) | ISBN 9781540964465
    (casebound)
Subjects: LCSH: Jesus Christ. | Emotions—Religious aspects—Christianity.
Classification: LCC BT218 .S64 2021 | DDC 232.9/03—dc23
LC record available at https://lccn.loc.gov/2020037104

21 22 23 24 25 26 27   7 6 5 4 3 2 1

To Lauren and Mark, Meredith and Jimmy
(and Oscar, Lucinda, and Seamus)

Contents

Preface

About a dozen years ago I began to notice how hot the study of emotions had become across a wide array of disciplines in both the humanities and the sciences. As the historian Jan Plamper reflected in 2012, "I write during a boom in the history of emotions; there is gold rush fever in the air."[1] As it happens, that was the same year I cofounded and cochaired with Matthew Schlimm the new "Bible and Emotion" consultation for the Society of Biblical Literature (it became a continuing group in 2015), with the aim of "understanding the spectrum of emotions displayed throughout the Bible in their literary and cultural contexts, informed by the burgeoning cross-disciplinary study of emotion."[2] Paper and panel sessions ensued at the annual SBL meetings, along with a published collection of seventeen essays by an international team of scholars, which I edited for SBL Press under the title *Mixed Feelings and Vexed Passions: Exploring Emotions in Biblical Literature* (2017).

The present volume represents the fruit of my particular interest in the emotional life of Jesus portrayed in the canonical Gospels, interweaving close textual analysis of relevant Gospel texts with ancient and modern theological, philosophical, and psychological approaches to emotion study. It offers, I believe, the most thorough exegetical-cum-interdisciplinary investigation of the subject to date.

A handful of other recent studies of Jesus's emotions (biblical scholars paid little attention to the matter until this century) have also capitalized on the broader surge of emotion research to various degrees. Matthew Elliott's

1. Plamper, *History of Emotions*, 297 (English translation of 2012 German original).
2. Spencer, *Mixed Feelings*, 2.

Faithful Feelings: Rethinking Emotion in the New Testament (2006) admirably
engages with overarching Greco-Roman and Jewish contexts and cognitive
theories of emotion in particular in its helpful survey of the emotions of love,
joy, hope, jealousy, fear, sorrow, and anger across the New Testament writings.
Its broad scope of coverage, however, necessarily limits its depth of probing
any single part of the New Testament, such as the four Gospels. Karl Allen
Kuhn's *The Heart of Biblical Narrative: Rediscovering Biblical Appeal to the
Emotions* (2009) is also attuned to current developments in emotion theory;
however, it makes no attempt to be comprehensive, telescoping its textual
focus on Luke 1–2 as a test case for "affective-rhetorical analysis" of biblical
narratives, leaving the bulk of Jesus's life and ministry unexamined.[3] By contrast, Stephen Voorwinde's *Jesus' Emotions in the Gospels* (2011) canvasses
the whole terrain of the four canonical Gospels with solid exegesis informed
by Old Testament interlinks, but it shows scant interest in Greco-Roman or
modern multidisciplinary assessments of emotions.[4]

Standing most apart in the group, Roy M. Oswald and Arland Jacobson's
The Emotional Intelligence of Jesus: Relational Smarts for Religious Leaders
(2015) tracks Jesus's overall "emotional intelligence" or EQ (distinct from
IQ) profile—in terms of self-awareness, transparency, empathy, inspiration,
assertiveness, optimism, and stress resilience, among other traits—as a model
for modern pastors and congregations. Although sketching a winsome picture
of Jesus's emotional demeanor in the Gospels (Jacobson is a trained New
Testament scholar as well as a pastor), it does so in broad strokes; cursory
examination of Gospel texts offers a thin springboard for diving into extended
applications to contemporary religious leadership.

I appreciate the contributions these monographs and their authors (and
others I might have overlooked) have made to kick-starting interest in Jesus's
emotional life in the Gospel narratives in dialogue with cross-disciplinary
emotion research. Again, however, I hope that this book significantly moves
the discussion down the field, covering more textual and theoretical ground
in a compelling way.

A quick glance at the table of contents will disclose roughly equivalent
concentrations on Jesus's negative/vehement (anger, anguish, disgust) and
positive/virtuous (surprise, love, joy) emotions, resisting simplistic assessments of Jesus's high EQ.[5] Increasingly, however, researchers in the arts and

3. See Spencer, review of *Heart of Biblical Narrative*.
4. See Spencer, review of *Jesus' Emotions*.
5. As suggested in Oswald and Jacobson, *Emotional Intelligence*, 11: "The portrait of Jesus
in the Gospels is remarkably consistent: he eschewed negative emotions such as fear, anger, and
hatred, and he displayed as well as demanded only positive emotions."

sciences have questioned the validity of strict, binary negative versus positive valences in emotion labeling.[6] Humans are emotionally complex beings, intertwining a welter of dynamic feelings for good and ill and everything in between. All feelings are mixed to some degree betwixt and between intricate neural circuits, social networks, and environmental ecosystems. Although the Gospels provide nothing close to a full psychological profile of Jesus, they do provocatively illustrate some rich facets of his emotional life, the Word made *feeling* together with flesh.

While I've experienced a raft of mixed emotions over the years I've worked on this project, overall it has been an immensely enjoyable undertaking, made all the more so by the continuing support of my life partner, Dr. Janet M. Spencer, who has just begun her well-deserved retirement from a long and fruitful teaching career. Looking forward to many more happy, adventurous years together!

I'm also grateful for the stellar team at Baker Academic shepherding this project to publication. Particular shout-outs go to senior acquisitions editor Bryan Dyer for believing in this book from the start, nudging me along the way, and making some key structural suggestions at the end and to my stellar project editor, Melisa Blok, for her eagle eye, keen judgment, and meticulous attention to the myriad final details of producing a first-rate manuscript. I'm also thankful for continued access to the resources of the Morton Library at Union Presbyterian Seminary, one of the top theological libraries in the country.

Finally, a couple of nuts-and-bolts matters for readers' attention: sources in footnotes are cited in abbreviated form, and full bibliographic information is provided at the back of the book; and unless otherwise noted, I quote from the New Revised Standard Version (NRSV) of the Bible.

---

6. See Kashdan and Biswas-Diener, *Upside of Your Dark Side*; Ivtzan, Lomas, Hefferon, and Worth, *Second Wave Positive Psychology*; Kaufman, *Transcend*, 274–75.

Abbreviations

General and Bibliographic

ABD	*The Anchor Bible Dictionary*. Edited by David N. Freedman et al. 6 vols. New York: Doubleday, 1992.
ANF	*The Ante-Nicene Fathers*. Edited by Alexander Roberts and James Donaldson. 10 vols. New York: Christian Literature, 1885–96. Reprint, Grand Rapids: Eerdmans, 1950–51.
art(s).	article(s)
AT	author's translation
BCE	before the Common Era
BD	Beloved Disciple in John's Gospel
BDAG	Walter Bauer, Frederick W. Danker, William F. Arndt, and F. Wilbur Gingrich. *A Greek-English Lexicon of the New Testament and Other Early Christian Literature*. 3rd ed. Chicago: University of Chicago Press, 2000.
CE	Common Era
CEB	Common English Bible
chap(s).	chapter(s)
KJV	King James Version
L&N	Johannes P. Louw and Eugene A. Nida, eds. *Greek-English Lexicon of the New Testament: Based on Semantic Domains*. 2nd ed. 2 vols. New York: United Bible Societies, 1988–89.
LCL	Loeb Classical Library
LXX	Septuagint/Greek Old Testament
MM	James H. Moulton and George Milligan. *The Vocabulary of the Greek New Testament*. London: Hodder & Stoughton, 1930.
n.	note
NAB	New American Bible
NASB	New American Standard Bible
NETS	New English Translation of the Septuagint
NIDB	*New Interpreter's Dictionary of the Bible*. Edited by Katharine Doob Sakenfeld. 5 vols. Nashville: Abingdon, 2006–9.

NIV   New International Version
NJPS   *The Tanakh: The Holy Scriptures: The New JPS Translation according to the Traditional Hebrew Text*
NPNF²   *A Select Library of Nicene and Post-Nicene Fathers of the Christian Church.* Edited by Philip Schaff and Henry Wace. 2nd series. 14 vols. New York: Christian Literature, 1890–1900. Reprint, Grand Rapids: Eerdmans, 1952.
NRSV   New Revised Standard Version
pt.   part
q.   question
RSV   Revised Standard Version

Old Testament

Gen.	Genesis	Song	Song of Songs
Exod.	Exodus	Isa.	Isaiah
Lev.	Leviticus	Jer.	Jeremiah
Num.	Numbers	Lam.	Lamentations
Deut.	Deuteronomy	Ezek.	Ezekiel
Josh.	Joshua	Dan.	Daniel
Ruth	Ruth	Hosea	Hosea
1 Sam.	1 Samuel	Joel	Joel
2 Sam.	2 Samuel	Amos	Amos
1 Kings	1 Kings	Jon.	Jonah
2 Kings	2 Kings	Mic.	Micah
Ezra	Ezra	Nah.	Nahum
Neh.	Nehemiah	Hab.	Habakkuk
Job	Job	Zeph.	Zephaniah
Ps(s).	Psalm(s)	Hag.	Haggai
Prov.	Proverbs	Zech.	Zechariah
Eccles.	Ecclesiastes	Mal.	Malachi

New Testament

Matt.	Matthew	Col.	Colossians
Mark	Mark	1 Tim.	1 Timothy
Luke	Luke	2 Tim.	2 Timothy
John	John	Philem.	Philemon
Acts	Acts	Heb.	Hebrews
Rom.	Romans	James	James
1 Cor.	1 Corinthians	1 Pet.	1 Peter
2 Cor.	2 Corinthians	2 Pet.	2 Peter
Gal.	Galatians	1 John	1 John
Eph.	Ephesians	Rev.	Revelation
Phil.	Philippians		

Old Testament Apocrypha

Jdt.	Judith	Sus.	Susanna
1–4 Macc.	1–4 Maccabees	Tob.	Tobit
Sir.	Sirach	Wis.	Wisdom (of Solomon)

Rabbinic Sources

m. Hag.	Mishnah Hagigah

Other Ancient Sources

Abr.	Philo, *On the Life of Abraham*	*Nem.*	Pindar, *Nemean Odes*
		Ol.	Pindar, *Olympian Odes*
Acts Pet.	*Acts of Peter*	*QG*	Philo, *Questions and Answers on Genesis*
Ant.	Josephus, *Jewish Antiquities*		
De. an.	Aristotle, *De anima*	*Rhet.*	Aristotle, *On Rhetoric*
Eth. nic.	Aristotle, *Nicomachean Ethics*	*Rust.*	Varro, *De re rustica*
		Satyr.	Petronius, *Satyricon*
Hist. eccl.	Eusebius, *Historia ecclesiastica*	*Theaet.*	Plato, *Theaetetus*
		Tim.	Plato, *Timaeus*
J.W.	Josephus, *Jewish War*	*Tusc.*	Cicero, *Tusculanae disputationes*
Lael. Amic.	Cicero, *Laelius de Amicitia*		
Let.	Seneca, *Letters on Ethics*	*T. Zeb.*	*Testament of Zebulun*
Lives	Diogenes Laertius, *Lives of Eminent Philosophers*	*Worse*	Philo, *That the Worse Attacks the Better*
Mart. Pet.	*Martyrdom of Peter*		
Men.	Lucian, *Menippus*		
Metaph.	Aristotle, *Metaphysics*		

PART 1

MISSION IM/PASSIBLE: THEORY AND THEOLOGY

*M*ission Impossible, one of the most popular television series of the 1960s and '70s and later a successful movie franchise, features the super-secret Impossible Mission Force (IMF) tackling the most difficult espionage cases—and solving them, of course, making the impossible possible. But don't try this on your own! By definition, the agents of IMF with their genius talents and high-tech gadgets are exceptional: if not superheroes or gods, certainly not your average Joes and Joans.

Sober theological analysis, however, outside the fantasy moving-picture world of TV and cinema, demands a firm grip on reality and, typically, a strict distinction between divine and human capacity: "I am God and not a human being, the holy one in your midst" (Hosea 11:9 CEB); "Nothing is impossible for God" (Luke 1:37 CEB); "What is impossible for humans is possible for God" (18:27 CEB). God's power is infinitely greater than any human effort, just as God's ways and thoughts are unimaginably higher than our ways and thoughts, "as the heavens are higher than the earth" (Isa. 55:8–9). Greater, higher, wholly Other in action and thought—and certainly *feeling*, too, if in fact God has feelings in any sense comparable to our feelings.

Therein lies the problem. Feelings, emotions, passions, sentiments, by whatever name, are quintessentially volatile human responses to a volatile world, "geological upheavals of thought," as Proust labeled "Love," especially, but

also "Rage, Jealousy, Curiosity, Envy, Hate, Suffering, Pride, Astonishment."[1]
If God has such emotions, surely they must be categorically different from
ordinary human feelings. God's anger or jealousy—both attributed to God
in the Bible—must be of a higher order than their human correlates. And
the very core of God's being, love—God Is Love! (1 John 4:8)—certainly
transcends the imbroglio of emotions we call "love," subject to so many vicis-
situdes and vulnerabilities. Whereas we weak humans are utterly passible—
subject to an array of passions impossible for us to control fully—the God
of all potentialities and possibilities is thoroughly impassible, according to
traditional thought. In contrast to an ever-feckless people, God's faithfulness
remains immutable. In the face of an ever-changing world God declares, "I
am the LORD, and I do not change" (Mal. 3:6 CEB). The mission of God is
Mission Impassible.

Or is it? Is it not possible for God to opt to be passible, especially since all
things are possible with God? Is it not possible that God fully plunges into
the creational process, with "hands"-on involvement in the earth, "breathing"
in-and-out with human beings molded in God's image (Gen. 1:26–27; 2:7)?
Is it not possible that God moves with creation and is moved by it, that God
evolves and emotes in some fashion, feeling God's way through, so to speak,
the unfolding experiences of a "groaning" creation and "children of God"
(Rom. 8:18–28)? Or is there some middle way to incorporate a sincerely sympathetic, compassionate, emotional God into the doctrine of the impassible
God? In the wake of two devastating world wars wreaking unprecedented
hell on earth, Christian theology of the latter twentieth and early twenty-first
centuries has passionately engaged the matter of divine passion anew, as I
will discuss in chapter 2.

This critical matter of the "passion of the passionate God"[2] bears on our
interest in the passions of the Christ in the Gospels because these narratives
present Jesus, each in their own ways, as the incarnation of God: "God with
us" (Matt. 1:23 CEB), "Jesus Christ, the Son of God" (Mark 1:1), "a Savior,
who is the Messiah, the Lord" (Luke 2:11), and "the Word became flesh"
(John 1:14). In telling their dynamic stories of Jesus the Christ, the embodied
Son of God, the Gospels are not interested in calibrating the metaphysics of
Jesus's human and divine "natures." Jesus is one holistic person, not a hybrid
or a composite. He is a unique person to be sure, not simply as every human
being is unique in some respects but uniquely filled with God's Spirit, wholly

---

1. Proust, *Remembrance of Things Past*, quoted in and providing the title for the monumen-
tal work on emotions by the philosopher Martha C. Nussbaum, *Upheavals of Thought*, vii.
2. Moltmann, "*Crucified God* Yesterday and Today," 74.

attuned with his Father's will, totally obedient to God's word, utterly "intoxicated" with God's love.[3] He is divinely human and humanly divine through and through, not a specimen to be dissected in a theological laboratory. The Gospels show and tell the nature of Christ by how he lives and dies in flesh, blood, bone, breath, voice—and *feeling*—on earth.

Without full emotional capacity, Jesus can lay no claim to full participation in human experience. By the same token, whatever the human Jesus feels, he also feels *as* God's Son. The human capacity for emotion within Jesus is not cordoned off in some separate compartment from his divine character, as if suffering from a split personality or struggling with a genetic duality like the fictional Commander Spock of Vulcan-human descent. Without attempting to explain in philosophical terms the profound mystery of Jesus the God-Man, the Gospels implicitly accept a certain integral logic regarding the person of Jesus Christ. Whatever he feels (and thinks and says and does) in the Gospels, he feels (and thinks and says and does) as the unitary God-and-Man; or put another way, Jesus the Son reveals the passions of his divine Father. In the words of the Fourth Gospel's prologue: "No one has ever seen God. It is God the only Son, who is close to the Father's heart, who has made him known" (John 1:18). We may thus discern a certain *pathos logic* pulsing throughout the Gospel portraits of Jesus the Christ, while acknowledging the need to defend this proposition in the face of more hardnosed, "higher" Christological thinkers who might regard exposing a spectrum of Jesus's emotions—including anger, anguish, disgust, and surprise as well as love and joy—as just plain "pathological" (degraded, deformed, diseased).

If passions or emotions associated with God and Christ have remained suspect in much of Western Christian theology, they have not fared much better in Western philosophy and psychology under the aegis of Lord Reason. Descartes declaimed "I think, therefore I am," not "I feel," though he did write a thoughtful work titled *The Passions of the Soul*. Nonetheless, the dichotomy between reason and passion, head and heart, runs deep in the Western tradition, with no doubt about which side is superior.

But recent decades have seen a remarkable renaissance of emotion theory and research across disciplines in the humanities and sciences. Scarcely any field of study has been untouched by this burgeoning interest in emotions—not

3. See Borg, "Jesus and the Christian Life": "Jesus is for us as Christians the decisive revelation of what a life full of God is like. . . . The human Jesus is the Spirit of God embodied in human life. . . . He was like the great social prophets of the Hebrew Bible or the Old Testament—people who also had vivid experiences of God and who in the name of God became God-intoxicated voices of religious, social protests directed against the domination systems of their day." Cf. Borg, *Heart of Christianity*, 91, 130.

least an emphasis on "the intelligence of emotions"[4] and the interplay between cognitive and affective experience—although biblical studies has been slower to join the party. While it's impossible to survey the total landscape of contemporary emotion analysis, I endeavor in chapter 1 to sketch some broad, "reasonable" interdisciplinary frameworks for investigating Jesus's emotions in the Gospels.[5] While the heart of this study features close contextual readings of relevant Gospel texts, these introductory chapters provide theoretical and theological lenses to sharpen those readings.

4. The subtitle of Nussbaum, *Upheavals of Thought*.
5. Subsequent chapters provide additional theoretical frameworks, each pertinent to the specific emotion under investigation.

1

Emotion Theory
and the Passional Christt

The "Passion" pulses at the heart of Christian history, theology, liturgy, and media and is focused on Jesus's final days from the Last Supper to his crucifixion. The capitalized term, which has appeared in English dictionaries since the Middle Ages,[1] derives from the Latin *passio*, "suffering." Memorialized in countless sermons and commentaries, but most dramatically in scores of paintings, sculptures, plays, hymns, and films, the Passion of the Christ has left its deepest defining marks—virtual stigmata—on the church, the collective body of Christ. The way of Christ that his disciples must "take up" is quintessentially the way of the cross (Matt. 16:24; Mark 8:34; Luke 9:23), the Via Dolorosa.

In Christian parlance, then, "Passion" functions as a technical term for Jesus's redemptive suffering, strictly demarcated from more common (vulgar) ancient and modern meanings of the word. Ironically, though the Greek verb *paschō* ("suffer") appears frequently in the New Testament, the related noun *pathos* appears only in lists of vices that proscribe acting on immoral "passions" or lusts (Rom. 1:26; Col. 3:5; 1 Thess. 4:5). Apart from having nothing to do with the events surrounding Jesus's death, this (im)moralized usage of "passion" language does not account for a wider semantic range in Greek and English encompassing a swath of emotions associated not only with painful experiences but also with pleasurable ones. Today's English associates "passion" not only with ardent

---

1. Fisher, *Vehement Passions*, 4–5.

sexual desire, variously celebrated or censured, but also with rapt dedication to some pursuit, serious or frivolous, attended by a spate of emotions. We may declare ourselves, for example, deeply passionate about social justice or cancer research, on one hand, or about chocolate pie or argyle socks, on the other.

Be Aware of Greeks Bearing Emotions

Since Aristotle, generally regarded as the father of emotion theory, the "passions" (*pathē*) correlate with our conception of common emotions like fear (*phobos*) and anger (*orgē*)—"and their opposites," calmness (*praotēs*) and love (*philia*) (*Rhet.* 2.1.8–2.4.29 [1378a–81b]). This is not to say, given the cultural shaping of emotional experience, that Aristotle and I would understand the concept of fear, for example, in precisely the same way, still less that we would dread the same threats. (For all the precariousness of life for ancient peoples, they didn't need to worry about nuclear annihilation or global warming.) But with a good translator, Aristotle and I could have a reasonable conversation about human emotions based on broadly shared feelings "accompanied by pain and pleasure" (2.1.8 [1378a]).

Classics scholar William Harris sums up the expanding notion of emotion-laden pathos: "The principal [Greek] verb for suffering, *paschō*, eventually [by the fourth century BCE] came to include the specialized meaning 'experience emotionally,' while in the same period the noun *pathos* came to mean 'passion' or 'emotion.'"[2] This fleshed out and felt out concept of emotionality bridges ancient and modern psychology, without denying the difficulties of crossing the divide with sympathetic understanding, fully "feeling with" ancient Mediterranean persons; we have a hard enough time sympathizing with current neighbors, even more with strangers. Harris, however, narrows bridge traffic to a single negative lane with his assessment that "the Greeks often thought of emotions as hostile disease-like forces outside the person."[3] So much for the positive role of pleasurable passions/emotions in Aristotle's thought, though his writings admit to various interpretations on the subject.[4] Harris's medical-viral model seems more suited to Hellenistic Stoic ideas than to Aristotle's, but in any case we can readily relate to feeling overwhelmed—attacked, even—by waves of anger or despair, as if they were alien, invading forces, even though modern emotion scientists dispute this etiology.

---

2. Harris, *Restraining Rage*, 342.
3. Harris, *Restraining Rage*, 342.
4. Fortenbaugh, *Aristotle on Emotion*; Nussbaum, *Therapy of Desire*, 78–101; Frede, "'Mixed Feelings.'"

Another classics specialist, David Konstan, has examined a wider range of emotions in ancient Greek thought than has Harris, who focuses on anger. Konstan cautions against assuming facile correspondences of emotion language across cultures; translation often betrays as much as it conveys (*traduttore, traditore*). Yet all is not lost in translation: "The *pathē* [still] appear to correspond broadly with the kinds of sentiments that we typically or at least sometimes classify as emotions. Often, however, the context will demand some variation."[5] A sensible, balanced framework for fruitful research, it seems to me.[6]

Getting Emotional about Jesus

From this springboard we launch, with both keen interest and due caution, into studying Jesus's "passions" in relation to his overall emotional life recounted in Greek by the four canonical Gospels. These ancient writings provide no catalog of Jesus's *pathē*, nothing approaching the kind of in-depth psychological profile we find in many modern biographies and novels. Like other biblical narratives, the Gospels chiefly tell about and show characters in action—what they say and do more than what they think and feel. Yet while the Gospels do not detail Jesus's introspective broodings, neither do they completely efface his emotions as somehow unworthy (irrational, unmanly, undisciplined) of his noble nature as Son of God and Humankind.

Still, as we consider the Passion accounts, we must not gloss over, either by omission or emendation, the emotional episode at Gethsemane/Olivet that depicts Jesus passionately pleading—punctuated by grief, sweat, and anxiety—to bypass his looming execution.[7] While the Synoptic Gospels negotiate this fraught scene in different ways, none attempts to sap its emotional poignancy (Matt. 26:36–46; Mark 14:32–42; Luke 22:40–46). The Fourth Gospel, however, all but annuls the Gethsemane tradition: "Now my soul is troubled. And what should I say—'Father, save me from this hour'? *No, it is for this reason I have come to this hour*" (John 12:27). At least John allows for some "troubling" of Jesus's "soul" (*psychē*) here, for intense emotions (including grief) at Lazarus's tomb in the previous chapter (11:33–35, 38), and elsewhere.[8] Nonetheless, John sets a precedent for discomfort over Jesus's vulnerable emotional state in Gethsemane on Maundy Thursday, abundantly evidenced in later interpretation.[9]

5. Konstan, *Emotions of the Ancient Greeks*, 4.
6. See Spencer, "Getting a Feel," 4–15, 30–32.
7. See a detailed discussion of this incident in chap. 5 of this study.
8. See Voorwinde, *Jesus' Emotions*.
9. See Madigan, "Ancient and High-Medieval Interpretations."

My project aims to correct skewed images of Jesus as a tough-as-nails strongman and hyper-stoical martyr (like Socrates), images based on a dispassionate interpretation of his Passion, oddly enough, and a disproportionate reading of the Gospel narratives. Martin Kähler's famous footnote casting Mark's Gospel as a "passion narrative with an extended introduction"[10] encapsulates the dominant preoccupation with Jesus's death in Christian faith, abetted by the centrality of "Christ crucified" in Paul's gospel (1 Cor. 1:23; 2:2), with lesser interest in Jesus's earthly career. In the four Gospels, however, reports of Jesus's baptism and temptation, preaching and teaching, healing and feeding, calling and guiding disciples, and challenging and debating authorities, while propelling him toward his crucifixion are no mere preludes to it but rather integral parts of the whole gospel (good news), carefully unfolded in the Gospel books. Taken in toto, Matthew, Mark, Luke, and John represent multifaceted *passional* narratives of Jesus's overall restorative mission—from birth to death (and resurrection)—to a suffering world, carried out with fervent *passion(s)*.[11]

Along with displaying Jesus's grief, the Gospels also feature, in varying degrees, his emotions of anger, disgust, surprise, joy, and, of course, compassion (this "passion" has always gotten a special pass, especially when apotheosized as "agapic" love). Most lists of basic emotions include all these, but they typically also include fear, which is conspicuously absent from Gospel portraits of Jesus's own feelings.[12] Though provoking fear among his adherents and opponents alike, Jesus is never explicitly said to be afraid. Yet fear terminology in any language can cover a swath of feelings, variously nuanced by related notions of terror, dread, fright, panic, timidity, shock, or awe. How we divvy up emotions proves less useful for understanding them than delving into the granularity and differentiation of each emotional situation and the language used to conceptualize it.[13] We thus seek to discover and unravel the thick texture of Jesus's emotional experience presented in the intricate narrative webs of the Gospel texts.[14]

Sympathetic Theology

Beyond giving due attention to Jesus's emotions in the Gospel records, I aim to view these emotions considerately rather than combatively, sympathetically

10. Kähler, *So-Called Historical Jesus*, 80n11; Kee, *Community of the New Age*, 30–31.

11. See my discussion of Luke's "passional theology" in Spencer, *Luke*, 706–32.

12. See Ekman and Cordaro, "What Is Meant?"; Cowen and Keltner, "Self-Report."

13. L. Barrett, *How Emotions Are Made*, 2–3, 121, 180–83, 246; Tugade, Fredrickson, and Barrett, "Psychological Resilience"; Nook et al., "Nonlinear Development."

14. See Robbins, *Exploring the Texture of Texts*.

rather than apologetically. In other words, rather than sanding off the rough edges of Jesus's emotional life that don't fit some dogmatic christological mold, I try to examine his reported passions in light of "normal" human experience as understood by ancient and modern emotion theorists and scientists. The Jesus of the Gospels feels with us, and we with him.

Yet I stay attuned to theology as well as anthropology. Each Gospel in its own way presents Jesus as the incarnation of God in the world. He is a human male reflecting God's image, like Adam and all men—and like Eve and all women (Gen. 1:27)—but to the ultimate degree: "the light of the gospel of the glory of Christ, who is the image of God" (2 Cor. 4:4); "the image of the invisible God, the firstborn of all creation" (Col. 1:15); "the exact imprint of God's very being" (Heb. 1:3). While the Gospels do not use this "iconic" (*eikōn*) language about Jesus, their stories patently depict his extraordinary relationship with and reflection of God. He is God's Son, with distinctive as well as associative status among all God's children.[15] He is Lord, Savior, and Messiah of God's household. Accordingly, he is passionately engaged with God, God's people, and God's world—as God is.

This affirmation of divine emotionality flies in the face of longstanding doctrine on God's impassible, immutable nature. In the next chapter I will argue the case for God's pathos. For now, I simply clarify my reading of Jesus's emotions in the Gospels as positive and appreciative from both divine and human perspectives. This is not to foreclose critical readings. When Jesus's emotions "get the best of him," is it always in the most salutary way? Perhaps not. We will certainly see the Gospels differing among themselves in evaluating Jesus's emotional responses in various situations. But overall, I approach Jesus's passions, whether painful or pleasurable, rough or smooth, not as alien forces to be extirpated by him or his interpreters but as integral feelings to be embraced, unpacked, and understood as formative components of Jesus's person and work. A dispassionate, unemotional Jesus is simply not believable.

The Importance of Being Emotional

The recent explosion of interest in emotion study across the humanities and sciences has provoked much debate, as should be expected with new methodologies and theories about the complex and often unconscious phenomena we designate "emotions"—or "passions," "feelings," "sentiments," "affections," and so on. We're not even sure what to call them![16] Functional magnetic

15. See Peppard, *Son of God*; Spencer, "Son of God."
16. See Izard, "Many Meanings/Aspects"; Dixon, "'Emotion.'"

resonance imaging (fMRI) of neural traffic in the brain has revolutionized emotion research but hardly settled every question. What exactly does mapping a particular emotional experience onto an electrochemical grid *mean* for that experience?[17] As important as our brains are to everything we do, to feeling as much as to thinking, we are not simply (or essentially) brains ensconced in a bone helmet perched on a skin-bagged skeleton for transport. The most persuasive theories of mind (ToM) advanced by psychologists and philosophers are expansive and connective rather than reductive and partitive. Daniel Siegel, for example, pushes beyond "enskulled" or "brainbound" models of "mental activities, such as emotions, thoughts, and memories," to incorporate the "body's whole state" in relation to, "within and between," other persons and objects.[18] In short, the mind, not least its emotional processes, operates in "both a fully embodied and relationally embedded" circuit of energy.[19]

Consonant with this dynamic "extended mind"[20] is a consensus about the vital importance of emotions to human functioning. Emotions matter to surviving and thriving in life. Pure reason, for all its vaunted value to advance our welfare through "enlightened" scientific method, is too measured and cumbersome to save us without emotive oomph. While I'm deliberating on a hiking trail whether the serpentine image flashing across my field of vision is a snake or a stick—and, if the former, a poisonous or harmless variety—I might well feel the venomous fangs before I'm through thinking. Thankfully, however, before it came to that perilous puncture, gut-level fear would kick in and hopefully propel me out of harm's way; then, at a safe distance, I might undertake a more considered examination of the object—with binoculars!

Fear is not the only emotion that can save our lives. Anger can stoke us to defend ourselves in a fight; disgust can deter us from consuming or coming into contact with lethal polluted substances; love can draw us into healing and nurturing relationships. Emotions are far from foolish or irrational. They are smart, quick smart. They make judgments about an object or situation often before we know it, snap judgments, sharp judgments, sensible judgments. Strict Cartesian dualism between reason and emotion doesn't fly anymore.

Yet emotional judgments are hardly infallible; then again, neither are more disputative, dispassionate decisions—"no *actual* mental process is infallible."[21] Just as one can think a thought to death, reason oneself into a corner, or refuse

17. See Adolphs and Anderson, *Neuroscience of Emotion*.
18. Siegel, *Mind*, 10, 14; on "brainbound" models, see Clark, *Supersizing the Mind*, xxv–xxix.
19. Siegel, *Mind*, 47 (cf. 10–16, 33–41, 46–48).
20. Clark and Chalmers, "Extended Mind."
21. Railton, "Morality and Prospection," 238 (emphasis added).

to consider counterevidence to one's conclusion, emotion can lead one astray. Fear can paralyze critical action or metastasize into crippling phobia. Disgust can bleed over from contaminant elements to despicable persons, as we might color them for all sorts of emotionally skewed "reasons." Anger, including so-called righteous indignation, can explode into cruel and disproportional vengeance, and even love can become obsessive and possessive to the serious detriment of the parties involved. In any case, emotion, cognition, volition, and other ways we categorize "mind" operations do not constitute discrete components. Though serving a certain heuristic purpose for analysis, they are dynamically interconnected, for better or worse, in embodied personal and social networks. With Walt Whitman, we "sing the body electric."[22]

While brain lesions or injuries can severely hamper emotional intelligence,[23] emotional capacity in general or particular emotions like fear do not strictly isolate in a single module of the brain or neural channel. Neuroimaging techniques can discover traces of emotional mechanics, but emotions cannot yet be—and may never be—pinpointed on an anatomical map, like bones and muscles; emotions do not have fixed "fingerprints."[24] Emotions flow more like the bloodstream than slot in place like the skeletal system.

For good or ill, we are emotional-rational, rational-emotional beings. Any way you slice it, emotions matter a great deal for human life. Correlative with emotions' importance for survival and well-being is their critical role in assessing what is particularly important to a person or group: what matters most, what drives beliefs and behaviors, what shapes the dreams and goals one pursues. Contemporary psychologists and philosophers agree widely on this fundamental motivational purpose of emotions, if not on the fine points of how this goal orientation plays out. Psychologist Richard Lazarus propounds "the motivational principle" of emotions within a broad-based "cognitive-motivational-relational theory."[25] Central to this approach is unpacking various "appraisal components" of emotions, first and foremost that of "goal relevance" concerning "the extent to which an encounter touches on personal goals—that is . . . issues in the encounter about which the person cares or in which there is a personal stake. If there is no goal relevance, there cannot be an emotion." Lazarus goes on to subdivide emotional appraisals into "congruent," "incongruent," and "ego-involved" elements. In other words, an emotion may signal and spur active support for valued goals

22. Whitman, "I Sing the Body Electric."
23. See Damasio, *Descartes' Error.*
24. L. Barrett, *How Emotions Are Made,* 1–24.
25. R. Lazarus, *Emotion and Adaptation,* 92–112; cf. R. Lazarus and B. Lazarus, *Passion and Reason,* 39–51.

(congruence) or resistance to perceived obstacles to such goals (incongru-
ence) in the interest of advancing "personal commitments" and solidifying
self-identity (ego-involvement).[26]

Take, for example, an emotional encounter with a judge or city official
who unfairly enforces housing laws to favor racial segregation. More than a
knee-jerk outburst from my hot Italian blood on my mother's side, my anger
may reflect an affront to my commitment to social justice and fuel "action
readiness" to do something to rectify the problem.[27] Whether the case directly
involves me or not, I take it personally. I may or may not correctly construe
the magistrate's decision. I may not get all the facts straight. Appraisal is an
ongoing, adjustable process. But feelings are themselves "facts" of life, integral to sorting out the factuality of our lives: who we are, how we operate,
what we truly care about. Our emotions may shock us ("I didn't know I felt
so strongly about that"), shame us ("Dang, there my hypersensitive fairness
button goes off again"), or shore us up ("Wow, this is a serious problem that
must be redressed")—but they will never fail to instruct us about important
matters.

In a similar vein, philosopher and ethicist Robert Roberts understands emotions as "concern-based construals" that signal "what the subject cares about,
what is important to him or her," including matters of "moral importance."[28]
What we feel passionately about betrays our critical moral values, not simply
our whimsical personal tastes in a conceptual buffet line. The current "mattering" project of philosopher and novelist Rebecca Goldstein contains a key
emotion component: "Strong emotions often carry us over the gap from is to
ought, and our conatus [striving] projects, providing us the motive force to
propel us into the future, are chock full of emotions."[29]

Likewise, the eminent philosopher, classicist, and public thinker Martha
Nussbaum stresses what we might call the "salience property" of emotions.[30]

26. R. Lazarus, *Emotion and Adaptation*, 149–50; cf. Moors, "Flavors of Appraisal Theories."
27. "Action readiness" or "action tendency" has been a major component of modern
psychological emotion theory. As Frijda ("Laws of Emotion," 351) summarizes, "State of action readiness is a central notion in emotion. All emotion—all states, that is, that one would
want to call 'emotions'—involve some change in action readiness: (a) in readiness to go at
it or away from it or to shift attention; (b) in sheer excitement, which can be understood as
being ready for action but not knowing what actions; (c) in being stopped in one's tracks or
in loss of interest." Cf. Frijda, *Emotions*, 69–93, 231–41; Fontaine and Scherer, "Emotion
Is for Doing."
28. Roberts, *Spiritual Emotions*, 11, 14; cf. Roberts, *Emotions*, 60–179; Baier, "Feelings
That Matter."
29. Goldstein, "What Really Matters?" (emphasis original); cf. Goldstein, "Mattering Matters"; Goldstein, "Mattering Instinct."
30. See my discussion of this property in Spencer, *Luke*, 710–11.

In her view, emotions are "suffused with intelligence and discernment . . . part and parcel of the system of ethical reasoning."[31] Emotions "involve judgments about important things, judgments in which, appraising an external object as salient for our own well-being, we acknowledge our own neediness and incompleteness before parts of the world that we do not fully control."[32] Nussbaum writes that "the object of the emotion is seen as *important for* some role it plays in the person's own life." She then gives incisive examples: "I do not go about fearing any and every catastrophe anywhere in the world. . . . What inspires fear is the thought of damages impeding that cut to the heart of my own cherished relationships and projects. What inspires grief is the death of someone beloved, someone who has been an important part of one's life."[33]

So what does all this emotion analysis mean for knowing Jesus? If "everything" sounds too grandiose, I'll settle for "quite a lot." To know what drove Jesus to carry out his messianic mission the way he did, to know what mattered most to him, what magnetized his moral compass, what moved him, *we must attend to his emotional life* as much as the Gospel evidence permits. Though theologically, again, we may accept the Gospel witness that the Holy Spirit impels Jesus's words and actions to fulfill the will of his Heavenly Father (see Matt. 3:16–4:1; Mark 1:10–12; Luke 3:21–22; 4:1; 10:21–22; John 16:12–15), this trinitarian supposition begs the utilitarian question of *how* this Spirit-force operates through the embodied, emotional Christ. It's clear in the Gospel narratives that Jesus is not a Spirit-programmed android; so how does the divine Spirit affectively shape Jesus's free, full-fledged human self, engaged with other feeling, thinking, speaking, acting selves and the surrounding environment?

First and Futurist

I've argued that the study of Jesus's emotional life in the Gospels is a matter of seminal importance to understanding his character and mission, not merely a dash of spice to make him somehow more appealing or relatable. Reinforcing the crucial role that emotions play in human nature, including Jesus's, ancient wisdom, clarified by modern research, stresses a double temporal function for emotions as (1) first responders to perceived stimuli and (2) forecasting simulators of possible outcomes.

31. Nussbaum, *Upheavals of Thought*, 1.
32. Nussbaum, *Upheavals of Thought*, 19.
33. Nussbaum, *Upheavals of Thought*, 30–31 (emphasis original).

First Responders

With the rapid-fire capacity of our intricately wired brains—a hundred billion neurons firing in milliseconds and running circles around any super-computer manufactured to date—it is difficult, as noted above, to situate and sequence physical and mental activities with cartographical precision. Yet, except in cases of extreme breakdown, order and method prevail over chaos and madness. However technologically limited we may be in mind tracking and however circuitous the track, looping back and forth, here and there, we live and move in some sensed temporal matrix of past, present, and future. Accordingly, sequential models help us understand how we navigate the world.

Nobel laureate Daniel Kahneman (with longtime collaborator Amos Tversky) has posited a two-stage, time-sensitive model of response systems.[34] System 1 kicks in fast, often before any conscious awareness, generating intuitions, gut feelings, and snap judgments—*emotional judgments*—not necessarily irrational or misguided, just less analyzed or thought out. Recall the impulsive flight reaction to a snaky object on the trail. Roman Stoics Cicero and Seneca categorized these first impressions as "pre-passions" (*propatheia*), "bitings," "slight contractions," "initial prickings," "first sparks," or "initial mental jolts" (Cicero, *Tusc.* 3.80–84; Seneca, *Anger* 1.8.1; 2.2–4; cf. Philo, *QG* 3.56).[35] In and of themselves, these first-feeling impulses are morally indifferent; only through considered "assent" do they blossom into deleterious, disturbing emotions or, if properly reasoned through, into "good emotions" or "proper feelings" (*eupatheia*).[36]

Better suited to the Stoic ideal is System 2 of Kahneman's scheme: a slow, deliberate, cost-and-benefit assessment of attitudinal and active responses to a person, event, or situation. Yet, despite the Stoics' aspiration to dispassionate tranquility, emotions cannot be completely overridden, since they themselves register indelible judgments (appraisals) that stay on the record, like emails that are never really "deleted" but remain floating in "the cloud." But neither should we strive for total eradication; as powerful, intelligent forces, emotions rightly demand a hearing in System 2 court, providing raw, "reasonable" materials for considered decision-making.

Loss of emotional capacity due to severe damage to key emotion-processing areas of the brain results in a deficit of discriminating "feel" for what to do

34. Kahneman, *Thinking*, 19–105.

35. This and other quotations of Cicero's *Tusculanae disputationes* are taken from Graver, *Cicero on the Emotions*, 36, 124–27, 134–39; for Seneca quotations, see Seneca, *Anger, Mercy, Revenge*, 21, 35–37, 110n29; see also D. Robertson, *How to Think Like a Roman Emperor*, 41–43, 62–68.

36. Graver, *Stoicism and Emotion*, 51–53, 85–108.

and where to go. Even with intact IQs, persons suffering from pathologically flat affect "see dozens of choices but lack immediate internal feelings of like or dislike. They must examine the pros and cons of every choice with their reasoning, but in the absence of feeling they see little reason to pick one or the other. When the rest of us look out at the world, our emotional brains have instantly and automatically appraised the possibilities."[37] Aristotle proves more on target than the Stoics with his nuanced "middle" perspective, seeking the "right" mix of emotion and reason in pursuit of "moral virtue." "To feel [passions like fear, anger, and pity] when one ought and at the things one ought, in relation to those people whom one ought, for the sake of what and as one ought—all these constitute the middle as well as what is best. . . . Virtue is concerned with passions and actions, in which the excess is in error and the deficiency is blamed" (*Eth. nic.* 2.6 [1106b.17–29]).[38]

While emotion and reason seep across these "systems" and inform each other, a common processing course starts with primary "affect laden," "emotionally charged" engagement (System 1), followed by secondary reason-rich, more "emotionally neutral" examination (System 2).[39] As social psychologist Jonathan Haidt puts it, the "emotional dog" wags the "rational tail"—which is necessary and beneficial but also prompts us, less helpfully, to rationalize intuitive emotional judgments through confirmation biases or confabulation ruses.[40] Another zoological image Haidt uses—his favored one, in fact—is that our rational "selves" function like riders trying to control a massive elephant plodding along with its bulk of "gut feelings, visceral reactions, emotions, and intuitions that comprise much of the automatic system."[41] A better "motion" picture to capture the force of Kahneman's fast, elegant System 1, might feature a rider on a racehorse.[42] In any event, let the student of human behavior—including that of Jesus—beware and be aware of the "dog" of emotional priority and of the emotional "elephant" that is always in the room.[43]

---

37. Haidt, *Happiness Hypothesis*, 12.

38. Unless otherwise indicated, quotations of *Nicomachean Ethics* throughout are from the Bartlett and Collins translation.

39. Railton, "Morality and Prospection," 232–36.

40. Haidt, "Emotional Dog"; Haidt, *Righteous Mind*, 27–51.

41. Haidt, *Happiness Hypothesis*, 17. He further stresses that "the elephant and the rider each have their own intelligence, and when they work together well they enable the unique brilliance of human beings" (17).

42. Haidt (*Happiness Hypothesis*, 16) briefly alludes to Plato's classic equine analogy of human drives in *Phaedrus* 246a–254e, featuring a charioteer attempting to drive two mighty winged horses pulling in opposite directions.

43. The eighteenth-century Scottish philosopher David Hume imaged emotion's power and primacy vis-à-vis reason in the form of a master/slave hierarchy, with emotion/passion in the

Forecasting Simulators

Increasingly, scholars correlate this primacy of emotional functioning with forecasting, as demonstrated in *Homo Prospectus*, a groundbreaking collaborative project among four leading psychologists and philosophers.[44] We would never have survived—much less evolved—as much as we have if we were only wired to be reactive to present danger or retroactive to prior experience. Threats come hard and fast from forces bigger and faster than we are. Forget the venomous snake for the moment; we cannot outrun or outfight a tiger with bare feet or hands any more than we can escape sudden overwhelming natural events like avalanches, floods, or earthquakes. We had to develop the brain power and social cooperation to learn to forecast: to think and plan ahead together, to anticipate crises and devise means to solve them on the basis of both filed and fresh information. In becoming proactive, prospective beings, past and present experiences arced toward future horizons.

Since we never know exactly what's coming around the bend any more than weather forecasters do, in the interest of maximizing our options we work around the clock, mostly subconsciously, in what some scientists and theorists of mind have dubbed the default mode network (DMN). In this mode our acutely alert, intricately wired brains keep running simulations of possible events and encounters, projecting various courses of action.[45] And what makes this powerful DMN "search engine" go? The network is primed for optimal readiness under the command of the chief affective-emotional operating system. As Gilbert and Wilson outline the process, "The brain generates mental simulations (*previews*) of future events, which produce affective reactions (*premotions*), which are then used as a basis for forecasts (*predictions*) about the future event's emotional consequences."[46]

This affective-emotional executive management team works 24/7 (the mind doesn't switch off in sleep mode) in a highly time-sensitive environment.

---

dominant position. For example: "We speak not strictly and philosophically when we talk of the combat of passion and of reason. Reason is and ought only to be the slave of the passions, and can never pretend to any other office than to serve and obey them" (Hume, *Treatise of Human Nature*, 266); "Morals excite passions, and produce or prevent actions. Reason of itself is utterly impotent in this particular" (294). Though hardly anti-reason, Hume is skeptical of reason's sovereignty.

44. Seligman et al., *Homo Prospectus*.

45. Sripada, "Free Will," 193–97; L. Barrett, *How Emotions Are Made*, 311–20; Mars et al., "On the Relationship."

46. Gilbert and Wilson, "Why the Brain Talks to Itself," 1335 (emphasis original); cf. DeSteno, *Emotional Success*, 77: "The brain isn't as much a response mechanism as it is a predictive mechanism. It's always guessing what's coming next based on what's come before. . . . In many ways, emotions constitute guesses about what's coming based on what has recently occurred."

Coolly calculated five-year plans that take five hundred committee meetings to devise are great (sort of) but not much help if you suddenly find yourself facing some hostile person or unsettling circumstance on five minutes' notice, which, let's face it, happens all the time. We need "emotional agility" and sophistication.[47] Social psychologist Roy Baumeister distinguishes between initial "twinges of feeling" or "automatic affect" and more developed "full-blown emotion" (somewhat akin to Kahneman's Systems 1 and 2), but he correlates both emotion-fueled operations around forecasting schemes to prepare for myriad eventualities: "That twinge (in the present) is a signal of what full-blown emotion one will have (in the future) if one acts that way, and it arises because of what one learned from previous, similar actions (in the past). The present affective twinge helps one anticipate future emotion."[48]

In economic language, we're not simply interested in firm, bottom-line projections about profit margins at the end of the day, month, year, or five-year block. We desperately want to know how we will *feel* about those numbers; how they will *affect* our own lives; how they will *move* us to act to reach our desired financial goals. The maddening reports, at least to non-economists, of investment values' fluctuation on the basis of "how the market feels" begin to make more sense, perhaps.[49] At any rate, whether we identify our species as *homo sapiens*, *homo economicus*, or some other brand, we are also, and maybe above all, *homo prospectus*, deeply invested in "emotional outcomes."[50]

Of course, just as economic history is littered with tales of rued decisions made on rash impulse ("If only I had not bought/sold all that seemingly booming/tanking stock at that moment of mania/panic!"), so the wider story of our lives remains susceptible to false projections. Though highly adaptive in learning from past mistakes, our default networks are not glitch-free; sometimes "gut feelings" have more to do with last night's spicy dinner than any prescient insight. Predictive errors continue to gum up the works,[51] during both "simpler" times (like Jesus's age) when there were fewer means of technological analysis and more "advanced" eras when it's near impossible to keep up with the pace of change. Still, we brazenly press on with our emotional prospective ventures, and amazingly enough, our continuing existence attests to the fact that we get it right more times than not.

Recalling the "mattering" matter discussed above and pressing the monetary metaphor further to encompass moral value—what is worth doing for

47. David, *Emotional Agility*.
48. Baumeister, "Emotions," 212.
49. See Akerlof and Shiller, *Animal Spirits*.
50. Baumeister, "Emotions," 209.
51. Gilbert and Wilson, "Why the Brain Talks to Itself."

the greatest good, personally and communally—we discover that anticipatory feelings play a critical evaluative role. In a brilliant essay titled "Morality and Prospection," philosopher Peter Railton unpacks the link between emotional prospection and ethical reflection in terms of "empathic simulation."[52] Railton explains how we routinely fast-forward into a future scenario, imagining not only how we will feel if we do this or that but also how others will be affected in the process, others we care about deeply (family and friends) or not so much (strangers and foes). Our affective moral compass takes a read on where a decision or plan of action might land us. For example, not only does the feeling of guilt arise after we engage in some conscious-pricking behavior, but the unpleasantness of such a feeling motivates us to predict its eruption in simulated cases, in hopes of preventing guilt-producing activity before the fact.[53] ("If I do this horrible thing I'm considering doing to you, I'm pretty sure we'll both feel bad as a consequence, and what will be gained from that? Except maybe it will at least help relieve the festering anger I've been feeling against you—and I don't really care how you'll feel, since I'm really mad at you.") Thus anticipated guilt and anger may rub hard against each other in emotional moral prospection. Again, this is not to say that "emotional reasoning"—emotion driving (wagging) reason—is always accurate or helpful.[54] But neither does reason do us any favors by trying to sever our emotional nerve, as if it could. Emotionally tone-deaf thinking misses important warning and guiding signals.

Passional Stories of Jesus

Railton goes on to discuss the rich resources of shared stories and gossip, describing them as "tightly intertwined with everyday moral thought and practice" and exerting "a powerful grasp on people's thoughts and feelings." These social narratives, formal (stories) or informal (gossip), are critically formative simulations of moral dilemmas and consequences. These narratives signal "not only about how people *do* think, feel, and act, but how they *ought* to. This ranges from the explicitly moralizing character of a children's story or a religious parable to the complex moral entanglements and ambiguities of a successful soap opera or television drama."[55]

52. Railton, "Morality and Prospection," 242.
53. Railton, "Morality and Prospection," 241–42.
54. Lukianoff and Haidt (*Coddling of the American Mind*, 38, 278) define "emotional reasoning" in cognitive behavioral therapy (CBT) terms as "letting your feelings guide your interpretation of reality. 'I feel depressed; therefore, my marriage is not working out'" (cf. 33–51).
55. Railton, "Morality and Prospection," 253, 255 (emphasis original).

This understanding of stories as emotionally charged frameworks for prospective moral evaluation aptly fits the Gospel narratives, the primary medium for encountering the life and mission of Jesus the Christ. Like all good literature, the Gospels move readers emotionally.[56] To read the Gospels dispassionately with some illusory goal of clinical objectivity is flatly to misread them. Beyond the Gospels' relatively spare, explicit references to particular emotions of Jesus, they convey his emotional character through their stories about him, culled from others' accounts orally transmitted through the years (gossip!) and constructed into a dynamic plot. In turn these Gospel stories feature Jesus's immersion in formative and affective stories, both inherited and invented: inherited from sacred Scripture and invented in poignant parables (many of which have scriptural resonance).

Accordingly, as we seek in this volume to understand Jesus's emotional life, we will attend to the stories Jesus tells along with those the Gospel narrators tell us about how he feels. Though Railton's comment rightly stresses the thrust of a "religious parable" to provide moral guidance via the interconnected feelings, thoughts, and actions exhibited by the parable's characters, his more particular association of parables with "explicitly moralizing" children's stories sorely misses the mark of Jesus's parables. Far from crystallizing his parables into catchy moral aphorisms, more often than not Jesus confounds his listeners, leaving his meaning dangling in the air, disorienting as much as comforting the audience but always challenging them with "complex moral entanglements and ambiguities." Any student of Jesus's parables who has not felt frustrated by what they think or feel Jesus may convey through these open-ended vignettes of common and not-so-common human feeling and action is not studying them very closely. Moreover, any student of Jesus's Gospel words and deeds who becomes so enamored with the "new" program he advances as to ignore his engulfment in the "old" religion of the Hebrew Bible, not least the fiery and teary impassioned prophets,[57] is reading with the narrowest of unifocal lenses, terribly distorting the "new" testament by dismissing the "old."

On we go with our quest to find the passionate Jesus, who in fact has been hiding all along in plain sight within the emotion-laden Gospel narratives. Let those with eyes to see, see, ears to hear, hear—and hearts to feel, feel.

56. See Oatley, *Passionate Muse*; Nussbaum, *Poetic Justice*.
57. See Heschel, *Prophets*.

2

The Pathos Logic of Theology
and Christology

The validity of this study of Jesus's emotional life ultimately rests on the reasonableness and persuasiveness of the close readings I offer in chapters 3–10 of Gospel passages referencing particular emotions. The proof is in the rich emotional ingredients of the Gospel pudding. But as I've already mentioned, the theo*logical* and christo*logical* basis for investigating God and Christ's passions/emotions suffers a fatal *logical* flaw from the start in much scholarly and popular Christian thought. Unlike fallen human beings subject to volatile and often virulent passions, the divine Father and Son, in their perfect natures, remain *impassible*, incapable of being perturbed by external forces. So the argument runs. Thus any presumptions of vacillating feelings on God's part are vain human projections onto the divine, tainted by our imperfect, skewed feelings. A purely impassible God and Christ would pose an impossible impasse for our project.

Therefore, though I cannot undertake here a full-scale analysis of the complex doctrine of divine impassibility, I do need to provide some explanation of the biblically based logic of a genuinely passionate God—a pathos logic—that I accept, following in the tradition of Abraham Joshua Heschel and Jürgen Moltmann, among other postwar theologians.

God as Moved and Moving Mover

As I will usually begin subsequent chapters by sketching Aristotle's foundational analysis of particular emotions, so I start here with his influential view of the deity as Prime Mover, which by Aristotle's logic means that God, who sets everything and everyone else in motion, cannot personally be *moved* by anything or anyone else in any way, not least *e-motion-ally*.

> There is some substance which is eternal and immovable and separate from sensible things; and it . . . is impartible and indivisible . . . and moreover . . . it is impassive [*apathes*] and unalterable. . . . The first principle and primary reality is immovable, both essentially and accidentally, but it excites the primary form of motion, which is one and eternal. Now since that which is moved must be moved by something, and the prime mover must be essentially immovable, and eternal motion must be excited by something eternal, and one motion by some one thing . . . then each of these spatial motions must also be excited by a substance which is essentially immovable and eternal. (*Metaph.* 12.8 [1073a])

This singular immovable and impassive (*apathes*) deity stands apart from the chaotic and capricious gods of Greek mythology and closer to the Creator God of the Bible.[1] Theologians John Cobb and David Ray Griffin label this ancient Greek philosophical concept of God as "the Unchanging and Passionless Absolute." This "notion of 'impassibility' stressed that deity must be completely unaffected by any other reality and must lack all passion or emotional response"—"in no way conditioned by . . . unforeseen, self-determining activities of us world beings."[2] This view became bedrock, according to Cobb and Griffin, for prominent medieval Christian theologians, such as Anselm and Aquinas. But a strong "impassibilist" theology (and Christology) also characterized earlier church fathers.

To take one example, Clement of Alexandria (150–215 CE) "described [human] passions as excessive and runaway impulses that are disobedient to reason and to revelation." If such a strict view applied to human emotions, how much more to the divine nature! Accordingly, "one's first task . . . is to moderate and control" all passions; "the final goal is to achieve *apatheia* in order to become more like the impassible God."[3] In Clement's words, we "err impiously" when we "interpret the will of the impassible Deity similarly to our perturbations," since the wholly Other, self-sufficient God "has no natural relation to us" (*Stromata* 2.16, 18; see 4.23).[4]

1. See Moltmann, "Passibility or Impassibility of God," 166–67: "Why did Aristotle call God '*apathes*'? To exclude the moods and affairs of the Homeric gods. The God of Israel is not subject to such moods, but he is full of compassion for his people."
2. Cobb and Griffin, *Process Theology*, 8–9.
3. McClure, *Emotions*, 46.
4. For a balanced discussion of Clement's views, detecting some limited use of "emotionally colored terms" to describe God's character, see Lister, *God Is Impassible*, 98–99.

The esteemed theologian and churchman Anselm of Canterbury (1033–1109) also challenges the tendency to correlate God's emotional experience with our own (to make God in our anthropopathic image) but does so in a distinctive way. He starts with the seemingly oxymoronic premise that God is "at once compassionate and passionless," which he then clarifies as the myopic view from our vantage point: "God is compassionate, in terms of *our experience*, because *we experience* the effect of compassion. God is not compassionate, in terms of his own being, because he does not experience the feeling [*affectus*] of compassion." God is genuinely compassionate in saving "wretched" sinners who gratefully feel God's forgiving love within themselves. But in God's "own being," God is not motivated by compassionate feelings, since God is "affected by *no sympathy* for wretchedness" (*Proslogium* 8).[5]

In short, Anselm is no fan of feeling, especially ascribed to God. Rather, Anselm advocates a strict cognitive approach that is both elevated over and separated from affective experience in a manner opposed to much ancient and modern integration of cognition and emotion, of mind and heart, as argued in the previous chapter. In Anselm's terms, "whatever in any way cognises [reasons cognitively] is not inappropriately said, in some sort, to feel." Thus, if we are to say that God is "sensible" (feeling sensations) in any sense, it is only in distinctive terms of being "truly sensible in the highest degree," consistent with the fact that God "cognize[s] all things [only] in the highest degree; and not as an animal [including a human creature] cognises, through a corporeal sense" (*Proslogium* 6).

Thomas Aquinas (1225–74) also advances a qualified understanding of God's passionate nature (passibility), but he does so by stressing God's volitive agency more than God's cognitive capacity and the sovereignty of God's will more than the superiority of God's mind. On the one hand, as Cobb and Griffin indicate, Thomas makes dogmatic statements about God's impassibility, even applied to God's love: "For in God there are no passions. Now love is a passion. Therefore love is not in God. . . . God loves without passion" (*Summa Theologica*, pt. 1, q. 20).[6] Similar to Anselm's view that God acts to save and forgive sinful humanity without attendant feelings of compassion, Thomas maintains that God moves to help suffering humanity without accompanying feelings of sadness: "To sorrow, therefore, over the misery of others belongs not to God, but it does most properly belong to him to dispel that misery" (pt. 1, q. 21). Cobb and Griffin analogize Anselm's and Thomas's

5. Emphasis added; see discussion in R. Olson, *Mosaic of Christian Belief*, 127; Cobb and Griffin, *Process Theology*, 40–45; Lister, *God Is Impassible*, 108–9.
6. The *Summa* citations in this paragraph come from Cobb and Griffin, *Process Theology*.

concepts of God in terms of "the father who has no feeling for his children, and hence does not feel their needs, but 'loves' them in that he gives good things to them."[7] Of course, one might wonder how truly "good" such an unfeeling father would be, a question that certainly emerges from modern family systems perspectives, if not within medieval patriarchal structures (more on this below).

On the other hand, however, Thomas makes key distinctions in emotive terminology that ancient Stoics and modern thinkers (and certainly popular culture) tend to elide: "The Stoics made no distinction between sense and intellect, hence between the sensitive appetite and the intellectual appetite. Accordingly, they made no distinction between the passions [*passiones animae*] and movements of the will [*motus voluntates*], since the passions belong to the sensitive appetite, and movements of the will to the intellectual appetite" (*Summa Theologica*, pt. 1–2, q. 24). For Thomas, then, "whether an emotion is vicious or virtuous" (as Anastasia Scrutton puts it) turns on whether it stems from sensate "passions" of the physical/animal body or deliberate "movements" of the spiritual/rational will (Thomas also labeled these resolute movements "affections"). Since God is Spirit and not body (until the incarnation in Christ!), God is only moved *voluntarily* (sovereignly) with virtuous "affection," never with impulsive "passion." Within these parameters, "real emotional feeling and personal involvement with creation is attributed to God, yet this is never contrary to God's reason and will, and never results in fickleness or infidelity to the world."[8]

This carefully circumscribed "model of divine 'emotional life' that includes affections but excludes direct experience of passions"[9] follows a similar pattern sketched by Rob Lister, which he traces across Christian theological history, envisioning God as both "impassible and impassioned." In Lister's reading, "God has always purposed to respond volitionally *and* emotively . . . in the face of given actions by his creatures."[10] Though seeking a balanced interpretation, Lister maintains a bold bottom line with no room to budge: "The sense of impassibility for which we have been arguing, namely that God's love (or any of his other *ad extra* emotional expressions), cannot be wrung from him *involuntarily*."[11] We may capture this limited impassibility

7. Cobb and Griffin, *Process Theology*, 45.

8. Scrutton, "Emotion," 175–76 (my *Summa* quotation in this paragraph comes from this source). On this Augustinian-Thomist view, see also Scrutton, *Thinking through Feeling*, 34–54; Stump, "Non-Aristotelian Character"; McClure, *Emotions*, 50–54 (though this discussion focuses more on Thomas's view of human, rather than divine, emotions).

9. Scrutton, "Emotion," 177.

10. Lister, *God Is Impassible*, 178 (emphasis original).

11. Lister, *God Is Impassible*, 187 (emphasis original).

argument in a catchphrase: "Only where there's a will is there a way to God's heart." Or fleshed out a bit more: "Only where there's an *unforced will by external experiences or events* is there a way God allows God's Self to become impassioned." If God chooses to feel, fine. And thank God that God does choose to love, sympathize with, and save suffering humanity. But make no mistake: no one and nothing outside of God, however poignant, moves God against God's sovereign will.

So it might seem that this systematic theological approach to the nature of God—this theo-logic—sanctions orthodox affirmation of the impassible God without making God into an unfeeling boulder or block of wood, the very definition of impotent idolatry (see Deut. 4:28–29; 28:36, 64; 29:17; 2 Kings 19:17–18; Pss. 115:4–8; 135:14–18; Isa. 44:9–20; Jer. 10:1–16). But does this more traditional image of God (all concepts of the infinite God in our finite minds are "imagined" to some degree) not run the risk of perceiving God's freedom as limited by making God's absolute, autocratic will into an idol? More to the point, does a colder rational-volitional theology—God as Supreme Mind and Will—not effectively run roughshod over a warmer (not sappy or merely sentimental) relational-emotional God as Beloved Lover (not an idea of love or only love as action), as Moved Mover?

The eminent postwar German Reformed theologian Jürgen Moltmann, deeply affected by his personal experience as a young soldier and prisoner of war, has mounted a vigorous case throughout his prolific career for the passionate God who suffers and sympathizes with God's broken, beleaguered creatures and creation on an intensely interpersonal level.[12] Moltmann expounds this theological perspective not only in rigorous academic argument but also in judicious practical counsel, as evident in his rejoinder to a stunning rebuke offered by the renowned Catholic theologian Karl Rahner in his final interview. Rahner sharply denounced Moltmann's image of the passion-filled (passible) God as heretical and harmful to suffering souls who need the hope and assurance of God's indomitable power as well as love: "What use would that [weak view of God] be to me [Rahner] in consolation in the truest sense of the word?" All the "use" in the world, Moltmann claims. Though readily conceding that "God entered into our history of suffering in a different way . . . not subjected to it against his will . . . not as a finite creature," Moltmann does not regard this difference as incommensurate with God's succor of the afflicted *from below*, from a participatory position *within* their suffering, feeling their pain: "God is capable of suffering *because* he is capable of love. . . . I cannot imagine an impassible God as a God who consoles in a personal

12. See Moltmann, *Broad Place*, 13–18; Moltmann, *In the End*, 33–34.

sense." And in a direct counter to Rahner's question, Moltmann asks, "With what right do we human beings say that God is 'incapable'? Do we not 'cement' God in with the negations of this negative theology? . . . How can a God who is locked into his immobility and impassibility become a comfort for the person whose situation also seems like that?"[13]

Limited, cemented, locked in: a rigid notion of God's impassible sovereignty projects a diminished view of God's infinite capacity. Allowing for God's passionate involvement with humanity and the world—but only under God's strict unilateral, invariable, invulnerable control—truncates, if not vitiates, the intimate, interacting, inter-agential covenant of love binding together God and all creation.[14]

Returning to the parental biblical image of God that has influenced both academic theology and popular faith, it strains both sound logic and sensible feeling to conceive of God as a perfunctory patriarch who provides "good things" for his children in a purely clinical, transactional way. If anything, the analogy (the ana-logic) runs from lesser to greater: "*how much more* will the heavenly Father give to"—and care for and sympathize with—his beloved children than earthly fathers can ever approximate (see Matt. 7:11 // Luke 11:13)![15] The American evangelical theologian Roger Olson finds parental experience an especially fruitful reference point for understanding God's pathos. He starts with a candid assessment of the cost of parental love—a welcome, elective cost but costly all the same: "Some of the freedom of not being a parent is gone the moment one becomes a parent. A certain limitation of responsibility and love intrudes into life. One opens oneself up to vulnerability. A new kind of pain becomes possible—and inevitable—the pain of being rejected by one's offspring and the pain of watching helplessly as the beloved child makes terrible mistakes as he or she matures." Olson then draws the evocative comparison with God:

> What is wrong with seeing God in relation to us in a similar light? Does it detract at all from God's transcendent greatness to think of God as voluntarily undergoing such change that does not affect his existence or essence? While remaining who and what he has been from all eternity, God undergoes a change of mode of existence in creation and incarnation that may be best described as divine *kenosis* (from the Greek for self-emptying). God sovereignly restricts his unrestricted, all-determining power and blissful, triune joy and risks the pain of rejection, loss and death on the cross.[16]

13. Moltmann, "*Crucified God* Yesterday and Today," 80–82; cf. Spencer, *Luke*, 728–29.
14. See chap. 8 for a discussion of the covenantal roots of love/compassion in the Bible.
15. Reasoning from lesser to greater, or light to heavy (*qal waḥomer*), was a common method of early Jewish scriptural interpretation; see Longenecker, *Biblical Exegesis*, 20, 52–53.
16. Olson, *Mosaic of Christian Belief*, 133.

Olson rightly discerns that the two great mega-events in world history propelling the biblical story—creation and incarnation—indeed change God in the course of that story by virtue of God's intimate, passionate involvement as a character in the story. We may best consider the emotional effects of these two watershed events by expanding them to *creation-election* and *incarnation-crucifixion*.

Creation-Election

The Creator-Parent God of the Bible makes the first move, the primal choice ("God said, 'Let there be . . .'" [Gen. 1:3]), as human fathers and mothers choose to have children. But once that creative option materializes, once the child is generated from the parents, the child represents part of them with inherent power to affect them as much as be affected by them. The creative mover becomes moved by the creation for good or ill, depending on whether the created being moves forward in alignment with the creator's will or moves back against it. Either way, expanded or diminished, the creator's will is changed in the process.

Regardless of whether we interpret God's repeatedly "good" (*tob*) evaluation of creation (Gen. 1:10, 12, 18, 21, 25, 31) as including an emotive tinge of "pleasing, desirable, joyous" along with its positive moral judgment, it doesn't take long in the biblical-theological story for an emotionally impacted (not simply impassioned) Creator God to emerge, hit hard by the *unexpected* disintegration of the created order, fueled by destructive humanity. This magnanimous Creator who "saw everything that he had made, and indeed, it was very good" (1:31) soon "saw that the wickedness of humankind was great in the earth" (6:5), particularly that "the earth was filled with violence" (6:11)—a degradation so great that it moved God to become "*sorry* that he had made humankind on the earth, and it *grieved him to his heart*" (6:6); or put another way: "The LORD *regretted* making human beings on the earth, and he was *heartbroken*" (6:6 CEB).[17] The term for "be sorry/regret" (*naham*), in the form used here, means "allow [oneself] to be sorry" or "allow [oneself] a change of heart regarding" a person or situation.[18] In this context, however, the divine Self who allows sorrow/regret—accompanied by heartfelt grief—seems to have limited choice in the matter because of the prior, primal choice to

17. See Moltmann, "Passibility or Impassibility of God," 164: "This passage [Gen. 6:5–6] is rightly called 'the pain of God': God's remorse conflicts with his faithfulness to creation. God, however, remains faithful to his stubborn human creature and suffers the appropriate remorse." See also Fretheim, *Suffering of God*, 111–13.

18. Holladay, *Concise Hebrew and Aramaic Lexicon*, 234. Here *naham* appears in the Niphal (causative) form.

become integrally enmeshed in human life from the ground up and from the nose in: "The LORD God formed the human from the topsoil of the fertile land and blew life's breath into his nostrils. The human came to life" (2:7 CEB). This Creator Lord is thus *compelled* to accede to feelings of regret and grief, drawing the thinnest of lines between self-determination and capitulation to a tidal wave of surging emotion pumped by wildly dysfunctional and destructive creatures.

Picturing God's roiling primordial emotions as a violent storm surge forms an apt prelude to God's dramatic reactive move to drown all created life in a global tsunami, save for Noah, his family, and representative pairs of creatures. In forty days of deluge, God all but undoes the "good" six-day creative project God had wrought out of watery chaos. Or perhaps better put, God pulls the plug on an out-of-control human race intent on destroying itself and its environment. Nothing left to do but wipe out the world and start over. Move to Plan B, though the Genesis narrative presents this not as a Plan B that God formulated in advance just in case but more as a necessarily improvised measure in the process of God's relationship with the world.

After the great flood, God moves ahead with remaking the world through Noah and family but not without a further adjustment: an everlasting covenantal promise that "never again shall all flesh be cut off by the waters of a flood, and never again shall there be a flood to destroy the earth" (Gen. 9:11; cf. 9:8–17). Though no mention is made this time of God's sorrow or regret over the devastation God brought to the rebellious world, it does not seem far-fetched within the theo-logic of Genesis's story to presume that it deeply pained God to see this mass destruction of God's creation, prompting God's resolve never to have that experience again.

Of course, Noah and his descendants are far from saints, and human corruption proceeds apace. Eventually, God changes plans again—or more properly put, God changes strategy to realize the enduring overarching plan and purpose to renew planet Earth and all who dwell within it. Election comes to the fore, as God chooses to covenant with a particular people, Israel, the offspring of father Abraham—by no means to the exclusion of everyone else—in order that "in you [Abraham's people] *all the families of the earth shall be blessed*" (Gen. 12:3; cf. 22:17–18). In prophetic terms, God "gives" Israel "as a light to the nations, that my salvation may reach to the *end of the earth*" (Isa. 49:6; cf. 42:5–7).

Overall, however, the prophetic corpus of the Hebrew Bible confronts Israel and Judah's failure to fulfill this world-blessing covenant with God. And the prophets of God—speaking and acting for God, virtually as God's direct channel—confront the people with fervent force reflective of the passionate

God distraught over the people's suffering, much of which they have brought on their own heads through idolatry and injustice, through not loving God and neighbor faithfully. No modern scholar has perceived this passionate drive of the biblical prophets more keenly than the Jewish rabbi, theologian, and philosopher Abraham Joshua Heschel, a refugee from Poland who eventually settled in America and in 1962 penned a magisterial two-volume work on the prophets that centered on the pathos of God.[19]

In Heschel's view, the prophets decidedly ramp up the intensity and duration of God's emotions, such as mercy and anger, which emerge in the Torah: "New is the prophetic conception that [God's] mercy or anger are not sporadic reactions, but expressions of a constant care and concern. The divine pathos embraces all life, past, present, and future; all things and events have a reference to Him. It is a concern that has the attribute of eternity, transcending all history, as well as the attribute of universality, embracing all nations, encompassing animals as well as human beings."[20] This emphasis on God's passions, including anger, as reflecting "constant care and concern" squares nicely with contemporary philosophers' appraisals of human emotions as signals of what concerns us and matters most to us (as was discussed in chap. 1). The "constant" dimension of God's passionate concern, integral to "God's aliveness,"[21] features elements of eternality and universality: eternal inherence in the nature of God and universal extension to all creation. But Heschel does not equate the prophets' concept of eternality with absolute inalterability or equanimity: "This was the central endeavor of the prophet: to set forth not only a divine law, but divine life; not only a covenant, but also a pathos; *not eternal immutability* of his Being, but the presence of His pathos in time; not only absolute Lordship, but also direct relatedness to man."[22]

No prophet embodied the sympathetic, suffering God more palpably than Jeremiah, whose "whole being," Heschel remarks, "convulsed with the divine pathos" as he "depicted the dramatic tension in the inner life of God," its "inner oscillation" and "inner wrestling" fueled by "God's pain and disappointment," by "God Who felt shunned, pained, and offended."[23] To be sure, Jeremiah could push the divine emotional envelope over the edge in a "hypertrophy of sympathy for God," as Heschel diagnoses it; the prophet

---

19. Heschel, *Prophets.* On his indebtedness to Heschel and other Jewish writers including Gershom Scholem, Franz Rosenzwieg, and Elie Wiesel, see Moltmann, *Crucified God,* 270–74; Moltmann, *Trinity and the Kingdom,* 25–30; see also Jaeger, "Abraham Heschel."

20. Heschel, *Prophets,* 2:57.

21. Heschel, *Prophets,* 2:57; see also the stress on God's "overwhelming livingness and concern" (2:56).

22. Heschel, *Prophets,* 2:57 (emphasis added).

23. Heschel, *Prophets,* 1:118, 108–12.

huffily demanded that God "bring down retribution . . . on my persecutors" (Jer. 15:15) and "not forgive [the people's] iniquity" (18:23). Thus God is compelled to rein in the "independent pathos" of the volatile, vengeful prophet who is wildly out of step with truly righteous anger. This anger is always constrained by "nonfinality," as Heschel puts is, by openhearted longing for reconciliation and restoration (see 15:19).[24]

Incarnation-Crucifixion

We will further consider the pathos logic of Christ's incarnation in the next section of this chapter, focusing on the Gospels' theological narratives, and will give particular attention in chapter 5 to the gut-wrenching scenes at Gethsemane and Golgotha, which Moltmann stakes as "Ground Zero" for the interpenetrating passions of the Father and Son.[25] Here I simply aim to bolster some of the theological argument adumbrated in the introduction to part 1 concerning the divine-human emotional "nature" of Christ.

In the history of Christian doctrine, the fourth-century Apollinarian debate provides a critical foundation for thinking about the incarnation. Apollinarius of Laodicea (310–390 CE) was concerned to safeguard the singularity of Christ as the "flesh-bearing God" (On Union 2), not in the sense of wearing a suit of flesh, as it were, but as "a compound unity in human form," "one nature composed of impassible divinity and passible flesh" (Letter to Dionysius 1.6–9).[26] Or "fleshed" out more fully in motion/moving terms (recall Aristotle): "The flesh, being dependent for its motions on some other principle of movement and action . . . is not of itself a complete living entity, but in order to become one enters into fusion with something else. So [the flesh] united itself with the heavenly governing principle [the Word/Logos] and was fused with it. . . . Thus out of the moved and the mover was compounded a single living entity not two, nor one composed of two complete, self-moving principles" (Anacephaleosis 16).

However, while we might applaud Apollinarius's unitary, holistic understanding of the person of Christ, it comes at the steep price of steamrolling

---

24. Heschel, Prophets, 1:126–27. In this discussion of Heschel, I draw on Spencer, Luke, 716–17. See further Fretheim, Suffering of God, 113–26, 156–61; and the incisive article by Schlimm, "Different Perspectives on Divine Pathos."

25. Moltmann, "Crucified God Yesterday and Today," 72; cf. Moltmann, Living God, 48; Moltmann, Trinity and the Kingdom, 76.

26. Kelly (Early Christian Doctrines, 291) encapsulates Apollinarius's view as that of being "joined in absolute oneness of being with the Godhead from the moment of conception." Most of his extant writings are embedded in polemical texts of the period. I'm indebted in this section to Kelly's key quotations of Apollinarius and clear analysis (289–301).

over the "passible flesh" of Jesus's humanity with "impassible divinity." In the "fusion" of divine and human "movements," the Mover deity effectively forces the human dimension to *move out*. As J. N. D. Kelly crisply describes the Apollinarian position, "The divine Word was substituted for the normal human psychology in Christ."[27]

We might thus call this view "substitutionary," with significant ramifications for atonement—but not in terms of Christ's taking the place of sinful humanity on the cross, of "substituting" his innocent, sacrificial death to redeem "cursed," corrupt human beings. Rather, Apollinarian substitution virtually replaces Christ's human nature with pure divinity, thus separating Christ from flesh-and-blood creatures. Instead of the Word assuming flesh (John 1:14), the Word consumes flesh in this scheme. And such a view cuts the very nerve of God's saving plan in Christ, as one of the influential Cappadocian fathers, Gregory of Nazianzus (329–390 CE), pithily declares: "That which He [Christ] has not assumed He has not healed" (*Letter* 101).[28] The fuller statement particularly focuses on Christ's human mind, his assuming full human mental faculties: "If anyone has put his trust in Him as a Man without a human mind, he is really bereft of mind, and quite unworthy of salvation. For that which He has not assumed He has not healed; but that which is united to His Godhead is also saved. If only half Adam fell, then that which Christ assumes and saves may be half also; but if the whole of his nature fell, it must be united to the whole nature of Him that was begotten, and so be saved as a whole" (*Letter* 101).

Gregory's polemic against Apollinarius and affiliates who would "begrudge us our complete salvation, or clothe the Savior only with . . . the portraiture of humanity" stresses that since Christ has a human "soul . . . which gives motion to the body . . . which suffers," he must also have "human intellect . . . the most essential part of man." Otherwise, Gregory asks, "How does this touch me?" Without a fully physical, passional ("which suffers"), and especially, intellectual nature, how could Christ move to save him or any of us? How could we know, feel, and experience true salvation through and through? "Keep then the whole man [of Christ], and mingle Godhead therewith" in order that we may "benefit" from Christ's "completeness" (*Letter* 101).

This orthodox broadside against Apollinarian "divinization of Christ's flesh" without remainder, leveled by Gregory of Nazianzus and others

27. Kelly, *Early Christian Doctrines*, 292.
28. Bird (*Evangelical Theology*, 462) glosses this nicely: "Only if Jesus has taken on a fully orbed humanity can humanity be fully redeemed."

including Gregory of Nyssa (another Cappadocian) and Athanasius of Alexandria (Pseudo-Athanasius), insists on the total "mingling" of the incarnate Christ's "two natures"—divine *and* human—"concurring in unity" (Gregory of Nazianzus, *Orations* 37.2). Such a Christology aligns with the Gospels' characterization of the redemptive Jesus as a person with "a normal human psychology" (denied by Apollinarians), "a Savior Who developed, exhibited signs of ignorance, suffered and underwent all sorts of human experiences."[29]

Curiously, however, for all his conviction that Christ had a human mind, Gregory of Nazianzus could not bring himself to believe that Christ progressively learned and discerned God's will over the course of his life and ministry (*Orations* 43.38 [more below]; see Luke 2:40, 52) or that he remained ignorant of anything, such as the "day and hour" of his return to earth, known only to the Father (Matt. 24:36; Mark 13:32). To massage this latter case, Gregory resorts to a split personality profile of Christ that is at odds (oddly) with the strong unitary view he otherwise advances: "Everyone must see that [Christ] knows as God, and knows not as Man." Thus, "we are to understand the ignorance [regarding when he will return] in the most reverent sense, by attributing it to the Manhood, and not to the Godhead" (*Orations* 30.15). Further, Gregory downplays any sense of Jesus's anguished struggle with God's will in Gethsemane or abject forsakenness by God at Golgotha (*Orations* 30.5, 12).[30]

Apart from these Gospel narrative examples of Jesus's human psychology, exhibited not least in the crucible of suffering and death, the conceptual theology of the cross (*theologia crucis*)—particularly Paul's classic paradoxical exposition of the "foolish wisdom" and "weak power" of the cross in 1 Corinthians 1:18–25—also has profound implications for God's affective immersion in the world. The Catholic-trained philosopher John Caputo, a leading proponent of so-called radical theology, pushes this theology to the brink but within bounds Paul might well approve:

> A *theologia crucis* radically conceived requires the crucifixion . . . of the God of wisdom on the cross of foolishness, of the God of power on the cross of weakness (1 Cor. 1:20–25). Everything is demanded of theology . . . requiring it to be poor and itinerant, naked and obedient, even unto death. Still more, the same thing is asked of God in the highest. Even what has been called the theology of the cross up to now . . . has preserved the eternity, transcendence, and sovereignty of God, so that if God suffers it is because God is strong enough

29. Kelly, *Early Christian Doctrines*, 296.
30. Kelly, *Early Christian Doctrines*, 298. Again, we will consider the Gethsemane ordeal and cry of dereliction from the cross in some detail in chap. 5.

to take on suffering, to absorb suffering into the eminence and immensity, the mystery and abyss, the sovereign of the Godhead.[31]

Deconstructing—by way of the crucified God—absolutist concepts of God's eternality and sovereignty that figure prominently in discussions of God's impassibility (even those also allowing for God's voluntary "impassioned" response), Caputo reinforces his "weak theology," as he calls it, which embraces God's variable, vulnerable, emotive ([e]motivated) being.[32]

Working within a more conservative tradition, the Scottish Protestant theologian T. F. Torrance still argues forcefully for the pathos of God at "the intersection of God's reality with worldly reality" and from "the depth of its penetration into our creaturely being." "If God is merely impassible," Torrance continues, God "has not made room for Himself in our agonied existence, and if He is merely immutable He has neither place nor time for frail evanescent creatures in His unchanging existence. But the God who has revealed Himself in Jesus Christ as sharing our lot is the God who is really free to make Himself poor, that we through His poverty might be made rich." Torrance alludes here to Paul's emphasis on the freely offered "generous act of our Lord Jesus Christ" who "became poor" for our sake (2 Cor. 8:9), culminating in his self-emptying "death—even death on a cross" (Phil. 2:6–8). In a deft turn of phrase, Torrance ultimately affirms "the God invariant in love but not impassible, constant in faithfulness but not immutable."[33]

Pulling together these various biblical and theological threads surrounding God's faithful commitment to redeeming the world through personal, passionate participation in creation, election, incarnation, and crucifixion, we perhaps can do no better than turn to the book of Hebrews.[34] Although placing Christ in a priestly context (via the mysterious Melchizedek) absent in the Gospels, Hebrews captures, in its own way, a poignant narrative Christology supplementing the Gospels' presentation:

> Since, therefore, the children share flesh and blood, [Jesus, God's Son] himself
> likewise shared the same things, so that through death he might destroy the one
> who has the power of death, that is, the devil. . . . Therefore he had to become
> like his brothers and sisters *in every respect*, so that he might be a merciful and

31. Caputo, *Cross and Cosmos*, 17.

32. See, for example, these Caputo works: *What Would Jesus Deconstruct?*, 82–83, 88, 138; *Weakness of God*; *Folly of God*, 1–4, 53–71, 108–9, 119, 127.

33. Torrance, *Space, Time, and Incarnation*, 75; cf. R. Olson, *Mosaic of Christian Belief*, 133: "Torrance is simply affirming that in his greatness and out of his goodness God freely chooses to be God for the world in such a way that he allows himself to be affected by it."

34. See Bird, *Evangelical Theology*, 462–63.

faithful high priest in the service of God. . . . Because he himself was tested by what he suffered [*peponthen*, from *paschō*], he is able to help those who are being tested. (Heb. 2:14–18)

For we do not have a high priest who is unable to sympathize [*sympathēsai*] with our weaknesses, but we have one who *in every respect* has been tested as we are, yet without sin. (4:15)

In the days of his flesh, Jesus offered up prayers and supplications, with loud cries and tears, to the one who was able to save him from death, and he was heard because of his reverent submission. Although he was a Son, he learned obedience through what he suffered [*epathen*]. (5:7–8)

Christ as Embodied and Evolving Revealer of God

Just as we may come to accept, by faith, the perfect fusion or commingling of divine and human natures in the incarnate Christ, so we affirm, by faith, the essential unity within the divine nature (God is One) and, by science (along with faith), the integrated whole of the embodied human being of Christ. Of course, the science is modern science, especially more recent neuroscience, which has mapped a broad outline of the human network of interfacing physical, psychic, social, and environmental processes (though much remains unknown about their precise connections and circuitry). We don't simply have flesh, blood, bones, brains, organs, and such: we are all these "things" together, working as one (though not always in perfect harmony) within us, between us, and among us, as discussed in chapter 1.

The ancient Gospels refer to Jesus's body (*sōma*) and various body parts (hands, feet, fingers, knees, side) as well as to his flesh (*sarx*), blood (*haima*), psyche/soul (*psychē*), and spirit (*pneuma*). His teaching also references the human heart (*kardia*) and mind (*dianoia*). But the Gospels never mention his or anyone else's brain, nerves, hormones, or chemical components central to neuroscience research. As theological biographies (narratives of faith), the Gospels have no interest in anthropological theory and analysis; they simply describe various features of Jesus's embodied engagement with other people and his environment. Yet in the process, they do not itemize these features as separate parts operating independently of Jesus's entire being. We should not impose dualistic (body-soul), tripartite (body-soul-spirit), or any other divisible schemes proposed in some ancient (Plato) and early modern (Descartes) philosophy regarding the "self," including Jesus's self in the Gospels. As Joel Green, an astute scholar engaging in serious interdisciplinary dialogue between biblical theology and cognitive neuroscience, states, "If we would articulate an account of the human person that takes with utmost seriousness the biblical record, we would have far less conversation about the existence or importance of 'souls' and far more about the embodied human capacity and vocation for community with God, with the human family, and in relation to the cosmos. These are profoundly ecclesiological, soteriological, and missiological concerns."[35]

Likewise these are profoundly *christological* concerns pertaining to Jesus's emotional capacity intertwined with his intellectual, volitional, motivational, behavioral, and relational experience, carried out in and through his body. Like all human beings, Jesus feels his way through the tangled web of life in all its multifaceted complexity. As believers, we confess that Jesus has a better feel for life, to continue the colloquial image, than the rest of us—a perfect feel, in fact, "without sin," as Hebrews 4:15 puts it. But his sinless life is by no means a passionless or phantasmal one, merely simulating the human form (the "docetic" heresy) as an unfeeling android rather than an *anthropos*, a robot rather than a real person.

As emotions play an integral role in the full range of human experience, affecting and being affected by all dimensions of life to one degree or another, this necessarily includes the educative or developmental dimension. Recent research in social and educational psychology confirms what most of us know already: one's emotional state significantly affects one's motivation and ability to learn. A fearful, anxious, depressed, and/or ashamed student, self-preoccupied and closed off, makes for a poor learner, just as much as a positive, confident, openhearted, open-minded one will be a keen learner.[36] Further, as emotions play a critical part in the human learning and development process, they also represent a key learning and development objective. One must grow toward emotional maturity through persistent training in wisdom, both conceptual and practical, learned and lived in the rough-and-tumble of human existence. As surely as a well-functioning body requires work and discipline (exercise, diet, rest, etc.), so does an optimal emotion system. Even more so, perhaps, as we've all known physically grown adults with the emotional maturity of self-centered adolescents. I'm not thinking here of certified psycho- or sociopaths—just garden-variety narcissists.

As for Jesus, just as Hebrews 5:8 asserts that he "learned obedience through what he suffered," so Luke frames the incident involving the twelve-year-old

---

35. Green, *Body, Soul, and Human Life*, 34; further, "It is erroneous to allege that the NT authors lived in a milieu pervaded by body-soul dualism" (51).

36. See Immordino-Yang and Damasio, *Emotions, Learning, and the Brain*; Immordino-Yang and Damasio, "We Feel, Therefore We Learn"; Brackett, *Permission to Feel*, 190–218.

Jesus with two parallel statements: "The child grew and became strong, filled with wisdom; and the favor of God was upon him" (Luke 2:40); "And Jesus increased in wisdom and in years [or in stature], and in divine and human favor" (2:52). The focal scene, the only snapshot in the canonical Gospels from Jesus's childhood (beyond his infancy), primarily features his precocious intellectual wisdom or "understanding" (2:47) evidenced in his remarkable question-and-answer exchange with the temple teachers. On a first reading that has dominated popular interpretation, this episode showcases a wunderkind Jesus brilliant beyond his years, a true genius unencumbered by the mental limitations—or emotional volatilities—of a typical preteen. But we scarcely expect anything less than exceptional ability from the Son of God! Whatever "growing" he has to do must be way off the charts of normal learning curves.

Such a reading is by no means limited to common Christian folk who delight in a Superboy image of Jesus in advance of his Superman identity. Returning to the Cappadocian theologian Gregory of Nazianzus, who argued for the divine Son's "assumption" of full humanity, especially the human mind, we mentioned above that he nonetheless blanched at any notions of Jesus's progressive learning or mental development *as a human*. Though affirming Christ's conjoined "two natures," making him a "specially wise man . . . [who] was with us in that form which surpassed us and yet is ours," Gregory quickly qualified this view in relation to Luke's assessment of Jesus's growth following the temple scene: "For He also, the gospel says, increased in wisdom and favor, as well as in stature [Luke 2:52], *not that these qualities in Him were capable of growth*: for how could that which was perfect from the first become more perfect, but that they were gradually disclosed and displayed?" (*Orations* 43.38; emphasis added). Thus Gregory falls into a "docetic" (from the Greek *dokeō*, "seem, suppose") trap of his own making, whereby Jesus only *appears* to follow a human course of development. In other words, his apparent growth is only for the sake of others' perceptions; it's only *to* and *for* the people that his process of maturation is "gradually disclosed and displayed," presumably because they couldn't handle the full impact of his infinite greatness at one blast.

A closer reading, however, of Luke's account in 2:41–51 reveals a more variegated scene incorporating ordinary family dynamics and emotional textures. In tension with Jesus's independence, extraordinary knowledge, and involvement in his heavenly Father's work in his Father's house is his continuing relationship with his earthly parents as a minor in their household. And this tension sparks heated emotions on both sides. Young Jesus stays behind in the temple compound, unbeknownst to his parents (who are already en route home with fellow travelers from Nazareth; they assume he's in the caravan). When they learn of Jesus's absence from the group, they launch a frantic search; it takes them three days to find him back in the temple, and they are none too happy when they do. Mary blurts out, "Child, why have you treated us like this? Look, your father and I have been searching for you in great anxiety" (2:48). Any parent who's ever misplaced a child for even three minutes understands Mary's emotional distress. And Jesus doesn't make things any better for her, whipping back: "Why were you searching for me? Did you not know I must be in my Father's house?" (2:49). One might be forgiven for detecting a tone of insolence in Jesus's response. He appears indignant, righteously or not, at his parents' ignorance and agitation.

Of course, Jesus has come to serve his true Father's priorities, and this will not be the last time his earthly family and community will be put in their proper places (see Luke 4:16–27; 8:19–21). But this is not the time to inaugurate Jesus's public mission. Jesus, it seems, has jumped the gun—by some eighteen years! Stunningly, after this clash with his parents in the temple, "Jesus went down *with them* to Nazareth, and was *obedient to them*" (2:51)—until he properly "began his work" at around *age thirty* (3:23). Apparently, he still has much to learn from his earthly parents and much growing up to do, emotionally as well as physically, socially, and spiritually (which are all of a piece).

Another Cappadocian scholar named Gregory (Gregory of Nyssa [335–395 CE]) believed in the "close conjunction [*synapheian*] and fusion [*symphyian*]" of divine and human natures in Christ,[37] the incarnate Word and Wisdom of God, who "preserves the due proportion with regard to our conception alike of the Divinity and of the Humanity" (*Against Eunomius* 3.2). Nonetheless, like his namesake from Nazianzus, he often conceived of Christ's two natures as discrete entities, with the more "active" divine Logos overriding the "passive" human side. As Kelly delineates Gregory of Nyssa's trinitarian view, "The Godhead, being impassible, remained unaffected, although through its concrete oneness with the humanity it indirectly participated in its limitations and weaknesses."[38] Such divine involvement in human finitude, though indirect, allows for a more nuanced interpretation of Luke 2:52 than Gregory of Nazianzus presented, to the effect "that Christ's human soul, through its union with the divine Wisdom, itself gradually developed in wisdom and knowledge, in much the same way as His body grew as a result

---

37. Kelly, *Early Christian Doctrines*, 299.
38. Kelly, *Early Christian Doctrines*, 299; on Gregory of Nyssa's trinitarian theology, see LaCugna, *God for Us*, 61–63.

of the nourishment it consumed from day to day."[39] Not merely was Jesus *perceived* as developing, but he actually *participated* in it as a human being and, at least obliquely, as God.

Again, Luke and the other Gospel writers are not preoccupied with ontological fine points about Jesus's nature(s). They are narrative, not systematic, theologians; storytellers, not philosophers. With compelling vividness but little argumentation, Luke shows and tells the story of Jesus Messiah, Son of God, conceived by God's Spirit in lowly Mary's womb (Luke 1:35), growing in wisdom and goodwill with other human beings and with God his Father (2:40, 52), loving God and people with his heart, soul, strength, and mind (10:27), and being loved by God (wholly) and people (partially). Luke's Jesus embarks on a progressive journey of love, full of obstacles and opportunities, twists and turns. As he powerfully affects others, he cannot help but be poignantly affected himself along the way. That's what love does to the divine-human Jesus; that's how love forms the divine-human Jesus, through and through.

Such is the pathos theology and Christology of the Gospels.

39. Kelly, *Early Christian Doctrines*, 299; here Kelly distills key ideas from Gregory of Nyssa's *Antirrheticus* (*Refutation of the Views of Apollinarius*) 21, 24, 28, 32; see Gregory of Nyssa, *Anti-Apollinarian Writings*, 91–258; Meredith, *Gregory of Nyssa*, 46–58.

PART 2

THE VIRTUE OF JESUS'S VEHEMENT EMOTIONS

A part from whatever emotions may be about in terms of content, their influence for good or ill has a lot to do with their *intensity*, with how they affect us.[1] While I and my nerdy academic friends can get pretty excited about a new idea and heated over a disputed issue, it's nothing compared with the gob-smacking rage and panic when some maniacal driver cuts you off or the gut-punching fear and despair when the doctor delivers a terminal diagnosis. Intense positive emotions can also spike the mercury, such as the burst of joy and pleasure upon hearing "I love you" in the throes of passion or, more trivially, the explosion of pride and excitement when your favorite team scores a dramatic comeback goal. But mostly we associate forceful emotions with negative, devastating hits.

In his stimulating book *The Vehement Passions*, the literary critic Philip Fisher focuses primarily on "the strong emotions or passions" of anger, fear, shame, and grief, though he also considers "wonder" and "spiritedness" on the more upbeat side.[2] But even with downbeat emotions more typically regarded as vehement, issues of value and valence on the pleasure-pain spectrum are more fluid than fixed. Fisher discerns a salutary purpose behind the vehement

1. "Intensity" is a major concept in recent affect theory. See Massumi, *Parables of the Virtual*; Bertelsen and Murphie, "Ethics of Everyday Intensities."
2. Fisher, *Vehement Passions*, 2, 227–45.

passions in "design[ing] for us an intelligible world . . . that we can come to know only in experiences that begin with impassioned or vehement states within ourselves." For example, anger plays a critical role "in discovering or marking out for us unmistakably the contours of injustices and of unjust acts in certain moments of time." Likewise, shame, grief, fear, and anger, in various configurations, "announce to us the presence within ongoing life of the fact of mortality, and . . . they do so by marking . . . the limited radius of our will by means of the injuries and humiliations of that will that are signaled to us by the moments when we find ourselves in a state of vehemence."[3] In sum: volatile, vehement emotions signal vital matters concerning justice and mortality, life and death.

But the virtue of these passions always teeters on the edge of vice. Most anger, with its penchant for revenge, does not prove to be *righteous* indignation, though it may lead us there if we pick up the right cues and respond rightly. In any case, human life provokes irksome feelings from the get-go. A baby's first wail and many others thereafter, while pleas for attentive care, also suggest that little Johnny is more than a little upset about being rudely wrenched from mama's cozy womb. Of course, he normally gets the attention he demands early on, thus vindicating anger's adaptive value. But it gets more complicated as Johnny grows up.

And what about the Lord Jesus? In the previous chapters, we set to rest naive portraits of a perpetually calm, cool, and collected Christ. Certainly he felt things deeply in the core of his flesh-and-blood being. Certainly he felt anger (though somehow "wrath" sounds more dignified and divine) but always in a pristinely "righteous" way, right? Perhaps, but we won't know for sure until we unpack the Gospel evidence.

And what about Jesus's experience of other vehement passions? The Stoic Roman emperor Marcus Aurelius greatly admired the philosopher Sextus of Chaeronea, who "never displayed even a sign of anger or of any other passion" (*Meditations* 1.9). But is such utter dispassion a worthy goal of human character in a fraught world? Mark clearly doesn't think so, as he reports Jesus's mixed responses of anger (*orgē*) and grief (*syllypeomai*) to a distressing event in a synagogue (Mark 3:5) and Jesus's anguished resistance to his impending death (14:32–42), as I will discuss in chapters 4–5. Although useful for analytical purposes, emotion terms and categories remain fluid.

I also examine disgust as a vehement emotion (chap. 6), which Fisher acknowledges but treats more tangentially.[4] In addition to unraveling Jesus's

---

3. Fisher, *Vehement Passions*, 2–4.
4. Fisher, *Vehement Passions*, 10, 12, 42, 94, 136, 138, 181.

viewpoints about disgusting matters, I will assess Stephen Moore's provocative argument that Jesus himself feels disgust at Lazarus's graveside.[5] Indeed,
this poignant scene in John 11 merits special attention as a maelstrom of all
three vehement passions—anger, anguish, and disgust—swirling within and
around Jesus at the same time!

Informed by ancient and modern perspectives on this triad of emotions,
and as much as the Gospel narratives allow, I try to discern how the incarnate
Christ "adapts" these passions in life-affirming ways. But such a basic constructive aim does not demand an airbrushed image of Jesus as a paragon of
"righteous anger," "good grief," and "pure disgust." Human emotions don't
function as static states. Though some are more volatile than others, all passions are mixed to some degree, in vigorous (e)motion in and between minds
and bodies. The line between righteous and unrighteous anger, for example, is
not clear-cut but depends on moral judgments in particular situations (which
is not to endorse squishy "situational ethics"). Doing justice to the Gospels'
complex portraits of Jesus requires a careful, properly critical evaluation of
his emotional responses.

5. Moore, "Why the Johannine Jesus Weeps."

3

That's Enough!

The Angry Jesus

S ince the classical period, the Greek term *orgē* has designated "intense and active anger,"[1] not mild irritation or mere thoughts of meanness. Oddly enough, expressions of Jesus's *orgē* in the Gospels are embedded in three stirring stories of Jesus's miraculous restorative powers, involving (1) a leper healed by Jesus's touch (Matt. 8:1–4 // Mark 1:40–45 // Luke 5:12–16), (2) a man's dysfunctional hand rehabilitated in Jesus's presence (Matt. 12:9–14 // Mark 3:1–6 // Luke 6:6–11), and (3) the four-day-old corpse of Lazarus resuscitated by Jesus (John 11:32–44). Why should such joyous events raise Jesus's ire? Anger often springs from suffering and victimization. As the "great physician" capable of curing the infirm, freeing the captive, and even raising the dead (Luke 4:18–23; 7:21–22), Jesus would seem to have little reason to succumb to vehement emotions like anger. He relieves sufferers and releases victims. He's in the "happiness" business—not in the trivial, sappy sense but in the substantive sense of true flourishing. So what gives?

While Jesus relentlessly pursues a restorative, redemptive mission endued with considerable power to help others, he is no superhero, no panacea for all ills. He does not eradicate sickness, sin, and sorrow from the planet. He heals many afflicted persons, but by no means all, and raises only a few from the grave, according to the Gospels.[2] He does not go around as a merry medic,

---

1. Harris, *Restraining Rage*, 401.
2. Jesus revives only three deceased persons: Lazarus, Jairus's daughter (Matt. 9:23–26 // Mark 5:35–43 // Luke 8:49–56), and a widow's son (Luke 7:11–17); see, however, the unique

whistling a happy tune and providing universal healthcare throughout the land. Throughout his life, he still struggles in a broken, hostile world that is ripe for provoking anger. The fact, then, that his anger erupts during his healing operations is not so surprising after all. For these events occur not in some antiseptic clinic but in public spaces of fraught everyday life (and death) inhabited by flawed, fragile, and frustrated people who inevitably affect Jesus as he affects them.

"Right" Angles on Anger

Before delving into these jolting, angry miracle episodes and other contexts in which Jesus either shows or speaks about anger, I will sketch some useful analytical frameworks from ancient and modern philosophers and psychologists. Aristotle treats anger (*orgē*) as his prime example of how to evaluate emotions (*pathē*): "In speaking of anger," one should assess "what is their *state of mind* when people are angry and against *whom* are they usually angry and for what sort of *reasons*" (*Rhet.* 1.1.8–9 [1378a]). In other words, one may profitably examine attitudinal, relational, and motivational factors that influence anger. Such a perspective undercuts the popular notion that people often impetuously blow their tops, as if possessed by a mad demon. While Aristotle agrees that some anger erupts for no good reason, he asserts there are proper times, types, and targets of anger: when, how, and at whom it *ought* to be expressed (2.2.1–2 [1378a–b]). Indeed, failure to become angry in requisite situations betrays a pathetic foolishness and slavishness (*Eth. nic.* 4.5 [1125b–26a]). Aristotle has no sympathy for doormats.

So what occasions might prove ripe for righteous, reasonable anger? In the Sermon on the Mount, Jesus drills down on the Decalogue's prohibition against murder to include heartfelt anger as tantamount to vituperative speech or violent action against a "brother" (Matt. 5:21–22). Does *any* twinge or feeling of anger count or just the full-blown variety?[3] Jesus doesn't elaborate. Since the second century, however, some Christian scribes began to mitigate this radical anger-equals-murder stance by adding a single little word in Greek: *eikē*, meaning "without cause/reason."[4] In this view, Jesus really meant to say, "If you are angry with a brother or sister *without cause*,

---

report in Matt. 27:52–53 that the entombed bodies of deceased "saints" came out alive at the moment of Jesus's death.

3. On "twinges of feeling" and "full-blown emotion," see discussion of Roy Baumeister's work in chap. 1.

4. See Omanson, *Textual Guide*, 6.

you will be liable to judgment" (5:22). Whew, that's better—except it's not what Jesus (or Matthew) actually said. And if it were, it doesn't so much solve anything as open a cavernous legal loophole: Who's to say what a justifiable reason might be for anger? Again, Jesus offers no legal brief on the subject. So we're left with scant teaching by Jesus to explain his displays of anger. Any right reasons for his anger must be discerned within the emotional scenes.

Other sages, however, have expounded more fully on causes for anger, both virtuous and venomous. Aristotle correlates justified anger with unjustified abasement: "Let anger be [defined as] desire, accompanied by [mental and physical] distress, for apparent retaliation because of an apparent slight that was directed, without justification, against oneself or those near to one. . . . The angry person always becomes angry at some particular individual. . . . And a kind of pleasure follows all experience of anger in hopes of getting retaliation" (*Rhet.* 2.2.1–2 [1378a–b]). The trigger of "slighting" or "belittling" (*oligōria*)[5] connotes a perceived "diminution"[6] or "down-ranking"[7] by the aggrieved party, loss (of status) related to a kind of grief. Martha Nussbaum quibbles somewhat with Aristotle, noting that one can also be angry at an unjust policy or harmful phenomenon (think slavery or cancer) as well as a derogatory person. But overall, she grants Aristotle's point that "anger is . . . very often about status-injury," especially in honor cultures associated with "personal insecurity or vulnerability . . . or lacking control with respect to . . . goals that have been assailed."[8]

Since anger often springs from other people's offensive words and actions that we take personally, it is especially sparked by particular offenders who have no "right," as we perceive it, to demean us. ("How dare they!") Here Aristotle reasons in hierarchical and parochial terms, justifying and even enjoying ("a kind of pleasure") angry retaliation against insolent subordinates markedly lower than oneself and one's "near" associates on the social ladder. Accordingly, "righteous" anger serves a more protective than reformative purpose, more to maintain the status quo than to effect social change.

5. "One who shows contempt belittles [*oligōrei*] (people have contempt for those things they think are of no account, and they belittle [*oligōrousin*] things of no account)." Aristotle, *Rhet.* 2.2.4 (1378b).
6. Fisher, *Vehement Passions*, 171–98.
7. Nussbaum, *Anger and Forgiveness*, 16–21.
8. Nussbaum, *Anger and Forgiveness*, 21; cf. her crosscultural assessment: "The idea of down-ranking proves . . . explanatorily fertile. . . . There is something comical in the self-congratulatory idea that honor cultures are in another time or at least another place (such as, putatively, the Middle East), given the obsessive attention paid by Americans to competitive ranking in terms of status, money, and other qualities" (20).

To be sure, in his moderating ethics Aristotle concedes that some slights are slighter than others, more "apparent" than actual, not worth getting het up over. But the Roman Stoic philosopher Seneca contends that no slight is worth getting angry about and disturbing one's tranquility. This is undoubtedly a pragmatic perspective, since one could spend excessive time being yanked around by all sorts of trivial offenses, like a mussed bed, a carelessly set table, water too hot to drink, or the grating sound of a bench being dragged (think fingernails on a chalkboard)—all examples Seneca dashes off, illustrating that "to get riled at such things is crazy" (*Anger* 2.25.1; 3.30). Fair enough, but to eschew anger in extreme cases like the monstrous murder of one's father or rape of one's mother, as Seneca also advises (1.12.1), seems even crazier! Surely these and other threats to vitally "important components of well-being"[9] do not merely allow vehement resistance but demand it.

Whether one takes Aristotle's middling position or Seneca's absolutist anti-line on anger, both approaches involve considered, deliberate judgment—a complex interface of cognitive and affective operations. This ancient perspective on emotions has been refitted under the modern rubric of appraisal theory, which regards emotional experiences as "episodes" or "processes, rather than states," involving interlacing physiological, psychological, evaluative, motivational, and behavioral responses to events and people (object relations).[10] One comprehensive framework supported by abundant cross-cultural testing has been developed by Klaus Scherer and associates.[11] They collate self-perceptions of emotional episodes into a multilevel, interactive grid of components under five broad categories: appraisals, bodily symptoms, expressions, action tendencies, and subjective feelings. All these (though not every instance) may apply to anger.

- *Appraisals* assess the expectedness (suddenness/predictability) of the emotional response to an eliciting event and its effectiveness in attaining goals (realization/obstruction) of salient concern; *anger* may signal frustration of a valued, goal-like status maintenance or enhancement.
- *Bodily symptoms* represent felt reactions in skin, muscles, joints, and organs; *anger* may manifest as hot and tight sensations in the face or chest, not actually boiling the fluid around the heart, per Aristotle (*De an.* 1.1 [403a.28–31]), but possibly feeling like that (cf. Seneca, *Anger* 2.19.3–5).

9. Nussbaum, *Anger and Forgiveness*, 153.
10. Moors et al., "Appraisal Theories of Emotions," 119–20.
11. Fontaine, Scherer, and Soriano, *Components of Emotional Meaning*. They call their method the Component Processing Model (CPM). See also the broader overview by Moors, "Flavors of Appraisal Theories."

- *Expressions* entail various facial, vocal, tactile, and gestural displays of emotion, typically in social exchanges and communal rituals; manifestations of *anger* may include bared teeth, raised voice, pressured touch, clenched fist, pointed finger, and collective protest demonstrations.
- *Action tendencies* designate the motivational thrust of emotions to move toward, away from, or against an individual or group; seldom self-contained, *anger* often drives the antagonized subject toward ("Charge!"), away from ("Good riddance!"), or against ("No way!") offending objects in aggressive, evasive, or retributive actions.[12]
- *Subjective feelings* constitute personal, self-conscious interpretations of feeling states, especially their agreeability (calm/chaotic), intensity (weak/strong), and controllability (safe/vulnerable); *angered* persons may develop a heightened sense of power surging beyond manageable limits.

Although definitions of emotion terms overgeneralize within and across cultures, the following précis comparing Spanish and Russian emotion language provides a helpful baseline for appraising anger: "In the psychological and linguistic literature, anger is generally described as a high-power, expressive, and confrontational emotion triggered by a demanding offense against the self or relevant others, leading to the experiencer's loss of control and the desire for retribution."[13]

This appraisal packs a lot of punch into anger! We should not expect Jesus's angry displays in the Gospels to reflect all these components. But they alert us to possible aspects we might otherwise miss in the "confrontational" Gospel episodes in which Jesus clearly cares about the belittling of underlings by abusive authorities. But does he care as much about slights against himself? And regarding the more extreme elements of the definition, does he ever let his anger extend to "loss of control and the desire for retribution"—what we might casually call "freak-out" and "payback"? Few among us are strangers to these reactions, but Jesus? Let's see.

Thin Skin (Mark 1:40–45)

In many ways, Jesus's first angry reaction is the weirdest.[14] It comes early in his ministry in a healing incident reported in the first three (Synoptic) Gospels,

12. See Frijda and Mesquita, "Analysis of Emotions," 283–84.
13. Soriano et al., "Types of Anger," 351.
14. In this section, I draw in part on my article, Spencer, "Why Did the 'Leper' Get under Jesus' Skin?" (used with permission).

but only Mark includes the anger component. When a "leper"[15] implores Jesus, "If you choose, you can make me clean," Mark prefaces Jesus's curative touch and affirmative speech ("I do choose. Be made clean!") with the single-word emotion descriptor "incensed" (*orgistheis*) (CEB; cf. NIV: "Jesus was indignant") (Mark 1:41). If you think that intense anger (*orgē*) is a peculiar motivator for Jesus's "cleansing" a poor leper, you're not alone. Matthew and Luke recount the miracle with no indication of Jesus's emotional state (Matt. 8:3 // Luke 5:13), and a number of early manuscripts of Mark simply replace "anger" with "pity/compassion"! As the NRSV reads, following these early manuscripts, "*Moved with pity [splanchnistheis]*, Jesus stretched out his hand" (cf. KJV's "And Jesus, moved with compassion, put forth his hand"). Well, that makes so much more sense! Somehow that's what Mark must have *meant* to say, right?

Not so fast. Actually, making too much sense sets off caution signals for textual critics seeking to determine the original text among manuscript variants. A rule of thumb is that the most difficult reading (*lectio difficilior*) is most likely the earliest. In other words, a scribe is more apt to change an awkward or controversial reading to a smoother or more amenable one than the other way around. In the case at hand, while we can easily imagine a scribe altering a received copy of Mark that reported Jesus's enraged (and outrageous) bedside manner toward the leper, it's hard to conceive of the reverse operation, changing "compassion" to "anger." No reasonable Christian scribe would bat an eye at Jesus's compassionate motivation. Hence, precisely because of its internal oddity, and matched with sufficient external evidence,[16] the "anger" reading lays a stronger claim to priority. The raw, vehement emotion assigned to Jesus cannot be cleaned up as easily as Jesus cleanses the man's psoriatic condition.

We must seriously grapple with the probability that something or someone elicits Jesus's ire, if only as an initial twinge of passion (*propatheia*). Yet, while it might be tempting to regard Jesus's anger as a knee-jerk reaction that he promptly tamps down in good Stoic fashion, that doesn't square with the remainder of Mark's scene: after the healing, Jesus remains upset with the leper! Following Jewish law, Jesus dispatches the man to the priests authorized to certify his "cleansing" and reincorporation into society, but

---

15. In the biblical world, a "leper" (*lepros*) was a generic designation for one suffering from various "unclean" skin conditions (see Lev. 13–14). Mark provides no specific dermatological diagnosis.

16. According to Ephrem's fourth-century commentary, Tatian's *Diatessaron* (second century) read "became angry" in Mark 1:41. See Ehrman, "Leper in the Hands of an Angry Jesus," 79–80.

he doesn't send him along very nicely: "After sternly warning him"—with a gag order against speaking to anyone but the priests—Jesus "sent him away at once" (Mark 1:43). Actually, Mark's language is stronger than the NRSV renders, more like: "After snorting [*embrimēsamenos*] at him, Jesus immediately threw him out [*exebalen*]" (AT). Jesus remains rather hot throughout this encounter.

What, pray tell, rubs Jesus so raw about this leper's case? What gets under Jesus's skin? Unfortunately, Mark's crisp narrative offers nothing close to an inventory of anger components: no indication of Jesus's bodily symptoms or facial expressions and no elaboration on his subjective feelings. The accompanying action of huffily dismissing the leper with a nondisclosure mandate fits Jesus's desire for privacy and secrecy in Mark (1:34; 3:11–12; 7:24; 8:30; 9:30), but it's not clear how this action connects with his initial angry response before he cures the leper. Jesus's first words to the leper—"I do choose. Be made clean!"(Mark 1:41)—come right on the heels of Jesus's anger. But again, the causal nexus is not immediately obvious: "I'm so mad at you that I choose to heal you!" Say what?

Maybe the best approach depersonalizes the situation by focusing Jesus's anger not on the leper but on the terrible ravages of his skin disease that results in the kind of brokenness and alienation that Jesus fervently seeks to overcome in the world. Anyone who has suffered from cancer or tended a loved one afflicted by this scourge knows something about anger. Yet while it's plausible that Jesus views leprosy as an enemy of human flourishing worthy of vehement resistance, we should recall from the discussion above that anger typically lashes out at someone who has offended or belittled us in some way. Anger is a quintessential personal emotion. The platitude "Hate the sin, not the sinner" is much easier said than done. Our actions, attitudes, and (dis)abilities necessarily contribute to who we are. Though the leper in Mark is never called a "sinner" ("cleansing" language is ritual-restorative, not moral-punitive),[17] it still appears that Jesus becomes incensed at *him*, rather than at his scabrous body (as if that could be separated from "him").

Granting, then, that Jesus somehow takes personally something the leper says or does, we might highlight his disobedience—not as the cause of his disease but as the source of Jesus's wrath. Two possible lines of disobedience might be considered. First, by directly approaching Jesus and coming close enough for physical contact, the leper violates Levitical law regarding quarantine "outside the camp" and the requirement to shout "Unclean, unclean" to

17. See Baden and Moss, "Origin and Interpretation."

warn off unwitting bypassers (Lev. 13:45–46; cf. Luke 17:12).[18] Fine; but who cares? Or rather, does Jesus care? While he faithfully adheres to Jewish law, as in his insistence on priestly authentication of the leper's cure "as Moses commanded" (Mark 1:44), Jesus doesn't appear bothered by the leper's proximity. He expresses no objection ("Whoa there, keep your distance, man!"), and given his purpose and power to heal, he need not worry about personal "contamination," hygienic or ritual.

Second, once the leper is cured, he disobeys Jesus's command to keep this matter private (before giving "testimony" to the priests) by blabbing word across the country such that Jesus scarcely enjoys a moment's peace thereafter, as sick people flock to him (Mark 1:45). But while Jesus doesn't want this kind of fame and likely finds it annoying, it beggars belief to conclude that this consequence of the leper's broadcast explains Jesus's earlier anger. Appeal to Jesus's future (prospective) insight[19] does not flatter him in this situation, as if he thinks, "I know this guy is going to rush out and tell the world about his miracle cure, against my explicit order. He's going to make my life miserable, and that makes me mad now—but I'll heal this pain-in-the-neck blabbermouth anyway." Even toning down this made-up interior monologue (I push the language for effect), it's hard to see Jesus getting "righteously" angry about the man's widespread witness before, or even after, Jesus cures him. You don't have to be the Messiah to predict that someone "immediately" relieved of a horrible disease (1:42) will shout the good news from the rooftops. And what's so bad about that, anyway? Privacy is nice, and the loss of it is frustrating. But is that the primary slight, the demeaning jolt, that provokes Jesus's anger at the leper?

I propose that what moves Jesus to anger is something other than the leper coming too close, transgressing the law, disregarding Jesus's word, and/or disturbing Jesus's privacy—something more integral to Jesus's identity and mission that this leper threatens from the outset. I suggest we concentrate not on the leper's physical approach to Jesus or his subsequent publicizing of his cure but rather on the particular plea he makes to Jesus: "If you choose [or will (theles)], you can make me clean" (Mark 1:40). That seems like a perfectly nice request, suitably polite and faithful: "You can [dynasai] make me clean. I believe you have the power to heal me." Doubtless, that's what the leper intends.

18. See, e.g., Loader, "Challenged," 56: "Jesus is angered at the man's aggressive disrespect for the Law; the man has crashed the barriers"; Beavis, Mark, 55–56.

19. See Voorwinde, Jesus' Emotions in the Gospels, 74: "Jesus . . . could foresee [the man's] disobedience and its consequences. The very thought made [Jesus] understandably irate" (cf. 72–74); Loader, "Challenged," 56.

But emotion, not least anger, often trades on *perceived* belittlement, irrespective of others' intentions. I take offense at some slight that I sense you're leveling against me before I take time to clarify what you actually meant to say or do. That's the way we're wired, which is why counselors across the ages urge being "slow to anger" and "quick to listen" (James 1:19) more considerately and deliberatively beyond our instinctive first and fast thoughts and impressions. On the other side, there's the familiar frustration of not understanding why someone has suddenly become angry with us; we then protest the explanation: "But that's not what I meant at all!" Overreaction and misunderstanding fuel the anger engine.

Yet emotional overreaction sometimes has its purpose: to make a point, especially a public point, about something of vital importance that's at risk of neglect (like vociferously appealing to people's sense of decency and morality during a pandemic, even rebuking careless people to their maskless faces). In such cases, the immediate targets of the emotion become props for the bigger issue at stake. Although Mark does not specify, as Matthew does, that the leper approaches Jesus among "great crowds" (Matt. 8:1), Mark's scene, which follows the summary in Mark 1:38–39 of Jesus's ministry throughout the towns and synagogues of Galilee, implies a public setting. The leper doesn't buttonhole Jesus in some corner or alleyway. A rapt audience looks and listens, and of course that audience includes us today, as readers/hearers. Mark, like all the Evangelists, writes his Gospel for publication, for public consumption, to publicize Jesus's primary purposes.

So what's the issue here? I propose that Jesus takes the leper's "If you choose/will" conditional introit as a personal affront and uses it—through the vehicle of vehement anger—to boost his own willpower, to broadcast what he most wills to do. If Jesus perhaps over-interprets the leper's language in the process, it seems fair to say that the leper doesn't mind, since he "immediately" gets the cure he desires. If Jesus snaps at the leper in the process, so what? The infirm man happily takes his healing and runs.

Still, we might wonder at Jesus's move to assert his will in such a testy way at this time. Why not just touch the man's diseased skin, say "Be made clean!" and be done with it? Why announce "I do choose" (Mark 1:41; single headword in Greek: *Thelō*), when his choice (his will) is made obvious by his action? While anger, like other vehement emotions, marks out "the radius of the will," as Fisher writes,[20] it takes none too kindly, as Aristotle stressed, to delimitations or belittlements of that boundary. Whether infants or adults, we're all prone to lash out when we don't get what we want. For spoiled brats

---

20. Fisher, *Vehement Passions*, 157–70.

and the narcissists they grow into, any impingement on their entitled wills becomes a federal case.

In the case of Mark's Jesus, however, the last thing that characterizes him is whiny, willful narcissism. He may be the Messiah (Mark 1:1), but he doesn't go around trumpeting it or encouraging others to adore him. He may promote the "way of the Lord" (1:3), but he doesn't insist on getting his way in everything. And while he protects his willpower on some matter of dire importance in the present scene and patently possesses extraordinary power (*dynamis*) to heal, Jesus does not display a consuming will to power.[21]

It comes down, then, to the specific slighting of Jesus's indomitable *will to flourishing life* intimated in the leper's "If you choose" proviso. As polite as that phrase sounds and as popular as it is in Christian prayer ("If it be thy will"), it insults Jesus and incenses him by striking at the very heartbeat of his restorative mission. Doubt him, mock him, beat him, kill him, and he scarcely utters a word of protest as long as his suffering serves the higher purpose of saving a hurting world (Mark 10:45). But question his life-giving purpose and you cross the line! "'If I want to help you?!' Are you kidding me? Do you know anything about me?" (Supply narrowed eyes, reddened face, raised voice.) "Of course, I want to 'save' you. Nothing matters more!"

This won't be the last time Jesus vehemently fights to defend his will to life among the ravages of disease, decay, and death. On the last evening of his life, he will declaim in excruciating agony his own will to live, not only against vicious powers that threaten his life but even against the will of God. Full examination of the poignant Gethsemane ordeal awaits the next chapter.

Withering Look (Mark 3:1–6)

While the setting of Jesus's encounter with the leper remains vague—we know only that it takes place outdoors in Galilee with an implied audience of witnesses—Jesus's next angry experience clearly breaks out in a synagogue (Mark 3:1–6),[22] probably in Capernaum, an early base of operations and site of conflict for Jesus (1:21–28; 2:1–12). This time his public anger mixes with grief (3:5). I will take up this sad element in the next chapter and concentrate first on who and what make Jesus mad in this scene and why.

21. "Will to power" draws on Nietzsche's famous concept, with recognition that its meaning(s) remains much debated.
22. For a published sermon sketching the main emotion components of this text, see Spencer, "Withered Hand."

A sacred gathering for prayer, worship, and study on the Sabbath should provide peace, healing, and refuge, not strife, suffering, and alienation. So Jesus's anger here initially seems even more ill-suited to God's Messiah than his previous angry response to the leper. Once again, at the center of Jesus's emotional upheaval is a physically challenged man, this time one with a disabled, "withered" hand (Mark 3:1, 3).

A key difference, however, emerges in the target of Jesus's anger, now directed not at the infirm man but at a group in the congregation, specifically, some Pharisees (see Mark 2:24; 3:6) who "*watched him* [Jesus] to see whether he would cure him [the disabled man] on the sabbath, so they might accuse him" (3:1). In turn, Jesus "looked around at them [the Pharisees] with anger," just before inviting the man to stretch out his shriveled hand. When the man does so, his hand is restored in quick order. Then the Pharisees storm out and "immediately" plot to "destroy" Jesus (3:5–6).

The affective dynamics of this scene coordinate hand and eye movements in a vehement swirl of anger, suspicion, and moral opprobrium. If looks could kill! Ancient optics mixed an "extramission theory of vision" with an "evil eye" intention of venom. The eye was regarded as the chief moral-perceptual organ, the "lamp of the body" as Jesus imagines in Matt. 6:22–23 // Luke 11:33–36, emitting light rays from within the body to illuminate objects and direct one's way.[23] Accordingly, the eye *betrays* the quality of one's inner life (light). If it is "healthy," blazing clearly and brightly, the eye reveals an inner being suffused with benevolent power and purpose (Matt. 6:22 // Luke 11:34). Conversely, an "evil eye" shooting poison darts against perceived enemies betrays a heart full of malice and misery.[24] In any case, what fuels one's inner life will come out in conduct, both verbal and behavioral (cf. Mark 7:14–23). And eyes can play tricks on us; appearances can be deceiving. Hence the incisive warning: "Consider whether the light in you is not darkness" (Luke 11:35).

So who sees rightly in the synagogue scene? From the start, the Pharisees keep a close, wary eye on Jesus,[25] particularly monitoring his curative outreach to the disabled man, as if it would be a bad thing if Jesus healed him—bad for Jesus, that is. As we grant Jesus's better reading of the situation, we should still be fair to the Pharisees, who for centuries have had their good name dragged through the mud as the epitome of prejudicial hypocrisy and pettifogging legalism. This and similar Gospel Sabbath scenes appear to cast

23. Plato, *Tim.* 45B–46A; Empedocles, frag. 84; Philo, *Abr.* 150–56; for these and other references concerning the "extramission theory of vision," see Allison, "Eye Is the Lamp."
24. On the "evil eye," see Derrett, "Evil Eye"; J. Elliott, "Paul, Galatians and the Evil Eye."
25. The verb for "watch" (*paratēreo*) in Mark 3:2 connotes close, suspicious surveillance, "watch maliciously, lie in wait for" (BDAG 721).

the Pharisees as callous, strict constructionists of the law, unconcerned about the sick and sinful, ever poised to throw the Book at any bleeding hearts, like Jesus, who try to help them. To put it mildly, that is a gross caricature of a dynamic (not monolithic) reform group in early Judaism seeking to apply scriptural instruction to everyday life. And any strategy to exalt Jesus by unjustly belittling others, not least other Jews, belies Jesus's ethic of love. That kind of bigoted belittlement (*oligōria*) is worth getting angry at.

But in this case, as often in the broader Gospel record, when Jesus and the Pharisees engage in testy disputation, Jesus vents plenty heat of his own. Name-calling and put-downs can get nasty on both sides. These altercations, however, have the feel of in-house wrangling over contested matters of importance within the common family. Among the various "parties" within early Judaism, Jesus was closest to the Pharisees, a lay group of Scripture scholars and teachers devoted to studying and practicing God's law (Torah). Jesus and most Pharisees had more in common with each other than with the priestly Sadducees, Qumran sectarians, and militant Zealots.[26] Jesus and the Pharisees shared a deep concern to reform society in accord with scriptural teaching. And because they cared so much about rightly interpreting God's word for God's people, they argued their cases vehemently. No one fights more passionately than family members. The Pharisees argued among themselves as seriously as they did with Jesus about scriptural interpretation and application.[27] Even in the most loyal, loving families, few of us are strangers to exasperated feelings like "You make me so mad, I could just kill you!" We don't mean it literally, of course (though Cain haunts our human lineage), but we feel it all the same. Mark's parting notice in our scene that the Pharisees conspired with Herodians to destroy Jesus is exaggerated invective. Most Pharisees had little affinity with Herod and his opportunistic politicians and cronies, and the Pharisees play no significant part in Mark's account of Jesus's death.[28]

Ironically, what some Pharisees and Jesus get all worked up about is what constitutes true Sabbath rest. Both wholeheartedly affirm the principle of Sabbath rest, rooted in the sacred soil of creation and exodus. Jesus hits the

26. It should be noted that Saul/Paul was an extremist, an outlier among the Pharisees in his former life of violently persecuting followers of Jesus—not typical of Pharisees overall.

27. Early schools of Pharisee thought developed around Rabbis Hillel and Shammai. Generally speaking, Hillel adopted a moderate, congenial interpretation of the law, while Shammai pressed a stricter, harsher position. See E. Sanders, *Judaism*, 421–38; L. Levine, "Judaism," 132–33.

28. "Some Pharisees and some Herodians" appear again in Mark 12:13 to question Jesus about his position on paying taxes to the emperor. But the principal Jewish collaborators with Roman authorities on Jesus's execution are the chief priests (with scribes and elders) (11:18, 27; 14:10, 53–65; 15:1, 10–11). Pharisees were laypersons, not priests.

nail on the head with his rhetorical question: "Is it lawful to do good or to do harm on the sabbath, to save life or to kill?" (Mark 3:4). The Pharisees' "silent" response is a silence of assent. Of course, the Sabbath stands for doing good, as God rested on the seventh day in peaceful communion with God's "very good" creation (Gen. 1:31–2:3; Exod. 20:8–11); and of course it stands for saving life, particularly from being worked to death in brutal enslavement (Deut. 5:12–15).

But in this case, the Pharisees' silence reflects grudging assent because Jesus appears to be heading down that slippery slope of allowing nonessential work on the Sabbath—good medical work, yes, but not life-saving work in the strictest sense. A withered hand is not a terminal disease, and the disabled man is in the safe environs of the synagogue, not stuck in a pit or a well (cf. Matt. 12:11–12; Luke 14:5). In all likelihood, he will live until sundown, when the Sabbath ends. Why not heal him then? As a critical sign of Jewish identity and faithfulness to God's way—all the more critical during a time of foreign domination—the Sabbath must be meticulously protected. Why, then, would Jesus appear to flout Sabbath observance, knowing full well the Pharisees were watching him? Who's being pettier here: the Pharisees in their hairsplitting judgment about acceptable Sabbath medical treatment or Jesus in poking the Pharisees' sensibilities and scoring points in a legal debate?

It all depends on the main point Jesus scores. While we cannot dismiss that Mark portrays the Pharisees as motivated not only by judicial principle but also by jealous concern to protect their professional turf against this upstart Galilean folk-healer and teacher (what rabbi did he study under?), Jesus himself seems unperturbed by political posturing. He's an idealist all the way, and his understanding of the "ideal" Sabbath anchors deep in his heart. Hence his boiling anger ignites when he perceives that these Pharisee inspectors miss the critical point of true Sabbath: rest. Again, anger betrays what matters most to Jesus.

Jesus's visual panning of the audience, literally "looking around" (*periblepō*; Mark 3:5), is no casual survey of surroundings but rather an intense physical/visceral capture of Pharisees and congregation in his conceptual web, a characteristic move in Mark when Jesus aims to drive home a "hard" teaching to a skeptical audience (10:23–24; cf. 3:35; 11:11–19). Perception, cognition, and emotion coalesce in fueling Jesus's anger at the Pharisees' misappraisal of the core Sabbath principle in this case. As with all complex affective experience, we have to assess the situation between the lines and spaces of embodied social interaction.

I suggest that once again Jesus is willfully and emotionally biased toward flourishing life. It's not that these Pharisees are anti-life or anti-health or take perverse pleasure in others' suffering or feel that the infirm somehow deserve their plight (this latter view had some currency in religious circles, even occasionally among Jesus's disciples, as in John 9:1–3). But Jesus consistently bends vital Sabbath law toward life-restoring and life-enhancing practice. Sabbath rest means *rest*oration in line with God's fruitful purpose for creation. So, in Jesus's view, we should not split hairs over what one should *not* do on the Sabbath—the rules of which early rabbis agreed "hang by a hair" at best.[29] If an action like revivifying a man's limp hand can be done on the Sabbath in the synagogue, what better time and place to do it! What better witness to Sabbath wholeness than a functional hand to lift in praise to the Creator-Redeemer God and with which to labor usefully for God and others the other six days of the week!

In Jesus's book, that's a point worth getting worked up about. Worth a passionate, angry riposte against any resisters.

Mad Snort (John 11:33–38)

Any Sunday school kid worth their salt knows that the shortest verse in the Bible is "Jesus wept" (John 11:35 KJV, NIV).[30] The few dedicated students who aspire to learn more than Bible trivia also know the setting of the famous verse: Jesus wept outside the village of Bethany, where his beloved friend Lazarus had recently died, leaving behind two grieving sisters, Mary and Martha. Weeping at a funeral is altogether fitting, even for Jesus, provided he doesn't overdo it, especially since he knows he's about to bring Lazarus back to life (11:11, 23). The succinct notice that "Jesus wept" keeps his grief in a neat little box (coffin), just big enough to capture a tear or two. I will have more to say about Jesus's weeping, but my main move now is to bust out the sides of the box and suggest that swirling amid Jesus's emotional reaction to Lazarus's death is a streak of anger.

Most of us have felt some admixture of grief and anger in dire situations of impending or experienced loss. Elisabeth Kübler-Ross famously codified anger as Stage 2 in the grieving process.[31] But cultures grieve in different ways according to different rituals, and no one consciously follows a prescribed sorrow checklist. Still, remembering our Aristotelian baseline of belittlement

29. "The rules about the Sabbath . . . are like mountains hanging on a hair, for [teaching of] Scripture [thereon] is scanty and the rules many" (m. Hag. 1.8); Danby, *Mishnah*, 212.

30. The NRSV ruins the game with its ingressive reading of the aorist verb: "Jesus began to weep."

31. Kübler-Ross and Kessler, *On Grief and Grieving*, 11–17.

as a trigger for anger, it's a short bridge from belittlement to bereavement, though not in terms of social acceptability. While both qualify as vehement emotions, anger tends to run hotter and more volatile than grief. And factoring in gender, women in antiquity were typically viewed as more prone to anger, especially frivolous, unjustifiable anger, than men.[32] Women also bore the brunt of public mourning of the dead. We expect Mary's weeping over her brother's passing, though maybe not for the reason she gives Jesus: "Lord, if you had been here, my brother would not have died" (John 11:32–33; Martha lodges the same complaint in 11:21). Is there a tinge of accusative anger here? At any rate, we are less prepared for Jesus's weeping with Mary and others (11:33) and for his eruption of anger in this situation. Here, among dear friends, at whom or at what can he possibly be mad?

The element of anger is not immediately obvious in English translations. Sandwiched between Jesus registering that Mary and company are weeping and Jesus weeping himself is the report that "he was greatly disturbed in spirit and deeply moved [or troubled]" (John 11:33 NRSV; NIV, CEB, and NAB vary only slightly). Clearly Jesus is overtaken by intense, distressing emotion but not necessarily anger. However, the two Greek verbs (for being greatly disturbed and deeply moved/troubled) push toward more roiling, boiling affect. The second verb, *tarassō*, signals a troubling effect on a material body, such as the turbulent eddying of a body of water. Its first use in the Fourth Gospel refers to the periodic whirling of the pool of Beth-zatha, thought to have therapeutic spa properties (5:7). But "troubled waters" more usually represented threatening, storm-tossed environments, literally (Matt. 14:22–26, 30, 32; Mark 6:47–51) or figuratively (Matt. 2:3; Luke 1:12; 24:37–38), sparking fear in anxious hearts. In figurative meaning, *tarassō* precipitates "acute emotional distress or turbulence" or "great mental distress."[33] In this vein, multiple Johannine references focus on Jesus's or his disciples' inner turmoil in the face of his imminent death.

- "My soul [*psychē*] is troubled [*tetaraktai*]" (John 12:27), Jesus confesses in anticipation of the approaching "hour" of his crucifixion (12:32–33). Far from defeatist and terror-stricken, however, he counters his angst with confident affirmation of God's glorious purpose (12:27–32).
- "Jesus was troubled [*etarachthē*] in spirit" (13:21), the narrator reports, when he announces to his disciples, whose feet he just washed, that

32. See Harris, *Restraining Rage*, 264–82; e.g., "To Greek intellectuals of the Roman period, female irascibility was generally a commonplace" (271).
33. L&N 2:315.

one of them would betray him to death-dealing authorities. Though we might imagine Jesus feeling pangs of hurt and disappointment over this suspected treachery, the text does not develop this point; again, he seems resolved to his fate rather than resistant ("Do quickly what you are going to do" [13:27]); and he shows no signs of fear.

- "Do not let your hearts be troubled [*tarassesthō*], and do not let them be afraid" (14:27; see also 14:1), Jesus counsels his disciples after they anxiously ask him to identify the traitor among them (which he does, but not in a way they recognize). Remarkably, Jesus proves more worried about his friends' "troubled" state than his own, assuring them of his legacy of peace that overrides the fearsome swells of death ("Peace I leave with you; my peace I give to you" [14:27]).

So the Johannine Jesus is no stranger to deeply felt, tumultuous emotions in the face of death. Yet while *tarassō* may connote an agitated state with the potential to erupt in hostile action (see Acts 17:8, 13) as well as hysterical fear, neither anger nor fear appear to be dominant components of Jesus's "troubled" heart in the Fourth Gospel.

Except, perhaps, related to Lazarus's death in close conjunction with another emotional term, *embrimaomai*, used only in this scene in John's Gospel, twice for emphasis. It appears first on the road into Bethany (John 11:33) and "again" (*palin*) at Lazarus's gravesite (11:38). It appears only three other times in the New Testament, two of them in Mark. One is in the leper incident discussed above, when Jesus "sternly warned" (*embrimēsamenos*) the cured man to go straight to the priests for certification without reporting to anyone on the way (Mark 1:43). We might presume that Jesus issues this strong order in an angry tone, consonant with the initial anger he felt toward the leper (1:41 CEB). As it happens, the other Markan instance of *embrimaomai* conveys irritation or indignation in another scene involving a leper. On this occasion, however, the anger is directed toward the leper not by Jesus but by certain guests in the leper's house who criticize an anonymous woman's extravagant anointing of Jesus's head: "But some were there who said to one another *in anger*, 'Why was the ointment wasted in this way? For this ointment could have been sold for more than three hundred denarii, and the money given to the poor.' And *they scolded* [*enebrimōnto*] her" (14:4–5). In response, Jesus defuses the angry situation and defends the generous woman.

As Mark sets *embrimaomai* in angry contexts, so does the LXX (Septuagint), though again with a small sample of cases. In the lone LXX use of the verb, Daniel predicts the Romans' stern denunciation of the volatile Hellenistic-Syrian tyrant, Antiochus IV: "And the Romans will come and will expel him and rebuke [*embrimēsontai*] him. And he will turn back [and will be angered (*orgisthēsetai*)] against the covenant of the holy one" (Dan. 11:30 NETS). And in the sole occurrence of the related noun *embrimēma*, the book of Lamentations recalls the tragedy of God's irate opposition to Jerusalem's unfaithful leaders during the Babylonian crisis: "The Lord made feast and sabbath to be forgotten in Sion, and he provoked in the indignation of his anger [*embrimēmati orgēs*] king and priest and ruler" (Lam. 2:6 NETS).

Of course, the nuances of a rare term like *embrimaomai* in Mark or the LXX do not automatically transfer to John. Nevertheless, an association with anger remains probable, following the cautious assessment of Moulton and Milligan: "We can produce no fresh evidence to throw light on the meaning of this difficult verb in the NT, but the LXX usage . . . is in favour of the meaning 'am angry,' 'express violent displeasure,' perhaps with the added idea of 'within oneself.'"[34] Wider ancient Greek literature attests to an animalistic tethering of *embrimaomai* to the "snort" of perturbed horses, whose "muzzles whisper in a barbarian way, filled with the breath of their haughty nostrils" (Aeschylus, *Seven against Thebes*, 460–64), and to an irascible mythical guardian of the underworld called Brimo, personifying *em-Brimao-mai*. Lucian of Samosata's pronouncement of postmortem judgment against wealthy oppressors of the poor concludes with a contemptuous "snort of Brimo and a bark [snarl] of Cerberus" (Lucian, *Men.* 20). It's tempting to supply dramatic sound effects of the aggrieved Jesus's snorting to the scene in John 11.[35] Though in no way invoking the pagan spirit of Brimo—Jesus remains in intimate communion with his divine Father (John 11:40–42)—Jesus may well express some bitter harrumphing at death.

Yet if we grant a degree of anger in Jesus's emotional reaction near (John 11:33) and at (11:38) Lazarus's gravesite, we again confront the thorny issue of what this anger is about and, more pointedly, with whom Jesus is angry and why. While some anger at the ravages of death and disease is understandable, it doesn't delve very deeply into the experience. Far from being an abstract principle, death, for all its universality, remains intensely personal. We may cry and even snort out in hostile horror upon hearing reports of a mass shooting or devastating famine miles or continents away, but we soon go about our

34. MM 206. In John 11:38, when Jesus is again said to be "greatly disturbed" (*embrimaomai*), the Greek adds *en heautō* ("in himself").

35. On the meaning of *embrimaomai* in John 11:33, see Zerwick, *Grammatical Analysis*, 321: "properly of horses, *snort*, so (as in Eng.) of persons snorting [with] suppressed rage or indignation. . . . [Perhaps] *he let out a groan of indignation from his innermost being*" (emphasis original); cf. C. Barrett, *Gospel according to St. John*, 399: "It is beyond question that [*embrimaomai*] . . . implies anger" (see also 398–401).

lives more or less unaffected unless it directly hurts us or a loved one and we
have some particular offender(s) to heap our anger on.

As with the leper incident in Mark 1, the best clue we have to who or what
sparks Jesus's irritation in John 11 comes from immediately preceding comments by characters in the story. John also provides a revealing visual element
that seems more in line with the disability case in Mark 3. Jesus's tumultuous feelings swirl among his hearing and seeing the speech and demeanor of
Mary and her "Jewish" friends (oddly designated, because Mary herself and
everyone else in the episode are "Jews").[36]

- *Mary says* to Jesus respectfully (she's kneeling at his feet), regretfully
  (she's weeping), yet pointedly: "Lord, if you had been here, my brother
  would not have died" (John 11:32).
- *Jesus saw* Mary and "the Jews who came with her . . . weeping" (11:33a).
- *"The Jews" say*, "See how he [Jesus] loved him [Lazarus]!" (11:36).
- *Some of "the Jews" say*, "Could not he who opened the eyes of the blind
  man [9:1–41] have kept this man from dying?" (11:37).

In this emotion-charged context, Jesus deals with deeply felt concerns
about delay and doubt wrapped up with poignant relational matters of love
and faith. Early in John 11, the narrator matter-of-factly weds Jesus's special love for the Bethany family with his considered decision not to rush to
Lazarus's bedside: "Though Jesus loved Martha and her sister and Lazarus,
after having heard that Lazarus was ill, he stayed two days longer in the
place where he was" (11:5–6). Though such delay seems like an odd, even
callous, way to show one's love, Jesus has everything figured out. Not to
worry, he tells his disciples, since he plans to arrive in Bethany *after* Lazarus's death precisely to raise him back to life! In fact, he has designed all
this for their benefit: "Our friend Lazarus has fallen asleep, but I am going
there to awaken him. . . . Then Jesus told them plainly, 'Lazarus is dead. For
your sake I am glad I was not there, so that you may believe. But let us go to
him" (11:11, 14–15). This is ultimately good for Jesus's reputation and for
the Twelve's education, but what about Martha's and Mary's experiences,

36. The Fourth Gospel's characterization of "the Jews" is complex and much debated.
Often (but not always) "the Jews" represent Jewish leaders and others who oppose Jesus and
his followers (who are also Jews, of course). In John 11, the story is mixed. While some of "the
Jews" operate as skeptics or enemies of Jesus (11:7, 36–37, 46, 54–57), others prove supportive
of Jesus and the bereaved family at Bethany (11:19, 45). On the overall "Jewish question" in
the Fourth Gospel, see Reinhartz, *Cast Out*; Reinhartz, "Gospel of John"; Bieringer, Pollefeyt,
and Vandecasteele-Vanneuville, *Anti-Judaism*.

to say nothing of poor Lazarus's, in the throes of his last breaths and four-day entombment (11:39)?

Whatever sympathy Jesus finally feels after the tearful Mary echoes her sister's lament that Jesus could have prevented her brother's death if he'd arrived sooner (John 11:21, 32) is laced with angry irritation. Jesus's tears seem to contain an excess of bitter salt. Did Martha and Mary merit this ire from Jesus? Their references to Jesus's late arrival may well represent affirmations of faith more than accusations of dilatory action ("Lord, we know you would have saved our dear brother, if you'd come sooner"). At any rate, there's no indication that they knew of Jesus's resuscitation plan, as previously disclosed to his disciples, who themselves don't fully understand (see 11:16).

But we know, and more critically, Jesus knows. Does he also expect the family and friends of Bethany to believe that death marks no barrier to Jesus's life-giving mission? Is he miffed, then, at their limited faith, overly constrained by physical boundaries of time and space? It's a big step from believing in a general resurrection of the dead at the end of the age, as Martha confidently averred (John 11:22–23), to believing in a personal revivification of a corpse back to life *now*, in this world. Nonetheless, Jesus is not shy about demanding bold faith in his power and authority in this episode (11:14–15, 25–26, 40–42) and elsewhere in the Fourth Gospel.[37]

The wider group of mourners echoes Mary and Martha's faith in Jesus's therapeutic prowess (citing the earlier case of giving sight to a blind man) but with a shade more doubt: "*Could not* he . . . have kept this man [he loved so much] from dying?" (John 11:37). In other words, was he *not able* (*ouk edynato*) to get the job done this time? Or did he not want to for some reason? Again, we knowing readers could quickly provide the reason. So once more, is Jesus simply upset that this bereaved audience does not intuit the bigger picture, does not believe that beyond giving a blind man sight, Jesus can bring a dead man back to life? The evidence tilts in that direction in Jesus's final statements just before he calls forth Lazarus from the tomb.

First, he somewhat testily reminds Martha, "Did I not tell you that *if you believed*, you would see the glory of God?" (John 11:40; cf. 11:23–26). Then, after the stone is removed from Lazarus's tomb per Jesus's order, Jesus utters a confident and grateful prayer to God for the benefit of the gathered mourners: "I knew that you [Father] always hear me, but I have said this for the sake of the crowd standing here, so that *they may believe* that you sent me" (11:42).

37. John 1:50–51; 2:18–22; 3:11–12; 5:43–47; 6:35–40, 47–48; 8:46–47; 9:35–38; 10:37–38; 12:35–36; 14:1, 10–14; 20:26–29. See Kysar, *John*, 93–114; Dodd, *Interpretation of the Fourth Gospel*, 179–86.

In this context, therefore, Jesus's anger appears to be associated with some deficiency in the people's faith. He's upset that they're upset about his delayed response to Lazarus's debility and death. Jesus's "If you only believed" pointedly counters Martha and Mary's "If you'd only been here!" Whew! Any way you slice it, that's a pretty gruff graveside manner, only slightly tempered by Jesus's weeping and scarcely recommended in pastoral care curricula. (Do *not* try this at the next funeral in your congregation.)

Of course, we probably wouldn't recommend the edgy way Jesus treats the leper in Mark 1 either. But setting aside the seminary grade Jesus might receive, we again mustn't lose sight of the core concern at the heart of Jesus's vehement emotion. The indomitable, fervent will to life evidenced in Mark's leper incident, the ardent commitment to restored vitality, appears just as central in John's Lazarus episode. Precisely because Jesus loves Lazarus and his sisters so much (John 11:3, 5, 36), he deeply desires their flourishing and adamantly aims to do everything he can to ensure and enhance their living. No statement from Jesus's lips throughout the Gospels asserts more forcefully his full embodiment of life than his response to Martha on the road to her house: "*I am the resurrection and the life.* Those who believe in me, even though they die, will live, and everyone who lives and believes in me will never die. Do you believe this?" (11:25–26).

Martha, amazingly, does believe but remains perplexed about Jesus's timetable. Well, aren't all we believers from time to time? Join the Martha club! With our laments of "If you'd only been here!" "How long, O Lord?" and such, we can question all we want: Jesus can take it and even invites our honest challenges. But we should also hear, see, and feel Jesus firing back with every fiber of his being: "Never doubt my love for you and my will to life!" That's not easy to do in the heat of trying ordeals. Such is the struggle of faith against faith, hope against hope—an intensely emotional as well as intellectual spiritual struggle.

Temple Tantrum and Royal Wrath (Matt. 21:12–17; Mark 11:15–19; Luke 19:11–27, 45–46; John 2:13–22)

Anger is more often shown than told, more often enacted than announced. Rarely will someone explicitly say "I'm really angry with you"; usually, you get the idea in the angry way someone speaks and acts toward you about some perceived irritating thing you've said or done. Likewise, narrative portrayals of characters' ire need not use specific lexemes denoting anger to convey the point. Although the primordial biblical anger case signals that "Cain was very angry," prompting God's query, "Why are you angry?" (Gen. 4:5–6), without these linguistic cues, we still would have readily discerned Cain's wrathful disposition from the stunning news that he "rose up against his brother Abel, and killed him" (4:8).

Thus in assessing Jesus's anger depicted in the Gospels, we should take into account reports of his seemingly volatile speech and action, absent specific anger language. Truth be told, Jesus is not prone to flying off the handle, which is not to say he is pusillanimous or passionless. But he generally acts and reacts in a reasonable, measured fashion, except to some degree for the incidents discussed above and perhaps, some would say, to a greater degree in that famous incident of cleaning the temple, narrated in all four Gospels (Matt. 21:12–17; Mark 11:15–19; Luke 19:45–46; John 2:13–22).

God's Faithful Prophet Acts

A kinetic Jesus dramatically upends tables of money changers and animal sellers and bounces these clerks out of the temple—with a whip in the Fourth Gospel's spicier version (John 2:15). Matthew indicates that such action sparks an "angry" response against Jesus by the chief priests and scribes (Matt. 21:15), but neither Matthew nor any other Gospel writer attributes anger to Jesus in this scene. Still, if any demonstration of Jesus's is anger driven, it would seem to be this veritable "temple tantrum," as one scholar has quipped.[38] In any event, the pressing question again concerns what motivates Jesus's emotive action. If he is moved with anger, against whom is it directed and why? Or maybe the lack of anger language points to a different affective state.

Of the episodes we've analyzed in this chapter, this one depicts the greatest physical movement on Jesus's part. More than simply stretching out his hand to a leper, looking around at a synagogue audience, or shedding a tear near a gravesite, here Jesus engages his whole body in turning over tables and throwing out (*ekballō*) tellers and sellers, with or without a whip. The Gospels differ somewhat on the scope of Jesus's expulsive action, the First and Fourth reporting that "he drove out *all*" the dealers (Matt. 21:12; John 2:14–15 [including sheep and cattle]), while the other two describe the action without quantification (Mark 11:15; Luke 19:45). At any rate, we should not imagine Jesus transforming into some "incredible Hulk" figure who suddenly sends every piece of temple furniture and all personnel flying through the air. A few toppled tables and dismissed persons would sufficiently disturb the

38. Fredriksen, *From Jesus to Christ*, xxi.

peace and drive home Jesus's point, an unmistakably emotional point that Jesus cares deeply about with his whole being.

But the precise nexus of Jesus's physical, mental, and emotional feelings is not altogether clear, particularly the extent to which anger fuels his actions. The matter-of-fact report that he "entered the temple and drove out" (Matt. 21:12; Mark 11:15; Luke 19:45) the merchants suggests a deliberate purpose, a planned protest, reinforced in Mark's Gospel where Jesus cases the temple compound the night before his public demonstration (Mark 11:11).[39] Of course, just because Jesus enters the temple intent on making a scene doesn't mean he executes it with cool, calm efficiency. But allowing for surges of adrenaline and tinges of anger does not turn this episode into a fit of pique. He knows exactly what he's doing; there is calculated method to the madness.

To discern this method, we focus on the literary setting of the event and Jesus's reported speech in the Synoptic parallels.[40] This temple incident slots in as the second stage of Jesus's climactic procession into Jerusalem, immediately following his dramatic entrance into the city to popular paeans of his Davidic royal authority. The core issue of God's kingdom—the right and just rule of God—is thus paramount in Jesus's mind. And not surprisingly, Jesus interprets that divine rule in reformative terms drawn from the biblical prophets. The only direct words from Jesus in this scene are direct quotations from Isaiah and Jeremiah: "Is it not written, 'My house shall be called a house of prayer for all the nations' [Isa. 56:7]? But you have made it a den of robbers [Jer. 7:11]" (Mark 11:17). In brief, then, Jesus enacts a shocking, symbolic drama to demonstrate that, in its current corrupt state, the temple and its leaders are undermining the rule of God they should be upholding, effectively creating a godless haven for rapacious, self-serving exploiters of God's people.

Instead of smashing a clay jug in the Hinnom valley at the base of the temple mount, as Jeremiah did to signify prophetic judgment against God's (un)holy city and sanctuary (Jer. 19:1–15), Jesus shatters tables and scatters people working in the temple courts. He's not opposed to the temple in principle or to these money changers and merchants in particular. They are necessary facilitators of temple business, ensuring proper sacrifices purchased with special temple coinage. Although it's possible that these functionaries were using their positions to line their pockets and "rob" the people, they are not so indicted in the Gospels, as tax collectors are numerous times. Rather,

---

39. The mention of Jesus "*making* a whip of cords" in John 2:15 also suggests premeditated action.

40. Prescinding for this analysis the Fourth Gospel's much earlier setting of this episode in John 2:13–22.

these temple workers represent the temple economic system, controlled at that time by compromised priestly authorities most responsible, in Jesus's view, for exploiting the people they should be serving, including poor, vulnerable widows (see Mark 12:38–44; Luke 20:45–21:4; see also Jer. 7:5–6).[41] By disrupting the business of these temple operatives for a while (they'll be up and running again soon enough), Jesus signifies his judgment that a total temple shutdown is in order until the institution returns to its God-ordained purpose.[42]

Jesus is clearly not happy with the present temple system, and it would not be surprising if he feels some anger amid his table-flipping and people-ousting actions. A bit earlier in Mark's narrative, Jesus becomes "angry" at his disciples for attempting to block those who are bringing little children to him for his therapeutic touch (Mark 10:13–16). Again, we can reasonably expect he has similarly cross sentiments toward uncompassionate temple officials obstructing pastoral care of the least and lowliest. Nonetheless, Mark and his fellow evangelists' Synoptic Gospels do not overly accentuate the physical-emotional force of the temple demonstration; it remains a more ambiguous example of Jesus's anger than the incidents examined above. Yet whatever trace of anger might motivate Jesus's temple drama, it is again associated with his fervent will to life: "King" Jesus vehemently resists any move, especially by religious leaders who should know better, to "rob" vulnerable people of God's gracious, life-giving nurture.

Before we close the book, however, on Jesus as milder, meeker, mule-borne prophet-king, we must scan a possible future horizon anticipating Jesus's return as militant, majestic, cloud-borne judge-king at the end of the age. No more Mr. Nice Guy. The enemies of God and Christ will finally receive the hard justice they deserve, the full force of divine wrath. This is not the place to engage in full-scale discussion of Jesus's eschatology and the kingdom of God. But one parable from Luke's Jesus merits reconsideration, especially its application to the fate of unfaithful servants "in the hands of an angry God" and angry Christ. Typical of other harsh judgment stories told by Jesus, the parable of the pounds (or *minas*, a monetary unit) in Luke 19:11–27 features a brutal king who exacts violent vengeance on his enemies.

---

41. The priestly leaders were particularly compromised by their dependence on Roman patronage, as nicely summarized by Skinner, *Companion to the New Testament*, 36: "The priestly aristocracy and the Roman prefect shared a relationship of complementary but unequal power during Jesus' lifetime. . . . Rome retained the authority to install and dismiss individual high priests. . . . To retain their status and cultural influence . . . the priests had to cooperate with and respect the empire's priorities. . . . The partnership was founded on political expediency and mutual benefit; tensions remained inevitable among the Jewish priestly elites . . . and a Roman sociopolitical order committed to upholding Roman economic and political values as supreme."

42. See E. Sanders, *Jesus and Judaism*, 61–71; E. Sanders, *Historical Figure of Jesus*, 254–62.

Caesar's Vengeful Client Axes

In the history of Gospel interpretation, authority figures depicted in Jesus's parables—king, ruler, landlord, judge, father—have commonly been assumed to represent God or Christ. Though a natural interpretive move, it is not a necessary one and can even be antithetical to Jesus's point. Jesus tells parables as part of his core curriculum concerning the kingdom (rule, reign, empire) of God. But these pithy stories are more illustrative than definitive, teasing out what God's realm is like, triggering fresh, imaginative reflection and reassessment.[43] Out of familiar, everyday scenarios, Jesus often springs a surprising punch to reorient traditional social attitudes rather than to reinforce moral platitudes. And in the process, while characters within the parables may evoke divine and messianic characteristics, they are not automatic stand-ins for God or Christ. God explicitly appears in only one parable (Luke 12:20) and Jesus not at all. Jesus's parables are not media of self-disclosure, still less of self-promotion. While the father figure in the famous parable of the prodigal son does fairly represent Father God, neither younger nor elder son matches Son Jesus (15:11–32); and the father in the parable of the friend at midnight contrasts as much as compares with the divine Patriarch (11:5–8). And we should be especially cautious about correlating God and Jesus with earthly rulers and managers, given their penchant for avarice, injustice, and abuse of power.

So what to do with the parable of the talents, which ends with the vicious killing of the "king's" enemies (Luke 19:27) and, in its Lukan setting, leads directly into Jesus's final entry into Jerusalem to adulatory cries of "Blessed is the king who comes in the name of the Lord" (19:38)?[44] How do we interpret this juxtaposition of "royal" parable and procession?

The simplest and clearest explanation, Occam's famed razor, marks a sharp antithesis between the king portrayed in Jesus's parable and the king Jesus exemplifies. Although he rides into town on a colt that he commandeers as "Lord" (Luke 19:30–34), he hardly flexes his lordly muscles before the adoring "multitude of disciples" that seems to assemble and burst out in song spontaneously (19:37). And then, in Luke's uniquely poignant account, Jesus breaks down in tears over what he perceives as Jerusalem's terrible fate. Because the city's leaders and those who follow them refuse to accept "the

---

43. C. H. Dodd's classic definition of a parable aptly captures core elements in Jesus's examples: "A metaphor or simile drawn from nature or common life, arresting the hearer by its vividness or strangeness, and leaving the mind in sufficient doubt of its precise application to tease it into active thought." Dodd, *Parables of the Kingdom*, 16.

44. And directly following Jesus's procession into Jerusalem, Luke narrates Jesus's forceful temple/house cleaning (Luke 19:45–48), discussed above.

things that make for peace," Jesus laments that they will soon be crushed by foreign "enemies"—not by God and certainly not by Jesus now, who wields no sword and commands no army (19:41–44).[45] He comes to his people via an *anti*-triumphal entry as the brokenhearted peaceful king (19:38; cf. 2:14), the very opposite of the hardhearted vengeful king of the parable.[46]

Perhaps, however, Occam's razor should be updated to more modern multi-blade instruments. Jesus's royal-messianic vocation is commonly conceived as a double-edged sword, cutting two ways: one edge he wields metaphorically as a shepherd king and a servant ruler who succors and restores his people during his earthly ministry; the other he wields more literally as a warrior king and a royal judge who punishes and banishes the wicked on the final day of reckoning. In this scheme, the Jerusalem procession depicts the former, humbler image culminating in Jesus's crucifixion, while the parable of the pounds projects the latter, stronger image at Christ's consummating return.[47]

Yet apart from the fact that this historical scheme reverses Luke's narrative order (the parable precedes the narrative of the entry incident), the parable admits to a very different reading, one more firmly rooted in first-century Roman-Palestinian soil and more consistent with Luke's overall portrait of Jesus, who eschews retaliation against enemies (Luke 6:27–36; cf. Matt. 5:38–48).[48] To be sure, Luke periodically depicts Jesus's frustration with his own disciples, as well as with religious and political leaders, and reports Jesus's pronouncements of judgment on unrepentant sinners.[49] But Luke also strategically deletes harsh prophetic statements of divine vengeance (the citation of Isa. 61:1–2 in Luke 4:18–19 stops right before Isaiah's reference to "the day of vengeance of our God") and Mark's attributions of anger and indignation to Jesus (compare Mark 1:41 CEB; 3:5; 10:14 with Luke 5:13; 6:8–10; 18:16, respectively). Comparing Jesus to a stern king who demands responsible stewardship from his following has its place in Luke and other Gospel presentations. But pushing the analogy toward a king who petulantly demands that his enemies be slaughtered in his presence because "they did not

45. Luke's Jesus elaborates on this expected destruction of the holy city in 21:5–24, when "Jerusalem will be trampled on by the Gentiles" (21:24). This reasonably refers to Rome's razing of Jerusalem and its temple in 70 CE, a devastating event that Jesus, like many others, could anticipate on the near horizon and that had likely already occurred at the time of Luke's writing.

46. See my fuller discussion in Spencer, *Luke*, 482–96.

47. This popular scheme presumes a direct correspondence between the royal official's "return" in Luke's parable (19:12, 15, 23) and Jesus's return to earth (second coming).

48. See, e.g., the stimulating readings by Vinson, "Minas Touch"; Schottroff, *Parables of Jesus*, 183–87; and Parsons, *Luke*, 280–85.

49. E.g., Luke 6:39–42; 7:31–35; 8:22–25; 9:41, 49–55; 11:37–53; 12:49–59; 13:1–5, 22–35; 16:14–18; 20:1–21:4; 22:39–53; 24:25–26.

want [him] to be king over them" (19:27) seems a bridge too far to traverse, and not just for squeamish bleeding hearts.

Here's the background to the parable's protagonist. He's a "nobleman"—that is, "a man of noble birth [*eugenēs*]" (Luke 19:12 NIV) and valuable estate—who journeys to "a distant [*makran*] country to get royal power [a kingdom (*basileian*)] for himself and then return" (19:12). From the outset, this profile ill fits Luke's Jesus.[50] The highfalutin figure in Jesus's story seeks promotional patronage (presumably from an imperial sovereign) to be a client-king over his home territory. But as it happens, he's not exactly the most popular aristocrat in the land. We soon learn that the local citizenry whom the nobleman seeks to rule hates him so much that they send an embassy to the (implied) emperor, pleading: "We do not want this man to rule [*basileusai*] over us" (19:14). The voice of the people, however, falls on deaf ears, as is usually the case in imperial politics. Despite the citizens' protests, the man receives his desired royal appointment, returns to his homeland, and promptly proceeds to exert his new authority.

He first assesses three slaves charged with managing a pound each in their master's absence. He happily rewards two for their exorbitant (fraudulent?) thousand and five-hundred percent returns, respectively, on his investment, granting them mayoral positions over multiple cities! And so this new "king" aims to cement control over his realm via his own patronage appointments. The third slave, however, is turned out on his ear for choosing to safeguard the pound and not risk the market. Significantly, his motivation stemmed from his assessment of the nobleman's character as anything but noble: "I was afraid of you," he tells his master, "because you are a *harsh* [*austēros*] man; you take what you did not deposit, and reap what you did not sow" (Luke 19:21). In other words, this slave played it safe because of his owner's reputation as a strict, stingy, exploitative plutocrat padding his own coffers by hook or crook.[51] Tellingly, the ignoble king agrees verbatim with the slave's character judgment ("Yes, I am a severe man; everybody knows that"), prompting him to query why the slave didn't at least deposit the money in an interest-earning

50. Three reasons stand out: (1) though Jesus is from the line of David, his birth in a manger to a lowly woman scarcely qualifies as a "noble birth"; (2) in contrast to the nobleman in the parable who must travel to seek royal power from the emperor, Luke's Jesus already has divine royal power now, on earth, before his ascension and return; (3) "distant country" (*chōra makran*) designates alien, godless territory in the parable of the prodigal son (Luke 15:13); it would be odd for this place suddenly to signify the heavenly realm in the pounds parable (19:12).

51. BDAG 151–52 notes that the term *austēros* (occurring only in Luke 19:21–22 in the New Testament) is "used [especially] of [persons] who practice rigid personal discipline or are strict in the supervision of others"; Luke's parable thus images "a tough, uncompromising, punctilious financier."

bank account (19:22–23). For his reasonable fear concerning the master's cruel disposition, the slave is stripped of his pound and his managerial status.

The emotional tenor of this story thus far generates scant sympathy for the autocratic royal figure, still less any affinity with Jesus. But the parable king's stern reaction to the self-protective slave is mild compared to what he does to those who lobbied against rule. While his severe, win-at-all-costs economic policy might seek "blood out of a stone," as one source has quipped,[52] he finally gets real blood out of the bodies of these "enemies of mine" (Luke 19:27). He takes all this very personally, dripping with bloodlust.

This parable mirrors Archelaus in first-century Roman Palestine, as reported by the Jewish historian Josephus (*Ant.* 17.206–344; cf. *J.W.* 2.80–100). The succession battles in the wake of Herod the Great's death brought his sons Archelaus and Antipas to Rome to appeal for Caesar's patronage. Archelaus had the greater testamentary claim and initial support from Jewish leaders who hoped he would rule more moderately than his tyrannical father. However, when a group protested the harsh policies of the deceased Herod at Passover, Archelaus had them slaughtered—all three thousand of them! So much for moderation. This vicious retaliation prompted fifty ambassadors to travel to Rome and join with eight thousand resident Jews in lobbying against Archelaus's royal appointment: "How then could they avoid the just hatred of [Archelaus], who, to the rest of his barbarity, has added this [slaughter of three thousand] . . . that they opposed and contradicted in the exercise of his authority?" (*Ant.* 17.313). Not surprisingly, Caesar sided with Archelaus against the Jewish embassy, though he limited Archelaus's position to ethnarch over Judea and Samaria, about half of Herod's kingdom. Moreover, after further accusations of Archelaus's "barbarous and tyrannical" actions, Caesar banished him to Vienna and placed Judea and Samaria under direct Roman military rule (*Ant.* 17.339–44). Whether Jesus's first hearers or Luke's first readers connected the nobleman-king with Archelaus, they would doubtless have heard the parable as an emblematic report of wicked royal affairs.[53]

---

52. From the entry on *austēros* in MM 93: "The epithet of Lk 19[21] is poorly rendered by the word we have borrowed ["austere"]. It obviously means 'strict, exacting,' a man who expects to get blood out of a stone."

53. For further analysis of Josephus's accounts of Archelaus in relation to this parable, see Schultz, "Jesus as Archelaus"; and van Eck, "Social Memory and Identity." Schultz ("Jesus as Archelaus," 112–19) persuasively argues that Jesus telling this parable en route from Jericho to Jerusalem sparks memory of Archelaus's reign, since according to Josephus (*Ant.* 17.340), Archelaus refurbished Herod the Great's palace in Jericho and also constructed a new city to promote his own honor in the vicinity. In my view, however, Schultz wrongly concludes that Luke's Jesus appeals to the Archelaus scenario to reinforce Jesus's stern message of judgment. By contrast, van Eck (rightly) interprets Jesus's use of Archelaus as a violent, voracious antitype to the peaceful, gracious aims of God's reign.

And most importantly *within* Luke's narrative, in response to his followers' pressing concern about the "kingdom of God" as he nears Jerusalem (Luke 19:11), Jesus tells this emotional story charged with anger and hatred, fear and violence as typical of the diabolical "kingdoms of the world" (cf. 4:5) opposed to God's realm embodied in Jesus Messiah. The grasping nobleman-king in the story is a veritable antichrist figure, from whose oppressive clutches Jesus—God's true viceroy, a man of humble origins and broken heart as he enters Jerusalem to die on a cross—seeks to deliver the lowliest of his people, slave and citizen alike.

We will sift his royal tears more finely in the next chapter. For now, we stress that whatever anger Jesus expresses toward those who would thwart his indomitable commitment to flourishing life, and however much he himself desires to live rather than die, he by no means concludes his final days of suffering in anger and bitterness. Indeed, following Luke's unique portrait, we marvel at Jesus's poignant display of forgiveness, salvation, and trustful commitment from the cross (Luke 23:34, 40–42, 46).

4

That's Heart Rending!

The Anguished Jesus in Ministry

The emotion of grief or sadness, common to ancient and modern lists of basic emotions, usually focuses on visceral responses to the death of beloved family members and friends. No passion certifies more strongly how "our relational life and our emotional life are indistinguishable."[1] As social creatures hardwired for nurturing attachment, we ache when ties that bind are severed in death.

As it happens, however, the Gospels provide scant evidence of Jesus's dealings with deaths of cherished relations. Jesus has no wife or children to lose, and he predeceases his mother and siblings. As for (step-)father Joseph, he likely died before Jesus did, given the average forty-year life spans of the time and Joseph's early disappearance from the Gospel narratives. That the Gospels say nothing about Joseph's death or Jesus's reaction to it is not surprising in light of their emphasis on Jesus's divine paternity.

Gospel portrayals of death and grief concentrate on Jesus's own crucifixion and resurrection, prefigured in his periodic revivification of deceased persons during his ministry. In the process, Jesus deals with others' weeping over lost children (Mark 5:35–43; Luke 7:11–17; 8:49–56) and with those who mourn his pending or past demise (Luke 22:45–46; 23:27–31; 24:13–53; John 19:25–27; 20:11–29). He responds with calm compassion for the bereaved, his emotions tempered by his aim to resuscitate dead children and restore them

---

1. Bosworth, "Understanding Grief," 126.

to their parents and by his hope that God will raise him from the dead (Mark 8:31; 9:31; 10:33–34; Luke 24:6–7). Overall, then, Jesus's personal experience of grief seems limited.

But it is not altogether absent from the Gospel tradition. Recall the poignant cases we broached in the last chapter, where Jesus weeps near Lazarus's grave (John 11:35) and the gates of Jerusalem (Luke 19:41–44). Also remember Jesus's grief (grievance) in Mark 3:5 at some Pharisees' callousness concerning the man with a withered hand, whom Jesus apparently meets for the first time and who, though disabled, is in no immediate danger of dying. Our main focus in the previous chapter was on Jesus's anger in these episodes. Yet the element of grief is not trivial and merits more careful attention, not least regarding how it mixes with anger.

Good Grief

Before diving into these Gospel grief-scenes, it is useful to set our investigation of this common emotion in a broader framework. While humans naturally grieve the loss of dear life, they do not all mourn in the same way or express the same feelings—at least not in public. While all emotions swirl within an affective network of physical, conceptual, and cultural exchange, none is more formally ritualized in public performance than grief. Mourning and funerary traditions both reflect and construct grief. In the US today, one only has to attend wakes, visitations, funerals, and other associated events in different religious contexts to observe distinctive emotional practices. And we should not expect to map modern patterns of grief onto ancient societies without some distortion.

In modern Western psychology, the influential five-stage process of grief (denial, anger, bargaining, depression, acceptance) delineated by Elisabeth Kübler-Ross derives from analyzing individuals coping with their own terminal diagnoses.[2] Though this scheme is not irrelevant to wider social experiences of loss, it does not provide a universal template for grief. Casting a broader cultural net and tracking responses to familial loss of a spouse or children under traumatic conditions, George Bonanno charts four possible "trajectories" of grief management, focused more on temporal duration than temperamental evolution: (1) resilience, (2) recovery, (3) chronic grief, and (4) delayed grief.[3] Generally speaking, the first two options mark a healthier course to wholeness,

---

2. Kübler-Ross and Kessler, *On Grief and Grieving*.
3. Bonanno, "Loss, Trauma, and Human Resilience"; Bonanno and Field, "Examining the Delayed Grief Hypothesis." More recently, however, Bonanno focuses on the first three

either with little lag between the event of the loss and moving on with life (resilience) or more extended—but not protracted—bereavement en route to more normal functioning (recovery). The latter two trajectories either lock one into a vicious dysfunctional cycle (chronic grief) or set one up for a major ambush of grief at some later point (delayed grief). Again, cultures reinforce these patterns through various norms and rituals.

For example, as Hebrew Bible scholar David Bosworth explains, whereas modern American clergy and counselors might blanch at King David getting on with business as usual right after learning that his sick child has died, this resilient response need not be regarded as callous. David's weeklong fasting vigil demonstrates his genuine concern for his "very ill" baby, and his riposte to his servants' query about his quick rebound is reasonable, even if curious by others' standards in David's day, as in ours: "But now [the child] is dead; why should I fast? Can I bring him back again? I shall go to him, but he will not return to me" (2 Sam. 12:23; see 12:15–22).[4]

Along with appropriating Jewish Scripture, the Gospel authors, writing in Greek, operated within Hellenistic frames of thought. A well-known Stoic system classified emotions (*pathē*) into four quadrants along moral (good/evil) and temporal (present/prospective) axes, as the classics scholar Margaret Graver charts.[5]

	Present	Prospective
Good	delight (*hēdonē*)	desire (*epithymia*)
Evil	distress (*lypē*)	fear (*phobos*)

The common assessment of Stoics as dispassionate intellectuals striving to extirpate all emotion from human experience is too extreme. Stoic sages acknowledged the inevitability of emotional impulses; the issue was how one dealt with these jolts, particularly resisting their irrational upheaval of one's tranquility. If properly regulated, certain "good" emotions (*eupatheia*) could be put to good effects in the present and future.[6]

For our interests, the category of "distress" proves most relevant, since the noun *lypē*, the verb *lypeomai*, and the compounds *perilypos* and *syllypeomai*

---

trajectories, omitting "delayed grief" for lack of evidence; see Bonanno, *Other Side of Sadness*, 8–10, 28–29. See also the helpful discussion in Bosworth, "Understanding Grief," 117–19.

4. Bosworth, "Faith and Resilience"; Bosworth, "Understanding Grief," 119.
5. Graver, *Stoicism and Emotion*, 54.
6. See the taxonomy of *eupatheia* charted in Graver, *Stoics and Emotion*, 54, 58:

	Present	Prospective
Good	joy	wish
Evil	—	caution

represent the main grief terminology used in Gospel passages denoting Jesus's anguish. In ancient Greek usage, *lyp-* applied to a broad range of unpleasant feelings "from physical pain . . . to psychological distress."[7] Under the "distress" (*lypē*) genus of Stoic passions, Graver lists several "species" of emotions associated with related terms, including "grief" (*penthos*) and "anguish" (*odynē*).[8] Of course, since synonyms may be used interchangeably in certain contexts, "grief" and "anguish" can also render *lyp-* terms in settings of severe loss.

In any event, the question of how much emotional force may be poured into any "distress" language must be evaluated case by case. Ancients and moderns readily grant overlaps among physical, mental, and emotional sufferings, but percentages of each type are impossible to calculate in different circumstances. If I bang my toe on the bedpost at night and break the poor digit, I will feel plenty of physical pain but probably not much mental anguish, beyond feeling stupid for not walking more carefully, and not much emotional depression either, unless I'm a kicker for a professional football team. As for more serious life-losses of loved ones or sudden confrontations with our own fragile mortality due to disease or disasters, we will no doubt experience the gamut of painful feelings but, again, in varying degrees of resilience, resentment, and resignation.

In Aristotle's catalog of fourteen emotions (*pathē*), which predates the Stoics, he conspicuously does not include grief or related feelings of sadness, despair, or anguish. Of course, he does not deny negative, depressive reactions in a world beset by evil, suffering, and loss. But he spreads the possibility of such feelings across the emotional spectrum under the macrocategory of *pain* (*lypē*). Distinct from the later Stoics, Aristotle sets up a polar binary (rather than quadratic) tension of *pleasure* (*hēdonē*) versus *pain* (*lypē*) that all passions negotiate one way or another, ideally in sober moderation: "The emotions [*pathē*] are those things through which, by undergoing change, people come to differ in their judgments and which are accompanied by pain [*lypē*] and pleasure [*hēdonē*]" (*Rhet.* 2.1.8 [1378a]).

In analyzing this Aristotelian scheme along with Greek drama and stressing the "ritualized aspect" of grief "under the jurisdiction of public authority and custom," David Konstan wonders if "grief might not qualify as a *pathos* at all" in the classical period.[9] Distinct from other passions, grief is more "passive" and "morally neutral." Then, as now, one may erupt in a paroxysm

7. Harris, *Restraining Rage*, 343.
8. Graver, *Stoicism and Emotion*, 55–56.
9. Konstan, *Emotions*, 258.

at some person or institution perceived to have caused the loss of a beloved partner, kicking into the emotional gear of retaliatory anger. But, as Konstan contends, for the classical Greek, grief manifested as a more inward, inactive (not "action ready") response to the matter-of-fact event of loss, externalized mainly in prescribed mourning ceremonies.[10]

This ritualized perspective on grief did not make flinty Spartans out of all ancient Greeks. Loss of life, however natural, was still painful and needed to be processed; one should just take pains not to get too over-wrought and unduly prolong the grief: "Grief . . . was reasonable and nec-essary in its proper place, or rather, in its proper moment. It is persistent, unrelenting grief that the ancients are unanimous in discouraging."[11] Fair enough: Greek philosophers were nothing if not "reasonable," and long-term, incapacitating grief seems anything but logical (what good comes from compounding loss with soul-strangling grief?). Yet logical or not, in the more immediate—and especially unexpected—experience of a loved one's death, it is altogether human to be hit with emotional pain and diz-zying disorientation: a shattering of one's world, hopefully temporary but no less disruptive for as long as it lasts.

Few modern philosophers have grappled more incisively with the phenom-enon of grief than Martha Nussbaum, who draws in particular on the robust view of the early Stoic sage Chrysippus.[12] As Nussbaum explains, "Chrysippus plausibly said that grief . . . contains not only the judgment that an important part of my life is gone, but that *it is right* to be upset about that: it makes a truth-claim about its own evaluations. It asserts the real value of the object, it says that getting upset is a response to something really important, not just a whim."[13] Because grief is so intimately attached to a lost, prized "object," it represents a "wrenching, tearing violation of [one's] self-sufficiency and . . . undisturbed condition. The passion is a 'very violent motion' that carries us along, 'pushing us violently' toward action."[14] While it tends to dissipate over time, it first delivers a thunder punch to the gut; or in Chrysippus's terms (quoted by Nussbaum), it is "*prosphaton*: not yet spoiled or digested, 'fresh.' . . . The 'fresh' acceptance is something tearing and wrenching. Since it concerns [one's] deepest values and projects, it upsets everything in me, all the cognitive structures of hope, cherishing, and expectation . . . built up

10. Konstan, *Emotions*, 244–58.
11. Konstan, *Emotions*, 256.
12. Nussbaum, *Therapy*, 375–89. See also Nussbaum's very personal as well as philosophical treatment of grief (and other emotions) in Nussbaum, *Upheavals*, 19–88.
13. Nussbaum, *Upheavals*, 47 (emphasis original).
14. Nussbaum, *Therapy*, 380.

around those values."[15] Perhaps a better label for this fresh upheaval of grief would be "raw."

Reinforcing this raw, rough, ragged edge of grief, inflicting a "cascade" of physical and psychological pain, the neuroscientist and molecular biologist Giovanni Frazzetto avers, "The physical pain sensed when we stub a toe or hit a wall is the effect of a *collision* that damages our tissue. The pain of loss or the breaking of an emotional bond, on the other hand, is the consequence of a physical *separation*. Something departs from our surroundings and from our lives. All the same its disappearance hurts us, causing pain just as would colliding with the wall."[16]

Accustomed as Christians may be to the risen Jesus's spectral passing through walls and doors (Luke 24:36–37; John 20:19, 26), Jesus adopts normal modes of transport (foot, boat, donkey) throughout his earthly life. And at distressing moments he stops in his tracks emotionally and "hits the wall," as we say, weeping outside Bethany near the stone structure entombing his friend Lazarus (John 11:35, 38) and again just outside the majestic walls of Jerusalem, which he envisions as soon crumbling, leaving not "one stone upon another" (Luke 19:41–44; cf. 21:5–6, 20–24). We turn now to a closer investigation of these and other "collision" episodes in Jesus's ministry that spark anguished grief.

Acutely Aggrieved (Mark 3:1–6)

Along with the anger Mark's Jesus feels when he meets the eyes of those suspiciously watching to see if he will heal a man's shriveled hand on the Sabbath, he also becomes "grieved at their hardness of heart" (Mark 3:5). Far from being two discrete sensations, however, in the way that one might feel both wet (because it's raining) and wobbly (because of a recent knee surgery) at a given moment, Jesus's anger and grief are closely related in the present context.[17] Grammatically, Mark 3:5's "look[ing] around [*periblepsamenos*] at them with anger" and "[being] grieved [*syllypoumenos*] at their hardness of heart" are parallel participle constructions, and the latter participle, a compound form of *lypeō* meaning "to feel hurt or grief with someone at the

15. Nussbaum, *Therapy*, 381–82.

16. Frazzetto, *Joy, Guilt, Anger, Love*, 120 (emphasis original).

17. At the Democratic presidential primary debate in Miami, Florida, on June 26, 2019, candidate Julián Castro responded to the horrific, viral picture of a dead refugee father and young daughter on the US bank of the Rio Grande River with an appropriate mix of searing grief and anger: "Watching that image of Óscar and his daughter Valeria is heartbreaking. It should also piss us all off." "First Democratic Debate."

same time,"[18] strengthens the connection. The *syl-* prefix, like *syn-* and *sym-*, connotes togetherness, socially ("with someone") and/or temporally ("at the same time"). While Jesus experiences anger and grief simultaneously, the relational component of the grief is more ambiguous.

What exactly does being grieved *at* (*epi*) the Pharisees' hardheartedness mean? Is this just another way of describing Jesus's anger or elaborating on it, conveying pained aggravation—being aggrieved—more than sadness or dejection related to loss? Or is it possible that Jesus grieves together or sympathizes with the man and his loss of dexterity and lack of therapy on this Sabbath, if certain legal hardliners have their way? On this score, Jesus could be mad at the lawyers and sad with the infirm man at the same time.

But acknowledging the presence of mixed feelings doesn't take us very far in understanding the chemistry of this confluence. Recent study has aimed for greater precision in tracking cause-and-effect links between emotions or, more simply, how we feel about feelings, a concept known as "metaemotion."[19] In chapter 1, I discussed prospective aspects of emotional reasoning involving our tendency to make decisions on the basis of anticipated future feelings. Metaemotional analysis, however, concentrates more on correlating a chain of past and present feelings in patterns of "reflexivity." Say, for example, that as a "first order" or "primary" emotion I persist for some time in being angry at someone who has demeaned me. Front and center in my experience, such ire assumes a life of its own, prompting secondary, reflective analysis concerning a cascade of "affective reactions *toward* the primary emotion"[20] or how I feel about the pressing vitriolic feelings. Perhaps I will find some sadistic joy in plotting revenge or, on the flip side, turning the attack on myself, some masochistic anguish at my corrosive bitterness and lack of self-control. Other factors may also prompt me to be sad about being mad, such as seeing the adverse effect that my bitterness has on my family or the disquiet that attends my increasing loss of faith in the goodness of humanity, God, or fate.

On a positive-negative scale that researchers use to evaluate metaemotions, the causal nexus of anger → grief tends to reflect a negative → negative valence.[21] In other words, grief typically feels out and fleshes out the vexatious pain of anger, adding more complex texture and tenor to one's hurt feelings

18. BDAG 956; cf. Aristotle, *Eth. nic.* 9.11 (1171b).

19. Norman and Furnes, "Concept of 'Metaemotion'"; Mendonça, "Emotions about Emotions"; see also the helpful summary of key ideas in Bailen, Hallenbeck, and Thompson, "How to Deal with Feeling Bad."

20. Bartsch et al., "Appraisal of Emotions," 16 (emphasis added); quoted in Norman and Furnes, "Concept of 'Metaemotion,'" 188.

21. Other possibilities are negative → positive, positive → negative, and positive → positive.

and harmful thoughts. Though grief may dial down the intensity of first-order anger to some degree and dampen the impulse toward vengeance, it scarcely makes one feel better about the situation and may well prolong the pain in a slide toward chronic depression.

Given the strong antipathetic (negative) link in Mark's account between Jesus's initial perception of the Pharisee-led synagogue audience's hypercritical mindset and his attendant anguish at their hardheartedness, any sympathetic (positive) feelings Jesus might have toward the man with the withered hand appear beside the point. Though Jesus aims to heal the man, in this case he's not particularly motivated by compassion (unlike in Mark 6:34; 8:2). The main surge of Jesus's emotional energy reacts to the assembly's emotional judgments against him, which are rooted in their restrictive interpretations of Sabbath law. Of course, the entire affective scenario significantly affects the disabled man, too—but only secondarily, as he finds himself in the crossfire between Jesus and the circle of onlookers.

In the last chapter, I suggested that Mark's Jesus becomes angry at public questioning, doubting, or diverting in any way, implicit or explicit, his passionate commitment to flourishing life and full capability for all people.[22] In the present incident he vehemently resists any misinterpretations of biblical law or suspicious investigations by religious teachers that might inhibit his whole-making, life-giving mission, especially on God's sacred day of rest/restoration. Accordingly, he has no qualms about the appropriateness (righteousness) of his anger. In no way does he turn his attendant grief back on himself, as if feeling sad and bad about feeling mad in the first place.

Revisiting Frazzetto's comparison of the pain of grief to a physical collision, we can see Jesus hit a grievous emotional wall in his angry encounter with critics in the synagogue, colliding with their hard, calloused (pōrōsis [Mark 3:5]) hearts, no less hard and hurtful for being set metaphorically rather than metabolically in stone. The classic biblical case of hardheartedness involves Pharaoh's repeated reneging on promises to free the Israelite slaves, whose lives he couldn't care less about.[23] But Pharaoh's obstinate refusal to comply with Moses's demand for his people's release does not perfectly parallel the Pharisees' adamant resistance to Jesus's plan to restore the man's withered hand. The Pharisees may exploit the disabled man on this occasion to score legal points against Jesus, but they do not own the man or work him to death. Indeed, they do not oppose the man's healing per se and would doubtless

---

22. For a robust "capabilities approach" to human flourishing, including physical and emotional components, see Nussbaum, *Creating Capabilities*; Nussbaum, *Frontiers of Justice*.
23. See Exod. 4:21; 7:13–14, 22–23; 8:15, 19, 32; 9:7, 12, 34–35; 10:1, 20, 27; 11:10; 14:8.

be happy to alleviate his physical debilitation—on any of the week's other six days. Accordingly, Jesus pushes back at the Pharisees' "block-hearted" obstruction not with punishing plagues like those Pharaoh received but with personal pain, aggrieved anguish, and persistent resolve to restore the man's hand to full function over the Pharisees' deep-seated objections. As a result, Jesus puts himself at risk of harsher attacks down the line (Mark 3:6).

A better match with the Pharisees' hardhearted response to Jesus involves Jesus's disciples in Mark's narrative. Following Jesus's tense exchange with the Pharisees in the synagogue, he "departed with his disciples to the sea" where he requested "to have a boat ready for him" (Mark 3:7, 9). On two subsequent boating ventures, each following Jesus's munificent feeding of a multitude over his disciples' objections (6:30–44; 8:1–10), they continue to evince *their* hardhearted lack of understanding "about the loaves" (and fishes) Jesus provided the crowd and what they signified about his life-sustaining mission.

First, after Jesus walks on windswept waters to his terrified disciples in a boat and calms the turbulence in both the lake and his associates' hearts ("Take heart, it is I; do not be afraid" [Mark 6:50]), the narrator concludes with a critical assessment of their condition: "For they did not understand about the loaves, but their *hearts were hardened [pepōrōmenē]*" (6:52). The disciples remained blocked from grasping Jesus's life-saving purpose and power. Second, on another lake excursion, Jesus notices that his disciples have brought no bread aboard and warns them about "the yeast of the Pharisees and the yeast of Herod." They miss his point by ridiculously literalizing the yeast analogy: "It is because we have no bread" (8:15–16). This thickheaded response sparks a lengthy rebuke by Teacher Jesus: "Why are you talking about having no bread. Do you still not perceive or understand? Are your *hearts hardened [pepōrōmenēn]*? . . . Do you not remember? When I broke the five loaves for the five thousand . . . and the seven for the four thousand? . . . Do you not yet understand?" (8:17–21).

Both episodes correlate the disciples' hardheartedness with diminished perception of Jesus's heartfelt compassion (Mark 6:34; 8:2) on the needy masses coupled with a dogged intention to meet their needs materially. Jesus's prime emotional concern for people's well-being aligns with dynamic "action readiness" to concrete ministry. Sadly, however, his disciples struggle to understand Jesus's fundamental, life-flourishing commitment amid the miasma of their cognitive-affective deficiency. They just can't seem to think and feel with Jesus. They just don't get it yet.

And naturally, this bothers Jesus. Though he is not explicitly said to experience "grief" (*lypē*) in these pedagogical sessions with his disciples, he seems implicitly aggrieved at their recalcitrance—much like he was with the callous

Pharisees who objected to his Sabbath-day healing of the man with the withered hand. Notably, this confrontation scene with the Pharisees aligns with the second of Jesus's corrective scenes with his disciples, not only in terms of the Pharisees' and disciples' common hardhearted conditions but also by shared mention of antagonistic Herodians (cohorts of Herod Antipas) in league with the Pharisees (Mark 3:6; 8:12).[24]

These scenes' shared characters (Jesus, disciples, Pharisees, Herodians), contexts (miracle episode followed by boat travel), and cognitive-affective states (hardheartedness) help us to understand the thrust in Mark 3:5 of Jesus's aggrieved (anger → grief) metaemotion toward the Pharisees' hardheartedness. As with his disciples later, Jesus deeply laments the Pharisees' misunderstanding of the core right-making, whole-restoring, life-flourishing purpose of God's realm. Closely following and mixing with his anger, Jesus's grievous anguish takes on the tenor of acute displeasure and disappointment at these hardheaded and hardhearted Pharisees for not apprehending the situation correctly, for not applying the law compassionately. He doesn't scream vengeful curses at them, excommunicate them from God's community, or throw them overboard for mutiny any more than he does his own obstinate disciples. But he is severely pained at the loss of their wholehearted participation with him in God's saving work. He needs all God's people partnering with him to reform the world according to God's life-giving will.

We miss the boat of Jesus's portrayal in the Gospels (not just in Mark) by driving too sharp a wedge between the Pharisees and Jesus's disciples. Both may be fairly described as students or learners. Above all, the Pharisees were dedicated students and scholars of Jewish law, desiring God's will to be done on earth as it is in heaven, and in Pharisee-circles as well as in Jesus-circles, the very term "disciple" (*mathētēs*) would have denoted a "student/learner" under the tutelage of authoritative teachers (rabbis) (see Mark 2:18). Moreover, from time to time both "disciple" groups fail to grasp the way of God charted by "Rabbi" Jesus (cf. 9:5–6; 11:21–23; 14:44–45). Both obstruct Jesus's life-affirming path through their obstinacy and obscurantism. And such resistance proves hard for Jesus to handle emotionally.

Anyone devoted to the teaching profession knows the frustrating pain of pouring your heart out to students who, for whatever reason, don't process

24. Among the Gospel writers, only Mark directly associates Pharisees with Herod/Herodians: first, as co-conspirators against Jesus after the hand-healing incident (3:6); second, as co-disseminators of corrupt "yeast," which Jesus enjoins his followers to "beware" (8:15); and finally, as co-interrogators of Jesus regarding his position on paying taxes (12:13).

the instruction and even snipe back in ignorant protest. It can make you mad as well as sad, thoroughly aggrieved, but it doesn't make these hardened students your enemies if they share your basic educational goals (e.g., to pass the tenth grade or the bar exam). Indeed, the aggravation becomes more acute the more potential the teacher sees in students. As I've mentioned before, among the various first-century Jewish parties, the Pharisees advocated the biblically based reformative platform closest to Jesus's gospel mission. Their heated debates with Jesus over theological and ethical fine points represent intramural turf battles, which can wage as fierce as or fiercer than external conflicts. Although no Pharisees in Mark are said to follow Jesus as his disciple, they remain potential allies; otherwise, it would be pointless for Jesus to keep butting heads and hearts with them.

More to the point of our concern, I suggest that Jesus expresses painful emotional energy toward the Pharisees in Mark 3:5 out of deep-seated grief, mixed with (*syl-*) anger, over their sadly missed opportunity to follow God's way. What better place (synagogue), time (Sabbath), and company (serious proponents and practitioners of Torah) to enhance one man's capability to enjoy productive life! Although Jesus presses through to restore the man's hand, the affective environment has turned sour. What should have been a joyous occasion of restoration among God's faithful people has been forfeited. Where this group of Pharisees should have shared together in both the man's suffering and his healing, they instead give vent to suspicion and disputation.[25] Such tragic loss of sympathetic response cuts Jesus to the heart.

Gravely Distressed (John 11:33–38)

Here we return to the complex emotional scene surrounding Lazarus's tomb site near Bethany, which greatly disturbs Jesus and brings him to tears. In the previous chapter, we explored his initial "roiling" (*tarassō*) and "snorting" (*embrimaomai*) responses (John 11:33) as anger-tinged expressions of frustration over family and friends' "faith deficiency" or failure to believe in Jesus's present power and purpose to glorify God by bringing Lazarus back to *this life*. Jesus "snorts" again later in the episode (11:38), just before commanding Lazarus to emerge from the tomb. But in between these angry

25. According to Aristotle, true friends naturally "share their grief" (*syllypein*) and feel "pain" (*lypē*) over each other's misfortunes. In fact, they suffer such deep mutual anguish that he urges friends to be "cautious" about sharing too much painful information with one another. *Eth. nic.* 11.9 (1171b).

expressions, "Jesus began to weep" (11:35). Although the common terms for "anger" (*orgē*) and "grief" (*lypē*) do not appear in the passage, this incident appears to embroil Jesus in another anger-grief metaemotional chain, which may be schematized as anger ↔ grief ↔ anger.

Our present focus is on the target of Jesus's teary grief—what exactly is he crying about, and why?—and how this colors and correlates with his anger. While weeping obviously reinforces the negative, painful valence of Jesus's experience (these are not tears of joy), it is not clear to what extent his tears reinforce or complicate his angry snorts. Without sound effects and more direct commentary on Jesus's weeping, we must seek to understand his emotional display in its wider narrative context.[26]

From the start, we again underscore that this episode marks the only reported occasion in the Gospels in which Jesus confronts the loss of a personally beloved friend. John 11 opens with an urgent message to Jesus from Martha and Mary about Lazarus's serious illness. Naming all three members of this Bethany family attests to their importance in Jesus's life, a point driven home by direct statements of intimate affection: "Lord, he whom you love is ill" (11:3); "Jesus loved Martha and her sister and Lazarus" (11:5). Jesus, however, lives out this love over the next days in puzzling fashion, deliberately delaying his visit to Bethany for two days as part of his plan to "awaken" Lazarus from the dead after four days of entombment (11:5–6, 11–15, 39–40).

So how does Jesus's weeping fit into this grand, "glad" (John 11:15), protracted miracle scheme for the glory of God and the disciples' instruction, punctuated by his "snorting" at the grieving community's lack of faith? I suggest that it *doesn't* fit well—for Jesus. Despite John's general portrait of calm, cool, and collected Jesus and the particular attempt in the current context to sweeten Jesus's tears with tender sympathy toward Mary and her companion-weepers (11:33) and touching sentiment toward Lazarus ("See how he loved him!" [11:37]), the salt of anguished grief still stings in the story. "Jesus began to weep"—suddenly, startlingly. This was not in the plan for Jesus. Others who are weaker in faith will naturally weep. But why should the powerful, prescient Jesus weep at this moment? The narrator seems not to have tied up all the loose ends; maybe he doesn't intend to.

From the larger narrative of John 11, we can home in on the most immediate trigger of Jesus's tears. Strictly speaking, Jesus's first response

---

26. On the fundamental narrative structure of emotional experience and the importance of interpreting emotions in their narrative contexts, see these works of philosopher Peter Goldie: *Mess Inside*; *Emotions*, 4–5, 11–16, 42–45, 69–72, 92–95, 102–6, 151–60, 176–89.

to seeing the weeping Mary and the mourners accompanying her is not mirroring their tears but rather erupting with inner turmoil and irritated harrumphs (11:33). He then asks, "Where have you laid him [Lazarus]?" (11:34a). More than a simple desire for directions seems to motivate Jesus's query. He wants to get on with what he came to do—namely, to restore Lazarus's life, likely with the double aim of stanching the tears of Mary and friends, on the one hand, and chiding their lack of resurrection faith, on the other. While he doubtless cares about his grieving friends, he has no interest in coddling them. Ultimately, Jesus rather coolly regards their weeping as unnecessary and excessive. This is not unlike the attitude reflected in his cheeky postmortem response to the distraught Mary Magdalene at his own empty tomb, "Woman, why are you weeping? Whom are you looking for?" (20:14–15a)—with the implicit subtext, "I'm standing right here alive and well. Can't you see?" Fortunately for Mary Magdalene, Jesus doesn't keep stringing her along in her befuddled bereavement. When she mistakes Jesus for a groundskeeper and pleads with him to tell her where he might "have laid" her Lord's formerly entombed body, the risen Jesus promptly reveals himself by speaking her name (20:15b–16).

While the central Lazarus narrative showcasing Jesus as the "resurrection and the life" (John 11:25) sets the stage for Jesus's culminating death and resurrection, it also evinces some notable contrasts—such as who weeps and wonders about where a dead body has been placed. In John 11:34, just before Jesus breaks down in tears with the other mourners, he asks where the Bethany folk "have laid" Lazarus's corpse. Of course, unlike Mary Magdalene later, Jesus does not fret over Lazarus's missing body. But some crack does emerge, it seems, in Jesus's omniscience: for all his keen insight into human nature (2:24–25), he does not possess superhuman GPS radar. He needs someone to lead him to the gravesite so he can execute his life-restoring demonstration. Even so, such a trivial need for guidance does not yet trigger Jesus's tears and scarcely qualifies as a source of grief.

It is actually Mary and company's response to Jesus's query that bursts the dam. When they answer, "Lord, come and see," *then* "Jesus began to weep." The word order of the Greek text conjoins "come/see" and "weep" in a tight sequence, which we may woodenly render, "Come and see. He-began-weeping, Jesus" (*Erchou kai ide. Edakrysen ho Iēsous*) (John 11:34b–35). Still, why should this simple invitation to usher Jesus to see Lazarus's tomb, per Jesus's request, suddenly set off his tears?

As it happens, "Come and see" is far from an empty conversation filler in the Fourth Gospel. As the centrally placed story of Jesus and Lazarus previews key aspects of Jesus's death and resurrection at the end of the narrative, it also reviews elements from early chapters in suggestive ways.[27] Urgent invitations to "come and see" Jesus more intimately or to meet him for the first time signal important revelatory encounters for would-be believers and disciples.

- First, Jesus himself invites two of John the Baptist's disciples to "come and see" his lodging place. This offer of hospitality comes on the heels of the pair's asking Jesus, "Where are you staying?" As a result, they visit with Jesus the remainder of the day, learning more about his unique mission. One of the two, Andrew, convinced he's now found the true Messiah in Jesus, then brings his brother Simon to meet Jesus, who promptly dubs Simon "the Rock" (Cephas/Peter) (1:37–42). Thus Jesus enlists his first followers.

- "The next day" Philip follows Jesus, at his command, and then proceeds to recruit Nathanael. When Nathanael initially balks, however, at Jesus's roots ("Can anything good come out of Nazareth?"), Philip compels him to "come and see" Jesus for himself. As Nathanael meets Jesus, he quickly changes his opinion, marveling at Jesus's personal knowledge of Nathanael's character (1:43–48).

- Not long thereafter, at a well-side encounter with Jesus, a Samaritan woman also becomes mightily impressed by his intimate knowledge of her life, so much so that she dashes into town announcing to everyone, "Come and see a man who told me everything I have ever done! He cannot be the Messiah, can he?" (4:28–29).

These three calls to come and see Jesus, issued by three distinct characters to different audiences, buttress the Fourth Gospel's emphasis on a transformative, individual encounter with the knowing Jesus as the foundation for faith and discipleship. Secondhand engagement with Christ is not sufficient: the relationship must be felt and formed in person (cf. 1 John 1:1–3).[28] Though Jesus's extended exchanges with Nicodemus (John 3:1–21), a paralyzed man (5:1–18), and a blind man (9:1–41) do not explicitly follow the same "come and see" formula, they reinforce the same personal pattern: meeting and seeing the potent and prescient Jesus reorients one's life.

27. On the plotting devices of previews (prolepses) and reviews (analepses) in Gospel narratives, see Culpepper, *Anatomy of the Fourth Gospel*, 54–70; Tannehill, *Gospel according to Luke*, 20–23, 61, 277–79.

28. Moule, "Individualism"; Dunn, *Unity and Diversity*, 128–29. Emphasizing individuals' encounters with Christ in the Fourth Gospel does not preclude these characters' representative and symbolic functions in the narrative. See Collins, *These Things*, 1–45.

Given the strong buildup of this revelatory theme in the first half of John's Gospel, the attentive reader notices in 11:34 a marked break in the framework, as Jesus now *receives* an invitation to "come and see" a place he does not appear to know. More importantly, this is not just any place but the place where an individual beloved to Jesus is buried. As Jesus is summoned to follow Mary and company to Lazarus's tomb, the prospect of a closer encounter with his deceased, beloved friend suddenly affects him physically and emotionally, triggering a flow of tears. As the research psychologist David DeSteno notes, "Emotions exist for one purpose: to influence what happens next. They're akin to mental shortcuts. They help the brain predict and adjust to the challenges it's about to face."[29] As Jesus's anticipation of reviving his "sleeping" friend becomes intensely immediate—from "I am going there [to Bethany] to awaken [Lazarus]" (11:11) to "Come and see" the deceased Lazarus right now! (11:34)—his emotional guidance system fires up.

Just as Jesus's anguished affective response on the cusp of "seeing" the entombed Lazarus breaks the dominant plot of preceding chapters, it also disrupts the flow of John 11. Up to this point, Jesus has everything under control, while others around him fall apart. Lazarus falls ill, dies, and is buried; Martha and Mary struggle throughout the whole ordeal, first sending Jesus word of their brother's illness and then each venting directly to Jesus some days later: "Lord, if you had been here my brother would not have died" (11:21, 32). As I suggested in chapter 3's discussion of anger, this statement carries tinges of faith and frustration, longing and lament. Yet as far as Martha and Mary know, as limited characters within the story, Jesus might have been delayed for reasons beyond his control, like bad weather or a washed-out road.

From the viewpoint of the omniscient narrator, however, Lord Jesus remains nonplussed, secure in his divine knowledge and power as the great "I am" of "the resurrection and the life" (John 11:25). Accordingly, Jesus resolutely "stayed two days longer in the place where he was" in order that he might not simply alleviate Lazarus's illness but "awaken" him from death, even after decay sets in, which it surely would after four days postmortem (11:6, 11–15, 39–40). When Jesus finally determines it's time to head to Bethany, he does so over his disciples' nervous objection that he's leading them all into a death trap laid by hostile Jewish authorities in the region. Nevertheless, the unflappable Jesus proceeds with his plan, which includes a boost in faith for his followers who will witness Lazarus's remarkable resuscitation (11:7–16).

Jesus's placid self-possession and providential purpose vividly contrast with his disciples' anxiety and Mary and Martha's anguish—until Jesus

---

29. DeSteno, *Emotional Success*, 36.

himself breaks down and cries as the stark concreteness of seeing head-on
the stone-cold tomb where his dear friend lies strapped in burial cloths (and
stinking from four-day rot) breaks through his heart and mind with searing
rawness. Here Jesus anticipates a deeper dive into the abyss of death than
he has ever experienced, made all the more agonizing by his intense love for
"this man" he has lost (11:36–37). Such emotional evaluation prompts Jesus
to "burst into tears."[30]

Like the other "come and see" cases, this one reflects a profoundly revelatory moment for Jesus and his associates. But it also reveals a stunningly
vulnerable side of Lord Jesus not only to his friends and followers but perhaps
to himself as well. Suddenly, he feels a poignant solidarity with mortal flesh
overwhelming previous sentiment. Maybe, too, the delay component of his
grand plan to resuscitate Lazarus doesn't seem like such a good idea as the
decisive moment presses in, with pangs of human grief that Jesus may never
have felt before. Though he regains his composure soon enough, completes
the plan, and inspires faith in "many of the Jews" who witnessed Lazarus's
loosening from the bonds of death (John 11:45), he can't take his tears back.
They remain, sinking into the ground with those of other mourners and
staining Jesus's cheeks, as it were, all the way to the cross.

Before leaving this complex emotive scene, we should further clarify the
temporal aspect of Jesus's grief. While Jesus does not get snarled in protracted grief on the back end, he does appear to get smacked on the front
end harder than expected. The blunt "come and see" directive accelerates
the pace of events, and perhaps Jesus's pulse as well. Suddenly, it hits home
hot and heavy, as grief and other anguished emotions can do. Unlike the
Markan Jesus's grieving response (sans tears) in the synagogue after a more
considered inventory of the situation ("he looked around" [Mark 3:5]), the
Johannine Jesus bursting into tears near Lazarus's tomb is more precipitous,
more impulsive, though not unconscious or devoid of thought. The Roman

---

30. This forceful connotation ("burst into tears") of the aorist form (*edakrysen*) is supported by BDAG 21; J. Sanders, *Gospel according to St John*, 272; C. Barrett, *Gospel according
to St. John*, 400; Voorwinde, *Jesus' Emotions in the Gospels*, 138. The verb *dakryō*, used only
here (11:35) in the New Testament, differs from *klaiō*, the more common term for mourners'
"weeping, wailing" that is used in 11:31, 33 to describe Mary and her companions' crying. While
klaiō may suggest somewhat more intense, vocal anguish than *dakryō*, this distinction does not
separate Jesus's tears from others' tears in the scene, as Moloney (*Gospel of John*, 331) thinks:
"The careful use of another verb for the weeping of Jesus . . . indicates that Jesus' tears cannot
be associated with the surrounding mourning process." In another place, however, Moloney
notes that "the noun *dakryon* appears in Heb 5:7 (significantly in the passage on Jesus' loud
cries and tears)," on the eve of Jesus's death (341). This apt observation more closely connects
dakryō and *klaiō* in mourning contexts.

sage and statesman Cicero, drawing on Greek Stoic philosophy, acknowledges the unavoidable impact of sudden trauma:

> Distress arises when something unexpected has occurred. . . . Suddenness is indeed a major contributor. Chrysippus is of the same view. I know: what is unforeseen strikes us with greater force. . . . When things happen suddenly, they invariably seem more serious than they otherwise would. There are two reasons for this. First, there is not enough time to gauge the seriousness of what is happening. Second, we sometimes think that if we had foreseen what was to happen, we might have been able to prevent it, and then our distress is keener because compounded with guilt. Thus the cause of distress is not solely that the events are unexpected. . . . The reason is rather that the event is fresh in one's mind. The proof of this is in the way our griefs are soothed in the passage of time. (*Tusc.* 3.52–53)[31]

For at least a few critical moments, Jesus seems to "see" the episode surrounding death in a fresher and rawer, bolder and balder light, including the fact that he indeed could have prevented it, as Martha, Mary, and fellow mourners tell him (John 11:21, 32, 37). Such sudden, fresh realization need not have induced any feelings of guilt in Jesus, but it certainly elicited an anguished outpouring of grief.

Regretfully Brokenhearted (Luke 19:41–44)

As Jesus collides in the Fourth Gospel with the imminent prospect of seeing the stone-sealed cave containing the rotting corpse of his beloved friend Lazarus, so he confronts in the Third Gospel, "as he came near and saw the city" of Jerusalem (Luke 19:41), the stunning picture of the stone-walled capital destined to be shattered in pieces in the coming days by vicious enemies (19:43–44). Both haunting prospective sights jerk Jesus's emotional system out of equilibrium. At first, he approaches Bethany in a confident "I am the resurrection and the life" mode (John 11:25) and traverses the path leading into Jerusalem amid paeans of "Blessed is the king! . . . Peace in heaven!" (Luke 19:37–38). But then, shockingly, Jesus weeps in both incidents (John 11:35; Luke 19:41).

Moreover, both emotional episodes associate Jesus's abrupt tear-filled grief with a poignant conditional concern, though with a key distinction regarding his involvement. Whereas Jesus is the target of Martha and Mary's "*if you* had been here" complaint (John 11:21, 32), he is the agent of the "*if you* had only

---

31. Graver, *Cicero on the Emotions*, 24; cf. Graver, *Stoicism and Emotion*, 79–80.

recognized" lament over personified Jerusalem: "If you, even you, had only recognized on this day the things that make for peace!" (Luke 19:42). Technically, these are counterfactual conditions, referencing "something that was not true in the past time (from the speaker's portrayal),"[32] a road not taken, an attitude not adopted, which nonetheless determined a particular outcome. Accordingly, we may modulate Martha/Mary's and Jesus's conditional statements into factual declarations: "Lord, since you were not here, my brother did in fact die"; "O Jerusalem, since you did not take the peaceful path laid out for you, you will in fact be destroyed."

In this latter case, however, the tragic effect doesn't become clear until the end of Jesus's tortured lament. He first breaks off his "if" condition without a "then" consequence. In his distress, he can barely get the words out in coherent form. Deviating from his polished Greek style, Luke matches the grammatical form of Jesus's speech with his frantic feelings, starting with a clumsy word salad: "If you'd known on this day, even you, the things of peace; but now it's hidden" (Luke 19:42 AT). And from there he stutters in "fractured syntax"[33] that "throbs with the agitation of his heart"[34]—"short, choppy sentences" conveying a vivid sense of spontaneous, emotional outburst.[35] As Jesus's tears fall down, his words fall apart in concert with his horrific visions of Jerusalem's devastating fall.

Luke's Jesus succumbs to a tidal wave of anguish on the brink of entering the Holy City at a critical time for its people and institutions—and for Jesus personally. This is no macho, militant, monarchical Jesus (he's an altogether different kind of king) staging crocodile tears so as to appear regretful that he has to bring the hammer down on a rebellious city.[36] And he maintains no stoic, stiff upper lip en route to his own noble martyrdom. He takes no delight in the horrible fate soon to befall his people "because you did not recognize

32. Wallace, *Greek Grammar*, 695.
33. Tiede, *Prophecy and History*, 79, 86.
34. Danker, *Jesus and the New Age*, 314.
35. Tannehill, *Luke*, 285; cf. Wilson, *Unmanly Men*, 218; Voorwinde, *Jesus' Emotions in the Gospels*, 149–50. Voorwinde associates the "broken grammar" of Luke 19:42a with the technique of *aposiopesis*, which (quoting A. Robertson, *Grammar*, 1203) is "a conscious suppression of part of a sentence under the influence of a strong emotion. . . . What differentiates [*aposiopesis*] from ellipses or abbreviations of other clauses . . . is the passion" (149).
36. Though Matthews ("Weeping Jesus," 384) acknowledges the weeping Jesus's "vivid emotional display," she argues that this apparent portrait of a mushy Jesus fits a heroic Greco-Roman pattern of generals weeping over cities they are about to destroy, so as to prove they're not being driven by uncontrollable rage. However, apart from the obvious distinction, which Matthews admits, that Luke's Jesus is no conquering military commander, she underplays his palpably weak, broken state, evidenced in the broken syntax (see above), which hardly strikes the pose of a triumphal hero.

the time of your visitation from God" (Luke 19:44). Such blindness is a terrible tragedy, pure and simple.[37]

Accordingly, God will not directly raise a retributive hand against God's beloved people, even in their obstinacy; rather, God will lift a restraining hand, as it were, against Israel's "enemies," allowing them to breach the walls of Jerusalem and brutalize its inhabitants, even its "children" (Luke 19:43–44). In this case, Rome will play the monstrous marauding role, reprising that of Babylon six centuries before. In turn, Luke's Jesus reprises the anguished, brokenhearted part of the weeping prophet Jeremiah.[38]

While unpacking these grammatical and historical elements underlying Jesus's tearful breakdown on the edge of Jerusalem helps us flesh out his emotional state, we've not yet gotten to the *moral* heart of the matter, to what concerns Jesus most at this juncture. Bewailing the people's stubborn disinclination to "recognize" God's peacemaking visitation in Christ (Luke 19:42, 44), thereby risking violent disintegration of their lives, focuses on the future consequences of past moral failure. In emotional terms, the grieving Jesus becomes potentially embroiled in painful "backward-looking emotions," such as regret, shame, remorse, guilt, and anger (again).[39] Though bearing a family resemblance, however, these feelings are not coterminous.

The focus on "if only" suggests feeling regret, which the Israeli philosopher Aaron Ben Ze'ev defines as "a counterfactual emotion . . . concerned with missed opportunities."[40] Regret may, but need not, affiliate with moral fault, as remorse, guilt, and shame inevitably do.[41] On the one hand, I may regret not getting a plum job teaching French literature because preference was given to a native speaker. But I could do nothing to change that fact: it's not my fault or that of the successful French candidate either (I might be jealous of her pedigree, but it would be irrational to blame her).[42] On the

---

37. See Tannehill, "Israel in Luke-Acts."

38. During Babylon's siege against Jerusalem, Jeremiah yearns "that my head were a spring of water, and my eyes a fountain of tears, so that I might weep day and night for the slain of my poor people!" (Jer. 9:1; cf. 13:17; 22:10). Tiede (*Prophecy and History*, 82) notes that Jesus's Jeremiah-evoking weeping "produces a striking effect, intensifying the rhetoric and pathos by reminiscence of a previous tragedy that is about to be repeated" (cf. 78–84); see also Wilson, *Unmanly Men*, 217–18; Fisk, "See My Tears," 170–75.

39. See Nussbaum, "Living the Past Forward."

40. Ben Ze'ev, *Subtlety of Emotions*, 498. Notice that "counterfactual" matches the second-class conditional Greek construction, discussed above.

41. See R. Lazarus, *Emotion and Adaptation*, 244–45: "Regret (like feeling sorry) is too ambiguous in relational meaning to be included within either the guilt or shame families with confidence, unless there is other evidence of its exact meaning."

42. See Solomon, *Passions*, 287: "The difference between [regret and remorse] . . . is very much like the difference between embarrassment and shame—a difference in responsibility. In

other hand, I may also regret spouting off on Facebook about the sorry state of current Francophone studies, throwing in a snide remark about French snobbery for good measure. That would be all on me and would merit a remorseful apology. In turn, however, if I discover that the person who got the post padded her transcripts along with the dean's bank account, I will regret her dubious behavior, though likely laced with resentment on my part. At any rate, the key distinction between types of regret and their proximity to remorse and anger lies in the degree of personal responsibility for the past regrettable experience.

Much recent philosophical discussion of regret concentrates on the personal variety, what Bernard Williams calls "agent-regret," understood in terms of what "a person can feel only toward his own past actions (or, at most, actions in which he regards himself as a participant) . . . the thought being formed in part by first-personal conceptions of how one might have acted otherwise."[43] Amélie Oksenberg Rorty adds an intensity factor: "Regret is characteristically felt as a particular sort of painful feeling, a pang, a stab, waves of stabs, relatively low keyed in comparison with remorse or guilt."[44] Painful and piercing, yes, and potentially engulfing ("waves of stabs"); but such experience doesn't quite fit with "low keyed," even in relation to other past-directed emotions. How intensely one regrets a missed opportunity depends on the value of the perceived loss.

In Jesus's case, his regret over Jerusalem's inhospitable treatment of God and God's peace-forging mission (in Christ) strikes him very hard, as we've seen, prompting a gush of tears and thickness of tongue. Although Jesus does not blame himself for Jerusalem's unresponsiveness to God's "visitation," given the self-involving nature of regret and its emotional cousins (shame, guilt, remorse, embarrassment) and the particularly collective consciousness of Jesus's world, we cannot rule out traces of personal regret.[45] Does Jesus wonder if he could have done more to get through to his recalcitrant people? It's not his fault that they have turned a blind eye to God's gracious revelation, but he nonetheless keenly feels their rejection and laments the terrible results

---

regret, one does not take responsibility, blaming . . . 'circumstances beyond one's control.' . . . Remorse, however, is more like shame and guilt in its acceptance of responsibility for past injuries to others." Cf. Ben Ze'ev, *Subtlety of Emotions*, 137.

43. B. Williams, *Moral Luck*, 27. For an ancient Stoic perspective see Marcus Aurelius, *Mediations* 8.10: "Regret is a kind of self-reproach for having let something useful pass you by."

44. Rorty, "Agent Regret," 496.

45. On SCE (self-conscious emotions), see Tracy, Robins, and Tangney, *Self-Conscious Emotions*; Tracy and Robins, "Self-Conscious Emotions." On collective, "dyadic" orientation of eastern Mediterranean culture applied to Luke's writings, see Malina and Neyrey, "First-Century Personality."

that will ensue. He cares deeply for his misguided compatriots, even as he has sought to guide them toward more penitent and peaceful paths.

But beyond letting his anguished feelings out, is there any point to Jesus's regretful grief over Jerusalem? Some thinkers, ancient and modern, decry the value of regret because of its pointlessness.[46] No use crying over spilt milk; since you can't change the past or inevitable future consequences of past decisions, why expend emotional energy over the past? But are all types of regret, including that displayed by Luke's Jesus, ultimately futile and fatalistic?[47] Is he simply resigned, albeit sadly rather than stoically, to Jerusalem's tragic demise, which could have been forestalled by more receptive prior behavior ("if only") but now is a foregone conclusion ("indeed, the days will come")?

Although Jesus's lament language in Luke 19:41–44 conveys a sense of final judgment, its fractured style stemming from a broken heart opens up cracks and crevices for fresh light and future conciliation. As we've repeatedly noted, a major purpose of human emotion is motivational, driving future life-preserving and -enhancing actions. In the case of regret, far from being pointless and helpless, Rorty notes, "The most effective assuagement of the pains of regret is *action*."[48] Though regret cannot erase the past, it can, in religious terms, spur repentance, a marked reversal of one's heart, mind, and behavior. No Gospel features Jesus's persistent call for his people to repent more than Luke (see 3:3, 8; 5:32; 10:13; 11:32; 13:1–5; 15:7, 10; 16:30; 17:3–4; 24:47). But at the rough end of his earthly road in Luke, maybe Jesus has finally reached the end of hope for his hardhearted people. Maybe there's nothing more he can do for them because there's now no chance they will change.

Without blunting the cresting "waves of stabs" of regretful grief engulfing Jesus on the outskirts of Jerusalem, the rest of Luke's narrative tracks his perseverant, outreaching activity in his final days. Although continuing to warn his people of the disastrous consequences of ignoring God's claim on their lives, he by no means writes them off. In his first move after entering

46. See Pigliucci, *How to Be a Stoic*, 38: "Epictetus tells us that regret is a waste of our emotional energy. We cannot change the past—it is outside of our control. We can, and should, learn from it, but the only situations we can do something about are those happening here and now." Whatever results from these present efforts, "whether you succeed or not, your levelheaded acceptance of outcome is best." By any reckoning, Jesus's brokenhearted lament over Jerusalem is not his most "levelheaded" moment.

47. The philosopher Robert C. Solomon (*Passions*, 288) notes that regret commonly features a "fatalistic" component in its "mythology." For a more positive assessment of regret, see Matheson, "More Than a Feeling," 664: "In this paper, I argue that regret is often reasonable because regret . . . communicates where we stand with respect to things we have done and outcomes that we have caused."

48. Rorty, "Agent Regret," 502 (emphasis added).

Jerusalem, with tears still streaming down his cheeks,[49] Jesus storms into the temple and enacts a dramatic demonstration, with the double-barreled aim of pronouncing judgment on the crumbling religious-political system *and* promoting radical reform before it's too late (Luke 19:45–48).[50] And at what appears to be the apex of brutal defeat, suspended from the cross, Luke's Jesus dares to pray that those who have misunderstood and mistreated him be forgiven, "for they do not know what they are doing" (23:34), as he also promises to usher the more receptive criminal hanging beside him into his kingdom (23:42–43). Finally, in his farewell words to his disciples, the risen Jesus commissions them to proclaim "repentance and forgiveness of sins . . . in his name to all nations, *beginning from Jerusalem*" (24:47; cf. Acts 1:8).

The book of Acts, Luke's second volume, makes clear from beginning to end that the kingdom of God established in Christ remains open to Jerusalem, Judea, and wherever God's people have scattered to the ends of the earth (Acts 1:8; 28:23–31). The last word—literally—in Luke's extended narrative is *akōlytōs*, "without hindrance" (28:31).[51] Whether from Jesus's perspective within Luke's story predicting the catastrophic fall of Jerusalem or from Luke's later vantage point in the aftermath of Rome's dismantling of Jerusalem in 70 CE, hope springs eternal regarding the persisting power of the gospel to save "everyone who calls on the name of the Lord" (2:21).

In sum, as he descends the Mount of Olives into Jerusalem, Luke's Jesus is struck by piercing pangs of grief; he bursts out in anguished tears over his people's past recalcitrance, setting the stage for tragic consequences. If only they had been more open to God's gracious visitation. How sad, how regretful that they missed this amazing opportunity for reformation and redemption! But Jesus's regret, while realistic, is not fatalistic. Though hitting a hard stone wall, the gospel journey has not ended. The dynamic word of God in Christ, fueled by God's Spirit, moves on "unhinderedly."

---

49. Here I imagine the continued streaming of Jesus's tears amid the seamless narrative flow from Jesus's tearful entry into the city to his blustery entry into the temple (Luke 19:44–45). Luke effectively depicts a single entry into the city and temple, unlike Mark, who has Jesus survey the temple on the night he enters the city and then return the next morning to carry out his temple demonstration (Mark 11:11–17).

50. See the discussion of this incident in chap. 3.

51. Stagg, *Book of Acts*, 1–4, 263–66.

5

That's Soul Crushing!

The Anguished Jesus at the End

In addition to examining scenes of Jesus's anguish set in the Capernaum synagogue, at Lazarus's grave, and on the road into Jerusalem, we must not neglect two major emotional upheavals at the end of his life when he gives vehement voice before God to his intense pain and grief: (1) at Gethsemane on the eve of his death, pleading for an eleventh-hour change of course; and (2) at Golgotha in the dark afternoon on the cross, lamenting his felt abandonment by God. Well-meaning Christian interpreters have attempted to massage the knotty tension out of Jesus's passionate final prayers. Yet I will argue that they are far from anodyne.

Sorely Pressed (Matt. 26:36–46; Mark 14:32–42; Luke 22:39–46)

After entering Jerusalem on the east side from the Mount of Olives, and after his disruptive, table-turning demonstration in the temple, Jesus spends a few tense days there debating with various teachers and scribes. Each night he and his disciples head back to the Olivet area, lodging with friends in Bethany on the mountain's eastern slope (according to Matt. 21:17 and Mark 11:11) or camping out on the mountainside (as Luke 21:37 suggests). Then, after celebrating the Passover meal in guest quarters in Jerusalem, he returns to the Mount of Olives but not to sleep. Now he pours his heart out to God regarding the violent death he knows awaits him. The first two

Gospels report that Jesus is accompanied by his three closest disciples: Peter, James, and John (Luke mentions an unspecified group). Although Jesus implores these associates to "stay awake with me" (Matt. 26:38; cf. Mark 14:34) and to "pray that you may not come into the time of trial" (Luke 22:40, 46), they succumb to slumber and provide scant support during Jesus's dark night of the soul.

And his emotional struggle with his divine Father over his impending demise is indeed dark and desperate, at least for a while. Matthew and Mark call the place where Jesus prays *Gethsēmani*, transliterated from the Hebrew, meaning "oil press"—aptly named not only for its mountainside olive groves and presses but also, in the Gospels, for its image of Jesus's squeezed, de-pressed mind and heart.[1] His anguished bereavement on this hill also evokes a scriptural link with King David's trudging "ascent of the Mount of Olives, weeping as he goes, with his head covered and walking barefoot," in the wake of Absalom's usurpation of his father's throne, abetted by David's treacherous counselor, Ahithophel (2 Sam. 15:30–31).[2] The distressed Jesus now comes to the same site on the heels of exposing his confidants as soon-to-be deserters, including the betrayer Judas and the denier Peter (Matt. 26:20–35; Mark 14:17–31; cf. Luke 22:21–34). Heretofore, Jesus has rather matter-of-factly predicted his execution on multiple occasions, to the consternation and confusion of his disciples (e.g., Mark 8:31–33; 9:30–32; 10:32–45). Now, however, in Gethsemane, the reality of his crucifixion begins to *press* in on Jesus himself with crushing emotional force, as "he [begins] to be distressed and agitated," confessing with disarming candor to his companions, "I am deeply grieved, even unto death" (Mark 14:33–34; cf. Matt 26:37–38).

Suppression of Passion

Yet despite such stark soul-baring by Jesus, the dominant pattern in the history of interpretation has been to suppress this passionate dimension of his Gethsemane ordeal. In his careful tracking of this event's tortured reception history, Kevin Madigan observes that "it was a plague and embarrassment to patristic and medieval interpreters. Few narratives in the New Testament were so inimical to received christological assumptions."[3] Generally speaking, the Christological trajectory has inclined toward higher notions of Jesus's divine

1. Thorsen, "Gethsemane," *ABD* 2:997–98; Powery, "Gethsemane," *NIDB* 2:561–62; Rousseau and Arav, *Jesus and His World*, 111–12.
2. Powery, "Gethsemane," 562.
3. Madigan, "Ancient and High-Medieval Interpretations," 157.

nature and operation at the expense of more volatile, vulnerable human experiences of thinking and feeling. Along this line, the cross became increasingly elevated as the essential crux of God's plan of salvation. We mustn't, then, have Jesus waver about playing his central part in this redemptive drama. Matthew and Mark's anguished Jesus in Gethsemane on the eve of his death cuts too close to the emotional nerve.

And we don't have to wait long for a Christian therapist to ease the pain. As we sketched in the previous chapter, the Fourth Evangelist, while admitting Jesus's and others' "troubled" (*tarassō*) emotional states in the face of death, also takes pains to highlight that Jesus calms agitated, death-fearing hearts with infusions of faith, hope, and peace (John 14:1–14, 25–29). As for Jesus's personal disclosure, "Now my soul [*psychē*] is troubled [*tetaraktai*]," he decisively tamps down such angst along with any escape route: "And what should I say—'Father, save me from this hour [of suffering and death]'? No, it is for this reason that I have come to this hour" (12:27). Such stark refusal to ask his Father to save him from excruciating death stands in contradistinction to the Synoptics' Gethsemane/Olivet portrait. Moreover, we look in vain in the rest of John's narrative for any scene where Jesus throws himself down and prays in agony. The "Lord's Prayer" Jesus offers in his final "hour" in the Fourth Gospel confidently affirms the Father's life-giving mission through the Son and also intercedes for the security and unity of his followers (17:1–26). Jesus's ensuing arrest is staged "across the Kidron Valley" in a garden (18:1, 26; cf. 19:41), a place of fruitfulness rather than stressful pressure (these verses make no mention of Gethsemane or Olivet). And the only ones who hit the ground are the arrest party, mysteriously knocked down by Jesus's "I am" identification before he allows himself to be taken (18:4–12).

So the interpretive struggle commences *within the New Testament* over Jesus's emotional state en route to the cross. A number of scholars also read Luke's version of the Olivet episode in dispassionate terms, partly because of text-critical doubts about Jesus's agonizing, sweat-drenched display but mostly because of supposed dilutions of Mark's more bitter depiction. But as I've argued elsewhere and will develop further below, I do not interpret Jesus's arrest scene in Luke as pathos-diminished.[4] Though Luke carves out his own way for Jesus, it remains physically rough and emotionally wrenching.

Attending more closely now to Mark's and Luke's accounts of Jesus's intense pleading with his divine Father on the night of his arrest, we concentrate

---

4. Spencer, *Luke*, 561–72; Spencer, *Dancing Girls*, 132–35.

on the affective context and volitive content of each scene, attempting to discern more precisely how Jesus feels and what he wants at this dire moment.

Passion at Passover

The affective context of Jesus's final prayer vigil in the Synoptic Gospels closely coordinates with the Jewish calendar. The prospect of Jesus's arrest and execution hits even harder under the weight of the weeklong Passover festival in Jerusalem (Matt. 26:1–5, 17–30; Mark 14:1–2, 12–25; Luke 22:1, 7–23). No event in Jewish life carries more historical significance and emotional resonance. Evoking vivid, vicarious memory of the seminal redemptive experience in Israel's history—God's liberation of Israelites from four centuries of brutal slavery and exile—Passover uniquely melds rituals of lamentation and celebration, sacrificing and singing, and eating and drinking, reenacting the original Exodus watershed. Before retreating to Gethsemane, Jesus shares the Passover meal in a rented Jerusalem room with his disciples, adapting the supper to this raw, "new" moment in salvation history.

The menu features bread and wine, symbols of sustenance and joie de vivre. Though lamb roasted with bitter herbs, the centerpiece of the original Passover meal, is not mentioned here, its blood—originally smeared on Israelite doorposts so that the Lord would "pass over" their homes while executing judgment on every Egyptian household (Exod. 12:1–32)—eerily mixes with the wine in Jesus's stunning commingling of the Passover elements with his sacrificed body. After breaking, blessing, and distributing the bread he says, "Take, this is my body"; then passing around a common cup of wine, he says, "This is my blood of the covenant, which is poured out for many" (Mark 14:22–24). In some mysterious fashion, Jesus's blood, like that of the paschal lamb, marks the passage from slavery to freedom, from death to life.

An odd Passover indeed, nothing like the disciples experienced before. Are they supposed to be happy or sad? And how does Jesus feel? In Matthew and Mark, the group caps off dinner with a hymn—likely a Hallel psalm of praise, not a dirge or lament—and then proceeds directly to Gethsemane. While this singing and strolling may seem pleasant enough, along the way Jesus baldly informs his followers they will "all become deserters," including Peter, despite his insistence that he would sooner die with Jesus than desert or deny him (Matt. 26:30–35; Mark 14:26–31). Jesus does not go out of his way to set a cheery mood for the evening; and the affective ambience only gets gloomier when they get to Gethsemane and Jesus starts to pray by himself, with Peter, James, and John nearby (and others a bit further away).

Expression of Passion in Mark 14:32–42

No more giving thanks or singing praises, as distress, agitation, and deep anguish overcome Jesus, "even unto death." The collocation of three strong emotion terms in Mark 14:33–34 amplifies the force of Jesus's struggle.

Ekthambeomai, a word used only by Mark in the New Testament, means "to be moved to a relatively intense emotional state because of something causing great surprise or perplexity, *be very excited*."[5] Before the Gethsemane incident, it applies to the crowd being "immediately overcome with awe" upon seeing Jesus after his transfiguration (does he still project some sort of aura?) when he drops in on their dispute over the perplexing case of a father's epileptic son (Mark 9:15). At the end of Mark, the verb aptly reports the women's initial "alarm" at Jesus's tomb, where they meet a mysterious, white-clad "young man" attempting to explain why Jesus's body is no longer there (16:5–6). Both instances reflect people's shock and awe, bordering on fear and trembling, in the face of Jesus's exalted experience. At Gethsemane, however, Jesus himself is overwhelmed by the pressing prospect of his excruciating, humiliating death. Though no stranger to the hope of resurrection, including his own (8:31; 9:31; 10:34), darker thoughts and feelings flood Jesus's psyche at this moment.

Adēmoneō, the second term, reinforces Jesus's upset state. Outside of Mark 14:33 and Matt. 26:37, the verb only appears in the New Testament in Philippians 2:26, where the imprisoned Paul recounts the "distressed" state of Epaphroditus, whom the Philippians had sent to minister to Paul. Ironically, Epaphroditus worried about his home congregation's anxiety for him, upon hearing about the life-threatening illness that beset him while caring for Paul. Epaphroditus also stirs Paul's emotions, as the apostle reports how he was spared "one sorrow after another" when his beloved "brother and co-worker" recovered (2:25–27). This Philippians case opens the possibility that Mark's Jesus is distressed less about his own demise than about how his disciples will feel and act over the ensuing hard days. Indeed, he admonishes them in Gethsemane to "keep awake and pray that you may not come into the time of trial" (Mark 14:38; cf. 14:34). Recall, however, that Mark's Jesus also distances himself in order to pray alone about his fate. Whatever concern he has for his followers, he has his own battle to fight with death.

---

5. BDAG 302 (emphasis original).

Perilypos, the third term, packs the most punch of the three anguish terms in this context because (1) it comes last in the sequence, (2) it comes directly from Jesus's lips, (3) it expresses what he feels in the depths of his soul (*hē psychē mou*),[6] (4) he is "afflicted beyond measure, deeply grieved, very sad,"[7] and (5) he is grieved "even unto death" (*heōs thanatou*)—as if to say, "I am so sorrowful as to almost die."[8] Jesus feels the pressure of his impending crucifixion so keenly as "to almost die" on the ground in Gethsemane before he gets to Golgotha. *Perilypos* shares the sense of pain and suffering associated with *lyp*-language (see above), punctuated by the intensifying *peri* prefix. Jarringly, Mark's only other use of this precise compound applies to Herod Antipas's "deep grief" over his wife's request, via her daughter, for John the Baptist's head on a platter (6:26). Not that Herod was normally squeamish about killing his critics, but for all the Baptist's annoyance, "Herod [still] feared John, knowing that he was a righteous and holy man, and he protected him" (6:20). Best to tread carefully with powerful men of God. Nevertheless, Herod had given his public word at his birthday party to grant whatever Herodias's dancing daughter wanted. Rather than risking his honor before his cronies, he had John beheaded. So much for his deep concern for John. Herod's regretful grief at his birthday bash runs pretty thin, in marked antithesis to Jesus's tortured wrestling with his own death at the end of the Passover festival, a death he ultimately submits to voluntarily, though by no means casually, as a "ransom for many" (see 10:45).

Of course, many Christian readers would hasten to stress that Jesus promptly surrenders all to his Father's will. Whatever natural, pre-emotional twinges of fighting death he might have felt, punctuated by a prayer shot in the dark asking for the lethal hour to "pass from him" (Mark 14:35), soon gave way to the more considered, conclusive avowal "Yet, not what I want, but what you want" (14:36). To be sure, the resolute, resilient Jesus does not become mired in protracted grief. But should we thereby throw out his first confession of intense anguish and plea for reprieve as inadmissible to his emotional case? While the

---

6. Here the NRSV simply has "I," which correctly captures the biblical usage of *psychē* as a unitary embodied self, not some separate, immaterial, "soulish" part of one's being. That said, however, a holistic model of personhood does not preclude introspective, "soul-searching" reflection by ancient people. As Dinkler ("'Thoughts of Many Hearts,'" 377) states: "Our options are not either/or—soul or body, individualistic or communalistic, introspective or anti-introspective. Like human interactions more generally ancient narrative depictions of the self are complex and often ambiguous. Characterizing all ancient Mediterranean people as 'anti-introspective' does not do justice to the 'diversity of opinion' on such matters found in the ancient texts themselves." Cf. Bovon, "Soul's Comeback."

7. B. Friberg, T. Friberg, and Miller, *Analytical Lexicon*, 309.

8. L&N 1:318.

durative force of grief is an important factor, as discussed above, a speedy recovery does not eradicate the initial sorrow. Whatever the time signature, however short or long one holds the sad notes, they remain an integral part of the score.

In Jesus's case, "Thy will be done" is not a magic formula for maximum pain relief. He does not simply swat away his depressive emotion like a pesky gnat. Affective and volitive elements inextricably intertwine in an honest struggle of wills—Jesus's and Abba's: what "*I [myself] want* [egō thelō (emphatic form)]" versus what "*you [want]*" (Mark 14:36). Jesus subjects his will to his Father's in a form of self-denial but one which still strongly asserts his counter-will. Jesus does not deny the way he feels or what he wants from Abba.

The volitive content of Jesus's plea to his Father, though brief, is clear and to the point. It is based on the firm premise that the Father is free and able, even at this eleventh hour, to change course and let death "pass from" his Son, as God "passed over" ancient Israel, collectively imaged as God's "firstborn son" (Exod. 4:22), in the process of liberating this beloved "son" from enslaving oppressors. Mark underscores this "possibility" of divine action, or what we might call God's *pass-over-ability*, through both indirect and direct prayer-speech.

> *Indirect Speech*: Jesus "prayed that, if it were possible [*ei dynaton*], the hour might pass from him" (Mark 14:35).
>
> *Direct Speech*: "Abba, Father, for you all things are possible [*panta dynata soi*]; remove this cup from me" (14:36).

Although the indirect narration also expresses a conditional possibility, it is not that different from the direct form's declarative statement. The "if" (*ei*) construction implies an assumed condition for the sake of argument,[9] thus providing an apt lead-in to Jesus's affirmation of his Father's all possible/powerful (*dynaton* means both) control over life and death. Make no mistake: Jesus knows that his Father can detour him from the cross, which is precisely what Jesus wants him to do at this hour.

Jesus's use of the "cup" as a symbol of suffering and death recalls the Passover cup he just drank as a token of his blood "poured out for many" (Mark 14:23–24). Whatever resolve he mustered at that instance has drained away, at least momentarily, in the olive grove. Such is the volatility of sorrow and grief in raw confrontation with death. Mark's Jesus is not Plato's Socrates. Jesus will not calmly down his lethal poison after coolly debating the philosophy of immortality with his tutees (see Plato, *Phaedo*). And he's not exactly the

---

9. See the discussion of first-class conditions in Wallace, *Greek Grammar*, 690–94.

Torah's Moses either, who mediated God's "ransom" of Israel with deadly plagues on Pharaoh's house and army, not by sacrificing his own life.

So why, pray tell, does Jesus assert his will so frankly and pray so fervently for release from death against his Father's wishes? To suggest that an overwrought Jesus succumbs to a fit of filial rebellion would offend not only Christological orthodoxy but also emotion/affect theory that takes seriously the complex of embodied thoughts, feelings, desires, and goals reticulated in any emotional episode, certainly one on the precipice of death at which Jesus stands, or rather prostrates himself. Jesus's passionate plea to be released from his death "cup" springs from the very core of his being and mission. It is no trial balloon launched heavenward just to see how the Father might react.

In his acute distress, sorrow, and grief unto death, Mark's Jesus, I suggest, does not blanch at his imminent crucifixion because he wants to escape pain and suffering but rather because he wants to continue living and restoring the lives of the beset and broken here and now, in God's realm on earth. I again stress Jesus's indefatigable will to life. To be sure, Jesus has had more tempered philosophical moments, expounding the profound paradox that "those who want to save their life will lose it, and those who lose their life for my sake, and for the sake of the gospel, will save it" (Mark 8:35; cf. 8:34–37; John 12:24–25). It is indeed the way of things for new life to spring from wintry death. But paradoxes are not cheap platitudes or palliatives; they stretch the heart and mind, even to the breaking point. However right they may be, they don't always *feel* right.

What Jesus knows and feels to his toes in Gethsemane is how much he has loved life—his own incarnate life in intimate connection with the lives of those he has touched, physically and emotionally. Indeed, his "greatest" insight into life, distilled from the Jewish Scriptures and borne out in his own experience, focuses on the nexus of loving God, others, and self—loving "neighbor *as yourself*," flowing out of holistic love of "the Lord your God with all your heart, and with all your soul, and with all your mind, and with all your strength" (Mark 12:28–34). If Jesus had not fully embraced his own life, he would have been no use to God or other people. Such genuine self-love, of course, has nothing to do with narcissistic preening, exploitative self-promotion, or personal pampering. By loving himself amid his personal suffering, Jesus is able to sympathize with and succor others in their struggles (see Heb. 2:17–18; 4:14–16). Yes, but terminal suffering—death!—is a harder pill to swallow.[10]

---

10. We might surmise that Jesus's death pill is all the more bitter because it's both premature and unjust. He will not die a "natural" death, "old and full of days," as even Job, the archetypal sufferer, ultimately experiences (Job 42:17).

How can one love from the grave (Eccl. 9:5–6)? Doesn't death "do us part"? Although willing to trust in his Father's larger wisdom and life-loving will at this pressure-cooker hour, Jesus nonetheless lodges his honest, heartbreaking protest and plea for another way—"what I *want*"—if at all possible!

Outpouring of Agony in Luke 22:39–46

Whether we view Luke as deliberately editing Mark's version or simply telling his own story, he puts his own distinctive cast on this moving Mount of Olives scene. While lacking Mark's stark opening three-note chord express-ing Jesus's depressed mood, and while featuring the disciples' grief (*lypē*), not Jesus's personal grief (Luke 22:45), Luke's account sounds its own death knell. Luke doesn't so much shunt the anguish away from Jesus as shift it into another gear: agony (*agōnia* [22:44]).

From the start, we must acknowledge that the passage depicting Jesus's sweat-soaked struggle with God (Luke 22:43–44) is absent in some ancient manuscripts (see NRSV annotation). Obviously, excising these verses removes Jesus's agony and reduces the emotional temperature of the entire scene. Yet, while I think the evidence supports including this material in Luke's narra-tive (see below), my argument for the passionate Lukan Jesus does not rest entirely on this judgment. Luke's preceding context matches Matthew's and Mark's in presenting Jesus's adaptation of the Passover meal to his bloody death, along with his acute awareness of his followers' betrayal and denial. To be sure, Luke's Jesus also sees a promising future for his disciples beyond their failures: "You are those who have stood by me in my trials; and I con-fer on you, just as my Father has conferred on me, a kingdom" (22:28–29); "Simon, Simon, listen! Satan has demanded to sift all of you like wheat, but I have prayed for you that your own faith may not fail" (22:31–32). Yet he has no illusions about the ominous fate awaiting him, as previewed in Isaiah: "And he was counted among the lawless" (22:37 // Isa. 53:12). Jesus heads to Olivet not only in the company of fickle apostles but also with a keen sense of unjust affiliation with criminals, among whom he will soon be crucified.

Upon arriving at the Mount of Olives, Jesus's palpable stress manifests in a double prayer movement: first, he exhorts the disciples, "Pray that you may not come into the time of trial" (Luke 22:40); then, he prays by himself for his Father to "remove this cup from me" (22:41–42). Naive presumptions about the power of prayer to magically smooth the rough road and ease the harrowed heart don't apply here. The trial (*peirasmos*) is on for Jesus, as it's been from the outset of his ministry (4:2, 13), and for his followers as well, though they aren't at all sure what's happening right now. Jesus urges them to

pray, precisely as he taught them earlier (11:4), that they might be spared full
entry into the trying ordeal.[11] But such relief is no foregone conclusion for the
supplicant, any more than daily bread is during hard times: that's why they
must pray to a loving Father and also put their prayers to work by mutually
sharing their burdens and bread (see 11:3, 5–13). While Jesus endeavors to
help the disciples find some prayerful refuge, they do not reciprocate, opting instead for a soporific anesthetic to their anguish. Waking them up after
finishing his own prayer session, Jesus repeats his initial counsel to pray for
trial protection (22:46). But "while he was still speaking," Judas and the arrest
party arrive (22:47). The disciples are wide awake now and right in the thick
of the worst trial of their lives.

Of course, Jesus bears the brunt of this trial. He's the main target of the
high priest's posse led by their informant Judas. Their apparent strategy: cut
off the head and the movement will die. So, even without their praying, Jesus's
followers get some reprieve, though hardly any true peace. Apart from their
tumult over Jesus's arrest, can they themselves rest easy? The authorities have
their number now and will be watching closely.

As Jesus enters headlong into this terrible, trying hour, he at least comes
forearmed not with clubs and swords, which he eschews (22:49–52), but with
prayer, as a "prayer warrior," we could say.[12] He finds himself embroiled in
the fight of his life—indeed, the fight *for* his life—against nefarious political
and religious forces who want him dead and gone. But first and foremost,
Jesus wrestles *with his Father* over his fatal destiny. The situation bristles
with tension. Luke stages Jesus's Olivet prayer as a dramatic earth-touching
experience. Some critics, however, make an emotional distinction between
Jesus kneeling in Luke 22:41 and him falling on the ground in Mark 14:35,
as if Luke's Jesus eased down to his knees in "upright" calm repose and then
confidently "got up from prayer" (Luke 22:45, another difference from Mark)
to exhort his groggy disciples in their "shrunken state of grief."[13] But while
lacking Mark's more dramatic depiction that Jesus "threw himself [*epipten*]
on the ground to pray" (NRSV)—which other versions more accurately render
"he fell to the ground" (Mark 14:35 CEB, NASB, NIV)—Luke's description
that Jesus "knelt" (literally, "put [down] the knees" [*theis ta gonata*]) leaves

11. Compound verbs prefixed by *eis* ("into") in 11:4 (*eispherō*) and 22:40, 46 (*eiserchomai*)
suggest full entry or headlong diving "into" a trying ordeal (*peirasmos*).

12. "Prayer warrior" is a common image in revivalist circles, based on Eph. 6:10–20, detailing
the "armor of God" capped off with triple emphasis on prayer in 6:18–20.

13. Neyrey, *Passion*, 53, 65–67; cf. Neyrey, "Absence." See also L. Johnson, *Gospel of Luke*,
51: "The description [in Luke 22:41] emphasizes Jesus' control and lack of emotional turmoil.
. . . Rather than 'fall on the ground' (Mark 14:35) or 'fall on his face' (Matt 26:39), he [Luke]
has Jesus simply sink to his knees"; Pope, "Downward Motion," 265–66, 280.

open how forcefully or emotionally he carried out this action.[14] He could have "dropped" or "fallen" to his knees. In any case, we can be sure that no padded kneeling bench supported his weight on the mountainside and that "getting up" from extended kneeling can strain the joints as much as rising from a prone posture.[15]

Moreover, Luke describes Jesus's separation from his followers in particularly intense terms. Whereas Mark has Jesus "going [ahead] a little farther" (*proelthōn mikron* [Mark 14:35]), Luke indicates "he *withdrew from* [*apespasthē*] them about a *stone's throw* [*lithou bolēn*]" (Luke 22:41). This move suggests a considered, deliberate, "not sudden"[16] or accidental, disjunction from his associates over some distance (one can hurl a stone pretty far).

In this aloof place and in an abased posture, Jesus lodges his plea with his divine Father. Although Luke uses slightly different terminology than Mark in recounting Jesus's request, the semantics are similar. "If you are willing" (*ei boulei* [Luke 22:42]) again carries an assumptive conditional force—granting the Father's freedom to choose and effect any course of action—albeit with a sharper focus on divine volition than on divine ability, as Mark 14:35 stresses ("if you are able" [*ei dynaton*] AT). The same imperative verb in Mark 14:36 and Luke 22:42 heads the direct entreaty, "remove [*parenenke*] this cup," but it resonates more strongly in Luke in relation to the Lord's Prayer: "Do not bring us to [*eisenenkēs*] the time of trial" (Luke 11:4; cf. 12:11). In other words, Luke's Jesus matches his foundational petition for God "*not* to lead us *into* a time of trial" (11:4) with his personal plea for God "*to* lead him *from* the time of trial" that presses hard upon him (22:42).

In sum, apart from the agonizing scene omitted from some early manuscripts, Luke maintains, even as he modulates to some degree, Mark's exposure of Jesus's passionate anguish in the face of death. A model Socratic or Stoic sage neither petitions God/gods to remove a painful roadblock from his life course nor instructs his students to plead for relief. One simply accepts

14. Examples in Luke's second volume, where Stephen (Acts 7:60), Peter (9:40), and Paul (20:36; 21:5) kneel to pray, all occur in tense, emotional situations. Paul's farewell to the Ephesian elders is particularly poignant: "When he had finished speaking, he knelt down with them all and prayed. There was much weeping among them all; they embraced Paul and kissed him, grieving especially because of what he had said, that they would not see him again" (20:36–38).

15. I grant that Luke's references to "getting up/rising" (*anistēmi*) often carry a symbolic association with resurrection (*anastasis*). If this resurrection image colors Jesus's "getting up" from prayer in Luke 22:45, then it must follow a rising up from a collapsed, deathlike posture of agonizing prayer.

16. L&N 1:190.

the divine will without demurral. What must be eliminated (removed) is any emotional desire resistant to providential fate. With calm composure, one dutifully takes up and drinks the cup one receives, however bitter or lethal (hemlock), without requesting a reprieve, as Jesus does. If you must speak on the brink of death, then muster up a valiant oration to engrave your legacy in the history books,[17] as Stephen does in Acts 7:2–53, but Jesus manifestly does *not* in Luke's Gospel. Even if we excise the "sweat . . . like great drops of blood" from Luke's account, we cannot expurgate the headline supplication, "Remove this cup from me."

In fact, we don't need to jettison the "agony" text. Though there may not yet be a consensus, many scholars support the Lukan provenance of 23:43–44 based on reassessments of external evidence as well as internal coherence with Luke's theology.[18] Claire Clivaz, for example, plausibly proposes that one of the earliest witnesses lacking this passage represents a deliberate omission by Gnostic-oriented scribes.[19] Luke's Jesus—fully flesh and blood, sweaty and dusty—is no more Gnostic than he is Stoic.[20] Accepting Luke 23:43–44 as original spikes the emotional temperature of Jesus's supplication on the night of his arrest.

Yet some scholars who regard Luke's Jesus as a stoical martyr also accept the authenticity of the "agony" passage. Arguing that the Greek notion of *agōnia* connoted masculine, muscular, martial, or athletic vigor more than emotional pain and weakness, they interpret Jesus's bloodlike sweat (not tears!) as signaling blood-pumping energy for combat or competition rather than a psychic meltdown. Such a lather is the stuff of stalwart religious martyrs like Eleazar in the Maccabean era, who withstood "the maddening waves of the emotions" and modeled a staunch commitment to God's law, "shield[ing] it with [his] own *blood and noble sweat* in sufferings even to death" (4 Macc. 7:1–8; cf. 6:11),[21] or like the apostle Paul, who "fought [*ēgōnismai*] the good fight [*agōna*]" to the end (2 Tim. 4:7; cf. 1 Tim. 6:12). In this vein, nothing mushy or gushy tempers *agōnia*; accordingly, Luke's Jesus faces his terrible

17. See Clivaz, "Angel," 428–29: "For most readers in antiquity, Jesus's demand that the cup pass from him was the most shocking element in the Gethsemane story. Ancient readers expected that an individual confronting death should make a noble speech, or at least maintain a dignified silence that could be interpreted as proof of that individual's sensibility."

18. See, for example, Brown, *Death of the Messiah*, 1:184–90; Green, "Jesus on the Mount of Olives," 35–37; Tuckett, "Luke 22,43–44."

19. Clivaz, "Angel," 425–32. The Gnostic-leaning witness is an early third-century manuscript (𝔓⁶⁹) from Oxyrhynchus, Egypt.

20. See Spencer, *Luke*, 562, 641–45.

21. See the "*agōnia*-as-combat" argument, supported by these and other references, in Neyrey, *Passion*, 63–65.

fate "like a man,"[22] like a macho man, like a warrior or gladiator in peak physical, mental, and emotional condition.

However, this battle-poised, self-controlled side of the agonistic Jesus only captures part of his experience. Though far from pusillanimous or panic-stricken, Luke's Jesus makes no pretense of dispassionate placidity in this critical hour. As much as *agōnia* fuels action-readiness for vigorous bodily combat, it also foments inner turmoil, "a state of great mental and emotional grief and anxiety—'anguish, intense sorrow.'"[23] Even the Maccabean literature attests to this emotional upheaval, though, tellingly, only among the priests and people of Jerusalem, not the freedom fighters and martyrs. When the Greek-Syrian officer Heliodorus raided the temple treasury, "There was no little distress [*agōnia*] throughout the whole city. The priests prostrated themselves before the altar. . . . To see the appearance of the high priest was to be wounded at heart, for his face and the change in his color disclosed the anguish of his soul [*psychēn agōnian*]. For terror and bodily trembling had come over the man, which plainly showed . . . the pain lodged in his heart. People also hurried out of their houses in crowds to make a general supplication" (2 Macc. 3:14–18). As it happens, the author only exposes these displays of psychic agony to ridicule them: "There was something pitiable in the prostration of the whole populace and the anxiety of the high priest in his great anguish [*megalōs agōniōntos*]" (2 Macc. 3:21). Real men and true leaders of God's people wouldn't be caught dead manifesting such pathetic angst; better to fight God's enemies and die bravely, if need be.[24]

But however "pitiable" it may be from a militant perspective, expressing emotional anguish is very natural, very human, and very Jesus, as he sinks his knees to the ground and pours out his heart to God in soul-wrenching, mind-stretching (*ektenesteron*),[25] pore-draining[26] supplication for relief from pain and

22. See Moore and Anderson, "Taking It Like a Man."
23. L&N 1:319.
24. *Agōnia* is never attributed to the Maccabean fighters and martyrs, though the noun *agōn* and verb *agōnizomai* ("struggle, fight") frequently characterize their tough-minded, courageous battle for independence.
25. The adverb *ektenesteron*, rendered "more earnestly" in the NRSV (Luke 22:44), is a comparative form related to the verb *ekteinō*, meaning "extend, stretch out." Wilson (*Unmanly Men*, 221; cf. 219–22) notes the link between Jesus's anguished praying and occasions of women crying out "fervently/earnestly" (*ektenōs*) to God in Joel 1:14; Jon. 3:8; Jdt. 4:12; 3 Macc. 5:9; and Acts 12:5.
26. Michael Pope ("Downward Motion," 261, 265–66, 280) argues that the flow of Jesus's sweat indicated by the participle *katabainontes* (Luke 22:44) denotes a "coursing/streaming down" of perspiration along the surface of the skin in a "gradual descent" to the ground rather than a "falling down" of sweat drops in a "gravitational free fall." While perhaps providing a

suffering. He seeks another way to accomplish God's will, a way out of death, not because of weak-kneed preference for leisure but because of strong-willed commitment to life. Grateful love for his own Spirit-generated life (Luke 1:35) has driven his life-saving vocation. While Jesus also knows that saving one's own and others' lives springs from denying and losing one's self (9:23–24), he never twists this paradox into a perverse desire for personal pain or martyr glory.

Recalling the discussion above comparing the psychological force of grief to a physical collision, Jesus's impassioned will for life collides with his Father's present will for the beloved Son's death, a clash all the more wrenching because of God's very nature as Creator-and-Sustainer of life. This is no small disturbance of the Father-and-Son communion; the agony stretches the bounds of finite comprehension. And Luke provides no transcript of the debate, no response from the Father. Even after Jesus concedes to the Father's will against his own, the Father remains hauntingly mute. For his part, Jesus presses as hard as he can—sweating, agonizing, wrestling with God—much like Jacob/Israel of old (Gen. 32:22–32). He does not submit without a fight for life, which his passion for life demands.[27]

Though Jesus's Father does not speak or appear at Olivet, an "angel from heaven" comes to "give him strength" (*enischyōn*) (Luke 22:43). But this angel wields no sword (cf. Josh. 5:13–15) and spearheads no heavenly host. Rather, this divine emissary provides the internal fortitude Jesus needs at this harrowing hour. Joel Green views this strengthening in the framework of "a great mural in which Jesus is pictured as the Servant of the Lord" from Isaiah.[28] For example, the Lord addresses the exiled nation collectively:

> You are my servant;
>   I have chosen you and not forsaken you;
> do not fear, for I am with you;
>   . . . I am your God
>   who has *strengthened* [*enischysas*] you,
> and I have helped you,
>   and I have made you secure
>   with my righteous right hand. (Isa. 41:9–10 NETS)

---

sharper physiological picture of the scene, Pope overinterprets it by taking Jesus's supposedly "measured," "more restrained" sweat flow as a sign of his disciplined self-control.

27. See Moltmann, *Passion for Life*, 22: "When the passionate devotion to life is missing, the powers to resist are paralyzed. Therefore if we want to live today, we must consciously *will* life. We must learn to love life with such a passion that we no longer become accustomed to the powers of destruction. We must overcome our own apathy and be seized by the passion for life" (emphasis original).

28. Green, "Jesus on the Mount of Olives," 42.

And again:

> I, the Lord God, have called you in righteousness,
>   and I will take hold of your hand and *strengthen* [*enischysō*] you.
>   (42:6 NETS)

God's beloved Son Jesus, who embodies all the hopes and dreams of God's corporate "son" Israel, is not spared the pain and agony of God's people in this "lawless" age, even as he is divinely strengthened to bear this suffering on their behalf (see Isa. 53:3–8, 11–12; Luke 22:37; Acts 8:32–35).

Utterly Forsaken (Matt. 27:45–49; Mark 15:32–36)

Although both Mark and Luke appropriate Isaiah's "great mural" of the Suffering Servant in their portraits of Jesus, Luke takes greater pains to balance the pain and suffering dimension with divine presence and strengthening. The prophetic promise that the Lord has "not forsaken [*enkatelipon*]" his servant (Isa. 41:9 NETS) finds some resonance in Jesus's last words from the cross: "Father, into your hands I commend my spirit" (Luke 23:46). Mark's (and Matthew's) Jesus, however, strikes a very different final tone, orally and aurally punctuated by Jesus's loud lament, reported twice for emphasis: first transliterated from Jesus's native Aramaic tongue and then translated into Greek by the Gospel writer. In English, we read or hear: "Eloi, Eloi, lema sabachthani?" which means, "My God, my God why have you forsaken [*enkatelipes*] me?" (Mark 15:34; cf. Matt. 27:46).

The way Jesus delivers this line—he "cried out [*eboēsen*] with a loud voice" (Mark 15:34)—expresses emotion at a fever pitch. The "distinguishing note of this verb [*boaō*]" conveys "a manifestation of strong *feeling*,"[29] with either positive valence as "emotionally charged cries of joy" or negative energy as "anguished cries."[30] Obviously, the dying Jesus cries out in blood-curdling horror at the apparent abandonment by "Eloi, Eloi!" The crowd mishears the cry and misses the point (Mark 15:35): Jesus is calling not for Elijah (*Ēlias*) but for God himself (*El*), after whom Elijah ("My God is the LORD") was named. Even more poignantly, Jesus cries out in a desperate doublet, "My God, My God!" No mention of "Abba, Father" here, as in Gethsemane (14:36). As bad as things were there, they've grown worse at Golgotha.

The Markan path from Gethsemane to Golgotha has gotten darker and starker, leaving Jesus increasingly alone and abandoned, stripped bare of

29. MM 113 (emphasis original).
30. BDAG 180.

both companionship and clothing. Illustrating the shameful fact that "all of them deserted him and fled" (Mark 14:50) after his arrest, Mark provides the unique vignette of a thinly clad young male follower of Jesus who almost doesn't escape. Members of the arrest party seize him by his single linen cloth, which comes off in their hands as the youth streaks away naked, his cowardly backside exposed for all to see (14:51–52). With terrible irony, this young man not only typifies the disciples' ignominious back-turning on their Lord but also exemplifies Jesus's own mounting isolation and humiliation. While the guards inadvertently stripped the fleeing disciple as they tried to nab him, they deliberately mock Jesus with a series of public re-dressings: first, they replace his clothes with a purple cloak and thorny crown; then, they strip him of this faux royal garb and put his own clothes back on him; and finally, they strip him once more and gamble for torn swatches to amuse themselves during the crucifixion (15:16–20, 24). Jesus dies utterly deserted and denuded. He has lost everyone and everything on the brink of losing his very life. If grief constitutes a characteristic emotional response to loss—to personal, social, and material loss—then the dying Jesus has reason to grieve, if anyone ever has.

But surely, when everyone else fails, Jesus's Abba is there for him, especially at the final hour when he submits to his Father's will to drink the cup of suffering to the dregs. Yet, six hours into the ordeal of being strapped to the cross and stripped to the bone, which culminates in an eerie three-hour span of "darkness . . . over the whole land" from high noon to three o'clock, the dying Jesus voices his deepest anguish over what *feels like* abject forsakenness by God (Mark 15:33–34). It's one thing for Abba not to remove the cup, not to forestall the cross; it's another to forsake the Suffering Servant Son at his most critical hour.

No elaborative emotion terms are required here, as at Gethsemane, to convey the depth of Jesus's psychophysical pain. The terse words of lament, four in Aramaic and ten in Greek, ring sharp and shrill on their own. Yet they also cry out for explanation. Without pretending to plumb all the emotional crevices of this haunting "cry of dereliction," as it's commonly called—which seems to charge God with dereliction of duty—I make two probes in quest of fuller understanding: one scriptural, the other theological.

On the scriptural side, Jesus's cry echoes the opening of Psalm 22: "My God, my God, why have you forsaken me? Why are you so far from saving me, so far from my cries of anguish?" (Ps. 22:1 NIV; cf. CEB, NJPS). It is scarcely surprising that Jesus turns to the Psalms in his distress, as myriad sufferers have done. And Psalm 22 makes a particularly apt choice, as a long, lugubrious lament attributed to David, bemoaning God's abandonment of

David during a season of unjust assault by vicious forces. Citing the opening line invites attention to the balance of the poem (and we can forgive the debilitated Jesus for not reciting the whole piece). Mark's context reinforces this larger perspective by further correlating Psalm 22 with the abusive mocking of Jesus (Ps. 22:7 // Mark 15:20) and gambling for his divided clothing (Ps. 22:18 // Mark 15:24).

The anguished emotional tenor of Psalm 22 reverberates for the first two-thirds of the lament in a torturous swirl of incredulous perplexity over God's distant inattention, passionate pleading for God's saving intervention, and vivid description of the Psalmist's joint-rending, heart-melting pain inflicted by beastly enemies (Ps. 22:1–21a). Such palpable despair, however, ultimately breaks through in the final third of the psalm to "a startling reversal and deliverance,"[31] to an exuberant confidence that God will yet come to the aid of his besieged servant as testimony of divine faithfulness "forever" to those "people yet unborn" (22:26, 30–31; see 22:21b–31). The hidden, abandoning God (*Deus absconditus*) is but a shadowy chimera in the desert, an empty terror in the night, for the truth is that God "did not despise or abhor the affliction of the afflicted; he did not hide his face from me, but heard when I cried to him" (22:24). All's well that ends well.[32]

Although Mark's Jesus does not explicitly resolve his desperate query to God with the confident answer of Psalm 22's conclusion, perhaps we should read in the answer for him. Other aspects of Mark's crucifixion narrative further intimate this positive resolution, such as (1) the audience's Elijah reference, evoking hope of final deliverance for God's people (see Mal. 4:5–6); (2) the temple curtain's parting in two, signaling renewed opening of God's saving presence to "all nations" (Mark 11:17 // Isa. 56:7); and (3) the Roman centurion's remarkable confession of faith inspired by Jesus's dying words and behavior: "Truly this was God's Son!" (Mark 15:39).[33]

Any crucifixion narrative—certainly one focused on God's Son, Jesus Messiah, by a Christ-believing Evangelist—is bound to teem with emotional tension. But must this faithful story, written from faith for faith, work out all this tension without remainder, leaving the reader/hearer with a final response of comfort without conflict, assurance without anxiety? Does the full Psalm 22 drown out the searing opening cry, which is all that Mark's Jesus utters and which Mark accentuates in two languages as Jesus's only words from the cross? Remember that raw lament dominates Psalm 22, intensifying the

31. Watts, "Mark," 236.
32. In the canonical Psalter, Ps. 23 strengthens the assurance of deliverance and protection from the last part of Ps. 22.
33. The points are nicely summarized in Watts, "Mark," 235–37.

force of the dramatic key change at the end by unleashing the full fury of its agonistic energy.

Moreover, the tearing (*eschisthē*) of the veil in Mark's crucifixion scene (Mark 15:38) marks more of a violent ripping (*schizō*, "to divide by use of force"[34]) than a precise scissor-cut, matching the rending (*schizomenous*) of the heavens at Jesus's baptism (1:10). While bridging heaven and earth and affirming the Son's union with his loving Father and the Dove-Spirit (1:10–11), this breakthrough of cosmological boundaries and bolstering of theological bonds is forged in a volatile crucible, not a clinical vial—on a desert battlefield, not in a garden paradise. It's no accident that after Jesus's baptism, "the Spirit immediately drove him into the wilderness" (this is no gentle, cooing dove) for a forty-day fight with Satan and "the wild beasts" (1:12–13). Only Mark uses the explosive, expulsive verb *ekballō*, stressing the Spirit's throwing/ hurling/ casting Jesus out into the desert, a virtual exorcizing *into* the realm of satanic conflict.[35] From start to finish, from the Jordan River to Skull Hill (Golgotha [15:22]), Mark's Jesus serves as commander-in-chief in the battle against evil, as champion restorer of God's just and right kingdom on earth (1:15). The struggle is real—physically, mentally, socially, politically, and emotionally—in and through all these interlaced facets of Jesus's experience.

Now, at the eleventh hour, the struggle ratchets up to an unfathomable theological dimension. Where is God the Creator and Sustainer of all, the Ruler and Redeemer of Israel, the Father of Jesus Christ the Son? No word now of paternal love and commendation (Mark 1:11), and no help from ministering angels (1:13). If Abba's silence was unsettling in the olive grove, it seems unconscionable on the skull-shaped hill. Resurrection beckons on the horizon, three days hence, as Jesus anticipated (8:31; 9:31; 10:34). But he never dreamed he would walk through the valley of the shadow of death without his divine Abba (cf. Ps. 23:4).

Of course, God will indeed raise Jesus from the dead on the third day (Mark 16:6–7). But again we ask: Does this blessed future eventuality nullify Jesus's present, horrible sense of forsakenness on the cross? Recall that emotions negotiate decisions and actions across the temporal spectrum, not least correlating current perspectives with anticipated ones: How *will I feel* down the line, in retrospect, about what I feel, think, and do at this moment? In the throes of such an excruciating death, is Jesus's emotional monitor misfiring, malfunctioning? One could hardly blame him for that as a human being—but

---

34. BDAG 981.

35. Mark typically uses *ekballō* to denote the "casting out" of demons. See Mark 1:34, 39; 3:15, 22–23; 6:13; 7:26; 9:18, 28, 38.

as God's beloved divine Son? That's harder to explain but should not surprise us. Is not the relationship among Father, Son, and Spirit that we call Trinity the ultimate ontological mystery, beyond the grasp of finite minds? For centuries, Christian theologians have struggled to understand this ineffable divine-relational concept, producing volume upon volume of analysis. In particular, it seems fair to say that no problem in the mystery of the Trinity has proven more acute than that of the "crucified God." And no modern theologian has wrestled more profoundly with this mystery than Jürgen Moltmann.

Moltmann reads Mark's tracking of Jesus's desolate Gethsemane-Golgotha path as an intertwining "perichoretic" dance set to the pulsing drumbeat of "the passion of the passionate God,"[36] which we briefly surveyed in chapter 2. God passes through Mark's stations of the cross, so to speak, and the endpoint where the Son dies is real (not metaphorical) and agonizing (not peaceful). As he cries out to his Father in unbearable anguish, it "kills" the Father to see and feel the Son endure this torture, as any human parent would react watching their beloved child suffer and die in this gruesome way. The Father intimately feels the Son's last painful pleas and gasps, as if it were the Father's own death. Moltmann suggests that the Father feels *worse* than the Son, because the loss of the Son lingers for the Father, while the Son finds a certain rest in peace after death.[37] And we might dare add that the painful memories of both Father and Son persist beyond the three days until resurrection, having become eternally etched in the heart of God as surely as pierce-scars forever mark the hands, feet, and side of Christ.

On the cross, the Father suffers and sacrifices himself with the Son and is consequently ripped apart (like the veil!), severed from part of God's very self. The brutal death of the Son cuts into the Father so deeply that the Father cannot bear this most vulnerable divine moment of seeming helplessness to rescue the Son (Gethsemane) or ease his pain (Golgotha). In turn, the Father's agonizing abandonment elicits the Son's bone-chilling cry of dereliction. Though not effecting any *essential* (ontological) dismembering of God's Trinitarian being—if anything, the Son's death grafts him even deeper into the Father's heart, if that is possible—the cross does mark an *existential* (emotional) crisis in the divine communion, a heartbreaking wound of compassion for a broken and alienated world.[38]

36. Moltmann, "*Crucified God* Yesterday and Today," 74.

37. Moltmann, *Living God*, 41; Moltmann paints a particularly poignant picture: "With evident pain, God the Father holds in God's hands the cross-beam of the cross on which God's Son hangs" (41); cf. Moltmann, *Crucified God*, 242–47; Moltmann, "*Crucified God* Yesterday and Today," 77–79.

38. Adapted from Spencer, *Luke*, 725.

In one of the most stunning passages in all of Moltmann's writings, he attempts to capture the piercing pathos of God between Jesus's two agonizing pleas to his Abba in the last hours of his earthly life:

> The *unanswered prayer* is the beginning of Jesus's real passion—his agony at the forsakenness by the Father. Of course there is also quite simply fear of the horribly slow death ahead of him. It would be ridiculous to say—as Augustine did—that, as the Son of God, Jesus could not have experienced the fear of death, because his soul lived in unbroken enjoyment of divine bliss and power; and that he only suffered in the body. But it would be equally foolish to see him . . . overcome by self-pity at the prospect of torments of death awaiting him. In the fear that laid hold of him and lacerated his soul, what he suffered from was God. Abandonment by God is the "cup" which does not pass from him. The appalling silence of the Father in response to the Son's prayer in Gethsemane is more than the silence of death. . . . The Father withdraws. God is silent. This is the experience of hell and judgment.[39]

Though not denying the probable admixture of fear/anxiety with anguish/grief in Jesus's experience, I would lay greater emphasis on the latter emotion in Mark's Passion portrait (the Gospels studiously avoid attributing *phobos* [fear] to Jesus). In any case, Moltmann lays bare the devastating "laceration" the incarnate Christ feels in flesh and blood, heart and mind, ensouled body—not from soldiers' flogging whips (see John 19:1) but *from, with, betwixt,* and *between* his absconding Father—bearing the full brunt of death and suffering, "hell and judgment," *within* the life of God.

---

39. Moltmann, *Trinity and the Kingdom,* 76–77 (emphasis original).

6

That's Gross!

The Disgusted Jesus

While we may grant Jesus the odd groan, sigh (Mark 7:34; 8:12), and even snort (John 11:33) in his stressful life portrayed in the Gospels, we would be hard pressed to imagine an outburst of "Eww!," "Ick!," or "Gross!," matched with scrunched nose, squinted eyes, and scowling mouth representing the near-universal facial expression of disgust.[1] Due to their scaly skin, open sores, and contaminating conditions, lepers were prime objects of disgust in the ancient world. But in notable contrast, the Synoptic Jesus freely ministers to such afflicted persons, touching them, restoring them to health, and urging their reincorporation into the community according to Jewish law (Matt. 8:1–4; 11:5; Mark 1:40–45; Luke 5:12–16; 7:22; 17:11–17). Although in Mark's episode (discussed in chap. 3), Jesus also becomes angry at the leper for challenging Jesus's willingness to cleanse him, this ire does not preclude Jesus from stretching out his hand, touching the diseased man, and making him whole. And while Jesus "sternly" orders him to tell no one about his healing until he has shown himself to a priestly examiner, Jesus never demeans him or shows a trace of disgust.[2]

1. Darwin, *Expression of the Emotions*, 250–60, 357–58, 376; Ekman, *Emotions Revealed*, 10–12, 172–89; Rozin, Lowery, and Ebert, "Varieties of Disgust Faces."

2. Note the distinction between disgust and indignation (anger) drawn by Nussbaum, *Hiding from Humanity*: "The core objects of disgust are reminders of mortality and animality, seen as pollutants to the human. Indignation, by contrast, centrally involves the idea of a wrong or a harm" (99). "However close the 'cry of disgust' lies to indignation, its content is antisocial. Its

On the flip side, as a branded criminal sentenced to crucifixion, Jesus himself is treated by the authorities as a disgusting blight on the body politic that must be humiliated and eradicated. That's the cruel way Rome preserved its vaunted "peace" against perceived threats. Isaiah's sketch of the Suffering Servant's contemptible state provides a vivid blueprint of Jesus's final degradation:

> He had no form or majesty that we should look at him,
>   nothing in his appearance that we should desire him.
> He was despised and rejected by others;
>   a man of suffering and acquainted with infirmity;
> and as one from whom others hide their faces
>   he was despised, and we held him of no account. (Isa. 53:2–3)

Hiding one's face from despised persons is a hallmark of disgust, tantamount to repudiating any fellow feeling or mirror imaging ("I am nothing like you!"), wishing they didn't exist, holding them of "no account," giving them no due consideration, and looking the other way while the authorities dispense with their worthless beings.[3]

The emotional valence of this dismissive avoidance of the suffering Christ is the polar opposite of the Son's perceived abandonment by the Father on the cross (as discussed in chap. 5). Whereas the brokenhearted Father couldn't bear to look upon his beloved Son in his brutalized condition, Jesus's executioners couldn't care less. The "converted" centurion represents the proverbial exception that proves the rule, and he reevaluated Jesus's status only at the end of the ordeal, when he "stood facing" Jesus and observed how he "breathed his last" (Mark 15:39). The gambling soldiers fixed their attention downward on Jesus's tattered garment, the only thing of remote value they attached to him. Jesus dies an object of abject shame, ridicule, and abuse.

Yet flipping the coin again to look at this from a biblical-theological angle, a paradoxical path to saving humiliated humanity comes to light. Jesus Messiah's dying as a stigmatized outcast uniquely qualifies him to succor and support, to redeem and restore fellow sufferers and pariahs:

> Surely he has borne our infirmities
>   and carried our diseases;

---

content is, 'I repudiate this ugly world as not a part of me.' . . . Indignation has a constructive function: it says, 'these people [or I] have been wronged, and they [I] should not have been wronged'" (105; cf. 99–107).

3. See Nussbaum, *Hiding from Humanity*; cf. Nussbaum, *Upheavals of Thought*, 205–6, 346–50.

> yet we accounted him stricken,
>> struck down by God, and afflicted.
> But he was wounded for our transgressions,
>> crushed for our iniquities
>
> . . . .
>
>> and by his bruises we are healed [physically, psychologically, socially, emotionally]. (Isa. 53:4–5; cf. Acts 8:32–33; Heb. 5:7–8; 1 Pet. 2:24–25)

So Jesus sympathizes and identifies with those labeled disgusting by "normal" society. He endures the slings and arrows of others' disgust without responding in kind or projecting his malignant experience onto some unfortunate third party. As is well known, victims of disgust tragically become enmeshed in an abuse cycle, inflicting their pain outward and downward on weaker individuals or groups in a self-defeating attempt to reclaim some personal dignity. Jesus aims, however, to short-circuit the abuse cycle and defuse the disgust dynamo.

Yet this anti-disgust mission may not capture the whole picture of Jesus's emotional journey in the Gospels. In fact, a couple of incidents hint at Jesus's own feelings of disgust toward others, which he surmounts but only by working through them and learning more about them. In short, Jesus exercises what we might call "disgust management" in two cases: one dealing with Lazarus's four-day rotting corpse (yes, we visit his gravesite one more time in John 11) and the other with a non-Jewish female supplicant Jesus compares to a scavenging "dog" (Mark 7:24–30). While we may bristle at ascribing the emotion of disgust to Jesus even in these rare examples, we may also broaden our sense of what Jesus truly accomplishes as a human being. He overcomes one of the most deep-seated, vehement human emotions by feeling it in his own gut and forging a way to a more embracive, compassionate vision. He knows firsthand what disgust feels like, and he comes to know a more excellent way through thoughtful interaction—with two women, as it happens: Martha in John 11:38–40 and an unnamed Syrophoenician woman in Mark 7:24–30.

In addition to investigating Jesus's disgust-evoking encounters with a rotting corpse and a cur-like intruder, we will examine a pair of his parables in Luke 18:1–14 that are linked by this narrative hinge: "He also told this parable to some who trusted in themselves that they were righteous and regarded others with contempt" (18:9). What exactly is Luke's Jesus teaching about self-righteous contempt/disgust toward others via the character relations between judge and widow and between Pharisee and tax collector in the two respective parables (18:2–5, 10–14)?

Before delving into these provocative Gospel passages, however, it will again prove useful to sketch an analytical grid for the emotion of disgust, drawn from ancient and modern perspectives.

Dissecting Disgust

Modern horror writers have nothing on Sophocles. He gets right to the bloody point in his gruesome description of Oedipus Rex's self-blinding, wielding his dead mother's gold brooches as daggers: "He struck his eyes with raised hand not once but often. At each blow the bloody eye-balls bedewed his beard, and sent forth not sluggish drops of gore, but all at once a dark shower of blood came down like hail."[4] A disgusting act by any standards and an eerily apt consequence of Oedipus's disgusting incestuous intercourse, albeit unknowingly, with his mother! In its tragic setting, audiences might find their way to pity poor Oedipus, once they recover from their shock of disgust. At a safe literary distance, they might also, as classics scholar Donald Lateiner suggests, find some relief from their own anxieties about transgressing taboo boundaries. Ancient comedies took a different tack, routinely depicting slapstick scenes of gory, gooey, smelly messes, thereby dispensing the medicine of mocking laughter to ease the threat of everyday disgusting contagions.[5]

Outside popular literature and theater, however, disgust does not seem to have registered much on the emotional radar of ancient Greek thinkers. Aristotle has no entry for "disgust" in his *Rhetoric* catalog of passions, probably because of the vulgar, nonpersonal, and viscous substance bases of disgust—the stuff of crude anatomy and animal science more than human psychology and sociology. As Konstan comments

> The emotions in Aristotle's catalogue are directed principally at agents, above all human agents. . . . The kinds of sentiments that find a place in Aristotle's discussion of the *pathê* seem to involve an awareness of other subjectivities. This is why such generalized moods as melancholy, the feelings inspired by music, wonder or awe at nature's grandeur, . . . *and disgust at pallid or slimy things* (as distinct from moral disgust) do not count as *pathê* for Aristotle, although they often qualify as emotions in modern inventories.[6]

Aristotle's list does include the *pathos* of *aischynē*, "shame" (*Rhet.* 2.6 [1383b–85a]), a close cousin to disgust; both shame and disgust involve feel-

---

4. Sophocles, *Oedipus Tyrannus*, lines 1275–80.
5. Lateiner, "Emotions of Disgust"; see also Lateiner and Spatharas, "Introduction."
6. Konstan, *Emotions of the Ancient Greeks*, 39 (emphasis added).

ings of degradation. Yet their motivations differ, though with some overlap. Aristotle defines shame as "a sort of pain and agitation concerning the class of evils, whether present or past or future, that seem to bring a person into disrespect" (2.6.2 [1383b])—especially disrespect from those on the same or a higher social plane: "A person feels shame toward those whose opinion he takes account of" (2.6.14 [1384a]). And such shaming opinion is based mainly on violations of behavioral norms rather than offensive bodily products, as with disgust. Aristotle singles out acts of "cowardice," "licentiousness," "shameful profiteering and stinginess," "flattery," "smallness of mind and meanness," and "boastfulness" as particularly shame-worthy conduct (1.6.3–11 [1383b–1384a]). Thus conceived, shame monitors impropriety more than impurity, external reputation more than internal repulsiveness, at the core of disgust. Shame counterpoises honor rather than hygiene, safeguarding one's standing in the body politic rather than one's health in the physical body.

A related "shame" term in classical Greek is *aidōs*, which Douglas Cairns defines as "an inhibitory emotion based on sensitivity to and protection of one's self-image," with prevailing concern to shield one's future good image more than contending with a guilty past.[7] Of course, if "normal society" came to regard someone or some group as totally worthless objects of contempt on the level of dirty animals and filthy scum, such stigmatization would doubtless affect that person or group's self-image as well as social status. But honor-shame codes apply across the spectrum, affecting elite classes as much as outcasts. A wealthy, healthy noble, for example, could suffer considerable shame by being snubbed from the guest register of an A-list banquet in his or her community (see Luke 14:12–24). This might arouse feelings of outrage, anxiety, depression, and a welter of other emotions along with dishonor—but not disgust.

As Konstan notes, the lacuna concerning disgust in ancient Greek emotion theory has been amply filled by modern psychological researchers and philosophers, who rank disgust among the most basic and universal of human emotions. Most everyone who's not a forensic scientist would experience disgust in a close encounter with a rotting, oozing corpse, accompanied by various possible physical reactions (hand over mouth and nose, gagging, vomiting), mental glitches (disorientation, dizziness, fainting), moral judgments ("That's so vile!"), and social aversions ("Get me out of here!")—all part of a

7. Cairns, *Aidōs*, 2 (cf. 13–14, 145), quoted and discussed in Konstan, *Emotions of the Ancient Greeks*, 94–95. Commenting on Aristotle, *Eth. nic.* 4.9 (1128b.32–33), Konstan states, "*Aidôs* is clearly understood to inhibit bad behaviour, while *aiskhunê* [*aischynē*] reflects back on it with regret" (95).

powerful, reactionary complex. One can scarcely help being moved to disgust by certain revolting sights, smells, and sensations.

Though recognizing that different cultures may direct their disgust toward different objects, extensive research conducted by the psychologist Paul Rozin and associates has exposed three broad categories of disgust related to a range of "unclean" bodily conditions and moral sensibilities:

- *Core oral disgust*: regulating what one ingests into the body through formal dietary laws and widely accepted taboos concerning polluting consumption
- *Sociomoral disgust*: stripping individuals or groups of their human dignity because of some assigned deviant label based on race, gender, class, disability, and other markers, which may or may not include immoral sexual behavior
- *Animal nature disgust*: monitoring an array of bodily functions, especially glutinous eruptions and emissions (blood, semen, vomit, excrement) that humans share with other animals, confirming to our great discomfort that we, too, are mortal creatures with life forces ebbing away and seeping out of us[8]

On a more elemental level, people prove particularly susceptible to seven "disgust elicitors": (1) food, (2) animals, (3) body products, (4) sex, (5) body envelope violations, (6) death, and (7) hygiene. Though common triggers of disgust, these manifest in different ways and situations according to people's "disgust sensitivity" both across and within societies.[9] A modern parent, for example, normally repulsed by others' feces, feels differently about changing the diapers of one's own little darling (though still not exactly enjoying the process). So, too, medical personnel, by dint of practice and vocation, become inured to bodily emissions in a clinical context (although outside that environment is another story). Moreover, it's no secret that sexual and hygienic standards and practices vary widely across cultures.

On the level of *moral disgust*, often interlaced with "religious" passions and precepts, Rozin and colleagues have established a triadic CAD grid, as they call it, mapping three moral emotions onto three moral codes.

8. Rozin et al., "CAD Triad Hypothesis"; cf. Rozin, Haidt, and McCauley, "Disgust"; Rozin and Fallon, "Perspective on Disgust"; Beck, *Unclean*, 13–30.
9. Haidt, McCauley, and Rozin, "Individual Differences." For a related but more "evolutionary/adaptive" approach surrounding three domains of disgust—pathogen avoidance, mate choice, and social interaction—see Tybur, Lieberman, and Griskevicius, "Microbes, Mating, and Morality."

Moral Emotions	Moral Codes
Contempt	Community
Anger	Autonomy
Disgust	Divinity

I will allude below to the "C" and "A" pairs (related to "contempt" in Luke 18 and "anger" in John 11). For now I briefly note the link between disgust and divinity. The toxic, contagious elements of disgusting substances and their hosts are readily imagined as unseen mysterious, malignant forces, even among moderns who (should) know something about microbiology. Germs by any name, teeming in yucky bodies and objects and poised to jump into my body and community, take on personas of spooky operatives in the spirit world, the realm of deities and demons, gods and gremlins, life and death. In our supposedly advanced scientific age, hysteria still erupts in certain circles over the transmission and treatment of HIV/AIDS, ignorantly invoking the wrath of God against (putative) disgusting, degenerate sexual acts and actors. Researchers identify patterns of "magical thinking" (mis)informing and inciting disgusted feelings, "magical" being an umbrella term for a range of superstitious, supernatural worldviews.[10]

The Gospels' theological narratives, like virtually all literature in antiquity, presume a pervasive "magical" milieu, although Matthew does not celebrate the famous Magi (*magoi*) for their profession (recall the ineptitude of Pharaoh's magician-sorcerers in Exodus), and the book of Acts denounces the practice of "magic" (*mageia*) per se as false and demonic (Acts 8:9–24; 13:6–12; cf. 19:11–20; Rev. 21:8; 22:15). Still, it's not surprising that Jesus grapples with potentially disgusting matters in paranormal contexts of death and resurrection (Lazarus), unclean spirits (the Syrophoenician woman's possessed daughter), and temple rituals (the parable of the Pharisee and the tax collector in Luke 18).

In sum, affective complexes related to disgust stay on high alert, policing multilane traffic between multilevel bodies and borders within an intricate web of evolutionary and cultural norms, codes, and regulations, spoken and unspoken, conscious and unconscious. Surveillance focuses particularly on spaces of entry and exit, ingress and egress—with hypervigilance against a horde of perilous transgressions. Scarcely any area of life—somatic, psychosomatic, ethnic, political, cosmic, environmental—escapes the dragnet of disgust.

10. Haidt, McCauley, and Rozin, "Individual Differences."

Stench That Sticks (John 11:33–44)

In the preceding two chapters, we've probed Jesus's anger and anguish at Lazarus's gravesite in John 11: his angry, snorting reaction to perceived doubts about his power and purpose to restore Lazarus's life and his anguished, stunned realization of the imminent prospect of "seeing" Lazarus's crypt and staring into the abyss of death. As distressing as this episode is for Jesus and the Bethany community, however, dare we try to wring yet another emotion out of it (disgust, no less)?

Rozin's CAD hypothesis (sketched above) closely correlates anger, disgust, and contempt as vehement emotional reactions to violated moral codes, with anger marking resistance to impingements on autonomy (the free pursuit of individual rights). Although the politics of human rights is largely a Western Enlightenment "invention,"[11] indignant ire at those who seek to constrict one's autonomy broadly matches Aristotle's concept of anger as heated protest against the belittlement of one's character and aims. The Johannine Jesus claims no Jeffersonian "inalienable right" to raise Lazarus from the dead, but he does have a clear intention to do so (John 11:11, 23) and becomes highly agitated when others faithlessly impede this purpose. So in this swirl of Jesus's "greatly disturbed" moral outrage (11:33, 38), we might be inclined to add a dash of sneering disgust to his snorting anger—particularly disgust, in Rozin's terms, over what Jesus perceives as an affront to his divinity in the pure and holy realm transcending death and decay.

But according to Stephen Moore, disgust—viewed less as a matter of principled moral aversion and more as a profuse bodily affect—elicits Jesus's tears and permeates the gravesite environment.[12] Following the French philosopher and affect theorist Gilles Deleuze, Moore is skeptical of what we can know about interior feelings, given their preponderantly unconscious operations. Perceptions of feelings, whether our own or others', constitute the proverbial tip of the iceberg, with the vast bulk hidden below. If an iceberg is too cold an image for feelings, an undetected subsurface magma chamber makes the point on the hotter scale. Small external seepages belie underlying masses of energy, until it's too late (think BP's *Deepwater Horizon*).

If we're handicapped in plumbing the depths of our emotion-laden lives in the "real" world, how much more in literary worlds, which bind us to the surface of the text, of the page? For all our pretenses at probing beneath the text, we go in blind. To push the point, if I hold an open book—say, the

---

11. Hunt, *Inventing Human Rights*.
12. Moore, "Why the Johannine Jesus Weeps"; another version of this essay is Moore, "Why the Risen Body Weeps."

Gospel of John—in front of my face, all I see is the printed text glaring back at me, blocking whatever's behind it; if I drop it on the ground and take a scalpel to it, I succeed only in ripping up the text and rendering it unreadable. This surface feel, whether of life or literature, by no means consigns us to superficial readings, but it does orient us to an interpretive path.

Here Moore distinguishes between conventional "emotion" language and Deleuzian "affect": "The etymological trajectory of *emotion*—from Latin *emovere*, 'move' or 'move out'—evokes expressive transmission from the interiority of a sender to the interiority of a receiver. The etymological trajectory of *affect*, however—at least for Deleuze—does not evoke transmission from depth to depth, internal subject to internal subject, but from surface to surface, body to body, action to action."[13] Since I affiliate with broad-based emotion theorists who track emotions within a thick web of somatic sensations, social relations, and action tendencies, I quibble less about terminological distinctions between feelings, emotions, passions, and affect(s). But I'm under no illusions (or "deleuzians") about getting to the core of Jesus's emotions through the medium of a flat text.

The iceberg/magma metaphors above are mine. Moore launches his own nautical images to convey the fraught voyage to fathom the feelings of literary figures: "Oceans of ink have been spilled on the inner lives of paper people."[14] He gets particularly exercised about facile pretensions to chart the depths of paper people's psychologies, not least Jesus's putative "deep sorrow," "deep distress," "deep emotional disturbance," "deep feeling," and "deep affection" in the Lazarus narrative, with particular assessment of Jesus's tears as "the outward expressions of his [inner] sorrow."[15] While I agree that "deep" is something of a waffle word (the "deep end" of the neighborhood pool is nothing compared to "the face of the deep" primordial waters [Gen. 1:2]) and that I myself use it too often (there are not many good synonyms), I'm not ready to abandon altogether the quest for Jesus's "depth psychology"— what he feels in his gut, way down, affecting his organs, impulses, desires, and thoughts, both consciously and unconsciously.

And Moore is not ready to give up on the probe either, though not as a "deep" dive. For all his postmodern (and post-postmodern) theoretical sophistication, Moore remains at heart a Bible scholar aiming to interpret biblical texts rigorously and meticulously (I almost added "deeply"). For my money there's no better guide through murky, French literary-critical waters

13. Moore, "Why the Johannine Jesus Weeps," 299.
14. Moore, "Why the Johannine Jesus Weeps," 300.
15. Moore, "Why the Johannine Jesus Weeps," 300–301. His target here is Voorwinde, *Jesus' Emotions in the Fourth Gospel*; it could have easily been me.

to exegete ("draw out") and illuminate biblical literature in fresh ways. As for navigating the affective response of the weeping Jesus in John 11, Moore is buoyed by film critic Eugenie Brinkema's adaptation of Deleuze in the interest of "coupling affect theory and close reading,"[16] of "formulating a new approach to affectivity that regards its exteriority in textual form as something that commands a reading."[17] Of course, it's easier to "read" filmed affects (special effects), with or without 3D glasses, than the affective stylistics of printed words. Nonetheless, close literary encounters generate their own rhetorical-affective energy within the reader as reflective pools of characters' feelings within emotion-charged episodes.[18]

Or to use yet another aquatic image favored by Brinkema and Moore (modifying Deleuze), one can detect small signs of scripted (or screened) affects as tiny bubbles, pockets, or folds on the surface of the text, emerging from and surrounded by the wider affective environment, as a ship might be envisioned as a "folding of the sea."[19] Or, shifting to living beings' watery substance, a teardrop might reflect extended, distended—and subtended—sluices of affective meaning. "The tear has been a liquid volley in countless debates over whether emotion is an active production or passive subjection; the relationship between interior states, judgments or beliefs, and exterior expressions. . . . The little lachrymal drop has been deployed to work through some of the most significant debates in philosophy about the relationship between the body and the mind, the interior and the exterior, the will and that which overrides the will."[20]

While Brinkema briefly references Aristotle's *Poetics*—and also John's famous "Jesus wept" disclosure—within the history of tearful signs of tragic emotion, her main focus falls on a singular haunting frame of Hitchcock's *Psycho*, featuring Marion's single teardrop precariously poised between the corner of her open, staring right eye and the bridge of her nose, just above a gaping right nostril, the right half of her mouth, and the shower floor where her pretty face lies on a watery, bloody tile deathbed. What a poignant story this "small spherule" might tell, especially if it is a "small, fat tear," as it appears to be.[21] But it could also be a clingy shower droplet. Whatever it is, it packs the punch of a water bomb or, better, the residue of a piercing (knifing) water jet. The ambiguity only amps up the affective field.

16. Moore, "Why the Johannine Jesus Weeps," 297.
17. Brinkema, *Forms of the Affects*, 4.
18. For an insightful "affective rhetorical" reading of Luke's birth narratives, see Kuhn, *Heart of Biblical Narrative*.
19. Brinkema, *Forms of the Affects*, 23; Moore, "Why the Johannine Jesus Weeps," 299, 301.
20. Brinkema, *Forms of the Affects*, 3.
21. Brinkema, *Forms of the Affects*, 1–2; Moore, "Why the Johannine Jesus Weeps," 298.

So, too, Jesus's tears—falling on the Bethany countryside at the edge of the grave that has ensconced Lazarus for four days—enfold and are enfolded by the emotional episode stretching across John 11. But in Moore's reading, what Jesus's weeping reveals necessarily remains on the surface of the text, which by no means scrapes it down to the barest desensitized bone. But it does shift the interpretive horizon outward, across the earthy, bodily, material elements of the narrative, rather than inward, bubbling up from Jesus's turbulent psyche.

> Jesus's tears, then, far from welling up expressively from a deep, hidden, internal pool of emotion—bursting up from imagined depths to splash the surface of the page—are better seen as yet further folds in the Johannine text, tiny but highly consequential pockets of insideness within its paper-thin, infinitely extensible outside. . . . Consider . . . Jesus's tears not as an expressively outward sign of an abruptly unleashed (e)motion surging up from an imagined human interior but as an impersonal affect force impelling horizontal movement across the plane of the text.[22]

And what this impersonal affective force field in the Lazarus story generates above all, in Moore's reading, is *disgust*. How so? Consider two disgust-laden material elements lurking upon and wafting across the narrative: putrid corpse and fetid odor.

Putrid Corpse

"Every book about disgust is not least a book about the rotting corpse," writes Winfried Menninghaus.[23] Nothing marks the ominous, diaphanous borderland of humanity, animality, and mortality more than the rotting corpse. Our bodies die, decay, and degrade just like every other living thing. Slug and king come to the same eerie end; they become disgusting death-bedfellows.

Although the Torah is not obsessed with corpses and does not explicitly register disgust as a feeling state, it carefully regulates contact with dead, "unclean" flesh, prohibiting consumption of predatory creatures that feed on carrion and prescribing separation and purification rituals for those who handle the dead (see Lev. 11:24–40; Num. 19:11–22). Such contact is not morally deviant (sinful); indeed, proper burial of the dead is a necessary and honorable community practice. But corpse contact is socially disruptive, as it straddles that most sacred, scariest threshold between life and death. And while it may or may not trigger physical and emotional upheavals of disgust, it

22. Moore, "Why the Johannine Jesus Weeps," 302.
23. Menninghaus, *Disgust*, 1.

certainly affects the community on a visceral level.[24] Far from choking strong feelings, rituals channel feelings into acceptable, affective actions.

Though Lazarus's corpse does not appear until the end of the story (John 11:44), it hovers like a specter over the entire plot, even as it rests doubly enfolded in strips of cloth (around hands, feet, and face) in a stone tomb (a folding of the earth), eerily threatening to ooze out and contaminate Jesus, his disciples, and the Bethany villagers. Not that Jesus here, or anywhere else in the Fourth Gospel, is explicitly concerned about corpse impurity or visibly moved to disgust over mortal matters, unless some trace element of disgust adheres in those tears that burst from his eyes when he's pressed to "come and see" Lazarus's body. But trace elements suspended in watery solution are hard to detect with the naked eye. Other senses, however, might prove more perceptive.

Fetid Odor

No sense is more sensitive than smell. And none is more permeable across space and time, drifting into nose and mouth—you can veritably taste aromas, pleasant and pungent—and detonating vivid memories, good and bad, with a single evocative whiff. On the nefarious side, free-wafting vapors can be lithe carriers of lethal toxins, which in turn demands highly developed olfactory radar to sniff out invasive threats (odorless airborne pathogens are the nightmares of epidemiologists and counterterrorism agents). William Ian Miller remarks: "Smells are pervasive and invisible, capable of threatening like poison; smells are the very vehicles of contagion. Odors are thus especially contaminating and much more dangerous than localized substances one may or may not put in the mouth."[25] Of course, signals can get crossed: foul-smelling gooey cheeses can prove quite tasty (especially with the right wine); and however lovely one's eau de toilette might smell, it's probably best not to drink it. Even so, the nose remains a key security guard, and in Jesus's world, long before germ theory and biochemistry, its role as disgust monitor was all the more critical.

The Bible attests to anthropomorphic and apotropaic components of smell. When the postdiluvian Noah offered burnt sacrifices (charred carcasses) of every "clean animal" from the ark, "the LORD smelled the pleasing odor [and] said in his heart, 'I will never again curse the ground because of humankind . . . nor will I ever again destroy every living creature as I have done" (Gen. 8:20–21). But God's nose can also get out of joint with the people when they

24. See the wide-ranging study in Kazen, "Disgust in Body, Mind, and Language."
25. Miller, *Anatomy of Disgust*, 60.

do not live faithfully, justly, and mercifully. Then, as the prophet Amos insists, their burnt sacrifices are pointless: God "will not accept them," period (Amos 5:22; cf. 5:21–24). And in turn, to challenge them to change their ways, the Lord sent them "a pestilence after the manner of Egypt" and "made the stench of [their] camp go up into [their] nostrils; yet [they] did not return" (4:10). Our English metaphor that some malevolent scheme or action "stinks to high heaven," which Miller traces back to Shakespeare's Hamlet ("O, my offense is rank, it smells to heaven"[26]), reinforces this moral dimension of malodor. As Miller glosses, "Bad smells are evil, evil smelling; and bad deeds stink to heaven, because they smell like Hell."[27]

While Lazarus's corpse stays safely ensconced in a cave tomb and grave-clothes, its deathly odor begins to leak out into the atmosphere before Jesus beckons his deceased friend to "come out." Out of sight does not include out of smell. No amount of spices and ointments applied at Lazarus's burial could fend off the noxious assault of fetid emissions for long. It falls to Martha to state the obvious when Jesus orders removal of the boulder at the tomb's mouth, "Lord, already there is a stench because he has been dead four days" (John 11:39). Perhaps Martha is tempted to make another gibe about Jesus's tardy arrival. In any case, she resists exposing herself to more emotional upheaval in a (dis)gust of rotting vapors to which her beloved brother has been reduced.

Or so one might read Martha's emotional state. But if it's difficult to sense internal feelings from a textual plane, how much harder to register emanating smells! Odors do not waft off the page or screen. In a movie theater, the smell of the audience's tubs of buttered popcorn will dominate most screen shots, including those of stinking objects and actors' portray-als of disgusted reactions to them.[28] But a particularly evocative shot of a reeking substance might leak out enough on the surface to degrade the buttery atmosphere ("Ugh, I can't eat another piece of popcorn after see-ing [smelling] that!").

But what does Jesus care about the smell of Lazarus's corpse, especially right before he revivifies (refreshes) it? And by the same token, what does he care about Martha's sensitive nose? She'll quickly forget about it when she welcomes her brother back to life. So does odor affect Jesus at all in this scene, the only Gospel story that has the slightest whiff of a bad smell? Moore thinks so, retrojecting Lazarus's stench back a few verses and projecting it into

26. Act 3, scene 3.
27. Miller, *Anatomy of Disgust*, 78.
28. Moore, "Why the Johannine Jesus Weeps," 303; Brinkema, *Forms of the Affects*, 121, 144.

Jesus's tears: "What makes Jesus's eyes water in 11:35 is a certain smell, indeed a certain unmistakable stench, as yet only wafted on the breeze."[29] So these become rancid tears, drops of acid rain at the edges of the eyes and contours of the cheeks and chin, ultimately dampening the ground below. Again, for Moore, such tears do not bubble up from some inner emotional wellspring but poke out within folded environs. To what extent Jesus smells the stench and feels the disgust of Lazarus's rotting flesh is undetectable in the text and beside the point. What we can say is that the disgusting stench *sticks to* the story and its characters,[30] oozing from Lazarus's corpse into others' noses and adhering, at least for a while, to Jesus's tear-streaked visage such that he must face the revolting reality of his friend's recent death, to say nothing of his own impending demise. We might even read Jesus's angry "snorting" (*embrimaomai*) as a forceful, repelling reaction to the odiferous onslaught of Lazarus's decomposing body.

But while the characters are clearly affected to some degree, no one faints dead away from the fetid fumes. The story moves on—speeds on, in fact—to Lazarus's resuscitation, as if Jesus flicks off the acrid tears and gets on with fumigating the whole environment and reverse engineering the rotting process back to a healthy living organism. The negative affect does not stick like superglue or stink like a cesspit. But it doesn't entirely wash or waft out either. Moore sees a "paradox of disgust" threading through the Johannine fabric around the core pattern of *flesh*—that is, en-fleshing, enfolding of flesh, incarnating.[31] Within the narrative fold, this flesh pattern shifts shape and texture: one moment highlighting that the "Word became flesh," cozily hosting divine glory in fleshly tent flaps (John 1:14)[32] and the next moment dividing the terrain with a thick wall between mortal "flesh" and eternal "Spirit" (3:6). Yet flesh is not cremated to dust by Spirit but rather recreated, reborn, reconstituted in, by, and through the divine Spirit (3:6). Instead of eradicating mortified flesh, resurrection transforms it. The wall is at least semipermeable.

Enfleshed human life remains spooky and unstable, subject to death and decay, dying from the moment of birth. It is unbearably disgusting, which is why we obsessively anesthetize our consciousness of death, medically postpone death as long as possible, and cosmetically sanitize and spruce up our

29. Moore, "Why the Johannine Jesus Weeps," 303.
30. On the cultural significance of "sticky" substances evoking the emotion of disgust, see Ahmed, *Cultural Politics*, 96–100.
31. Moore, "Why the Johannine Jesus Weeps," 306–8.
32. Here I associate the "tent flap" image with the verb in John 1:14 related to "tent" (*skēnē*): "And the Word became flesh and lived [or tented; *eskēnōsen*] among us."

bodily veneers in the meantime. Or in the case of Jesus, just go straight to resurrection as soon as possible. Four days is long enough for poor dead Lazarus, too long even, Jesus may come to believe. Three days in the tomb will do for Jesus himself, if he actually stays that long. (In this Gospel, he takes time to neatly fold up his burial facecloth before exiting!—no rushed, last-minute departure before visitors arrive [John 20:7 CEB].) While Martha accepts the Jewish doctrine of a general bodily resurrection "on the last day" (11:24), Jesus begins to collapse the present-future time continuum with anticipated *particular* resurrections—namely, Lazarus's and his own—in the *now* and *near*, respectively. The last day is at hand; eschatology is realized partially, particularly, proleptically. Lazarus will be restored to life within the hour but will die again, rot again, stink again before the grand, general resurrection finale. And when Jesus rises to new life, he will boost his followers' faith in resurrection, while also maintaining spatial and temporal distance from them as he ascends back to his heavenly Father (see 20:17) awaiting the apocalyptic "last day," whenever that will be.

So, like most New Testament writings, the Fourth Gospel maintains an already/not yet tension between life and death. But across this threshold, the Johannine Jesus bends more toward the *matter* of life: "I am the bread of life . . . that comes down from heaven, so that one may eat of it and not die. . . . Whoever eats of this bread will live forever; and the bread that I will give for the life of the world is my flesh" (John 6:48–51). Jesus favors fresh bread, which is to say, fresh flesh that doesn't rot or reek like day-old manna (see 6:49; Exod. 16:19–21). The follow-up scene to Lazarus's revivification, set around the family dinner table with Jesus, all but entirely deodorizes the gravesite event and even pre-sanitizes Jesus's entombment ("for the day of my burial"), as Mary douses Jesus's feet with perfume such that "the house was filled with the fragrance" (12:1–7). Yet that disgusting whiff of Lazarus's decaying corpse cannot be completely wiped away. As Moore deftly concludes, "The scent of death sits lightly on the Johannine Jesus; it is not the stench of Lazarus. But it is a scent that cannot be scrubbed clean. And that, more than anything, is why the Johannine Jesus weeps at the tomb of Lazarus."[33]

Moore's compelling article persuades me that some element of disgust should be added to the affective mix of Jesus's dealings with Lazarus. At the same time, Moore's study, for all its expansive range, strikes me as too restrictive in bracketing out Jesus's internal feelings and too reductive in breaking down his tears to the core affect of disgust. Such can be the price of methodological rigor. No method can be expected to cover everything,

33. Moore, "Why the Johannine Jesus Weeps," 308.

and Moore covers more ground than most biblical scholars, not least in brilliantly demonstrating the exegetical fruits of affect theory. But while affect theory rightly challenges hyper-sentimental interpretations of characters portrayed on paper, canvas, and screen, good writers, painters, and filmmakers inevitably evoke various aspects of their subjects' emotional lives. All these centuries later, Sophocles still makes his readers and audiences feel Oedipus's poignant pain, or at least what we think Oedipus feels within the tragic drama.

For all the limited revelatory powers of the Fourth Gospel's text qua text, it doesn't simply close in or fold around itself in a sealed compartment. Like the stone rolled away from the tomb and the graveclothes unwound from Lazarus's corpse, the phrases "greatly disturbed" (twice) and "deeply moved" open and loosen the text enough to allow the stench of disgust to drift across the text and textual bodies and the snort of anger and squirt of anguish to burst out of Jesus's "round" character,[34] capable of portraying interior emotion as well as surface affect.

Closer attention to sequential plot movement across the textual plane still, I believe, links Jesus's snorts and tears most tightly to anger at his friends' unbelief in his life-restoring mission and to anguish in anticipation of seeing Lazarus's corpse (John 11:33–38). Stench does not come into the story until Martha injects it at 11:39. She strikes this nasal blow in sharp terms, which Jesus can scarcely ignore, but as noted above, he parries it immediately without acknowledging her pungent point. One could argue that what is most vigorously repressed is most viscerally felt. Jesus can scarcely bear the thought of his beloved friend vaporizing into a disgusting cloud of malodorous rot. He's much more comfortable with senses of sight and hearing (the spoken word) than of smell.

> Jesus said to [Martha, in response to her "stench" remark], "Did I not *tell you* that if you believed, you would *see* the glory of God?" (11:40)

> And Jesus *looked upward* [away from Lazarus's tomb] and *said*, "Father I thank you for having *heard* me. I knew that you always *hear* me, but I have *said* this for the sake of the crowd standing here." (11:41–42)

> When he had *said* this, he *cried with a loud voice*, "Lazarus, come out!" (11:43)

---

34. In line with the image discussed above of Jesus's out-folding, spherical teardrop, I draw here on the well-known delineation of "flat" (stock) and "round" (complex) literary characters in Forster, *Aspects of the Novel*, 73–81; cf. Culpepper, *Anatomy of the Fourth Gospel*, 102–3; Resseguie, *Narrative Criticism*, 123–26, 147, 152–53, 253–54.

It's as if Jesus aims to shine out and shout down all trace of morbid, mortal disgust from the affective atmosphere. In the process, however, he doth protest too much perhaps. To reprise Moore, the Johannine Jesus, for all his divine glory and dynamic word, cannot quite scrub himself clean of the stench of rotting flesh. Martha won't let him.

Going to the Dogs (Mark 7:24–30)

In the extraordinary story in Mark 7:24–30 (cf. Matt. 15:21–28), Jesus restores to health the demon-tormented "little daughter" (Mark 7:25) of a desperate mother who seeks his help for her stricken child. As it happens, Jesus exorcises the "unclean spirit" from the girl without meeting her or making a house call. Upon returning home, the mother finds her daughter "lying on the bed, and the demon gone" (7:30)—a remarkable displacing and disinfecting of toxic, "unclean" forces that had seized the girl but not yet squelched her life. Yet this case features no rotting flesh, fetid odor, or any physical proximity between Jesus and the "unclean" victim. Thus, Jesus appears to be well clear of any contaminating zone of disgust.

But that's not the whole story, or even the main story, which is less about the daughter's healing than the mother's solicitation of Jesus's aid. And Jesus responds to this pleading woman with more emotional vehemence than we might expect. In an earlier, similar case, when a distraught father bows before Jesus and begs, "My little daughter is at the point of death. Come and lay your hands on her, so that she may be made well, and live," Jesus promptly heads to the girl's bedside (Mark 5:22–24). But now, when a mother, also bowing and begging (7:25), pleads for Jesus to deliver her "little daughter" from her demonic plague, Jesus doesn't budge and even bristles at the mother's request before ultimately granting it. He is not said or shown to be moved with compassion, as in the surrounding feeding incidents (6:34; 8:2), and might even be fairly said, as Sharon Ringe puts it, to be "caught with his compassion down."[35]

What exactly about this encounter irks Jesus and what clues might the narrative provide to his emotional state? Neither Mark nor Matthew provides any direct statement of how Jesus *feels* here; but again, the story's dialogue bristles with affective tension. Much scholarly ink has been spilt trying to pinpoint Jesus's motives, aims, and thought processes in this provocative exchange. But the factor of disgust has not typically figured in these studies (beyond a

---

35. Ringe, "Gentile Woman's Story," 69; cf. Ringe, "Gentile Woman's Story, Revisited."

superficial link with "unclean" taboos in Jewish law).[36] Various aspects of this story and its context, however, "stick" rather aptly to the disgust categories sketched above. Though no explicit odors drift across the surface of the text, we might still smell a rat.

Oral Disgust

Recall, first, the core element of oral disgust, which regulates what one ingests into the body. Jesus's dismissive retort to the mother's plea for her child focuses on priorities of feeding: "Let the children be fed first, for it is not fair to take the children's food and throw it to the dogs" (Mark 7:27). At first blush, this statement seems extraneous to the situation: the woman's daughter does not suffer from hunger or malnutrition; she's afflicted by a malevolent spirit and thus needs to be freed, not fed. Yet material foods and spiritual forces share a dualistic classification as holy or profane, pure or polluting, salubrious or disgusting. Immediately preceding our focal scene, Mark's Jesus expatiated on "things that do and do not defile," including food in kosher systems (7:15–23). And now he's compelled to deal with a case of an "unclean spirit" (7:25).

Foodstuffs and spirit-beings presumed tainted by community standards represent insidious body invaders worthy of disgust. On one level, then, Jesus seems to associate the little daughter's condition—her infection in spirit and body—with a kind of food poisoning; by extension, this implicates the mother in not defending the child from harmful infestation. Might Jesus be implying that this mother has not been properly feeding her child "first," as a matter of prime importance, but rather letting the poor girl scavenge for cast-off scraps? By any standard, ritual or moral, such maternal malpractice would be regarded not merely as "unfair" but as thoroughly disgusting, debasing the daughter to a ground-licking dog.

But while the story of Jesus's encounter with a pleading mother is patently embedded in a network of material in Mark 6–8 about harmful and helpful feeding/food, the link between the condition of defilement and the emotion of disgust is not entirely clear. Serving up the Baptist's severed head on a platter (6:24–28) and assuming the position of salivating dogs slurping up dirty crumbs (7:27–28) are blatant, disgusting actions on a par with demonic predation. Yet on the matter of "things that defile," Jesus argues against

36. In his study of Matthew's version (my focus is primarily on Mark's account), Moore ("Dog-Woman of Canaan," 66) does mention "disgust" once in connection with the mother's Canaanite roots, a major biblical strike against her: "The woman . . . has most often been an object of disgust. The term 'Canaanite' evoked revulsion for an ethnic other."

common notions that polluting elements come from "outside a person" as alien invaders. Rather, the real defilers are evil words, thoughts, and behaviors that "come out of a person . . . from within, from the human heart" (7:20–21).

So where does that leave food? It seems to occupy a neutral "clean" zone, "since it enters, not the heart but the stomach, and goes out into the sewer" (Mark 7:19). In most cultures, fecal sewage epitomizes disgusting substances. But excrement is the byproduct of food consumption, not its essence. While the Markan narrator perhaps pushes the point too far by opining parenthetically, "Thus he declared all foods clean" (7:19),[37] Jesus does accentuate internal, moral components of disgust over external, ritual elements.

Does such a perspective, then, put the onus more on the little girl herself than on her mother, blaming the daughter, as it were, for her evil, "unclean" heart where demons take root and thrive? No more than other demon-afflicted victims in Mark, however, can the girl be expected to excrete these foul forces naturally into the sewer. She rather needs exactly what her mother asks from Jesus, that which he has provided for others: a supernatural casting out of nefarious interlopers. In short, while the issue of oral, gastronomic disgust hovers over the case of the demon-possessed daughter, it hardly settles it.

Sociomoral Disgust

The second element, sociomoral disgust, strips individuals or groups of their human dignity because of some perceived deviant status based on race, gender, class, disability, and other markers. Oral boundaries may be sketchy in Jesus's dialogue with the entreating mother, but social boundaries are sharply drawn. Juxtaposed against the Jewish, male Jesus, his interlocutor is profiled as "the woman . . . a Gentile [Greek; Hellēnis], of Syrophoenician origin" (Mark 7:26). Assuming a patriarchal and parochial milieu, however, does not automatically brand this female Gentile as an object of disgust in most ancient Jewish men's eyes, much less in Jesus's. Of the two categories, gender and race, the latter appears more dominant in Mark's story because of its particularity, designating not merely a non-Jew but a *Syrophoenician*. Bitter tensions between ancient Israelites and Syrian-Phoenician (Tyrian/ Sidonian) peoples simmered in biblical history, breeding mutual feelings of contempt. Jesus's riposte about "first children" likely refers to Jesus's own

37. Matthew eschews this blanket annulment of kosher requirements (see 15:10–20). Overall, Jesus remains devoted to the Jewish law across the Gospel tradition. He certainly mounts no crusade against food laws, as the narrative aside in Mark 7:19 might suggest.

ethnic people, the "children of Israel," the chosen ones (first!) of God.[38] Still, prioritizing service to one's own (charity begins at home) does not necessitate treating all foreigners with dismissive disgust. They just need to wait their turn in line and take what's left.

Of course, egregiously malevolent foreign actors might merit labeling as disgusting deviants. But however badly Syrian-Phoenician rulers, soldiers, and merchants might typically treat the people of Israel, Mark's narrative gives no clue about this woman's moral reputation beyond her immediate preoccupation with her daughter's health, an altogether natural and admirable concern.[39] Mark, however—unlike Matthew—casts the woman from the start as a kind of transgressor or invader of Jesus's private space. Following his extended lecturing to various audiences (Mark 7:1–23), Jesus "set out and went away to the region of Tyre. He entered a house and did not want anyone to know he was there" (7:24). This desire for private retreat after an intense ministry is nothing new for Mark's Jesus, along with the frustration of this desire by supplicants clamoring for his attention. But Jesus usually takes these interruptions in stride, either tending to the desperate seekers or moving on to help needy parties in other places.[40] In the present incident, Jesus again "could not escape notice," as the mother enters his lodging place and pleads her case (7:24–25). She thus crosses private boundaries and imposes herself upon Jesus, which could possibly agitate him more than usual and motivate his truculent response. But we should not forget that Jesus first crosses into her land and imposes himself on some (unknown) local host. Moreover, while the mother does press herself and her case upon Jesus, she does so in a deferential manner, bowing down low before him and begging for his help (7:25). Only after Jesus rebuffs her does she respond more forcefully, a move which actually turns his irritation into admiration and healing action on her behalf (7:28–30).

While the ethnic divide between Jesus and the Syrophoenician woman, between the "rights" of Jewish and non-Jewish "children" and "houses," explains some of the angst in Jesus's dismissive first response, it does not by itself sink to the emotional cellar of disgust toward this particular foreigner—on *her* turf!

---

38. Matthew's Jesus explicitly states, "I was sent only to the lost sheep of the house of Israel" (15:24).

39. Theissen (*Gospels in Context*, 61–80) infers the woman's wealthy, elite status by virtue of Syria-Phoenicia's operation at this time as the major food supplier ("breadbasket") for the region, which also put them in a position to exploit dependent clients, like Galilee (Ringe ["Gentile Woman's Story, Revisited"] supports Theissen's reading). But Mark's story provides no evidence that the Syrophoenician woman was herself rich or oppressive, characteristics Mark readily associates with other figures (10:22–25; 12:41–44); see Spencer, *Dancing Girls*, 62–63.

40. See Mark 1:35–37; 4:35–36; 5:1–2, 15, 21–24; 6:30–34; 6:45–46, 53–56; cf. 9:2–29.

Animal Nature Disgust

The third possible offensive element associated with Jesus's emotional state in his encounter with the Syrophoenician woman—animal nature disgust—proves harder to mitigate. Recall that this factor monitors an array of bodily functions that humans share with other creatures, confirming that we, too, are mortal beings with ebbing, seeping life forces. If Jesus had simply subordinated the needs of the Syrophoenician woman's daughter to those of his people's "first children" with a higher claim on his "feeding" ministry, that would have downgraded her status but not to the lowest level of ground-scrounging animals. But by "going to the dogs," by breaking down his family-feeding analogy to tidbits tossed to the dogs, Jesus ratchets up the intensity of his disgust-laden imagery. As noted above, canine eating habits, with which Jesus seems to associate mother and daughter, typify oral-oriented disgust. But dogs' notoriety in the ancient world as disgusting creatures extends beyond their love of table scraps.

We must acknowledge the dissonance between classifying dogs as despicable curs in antiquity and as "man's best friend," cuddly companion, and cherished family pet in popular culture today. Not that the latter notion was unknown in the ancient world, as evidenced in Odysseus's homecoming encounter with his beloved hound, Argos, whom he had trained as a pup before embarking on his twenty-year journey. Now old and decrepit, Argos alone "sensed" his disguised returning master, "thumped his tail, nuzzling low, and his ears dropped, though he had no strength to drag himself an inch." In turn, Odysseus "glanced to the side, . . . flicked away a tear," and struggled to maintain his masquerade with a diverting comment: "Strange, Eumaeus, look, a dog like this, lying here on a dung-hill . . . what handsome lines! But I can't say for sure if he had the running speed to match his looks or he was only the sort that gentry spoil at table, show-dogs masters pamper for their points" (Homer, *Odyssey* 17.329–41).

This emotional Homeric scene resonates with dog lovers today, to say nothing of the modern ring of pampered pooches fed at elite tables and shown off at competitions. Ancient art, including funerary inscriptions, sculptures, and reliefs, attest to the valued place of dogs, large (watchdogs) and small (lapdogs), in Roman society.[41] However, while not precluding the beloved pet status of some animals, the Roman scholar Varro classified owned dogs into two main working groups: "the hunting-dog suited to chase the beasts of the forest, and the other which is procured as a watch-dog and is of importance to

41. See Ferris, *Cave Canem*; Ferris, "Six Things"; Ferris, "If You Owned a Dog"; Brewer, Clark, and Phillips, *Dogs in Antiquity*.

the shepherd" (Varro, *Rust*. 2.9.2).[42] In both categories, hunting and guarding, a certain ferocity and wildness carry over from the dog's lupine origins. With watchdogs, the more fearsome, the better. Petronius's *Satyricon* describes Encolpius's stunned reaction to a vivid mural at the entrance of the wealthy Trimalchio's estate: "I was gazing at all this, when I nearly fell backwards and broke my leg. For on the left hand as you went in . . . a great dog on a chain was painted on the wall, and over him was written in large letters, 'BEWARE OF THE DOG [*CAVE CANEM*]'" (Petronius, *Satyr.* 29). Excavations of ancient Pompeii have uncovered similar mosaic panels from walls and floors at thresholds of Roman villas.[43]

Of course, the historical record in text and art accentuates the values and practices of societal elites. Rarefied images of tenderhearted masters and their "registered" hounds were hardly the norm and are certainly not the picture Mark's Jesus evokes in responding to the Syrophoenician woman. His use of the diminutive "little dog" (*kynarion*; Mark 7:27) is not a move, with a wink and a nod, to soften his retort with heartwarming allusion to cute puppies frolicking about the family dinner table and snapping up little treats tossed their way.[44] That's a Norman Rockwell painting, not a Markan Gospel scene. Most logically, the "little dog" reference fits the subordinating, be*littling* hierarchy in which Jesus slots the Syrophoenician mother and her "little daughter" (*thygatrion*; 7:27).

Further, most dogs in antiquity were neither chained nor trained but rather prowled about as wild predators. Accordingly, Jesus's primary scenario of "throwing/casting" (*balein*) good children's bread "to the little dogs" (Mark 7:27) conjures up images of indulging pesky, scavenging mutts at the expense of hungry human children. These little beasts should themselves be shooed away, indeed, thrown/cast out like marauding demons. The terrible irony is that Jesus rebuffs the Syrophoenician mother's plea to cast out (*ekbalein*) the demon that is mauling her little daughter (7:26) by casting the mother and/ or daughter in the villainous role of a no-account dog taking food from the mouths of precious little children. Such lowly, loathsome creatures—dogs and doglike people—do not deserve a place at the family table and must be kept outside the door or gate with sickly beggars whose oozing sores attract the salivating tongues of preying dogs.

42. Quoted in Grout, "Dogs in Ancient Greece and Rome."
43. Ferris, "Six Things."
44. See Pokorný, "From a Puppy to the Child," 324: "It is shocking to hear that the sick child together with its mother becomes a puppy (κυνάριον). This was not a euphemism and most probably in *koine* [Greek], κυνάριον was simply the expression for the dog—a defiled animal (Exod 22.31). The status of a dog or a puppy is the starting position for the female protagonist and her child in this dramatic story." Contra L&N 1:44.

Gospel students will recognize the last image from Jesus's parable of the Rich Man and Lazarus in Luke: the starving, suppurating Lazarus lies daily outside the callous rich man's gate, craving "what fell from the rich man's table" but receiving nothing but the crude ministrations of dogs licking his putrid pus (Luke 16:19–21). Of course, in that story Jesus's sympathies clearly lie with Lazarus against the stingy plutocrat and disgusting canines, which only makes all the more shocking the Markan Jesus's dismissive identification of the needy Syrophoenician mother/daughter with rapacious wild dogs.

For the sake of Gospel harmony in portraying Jesus's fundamental, compassionate treatment of suffering people, we might push harder to soften the dog reference in Mark, except for the fact that biblical literature evinces a nearly universal pejorative assessment of dogs as detestable creatures. Only the book of Tobit depicts a dog as a family pet, in this case a faithful companion of the youth Tobias and his guardian angel Raphael on their journey to procure money and medicine (Tob. 6:1b–2; 11:4).[45] Otherwise, as D. Winston Thomas states, "The dog in ancient Israel was hardly a domesticated animal,"[46] unlike examples in Greco-Roman life noted above. In fact, dogs ranked among the dirtiest creatures off-limits for God's people. The Torah stipulates in the voice of God: "You shall be people consecrated to me; therefore you shall not eat any meat that is mangled by beasts in the field; you shall *throw it to the dogs*" (Exod. 22:31). Here dogs occupy the lowest level of bottom-feeding, carnivorous predators, below other vicious beasts that have devoured animal flesh and blood. Such manifestly "unclean" meat, fit only for the garbage dump and rapacious curs, has no place on Israelite tables. In the Torah-grounded view of Matthew's Jesus, dogs join pigs as quintessential marauders and spoilers of holiness: "Do not give what is holy to dogs; and do not throw your pearls before swine, or they will trample them under foot and turn and maul you" (Matt. 7:6; cf. 2 Pet. 2:22).[47]

The raw and ragged politics of Samuel and Kings might well be characterized as "dog-eat-dog," as commanders and princes either hurl insults at each other or make ingratiating statements of self-abasement laced with canine slurs. Goliath, David, Abner, and Abishai all express disgusted offense taken against their enemies in the basic form, "How dare you treat me like

45. A more domesticated view of dogs also appears in the book of Sirach in an odd contrast with wild hyenas: "All living beings associate with their own kind, and people stick close to those like themselves. What does a wolf have in common with a lamb? . . . What peace is there between a hyena and a dog?" (Sir. 13:16–18).

46. Thomas, "*Kelebh* 'Dog,'" 419.

47. See also Phil. 3:2, where Paul exhorts the Philippians, "Beware of the dogs . . . who mutilate the flesh," invidiously comparing those who advocate circumcision for Gentile believers with mauling dogs.

a despicable dog?" (1 Sam. 17:43–44; 24:14; 2 Sam. 3:8; 16:9). As a prime example, note the taunting exchange between the giant Philistine and young shepherd on the battlefield: "The Philistine said to David, 'Am I a dog, that you come to me with sticks?' [Here the LXX adds David's response, 'No, but worse than a dog!']. And the Philistine cursed David by his gods. The Philistine said to David, 'Come to me, and I will give your flesh to the birds of the air and to the wild animals of the field'" (1 Sam. 17:43–44).

Mephibosheth and Hazael both rhetorically deprecate themselves as despicable "dogs" in delicate diplomatic situations. The former figure, the disabled son of Jonathan and grandson of Saul, receives kind treatment from the newly appointed King David, including the monarch's promise that "you yourself shall eat at my table always." In humble gratitude, Mephibosheth responds, "What is your servant, that you should look upon a *dead dog* such as I?" (2 Sam. 9:7–8). As Thomas notes, "The expression 'dead dog' is stronger than merely 'dog'. A dog is a vile, contemptible animal. A dead dog is more vile and contemptible and, like all dead bodies, unclean into the bargain. It is very strong language of self-abasement or invective."[48] David granting an honored place at the king's table for such a self-confessed "dead dog" constitutes a remarkable erasure of common boundaries of core oral and animal disgust, to say nothing of defusing political rivalry. Mark's Jesus eventually follows in his royal ancestor's footsteps in aiding a Syrophoenician "dog" but not without first blocking her access to the table.

Associations of dogs with dead, disgusting things extend to their grisly consumption of corpse flesh and blood. As such, they provide perfect fodder for biblical prophets' anathematizing of abhorrent northern kingdom rulers like Jeroboam (1 Kings 14:11), Baasha (16:4), and, especially, the notorious couple Ahab and Jezebel: "In the place where dogs licked up the blood of Naboth, dogs will also lick up your [Ahab's] blood. . . . The dogs shall eat Jezebel within the bounds of Jezreel" (21:19–24; see 22:38; 2 Kings 9:10, 36–37). Jezebel's doglike status as a polluted, foreign Sidonian (Phoenician) woman (1 Kings 16:31; cf. Rev. 2:20–23; 22:15) makes her a distant ancestress of the Syrophoenician woman in Mark, though the latter has no royal position.

Another suggestive backstory of the dog-designated Syrophoenician woman to the biblical world, this time on the Syrian side, may be traced to Hazael, the deputy and eventual successor to King Ben-hadad of Aram (ancient Syria). When Hazael comes to Israel's prophet Elisha to inquire if the critically ill Ben-hadad will live or die, Elisha forecasts the king's short-term recovery, followed by his "certain" death and Hazael's ascendancy to Aram's

48. Thomas, "*Kelebh* 'Dog,'" 417.

throne. Such a future makes Elisha break down in tears because he knows the terrible harm Hazael will inflict on Israel: "You will kill their young men with the sword, dash in pieces their little ones, and rip up their pregnant women" (2 Kings 8:12). Far from recoiling at this expected rapacity, however, Hazael himself welcomes the opportunity for violent conquest, but with a weird mix of self-deprecation and ingratiation before Elisha. Hazael asks, "What is your servant, who is a *mere dog*, that he should do this great thing?" (8:13; see 8:7–15). This twisted assessment of mass murder and mutilation of Israelites as a "great thing" is where Hazael proves himself aligned with the most repugnant behavior of predatory dogs.

This preponderant biblical picture of the dog species (*keleb* [Heb.]/*kyōn* [Gk.]) as a "vile and contemptible animal . . . the scavenger *par excellence*"[49] strongly suggests that Jesus's canine comparison carries the force of disgust toward the intrusive, pleading mother, in tandem with her social identity as a Syrophoenician (a historic enemy of God's people) and Jesus's allusion to the nasty oral habits of dogs. Animal, social, and oral elements (in that order of emphasis) comprise a trifecta of disgust, which Jesus conveys to the Syrophoenician woman. The extent to which Jesus viscerally feels this emotion cannot be determined in the absence of audiovisual effects revealing his tone of voice, facial expressions, and gestures. But we can suppose, indeed believe, that Jesus feels some disgust matching his words, since the worst form of disgust—and any negative social emotive action—is the kind carried out with cold detachment and callous banality. Jesus is anything but banal in his words and actions regarding fairness and justice ("*It is not fair* to take the children's food and throw it to the dogs" [Mark 7:27]).[50] The Syrophoenician woman has undoubtedly struck a nerve in Jesus, triggering a disgust reaction.

If suggesting that Jesus gets "caught with his compassion down" in this story proves unsettling to pious sentiments about Christ, then claiming that he entertains feelings of disgust toward a Syrophoenician mother who pleads for her daughter's deliverance seems to rock the very foundations. A disgusted Jesus who associates a "foreign" woman with nose-to-the-ground, scrap-grubbing dogs flies in the face of his messianic vocation as lifter of the lowly and deliverer of the downtrodden. But who among us is entirely exempt from twinges of disgust toward some individual or group who offends our innate and culturally conditioned sensibilities in some way? A basic part of adaptive survival entails both impulsive (better safe than sorry) and repulsive

49. Thomas, "*Kelebh* 'Dog,'" 414.
50. My use of "banal" here to characterize cold, unfeeling mistreatment of people draws on the famous work by Hannah Arendt, *Eichmann in Jerusalem*. As discussed below, some label cold disgust "contempt."

avoidance of infectious persons and substances; in this respect, fear and disgust closely align. Of course, first impulses may be wrong: remember, the thin, curvy object in the grass might really be a stick, not a snake; and HIV/AIDS is not transmitted by surface contact or proximity. The keys to healthy emotional regulation of the disgust reflex are expanded learning (observation, examination, contemplation) about the disgusting trigger and changing one's viewpoint, if need be, as soon as possible before repellent feelings fester into hard "us" versus "them" polarities. But such agile adjustment of the vehement emotion of disgust does not come easily; gut-level social prejudices die slow and hard.

Yet this is precisely what Jesus does. In short order he *learns* from the Syrophoenician woman and *changes* his initial, impulsive opinion about her and her child. Unlike with the begging leper who questions Jesus's willingness to heal (to whom Jesus responds with righteous indignation even as he cures the man's skin disease [Mark 1:40–45]), with the begging Syrophoenician mother, Jesus readily reverses his disgust-tinged dismissal and delivers the woman's demonized daughter *because* of her determination and insight. If Jesus wants her to play the dog, she will do so with dogged persistence and dexterous panache. From her begging, bowed position, she barks back a statement as clever as it is practical: "Sir [or Lord; *Kyrie*], even the dogs under the table eat the children's crumbs" (7:28). She proves herself to be clever in volleying Jesus's culinary canine reference back to him and practical in her relentless resolve to get what she needs from Jesus. We might also infer her remarkable faith in Jesus's power: even a crumb's worth will suffice. In any case, Jesus promptly answers her: "For saying that"—or more literally, "On account of this word" (*Dia touton ton logon*)—"you may go—the demon has left your daughter" (7:29).[51]

The Syrophoenician woman moves Jesus emotionally, cognitively, volitionally, and behaviorally from his off-putting position. And narratively and socially, this woman's word also sets Jesus on a wider course of healing a deaf and speech-impaired man and feeding the masses in the predominantly Gentile "region of the Decapolis" (Mark 7:31; see 7:31–8:10). Heretofore, he had made a brief foray into this area, where he encountered "a man out of the tombs with an unclean spirit"—a veritable Legion-horde of demons, as it happens—in a "disgusting" environment replete with unclean corpses,

---

51. The Markan narrator introduces the Syrophoenician woman's compelling words to Jesus with the adversative transition: "But she answered him" (7:28). Her persistent pleading ("Yes, Lord, *but . . .*" [NASB]) has become iconic in contemporary feminist biblical interpretation, "represent[ing] the biblical-theological voice of women, which has been excluded, repressed, or marginalized in Christian discourse," as Schüssler Fiorenza (*But She Said*, 11; cf. 10–15) puts it.

spirits, and pigs. After Jesus's assault on this polluted region, causing the violent death of two thousand swine, the local population "begged him to leave their neighborhood" (5:17; see 5:1–20). But after meeting—and heeding—the Syrophoenician woman, Jesus returns to the Decapolis and reconciles, as it were, with its people in a life-nourishing act of service.

Whatever Mark might take away from an antiseptically pure, perfect Jesus, he gives back much more in an authentically passible, perfectible Jesus who decisively stanches his rupture of disgust and extends his circle of compassion at the word of a wise woman. Such openhearted humility is the mark of the true person of God.

Contempt of Courts (Luke 18:1–14)

Disgust-related matters do not overly preoccupy Jesus's teachings any more than they dominate his actions. But what he does say about "unclean" and "clean" boundaries stands out. I've already noted his aphorism in the Sermon on the Mount against casting off holy things to filthy dogs and pigs (Matt. 7:6) and his extended purity lecture before meeting the Syrophoenician woman, prioritizing moral outflow from the heart over oral intake (Mark 7:14–23). Overall, Jesus affirms and adjusts, actualizes and internalizes traditional holiness codes. One other teaching section, however, also merits attention: a pair of parables in Luke 18:1–14 cohering around the emotion of contempt, which is closely related to disgust.

A hinge statement by the Lukan narrator juxtaposes two stories unique to this Gospel, the parable of the widow and the unjust judge (Luke 18:2–5) and the parable of the Pharisee and the tax collector (18:10–14): "He also told this parable to some who trusted in themselves that they were righteous [*dikaioi*] and regarded others with contempt [*exouthenountas*]" (18:9). The "also" (*kai*) clues the connection, along with official "court" settings and common themes of righteousness/justice/justification and contempt/disrespect/disgust. The first parable features an exploited widow pleading, and eventually winning, her case in a civil court before a contemptuous magistrate who has "no respect for anyone" (18:4; cf. 18:2). The second parable presents a Pharisee and a tax collector praying in the temple court about their relative standings before a gracious and merciful God.

Due to his widely despised profession of collecting revenue for Roman-Herodian overlords (with the opportunity to pad his own pockets in the process), the tax man was a frequent target of fellow Jews' contempt. And he knows it and regrets it, sincerely pleading with bowed head and beaten breast, "God, be merciful to me, a sinner!" (Luke 18:13). In conclusion, Jesus makes clear that God, the Supreme Judge, does not hold this penitent tax collector in contempt but rather declares him "justified" (*dedikaiōmenos*), made righteous, set to rights on a par with the Pharisee and, by implication, with all humble humanity (18:14). Whether or not the Pharisee in the parable shows contempt for the tax collector (the Pharisees' prayer can be taken either as genuine gratitude to God for inspiring his righteous lifestyle or as self-congratulation laced with snide contempt for the tax agent),[52] "some" (18:9) Pharisees in Luke's narrative do fall into the self-justifying, other-deriding trap (10:29; 16:15; cf. 5:30; 7:29–30; 15:1–2). Be that as it may, such Pharisees have no corner on the market, then or now, of religious bigots who pump up their own fragile egos by putting down those they label beneath contempt.

How, then, should we delineate this emotion of contempt more precisely in the orbit of disgust? In Rozin's CAD scheme, the "contempt" emotional component is connected with "community" moral values. It fits much better with the socio-moral dimension of disgust than with the oral and animal aspects. Contempt reinforces social norms and hierarchies, justifying the superior positions of elites and keeping inferiors in their low places.[53] As Miller remarks, "Where there are rankings, there is contempt doing the work of maintaining them."[54] As for emotional intensity, some scholars regard contempt as "cooler," more calculating and callous, than disgust. Carroll Izard states, "Of the three emotions in the hostility triad—anger, disgust, contempt—contempt is the most subtle, the coldest. . . . Contempt is cold and distant, more likely to foster aggression. . . . The feeling of contempt toward a human being tends to depersonalize the target individual, to cause the person to be perceived as something less than human."[55] It is thus more baldly sociopathic, etched in the emotional DNA of "cold-blooded" killers and genocidal butchers, though one need not take contempt that far.

While acknowledging that contempt coordinates with indifferent banality toward lesser-valued mortals (in ways that disgust, "always very present to the senses," never does), Miller also curiously paints contempt in somewhat softer and warmer tones than disgust. He rightly claims that "we can enjoy our feelings of contempt, mingled as they often are with pride and self-congratulations," unlike feelings of disgust which are, well, disgusting

---

52. See more below and the discussion in Spencer, *Luke*, 437–40, 451–57; cf. A.-J. Levine, *Short Stories*, 169–95; Friedrichsen, "Temple."

53. Rozin et al., "CAD Triad Hypothesis."

54. Miller, *Anatomy of Disgust*, 32.

55. Izard, *Human Emotions*, 340.

and miserable.[56] But such guilty pleasure derived from "abstract bemusement" at belittled others fits in with harder and colder facets of contempt, not softer and warmer feelings. I am thus hard pressed to associate contemptuous "looking down" with "softer and gentler sentiments" of looking down on sufferers with "pity, graciousness, and love." Likewise, I fail to feel the temperature contrast Miller draws: "Disgust does not have a pleasant warm side like contempt."[57] Frankly, both emotions send an eerie chill down my spine. The warm, fuzzy side of contempt just doesn't compute. There may be a way to condescend to someone in a benign fashion, but "contempt" is not the word for it.

Of course, whatever nuances attach to English emotion words like "contempt," our primary concern is with biblical Greek usage. The Greek verb *exoutheneō* in Luke 18:9, rendered in the NRSV as "regarded . . . with contempt," combines *ex*, meaning "out," with *outhen*, signifying "nothing." Accordingly, Luke's Jesus challenges those who expel and devalue others as no-account nothings and nobodies who "regard another as of no significance and therefore worthy of maltreatment."[58] The term Luke uses for "others" (*loipoi*) so regarded connotes "the rest, the remaining," further demeaning them as contemptible leftovers or remainders, not full human beings worthy of respect. Hence, while "contempt" captures the Greek meaning well, it is very close to "disgust," which the CEB prefers in our text: "Jesus told this parable to certain people . . . who looked on everyone else with disgust." Moreover, in other places biblical Greek twins *exoutheneō* with synonyms reinforcing shades of disgust and detestableness.

> Look kindly on those who are despised [*exouthenēmenous*] and detested [*bdelyktous*], and let the Gentiles know that you are our God. (2 Macc. 1:27 NAB)

> Though my condition put you to the test, you did not scorn [*exouthenēsate*] or despise [*exeptysate*; lit. "spit out"] me, but welcomed me as an angel of God. (Gal. 4:14)

Exoutheneō thus allows for hot and hostile emotional attitudes of contempt/disgust by self-righteous supremacists toward those judged to be lesser and lowlier—vehement attitudes that Luke's Jesus repudiates in these two parables. The judicial figure in the first story has smugly cultivated a hard-nosed reputation as one having "no fear of God and no respect for anyone"

56. Miller, *Anatomy of Disgust*, 32–33.
57. Miller, *Anatomy of Disgust*, 32–33.
58. BDAG 352.

(Luke 18:4; cf. 18:2). Under the veneer of an impartial adjudicator beats a heart that couldn't care less about anyone but himself. This judge's colder, harder contempt, however, evokes a vigorously bold and hot response from an exploited widow who pleads her case before him, initially to no avail. A poor, lowly widow means nothing to this magistrate, until she keeps coming to court, raising her voice of protest and petition and threatening to give him "a black eye," literally (shaking her fist at him), figuratively (shaming him and causing him to lose face), or both.[59] It seems this judge is not so self-confident after all. He can't bear to be shown up by this "pushy," persistent woman day after day, so he decides to cede to her demands (18:2–5)—ironically, just as Mark's Jesus did in the face of the dogged Syrophoenician woman (though note well: Jesus got the message immediately, not after prolonged nagging). In his brief commentary on the parable of the widow and the unjust judge, Luke's Jesus contrasts the exceptional, externally forced right verdict of the parable's judge with the characteristic commitment to justice in God's supreme court, not least for those least ones who cry out for justice.[60] Contempt—cold or hot—toward the left-out "remainders" of society has no place in the divine emotional, social, and moral economy.

In the second parable, Jesus trades on the implied contempt that most Jews in Jesus's day, not just Pharisees, would have had toward tax collectors as quisling extortionists (cf. Luke 3:13; 19:8). And we can imagine that such contempt typically ran rather "hot." By virtue of their calculating, injurious treatment of their compatriots, tax collectors in Roman Palestine would seem to deserve whatever contempt came back on their own heads. Taking advantage of the poor and oppressed as self-serving agents of an exploitative foreign power is legitimately abhorrent, disgusting behavior, if anything is. No wonder the tax collector stands "far off" in the temple courts. No one wants anything to do him, and he knows it.

If the Pharisee, however, in the story looks down on the tax collector, his contempt runs neither hot nor cold: no extended lambasting of the man or listing his sins; no hardhearted pronouncement of hellish judgment. Moreover,

---

59. The NRSV's rendering of the judge's words in Luke 18:5, "so that she [the widow] may not *wear me out [hypōpiazē me]* by continually coming," obscures the boxing image of the verb, *hypōpiazō*, which means "to blacken an eye, give a black eye, strike in the face" (BDAG 1043); cf. 1 Cor. 9:26–27. After surveying the usage of *hypōpiazō* in Greek writings, Cotter ("Parable of the Feisty Widow," 339) stresses "that the verb must be translated *literally* every time if the metaphor is to work" (emphasis original). Even in a figurative context, the punch of the image should not be pulled. Cf. L. Johnson, *Gospel of Luke*, 270: "In this case, the literal rendering of *hypōpiazō* ["give a black eye"] maintains the delicious ambiguity of the original. She [the widow] may in fact give him [the judge] a sock in the eye!"

60. See Spencer, *Salty Wives*, 294–302.

the language of the Pharisee's prayer, which is all we have to judge him by in
the story, beginning with "God, I thank you that I am not like other people,"
may well reveal an emotional tenor of gratitude toward God rather than self-
congratulation or other-condemnation—along the lines of the modern adage
"But for the grace of God, there go I."[61]

But regardless of whether Jesus uses the parable's Pharisee as a foil or an
ally, Jesus's own position is patent, leaving no place for emotional judgments
of contempt. He does not operate within strictures of merit systems and
popular stereotypes. He wants Torah-faithful reform and repentance as much
as the Pharisees do, but he prefers a mission strategy of direct therapeutic
engagement with sinners—at the dinner table, for example—over select segregation from them (see Luke 5:29–32). While by no means soft on sin, Jesus
is high on sinners' capacity to change through God's grace and power. Thus
he highlights in this tale the shocking action of a tax collector in the temple,
not hunting for tax evaders or putting on a show of piety for appearance's
sake but sincerely—passionately—with all his heart and body, beaten breast
and hanging head, pleading, "God, be merciful to me, a sinner!" And most
importantly, Jesus declares God's eager acceptance and "justification" (setting
to rights) of this repentant man (18:13–14).[62]

61. A.-J. Levine, *Short Stories*, 194; Friedrichsen, "Temple," 94; Spencer, *Luke*, 451–54.
62. In the next chapter of Luke, Zacchaeus represents a compelling case in point of a changed,
Jesus-seeking chief tax collector (19:1–10).

PART 3

THE POWER OF JESUS'S POSITIVE EMOTIONS

If speaking about vehement emotions like anger, anguish, and disgust as
somehow virtuous in the previous parts of this book seemed like special
pleading, referring in part 3 to "the power of positive emotions" may
seem at first like schlocky self-help peddling. Think it, feel it, make it happen.
Turn that frown upside down. On the modern Christian side, it may appear
to hew too closely to Norman Vincent Peale's *The Power of Positive Thinking* agenda or the prosperity-gospel claims of televangelists, neither of which
bears much resemblance to the teachings and actions of the suffering Son of
Humankind, Jesus of Nazareth.

However, we may pursue a serious, substantive investigation of positive
thoughts and feelings as part of a paradigm shift in American psychology
research, typically labeled "positive psychology." As nonacademic as that term
may sound, it has been undergirded by a tidal wave of fresh studies sponsored
by major universities, the American Psychological Association (APA), and
the National Institute of Mental Health (NIMH). The pivotal moment came
with the election of University of Pennsylvania psychology professor Martin
E. P. Seligman as APA president in 1998. Addressing his colleagues, Seligman
reaffirmed the prime directives of his field prior to World War II: "Psychology
had three missions: curing mental illness, making the lives of all people more
fulfilling, and identifying and nurturing high talent." While lauding the major

achievements of the first mission plank in the fifty years since World War II (including new wars in Korea, Vietnam, and the Middle East)—so desperately needed, with myriad soldiers suffering mental battle wounds as deep or deeper than physical traumas—Seligman candidly lamented the "all but forgotten" other two psychological agendas. "We became a victimology" as a society, he argued, damaged goods requiring an army of psychological experts who "treated mental illness within a theoretical framework of repairing damaged habits, damaged drives, damaged childhoods, and damaged brains." Hence Seligman's clarion call to get back on track: "Psychology is not just the study of weakness and damage, it is also the study of strength and virtue. Treatment is not just fixing what is broken, it is nurturing what is best within ourselves."[1]

In a word, American psychology needed to become more *positive*, not least in its emotional focus. Surely the human condition generates love, joy, and hope as much as anger, anguish, and disgust. Yet the last thing Seligman called for was a cheap, naive, feel-good psychology divorced from the rigorous demands of meaningful life.[2] The "pursuit of happiness," that quintessentially American (Jeffersonian) value with wide crosscultural resonance, is not some fluff piece but rather an integral part of the strong fabric of authentic human life, of robust spiritual life. Neither Jefferson the deist nor Seligman the secularist represent traditional Christian philosophy or psychology, but they nonetheless advocate a virtuous, character-based "spirituality." In Seligman's words, "The belief that we can rely on shortcuts to happiness, joy, rapture, comfort, and ecstasy, rather than be entitled to these feelings by the exercise of personal strengths and virtues, leads to legions of people who in the middle of great wealth are starving spiritually. Positive emotion alienated from the exercise of character leads to emptiness, to inauthenticity, to depression, and, as we age, to the gnawing realization that we are fidgeting until we die."[3]

In ancient reflections on the passions, considerable attention was paid to negative emotions like anger, fear, and shame, which prove so destructive to civil society and disruptive to personal tranquility. Hence the Stoic therapeutic goal of fending off and rooting out painful passions, as well as tamping down overly excitable bursts of pleasure. Aristotle, though starting his passion catalog in *Rhetoric* with "anger," allowed for a more moderate

1. Seligman, "Building Human Strength," 2; quoted in Snyder, Lopez, and Pedrotti, *Positive Psychology*, 4–5.

2. As claimed by Barbara Ehrenreich in *Bright-Sided*. Ehrenreich provides considered critique but rather too much of it, skewing the balance and "positive" therapeutic value of positive psychology.

3. Seligman, *Authentic Happiness*, 8.

assessment of emotions, as we've seen, balancing negative and positive poles, like anger/calmness, fear/confidence, indignation/pity. In any case, whatever place they allowed for positive emotions in their philosophies, both Aristotle and the Stoics linked them with sober thought and strong character, not with unbridled hedonism.

Though steeped in Israel's wisdom tradition, Jesus was no professional philosopher of emotion or anything else in the Gospel narratives. As far as we know, he wrote no formal lessons, catechisms, or treatises for his disciples. He taught them on the road by example as much as by precept. Our interest in Jesus's emotional life focuses primarily on his own felt and enacted experiences of emotion depicted in the Gospels and only secondarily on his reported teachings about emotion. We began by exploring less familiar and more controversial cases of Jesus's exhibition of oppositional/negative emotions. Yet, while uncovering an occasionally angry, anguished, disgusted Jesus safeguards us from misty-eyed, romantic delusions about the incarnate Son of God, this scarcely tells the whole tale of his emotional life. A mean, morose, demeaning Messiah Jesus was not.

On the inspirational/positive side of the emotional spectrum, love and joy most readily register in neon lights. It is impossible to imagine Jesus and the Christian movement without these feelings ("For God so loved the world . . ."; "Joy to the world!"). Of course, this popular tandem of positive emotions is subject to much squishy interpretation. Love is as many-splintered a thing as many-splendored, ranging from pure sap to total sacrifice. Joy bubbles up from frothy pop tunes and bursts out from majestic oratorios. Jesus epitomizes true love and joy; indeed, he veritably defines what these emotion terms mean on their highest levels. Much scholarship and spiritual writing has been devoted to apprehending Jesus's consummate revelation of these two passions, though not usually incorporating emotion theory.

With the aid of old and new philosophical and psychological perspectives, I seek to provide some sharper clarity and fresh insights into Jesus's love and joy. Regarding Jesus's love, for example, I aim to correlate it with a cluster of terms related to passion and pathos, such as "compassion," "sympathy," and "empathy." These terms may seem synonymous and semantically self-evident but can in fact carry some significant variances. For example, the incisive Yale psychology professor Paul Bloom has recently distinguished sympathy from empathy as constitutive of loving feelings, attitudes, and actions in a way that complicates the virtue of empathic responses to needy persons.[4] How does Jesus's passion and pathos theology fit into this nuanced model of

4. Bloom, *Against Empathy*.

love? I will probe these and other questions about the compassionate Jesus in chapters 8 and 9.

As for Jesus's joy, it is commonplace to differentiate it from garden-variety happiness or supercharged outbursts of excitement. Somehow Jesus's joy runs deeper and fills fuller, all the while remaining calmer and soberer. But what particular contexts and concepts, events and perspectives, spark Jesus's joy in the Gospels? And how does his joy hold up in the face of pain and suffering? I will focus on these aspects concerning Jesus's joy in chapter 10.

Before reconsidering Jesus's well-known positive emotions of love and joy, however, I will explore in chapter 7 a much less familiar (and some might say impossible) feeling state for Jesus—namely, surprise or amazement. How can the omniscient Christ ever be taken by surprise? And how can the omnipotent Christ who regularly evokes others' amazement ever himself be amazed? In fact, two Gospel passages moderate Jesus's supposed "omni"-status by reporting events that elicit Jesus's surprise/amazement: his rejection at Nazareth (Mark 6:1–6) and his healing of the centurion's servant in Capernaum (Luke 7:1–10; cf. Matt. 8:5–13).

But why include surprise/amazement in this part on positive emotions? Isn't this emotion a close cousin to fear, shock, and confusion—thus giving another good reason to suspect its relevance to Jesus? Although Jesus evokes others' fear in the Gospel narratives, these narratives never explicitly indicate that Jesus himself was afraid. There is no more basic, primal emotion than fear, designed to alert us to life-threatening dangers like snakes, predators, and unseen "spirit" forces. Indeed, the first human emotion mentioned in the Bible is Adam's shrinking in fear from a lurking God after he (Adam) succumbs to the serpent's temptation (Gen. 3:10). But God is by no means done with humanity at this point (though God comes close in Noah's day). Adam need not fear God's immediate destructive action, but he will also never lose a profound sense of fearing God on multiple levels. Every Bible student knows that "the fear of the LORD is the beginning of knowledge [or knowing]" (Prov. 1:7), but what it means to fear God is itself fraught with fearful anxiety (fearing fear itself), hovering between haunting and healthy fear, shock and awe, the woeful and the wonderful.[5]

The awe-full, wonderful side of fear makes room for surprise and amazement in a way that uplifts and enlarges human experience relative to the divine rather than denigrates and diminishes it. Research psychologist Jonathan Haidt describes this phenomenon as "elevation." As it happens, Haidt began his career working with Rozin on elicitors of oral and moral disgust. Becoming

5. See Spencer, "To Fear."

weary of gauging people's responses to icky fried grasshoppers, Adolf Hitler, and other repulsive stimuli, Haidt turned to investigate more positive, buoyant feelings of awe and wonder that enhance human happiness and flourishing.[6]

Along with fine-tuning our understanding of Jesus's emotions of love and joy in the Gospel narrative, this part aims to expand our vision of his wide-eyed, openhearted sense of surprise and amazement.

6. See, for example, Haidt, "Elevation," and the discussion of Haidt's work in Seligman, *Authentic Happiness*, 8.

7

That's Amazing!

The Surprised Jesus

The canonical Gospels' all-but-total silence regarding Jesus's childhood and youth in the Galilean hamlet of Nazareth implies a more-or-less normal, unremarkable upbringing.[1] Fanciful stories of a wonderworking Superboy Jesus await the later apocryphal Gospels. Accordingly, in the New Testament narratives, when the ordinary adult Jesus of Nazareth begins his extraordinary public mission, he takes his Galilean audiences by surprise, even shock, eliciting responses of utter amazement. For example, in his ministerial debut at Capernaum, Mark's Jesus "astounds" the synagogue audience with his authoritative teaching and "amazes" them with his expulsion of a boisterous "unclean spirit" who had possessed a man in the assembly (Mark 1:21–28). Likewise, in launching his messianic campaign in his hometown synagogue, Luke's Jesus sparks "amazement" from his relatives and neighbors for his audacious claims to Spirit-anointing and prophetic power (Luke 4:16–22). In both cases, as elsewhere in the Gospels, being amazed at Jesus does not equate to having faith in him or following him. Amazement may or may not lead to endorsement and affiliation; it may even lead to resistance or violence, as happens at the end of Luke's synagogue scene (4:28–29).

1. The lone exception is Luke 2:40–52, portraying twelve-year-old Jesus's "amazing" interaction with the temple scholars in Jerusalem; finally, however, he accompanies his parents back to Nazareth and remains "obedient to them" (see chap. 2 of this study). We don't see or hear from him again until he begins his public ministry around "thirty years old" (3:23).

Amazement hovers near the impulsive side of emotional response, which may quickly dissipate and be forgotten or may stimulate more extended cognitive evaluation. At base, amazement signals either some level of positive interest ("Wow! We've never seen anything like this!") or a frisson of negative suspicion ("Whoa! We've never seen anything like that!").

While fickle crowds' wide-eyed reactions to Jesus hardly take us Gospel readers by surprise, we are not primed for Jesus himself to respond with reciprocal amazement. Elsewhere I've mounted a case for Jesus being surprised, even somewhat unsettled, by a woman pressing through a crowd, touching his garment from behind, and eliciting a power surge from him.[2] Stopping in his tracks, he queries, "Who touched me?" When this woman, suddenly cured of her long-term bleeding disorder by triggering Jesus's healing energy, falls down before him in "fear and trembling," Jesus now learns what we readers already know (Mark 5:25–34; Matt. 9:20–22; Luke 8:43–48). In my judgment, this incident conveys a strong element of surprise on Jesus's part without explicitly calling it "amazement."

In two other miraculous healing incidents, however, the Gospel narrators overtly report that Jesus himself "was amazed" at the levels of faith exhibited by those seeing or seeking his wondrous works. Mark's version of the Nazareth synagogue episode concludes with the stunning note that Jesus "was amazed [*ethaumazen*] at their *unbelief*"—that is, at his home community's skeptical resistance to his "deeds of power" (Mark 6:2, 5–6). In the other instance, however, Matthew and Luke announce that Jesus "was amazed" (*ethaumasen*) at a Roman officer's extraordinary belief in Jesus's ability to heal one of his servants who had fallen gravely ill: "I tell you, not even in Israel have I found *such faith*" (Luke 7:9; see also Matt 8:10).[3]

In order to gauge the emotional content and intensity of Jesus's amazement, we could again wish for more than what the brief Gospel scripts deliver. A shot of Jesus's face would be particularly helpful, since surprise commonly registers there in clear fashion.[4] A tape revealing nonverbal sounds associated with surprise (gasps, shouts, oohs and aahs) would also be nice. But absent such audiovisual aids, we still have a narrated emotional episode offering hints of the affective environment surrounding Jesus's amazement. The associated faith component in these stories bears further investigation, especially if we allow for an emotional-relational dimension to faith involving trust (devotion) and its flip side, distrust (suspicion).

2. See Spencer, *Dancing Girls*, 57–61; Spencer, "Woman's Touch," 90–94.
3. Jesus also commends the bleeding woman's faith (Matt. 9:22 // Mark 5:34 // Luke 8:48), after being taken by surprise at her power-siphoning touch.
4. Ekman, *Emotions Revealed*, 148–52; Luna and Renninger, *Surprise*, 1–6.

That's Amazing!
153

The nexus of fear and surprise also merits exploration. Is Jesus anxious or apprehensive in any way about what these amazing events might mean? Just as the apparent stifling of his restorative powers by the Nazareth folks' unbelief ("he could do no deed of power there, except that he laid his hands on a few sick people" [Mark 6:5]) has puzzled interpreters, it might well worry Jesus himself; heretofore Mark's Jesus has known no limit to his power. Conversely, while modern Christians might rejoice in Jesus's praise of a Roman centurion's faith (Matt. 8:10 // Luke 7:9), Jesus himself might wonder with some perplexity, as well as positivity, about the greater trust he receives from a Gentile than from many of his own people. His thinking and feeling about Israel and "others" are shaking and shifting, elevating and expanding, reminiscent of his encounter with the Syrophoenician woman. What does this portend for Jesus's evolving mission? Whom can he trust and entrust himself to? With these questions, we recall the vital future (prospective) dimension of emotions, reflecting a range of anticipated feelings about events' possible outcomes.

To help us assess these various potential contours of Jesus's amazement in the two Gospel episodes, we again delineate some useful frameworks derived from emotion theory and research.

Mapping the Maze of Amazement

As is usual with emotion analysis, we encounter a terminological issue. The Bauer-Danker lexicon (BDAG) defines *thaumazō*, the verb used in our two focal Gospel texts, as "to be extraordinarily impressed or disturbed by something." Used intransitively, as in Mark 6:6, it means "wonder, marvel, be astonished" in the broadest sense, wherein "the context determines . . . a good or bad sense." With the preposition *dia* ("because/on account of"), *thaumazō* expresses "wonder at something," such as the Nazarenes' "unbelief" (*apistian*) in the Markan text. Used transitively (with a direct object), the verb means "admire, wonder at, respect" something or someone, as in Luke 7:9, where it pertains to Jesus's wonderment at "him" (*auton*)—namely, the centurion. In other instances of *thaumazō* and cognates, BDAG adds "be amazed/amazement" to the notion of "wonder."[5]

Apart from the key contextual variable of *thaumazō*'s emotional and moral valence, evoking a range of pleasurable or painful feelings about good or bad objects, English notions of wonder, amazement, astonishment, marveling,

5. BDAG 444–45.

admiration, and respect, though rooted in a common semantic field, may carry different nuances and associate with terms like "awe" or "alarm" (fear) on the more serious side and "surprise" or "start(le)" ("You gave me a start!") in a less freighted sense.

In English translations and discussions of this constellation of sentiments in ancient and early modern thought, "wonder" represents the principal term of choice. In the LCL edition of Plato's dialogue between Theaetetus and Socrates, for example, when the former confesses, "By the gods, Socrates, I am lost in wonder [*thaumazō*] when I think of all these things, and sometimes when I regard them it really makes my head swim," Socrates replies, "This feeling of wonder [*pathos thaumazein*] shows that you are a philosopher, since wonder is the only beginning of philosophy, and he who said that Iris was the child of Thaumas [Wonder] made a good genealogy" (Plato, *Theaet.* 155).[6]

Wonder also receives special attention, somewhat surprisingly perhaps, in the philosophy of the pioneering French Enlightenment thinker René Descartes. Better known for his rigorous advocacy of reason in *Discourse on Method* and *Meditations on First Philosophy*, he also published an important work on emotion, *The Passions of the Soul* (*Les Passions de l'âme*) in 1649, a few weeks before his death. In this volume Descartes identifies six "primitive passions" from which all other emotions derive: "Wonder, Love, Hatred, Desire, Joy, and Sadness" (art. 69).[7] The order is not arbitrary, as he regards wonder as "the first of all the passions" (art. 53) and, indeed, the priming fountain of all knowledge, vitally "useful in making us learn and retain in our memory things we have previously been ignorant of" (art. 75). Wonder represents "the first encounter with some object [that] surprises us, [that] we judge . . . to be new, or very different." Since wonder "can happen before we know in the least whether [an] object is suitable to us or not"—that is, suitable for further investigation—it acts as a critical filter of multifarious experience (art. 53). It signals that *this*, rather than that or a million other things, merits priority attention. Advancement in knowledge concerning *what matters most* cannot proceed without wonder. Conversely, "those who have no natural inclination to this passion are ordinarily very ignorant" (art. 75).[8]

Writing a few decades later in the seventeenth century, the Portuguese-Dutch philosopher Benedict de Spinoza proves less sanguine than Descartes

---

6. See Prinz, "Why Wonder"; Rowe, "Beginning in Wonder."
7. All citations are from Descartes, *Passions of the Soul*.
8. See the incisive analysis of Descartes's appreciation for the passion of wonder in Rosfort and Stanghelini, "In the Mood," 402–6.

about the value of wonder.[9] Rather than appreciating wonder as a passion or affect that moves (motivates) the mind to expansive thought and research, in his major work, *Ethics*, Spinoza disagrees with wonder's classification as an "affect" and decries its tendency to fixate the mind too arbitrarily and narrowly and distract it from the most worthwhile pursuits: "Wonder is an imagination of a thing in which the mind remains fixed. . . . So the imagination of a new thing, considered in itself, is of the same nature as the other [imaginations], and for this reason I do not number wonder among the affects. Nor do I see why I should since this distraction of the mind does not arise from any positive cause which distracts the mind from other things, but only from the fact that there is no cause determining the mind to pass from regarding one thing to thinking of others" (*Ethics*, pt. 3, "Definitions of the Affects" IV).[10]

Spinoza also finds the notion of wonder too nebulous to merit much analytical attention in itself. Fortunately, however, this judgment leads him to clarify particular emotional variants of wonder regarding specific objects, both positive (veneration, devotion) and negative (consternation, dread, disdain) (pt. 3, P52).

- *Veneration*: wonder at someone's extraordinary virtue, like "prudence" or "diligence," beyond our normal experience
- *Devotion*: wonder at the venerable virtue of someone we come to love
- *Consternation*: wonder at "*an object we fear*" (emphasis original) because of its perceived "evil" (not virtuous) effects on us
- *Dread*: wonder at someone's malign emotional attitudes, such as "anger" and "envy"
- *Disdain*: a disavowal or reversal of wonder, upon further consideration, at some formerly venerated or dreaded object or person, expressed as mockery of something previously hated or feared and as contempt for stupid ideas and actions ("folly")

While we might quibble over the best English equivalents of Spinoza's subcategories of wonder in the *Ethics* (originally written in Latin), the terms above drawn from Edwin Curley's translation help fill out a framework for understanding Jesus's amazement in the Gospels.

9. Descartes also warns in arts. 73 and 76 about *excessive* wonder, which he calls "astonishment," that leads to scattered, unfocused reflection. His remedy for fuzzy-headed astonishment calls for knowing everything one can about many things in order to make sound judgments.

10. See the discussion on wonder, with reference to both Descartes and Spinoza, in Fisher, *Vehement Passions*, 1–2, 28–29, 238–41.

Two centuries later, from a more experimental, scientific perspective, Charles Darwin turned his keen mind and observational skills to *The Expression of the Emotions in Man and Animals*. He devotes chapter 12 of this work to tracking "gradations from mere attention to a start of surprise, into extreme terror and horror," assessing evidence from the behavior of his children and animals, from pioneering facial photographs staged by the French neurologist Duchenne de Boulogne and others, and from reports on the phenomenon of human "surprise" by physicians and anthropologists around the world.[11] Across cultures, Darwin discovered remarkably similar physiognomic expressions of surprise, such as wide eyes, gaped mouth, upraised palm-outfacing hands, and splayed fingers—all signs, Darwin theorized, of "a desire to display surprise in a conspicuous manner," reflecting open alertness to the new, unexpected situation.[12]

Among the levels beyond the initial "start of surprise," Darwin includes *admiration* or "surprise associated with some pleasure and a sense of approval" and *fear*, which "seems to be derived from what is sudden and dangerous" and which may escalate to tremulous *terror* or "extreme fear."[13] Notably, he gives scant consideration to "wonder" or "awe," probably because of their mystical, metaphysical associations beyond the realm of strict scientific study (though see below).

American psychologist and anthropologist Paul Ekman has followed in Darwin's train, not only editing and commenting on the fourth edition of Darwin's *Expression of Emotions* but also doing fieldwork (in Papua New Guinea and elsewhere) and other research investigating emotions revealed in facial and gestural displays. Ekman is a leading proponent of a suite of "basic" emotions common to virtually all cultures, however otherwise distinctive they might be in their emotive contexts (while New Guineans and American college students might fear different objects, each group recognizes expressions of fear in the other). Six "basic" emotions predominate in Ekman's scheme—anger, fear, sadness, enjoyment, disgust, and surprise—though he grants that other emotions, including awe, are also widely experienced. Like Darwin, however, Ekman devotes little attention to awe, since this emotion proves difficult to study in the field and laboratory.[14] In his more recent work, he distinguishes awe from wonder, attributing to the former "a strong component of fear and dread," unlike wonder—the rare "feeling of being overwhelmed by something incomprehensible [which] . . . separate[s] it from fear, although the two

11. Darwin, *Expression of the Emotions*, 308 (see 278–309).
12. Darwin, *Expression of the Emotions*, 288.
13. Darwin, *Expression of the Emotions*, 289–90.
14. Ekman, "Argument for Basic Emotions," 170, 191.

emotions can merge when we are threatened by something overwhelming, hard to understand fully or grasp." Overall, however, Ekman classes wonder as a positive, "enjoyable emotion."[15]

Where Ekman gives only a brief nod to awe/wonder, he, like Darwin, delves deeply into the "basic" emotion of surprise and its relation to other emotions.[16] Concerning whether surprise qualifies as an emotion per se, Ekman responds in pragmatic terms: "I think surprise *feels* like an emotion to most people."[17] It's a slippery emotion to handle, however, because of its characteristic sudden onset and short duration ("surprise is the briefest of all the emotions, lasting only a few seconds"). Yet, in Ekman's view, it is not merely a startle reflex. Though surprise doesn't persist long enough to allow for concurrent evaluation, it prompts urgent assessment and analysis: What's happening here? What does this strange phenomenon mean? And, depending on the source of surprise, this sudden shock, upon evaluation, may vector out into a variety of emotions, including "fear, amusement, relief, anger, [and] disgust," or "no emotion at all if we determine that the surprising event was of no consequence."[18] Ekman thus attenuates the link between surprise and fear that other emotion theorists emphasize; he simply grants that fear may or may not ensue. Curiously, however, he also reports that both New Guineans and Americans failed to reliably distinguish facial representations of surprise and fear when viewing others' responses to stories designed to evoke *either* surprise *or* fear, not both.[19] In any case, surprise, like other core emotions, demands some explanation to direct our prospective feelings, thoughts, and actions, even if it turns out to be negligible ("No big deal; nothing to see here; let's move on").

One notable, even surprising, way that surprise can be significant relates to what we might call its *humbling effect*. Being taken by surprise brings us up short in some way, which is "rarely a problem," as Ekman notes, "unless we are in a situation in which we shouldn't be surprised," like one where we're supposed to be experts by training and experience or, worse, where we try to pass ourselves off as more competent than we are. Many a cocky student claiming to have done the assigned reading has had to reckon with the dreaded pop (surprise) quiz. Again, we confront the possibility that Jesus's

15. Ekman, *Emotions Revealed*, 194.
16. See chap. 7, "Surprise and Fear," in Ekman, *Emotions Revealed*, 148–71.
17. Ekman, *Emotions Revealed*, 150 (emphasis original).
18. Ekman, *Emotions Revealed*, 148.
19. Oddly, while respondents routinely distinguished both fear and surprise from anger, disgust, sadness, and happiness, they found it difficult to demarcate fear and surprise from each other. Ekman (*Emotions Revealed*, 150) candidly admits he has no explanation for this phenomenon.

surprise/amazement reflects something he does not know until a moment of fresh revelation hits him from surprising sources. It remains for us to assess below whether the Gospel accounts suggest Jesus's humble acknowledgment of new insight.

Whereas Darwin, Ekman, and other modern researchers have largely shied away from studying more ineffable experiences of surprise associated with awe and wonder, social psychologists Dacher Keltner and Jonathan Haidt have ventured to fill in the gap. By analyzing classic accounts of numinous events—including Saul's Damascus Road epiphany—along with surveys of contemporary awe-inspiring phenomena, they discovered five potential "flavoring themes" or appraisal factors affecting the "hedonic tone of awe": threat, beauty, ability, virtue, and supernatural causality. In turn, these elements may apply to "related states" of admiration, elevation, and epiphany.[20] Arcing over these variations of awe is a common perception of *vastness* accompanied by the pressure of *accommodation*—that is, the need to adjust one's conceptual framework to make room for a new, overwhelming experience. In other words, focusing on "powerful" concomitants of vastness and accommodation, Keltner and Haidt summarize, "Across disciplines, theorists agree that awe involves being in the presence of something powerful, along with associated feelings of submission. Awe also involves a difficulty in comprehension, along with associated feelings of confusion, surprise, and wonder."[21]

In other studies, Haidt has particularly examined the awe-related state of *elevation*, which he describes as a "warm, uplifting feeling that people experience when they see unexpected acts of human goodness, kindness, and compassion," inspiring them in turn to emulate such beneficent behavior. In Haidt's research, the most common scenarios eliciting elevation "involved seeing someone else give help or aid to a person who was poor or sick, or stranded in a difficult situation."[22] This heartwarming, prosocial dimension of elevation coordinates with Barbara Fredrickson's categorization of positive emotions as those which "broaden and build" our experience,[23] expanding our love for others, we might say, horizontally, as we are elevated vertically by extraordinary models of loving action. Haidt takes seriously that people often interpret elevated awe as divinely inspired or uplifted in some way. Accordingly, modern assessments of awe and wonder as merely welcome or happy surprises (surprise + approval) too readily desacralize and trivialize poignant

---

20. Keltner and Haidt, "Approaching Awe."

21. Keltner and Haidt, "Approaching Awe," 303.

22. Haidt, "Positive Emotion"; see also Haidt, *Happiness Hypothesis*, 193–206; Haidt, "Elevation."

23. Fredrickson, "Cultivating"; cf. Fredrickson, "Broaden-and-Build Theory."

experiences of elevation. Even more so, the current colloquial craze to label almost anything that's not painful as "awesome" sucks all the mystical life out of awe: when it's applied to everything, it means nothing.[24]

By reclaiming awe's socially and morally elevated and expansive potential, Haidt does not deny the prospect of overwhelming fear and trembling when facing a severe threat. But on this "awful" end of the awe-spectrum, fear shrinks, constricts, freezes, and triggers flight rather than elevates, expands, energizes, and embraces experience. Moreover, the elevation "flavor" of awe, combined with "broaden and build" action tendencies of altruistic emotions, places it in direct opposition to social disgust, which aims to diminish and degrade persons to the lowest levels.[25]

Informed by these wide-ranging analyses of the complex of emotions under the umbrella of awe and wonder, surprise and amazement, we will now seek to elucidate Jesus's amazement as reported in two Gospel incidents. To what extent, if any, is Jesus perplexed, threatened, frustrated, elevated, expanded, and/or motivated to change his viewpoint and behavior or, in Haidt's terms, his "thought-action repertoire"?[26]

Jesus's Amazement at Unexpected Unbelief (Mark 6:1–6)

Mark's Jesus launches his public ministry with remarkable acts of liberation and restoration on behalf of a man possessed by a nefarious spirit (Mark 1:21–28), a woman with a fever (1:29–31), a leper (1:40–45), a paralytic (2:1–12), and a man with a withered hand (3:1–6). Evidence of Jesus's "deeds of power" is patent (see also 1:32–34; 3:10–11) but not probative for most witnesses. Public responses to Jesus's miracles include astonishment and amazement (1:22, 27; 2:12) along with disputation and suspicion (2:6–8; 3:2, 6). The only exemplary faith/trust/belief (*pistis*) Jesus acknowledges is that of the paralytic's four friends who carry him and lower him through the roof into the room where Jesus is speaking (2:5).

As Jesus's mission ensues, faith in his ability to mediate the saving power of God's realm remains in short supply and increasingly seems to puzzle and frustrate Jesus. Even his closest disciples fail to trust him fully and voice their panicky, accusatory doubt on a storm-tossed lake ("Teacher, do you not care that we are perishing?" [Mark 4:38]), to which Jesus retorts—after calming the tempest—"Why are you afraid? Have you still *no faith*?" (4:40). Ultimately,

24. Haidt, *Happiness Hypothesis*, 202–3, 206.
25. Haidt, "Positive Emotion"; Haidt, *Happiness Hypothesis*, 194–95.
26. Haidt, "Positive Emotion."

the narrator reports that the disciples "were filled with great awe" about this whole incident, not least Jesus's taming of the turbulent winds and waters with but a word (4:41). The NRSV rendering "great awe," recalling the wide spectrum of emotions associated with "awe," misses the more menacing mark of standard "fear" language: literally, "they feared a great fear" (*ephobēthēsan phobon megan*) or more smoothly, "they feared exceedingly" (KJV) or "they were terrified" (NIV). Jesus was not aiming to scare his followers any more than they wanted to fail him with their faithlessness. But both were caught up in an emotional vortex amid the environmental storm.

After crisscrossing the lake, Jesus soon encounters another jolting fear-and-faith scenario, registering this time, however, on the *positive* pole of the faith meter. A woman with a chronic bleeding disorder and proactive faith in Jesus's healing power presses through the crowd, touches the back of his cloak, draws power from his body, and "immediately . . . felt in her body that she was healed of her disease" (Mark 5:29). As mentioned above, I've argued elsewhere that this sudden siphoning of Jesus's power takes him by surprise. When he stops in his tracks, wheels around scanning the crowd, and queries, "Who touched my clothes?" (5:30), I suggest he's not merely staging a publicity scene but seeking answers to a puzzling situation. No one thus far has elicited healing from him without his permission or knowledge. What's happening here?

In response to Jesus's investigation, the cured woman reveals herself, falls down before him "in fear and trembling" (no telling what this powerful man might do now), and blurts out "the whole truth" (Mark 5:33). Quickly processing the information (remember that the initial spurt of surprise tends to be short-lived, promptly giving way to further affect and assessment), Jesus tenderly commends her extraordinary faith—"Daughter, your faith has made you well"—and dispatches her "in peace" (5:34). Another rollercoaster emotional episode culminating in peace (cf. "Peace! Be still!" in 4:39).

Right after this incident with the bleeding woman (interleaved with Jesus's resuscitation of a synagogue ruler's daughter), Mark's Jesus heads with his disciples to the Nazareth synagogue, where he "astounds" (*ekplēssomai*) his kinfolk and neighbors with the exceptional words of wisdom and deeds of power emanating from this local carpenter fellow they thought they knew (Mark 6:1–3). Again, a basic notation of surprise, amazement, or astonishment characterizes a first response to unusual phenomena, and that first response awaits clarification and direction. Is this person or event good, bad, or negligible? What action, if any, should we take to celebrate or denigrate this experience?

In this case, the Markan narrator leaves no doubt as to the "flavor" of the Nazareth congregation's feelings about this young man's eccentric behavior. They've gone sour on Jesus, taking offense at him (Mark 6:3), being *scandalized* by him, as we would transliterate the Greek verb (*skandalizō*), which here aptly catches the force of the Nazarenes' shocked "reaction over what appears to be publicly offensive."[27] The CEB says, "They were repulsed by him and fell into sin."[28] We could just as easily say "They were disgusted by him" or "They held him in contempt."

While such a vehement response may seem excessive to us, it makes sense within a tight-knit, small-town culture, ancient or modern, but especially within a first-century milieu governed by deep-seated honor-shame codes (hardly absent in today's societies but not always as strong as in the ancient Middle Eastern world).[29] Jesus's highfalutin words and extraordinary feats—however impressive, beneficent, and unintentionally offensive on Jesus's part—prove so foreign to his upbringing as to appear threatening and humiliating to his hometown folk. "Where did this man get all this?" (Mark 6:2). ("Certainly not from around here!" they would answer. "What's happened to this carpenter son, brother, and friend of ours? He's gone off the rails. He's gotten above his raising. Where does he come off flaunting this power display? Something's not right here!") The community's amazement/wonderment at this alien Jesus, from their perspective, tilts hard toward the sense of dread, consternation, and disdain outlined by Spinoza.

At first, Jesus himself is scarcely surprised by his fellow Nazarenes' pejorative response, since he knows well from biblical models that God's prophets typically receive the least honor "in their hometown, and among their own kin, and in their own house" (Mark 6:4). Parochial communities become suspicious and offended when one of their own turns itinerant maverick claiming divine authority. We can easily imagine the villagers of Tishbe, Tekoa, and Anathoth wondering if Elijah, Amos, and Jeremiah, respectively, had lost their minds, much as the Nazareth folk question Jesus's sanity and fidelity to local norms and values. Before this present commotion in the Nazareth synagogue, Jesus's family had already fretted about his outlandish reputation as a healer and exorcist in other Galilean towns. His mother, brothers, and sisters became so worried about reports that "he has gone out of his mind" that "they went out [to Capernaum] to restrain [or seize] him" and presumably bring him back to Nazareth (3:21; cf. 3:31–35). When he returns, however, their concerns only heighten.

Although Jesus appears to take in stride his hometown's shock and shame at his display of prophetic authority, that doesn't mean he's not affected at

27. Danker with Krug, *Concise Greek-English Lexicon*, 322.
28. This CEB reading combines both the emotional (repulsion) and moral (falling into sin) nuances of *skandalizō*.
29. See Malina and Rohrbaugh, *Social-Science Commentary*, 212–14.

all. And soon we discover that the Nazarenes' unbelief (*apistia*) particularly throws him off balance emotionally, triggering his own upsetting bafflement (Mark 6:6). To ascertain why their unfaithful disposition amazes Jesus so much, we need first to appraise what it is about Jesus they don't believe; and to do that we need clarity about the Greek term *pistis*, typically rendered "faith" or "belief." Through the centuries of Christian history faith and belief have become encrusted with doctrinal and creedal notions—the faith, statements of faith, sets of beliefs—beyond their primary ancient usage. From her extensive investigation of the Greek *pistis* and its Latin counterpart *fides* in the epigraphy and literature of the early Roman era (including the Greek Bible), Teresa Morgan concludes, "'Trust,' 'trustworthiness,' 'honesty,' 'credibility,' 'faithfulness,' 'good faith,' 'confidence,' 'assurance'. . . are all widely attested as meanings of both lexica."[30] Notice the primary emphasis on relational trust, particularly, as Morgan evidences in numerous examples, between divine and other authority figures—political rulers, military officers, landlords, household heads—and their subjects. Accordingly, *pistis* (and *fides*) denote "first and foremost, neither a body of beliefs nor a function of the heart or mind, but a relationship which creates community."[31]

Individual and decisional affirmations of credos prove less relevant to New Testament "faith" than do social and experiential engagements of trust. Though downplaying emotional ("heart") and intellectual ("mind") dimensions of *pistis*, Morgan does not discount them altogether. Overall, she finds the ancient sources more holistic in their understanding of "*pistis*, *fides*, and their cognates . . . as simultaneously cognitive and affective, active and relational."[32]

Still, with the trust/trustworthiness factor most dominant in "faith" experience, the Nazarenes' no-confidence response to Jesus reflects further suspicion about his relational reliability, along the lines of his family's previous worries about his mental and emotional stability ("out of his mind") and the social embarrassment he's causing for his kin and village throughout Galilee. His own people thought they knew Jesus and could count on him as a supportive, dutiful son, brother, and friend. Now they don't know what to make of him. But they know they now have a trust problem with Jesus, a case of "bad faith."

Compounding their disquieting doubt concerning his relational reliability is their sclerotic skepticism of his remedial ability, implied in the stunning

30. Morgan, *Roman Faith*, 7; see also Gruen, "Greek *pistis*"; Spencer, "'Your Faith Has Made You Well'"; Jones, "Trust."
31. Morgan, *Roman Faith*, 14 (emphasis added).
32. Morgan, *Roman Faith*, 19; see Morgan's full discussion in chap. 11, "Relationality and Interiority in *Pistis* and *Fides*," 444–72.

statement of Mark 6:5 immediately preceding the report of Jesus's amazement at their unbelief: "He could do no deed of power there, except that he
laid his hands on a few sick people and cured them." This statement flatly
avers that Jesus was "unable to do any miracles there" (CEB). A more literal
translation conveys Jesus's surprising power outage in Nazareth: "He did
not have the power [*edynato*] there to do any powerful act [*dynamin*]." He
tries to perform restorative miracles in his hometown—not to show off but
genuinely to help the infirm—yet he's largely thwarted in his efforts, able to
cure only "a few sick people," not the "many" or "all" he's more accustomed
to helping (see 1:32–34; 6:53–56).

Nothing in Mark's narrative to this point has prepared us readers—or
Mark's Jesus—for this downturn of events. While some have opposed his
miraculous mission, none have blocked its progress. And while positive faith
in Jesus's curative ability can encourage or elicit therapeutic power (Mark
1:40; 2:5; 5:27–29, 34), evidence of the ailing party's proactive faith in him,
as commendable as that is, has not been a prerequisite for his saving work
(see 1:21–28; 3:1–6; 5:1–20, 35–43). In fact, even "*no faith*," like that of his
disciples on the tempestuous lake, has not diminished Jesus's powers one whit
(4:35–41)—until now, in Nazareth!

To be sure, Mark makes no direct causal connection between the Nazarenes' unbelief and Jesus's inability to perform many miracles among them, as
in Matthew's parallel account. But Matthew also makes a significant change
in Jesus's response, eliminating his "amazement" and modulating his power
reduction to a matter-of-fact occurrence or even a willful choice caused by
his hometown's distrust: "And he *did not do* [*ouk epoiēsen*] many deeds of
power there *because of their unbelief* [*dia tēn apistian*]" (Matt. 13:58). Matthew's apologetics are obvious, attempting to correct any misconceptions
that Mark's account might raise about Jesus's consummate knowledge (omniscience) and ability (omnipotence). In the process, Matthew intimates an
early interpretation of Mark that perceives an uncomfortable nexus between
Jesus's amazement at his people's lack of trust and his limited capacity to
heal. As with emotional scenarios generally, connections run more in loops
in and around, betwixt and between, subjects and environments than in hard
cause-and-effect lines.

It may seem odd to believers today that Jesus's family and neighbors would
doubt his ability to deliver the diseased and demonized, given the mounting
number of favorable witnesses to his supernatural power. But theirs was a
culture that worried more about the *source* of folk healers' power than the
product. While granting that God could heal through authorized agents, they
also believed that Satan and his minions could perform wonders through

human intermediaries driven by impure motives, like profit or popularity. The line between fraudulent magicians and hucksters, on the one hand, and benevolent miracle-workers and healers, on the other hand, was a fine one. The Nazareth villagers' mistrust of the nonconformist Jesus's reliability could easily extend to doubting his divinely graced restorative abilities. In the same incident in which Jesus's family seeks to restrain him due to increasing reports of his insanity, some Jerusalem scribes come to Galilee accusing him of demonic affiliation: "He has Beelzebul, and by the ruler of the demons he casts out demons" (Mark 3:22; cf. 3:20–35). Although Jesus decisively refutes this slander, the charge remains in the air and drifts back to Nazareth. Perhaps Mark's Jesus should have not been so surprised about the chilly reception he receives in chapter 6. But he would hardly be the only person in human history to expect conflict when he returns home and yet still be surprised, upset, and disappointed when it happens. Emotions never run higher, for good and ill, than at family reunions.

Of course, most of Jesus's upbringing and family relations remain in the shadows. We can only speculate about his feelings regarding family rejection. The Gospels are not soap operas, not even close. Absent more details, the amazement of Mark's Jesus over Nazareth's unbelief proves more evocative than definitive. I've teased out some possible explanations focusing on trust issues. Overall, Jesus's surprise/amazement/wonderment seems to hover somewhere in the middle of the spectrum of related emotions sketched above. On the one end, he is not consumed by dread or despair; and on the other end, he experiences no special revelation expanding his vision of God or the world but instead experiences a sudden sense of delimitation.

I tentatively propose that Mark's Jesus experiences an emotional reality check in Nazareth—a *humbling effect*, as I mentioned above—as he confronts limits on his knowledge and power, heretofore not fully apprehended, in a deep-rooted relational environment. Not that Jesus is a narcissist obsessed with his authority and popularity. Far from it! His indefatigable cross-bearing, self-sacrificing mission embodies humble service, which he also enjoins on his followers (see Mark 8:31–37; 9:30–37; 10:41–45). Humility ranks as a prime virtuous emotional attitude in Jesus's life and teaching.[33] Adapting the christological tenet in Hebrews 5:7–8, "In the days of his flesh . . . although

---

33. See the self-evaluation of Jesus the Teacher in Matthew's Gospel: "I am gentle [*praus*] and humble [*tapeinos*] in heart" (Matt. 11:29); likewise Matthew's citation of Zech. 9:9 uniquely characterizes Jesus the King as entering Jerusalem (on what we call Palm Sunday), "humble [*praus*], and mounted on a donkey" (Matt. 21:5). On Jesus's teaching about humility, see Matt. 18:4; 23:12; Luke 14:11; 18:14. For a thoughtful exposition of humility as an emotional virtue and "moral project," see Roberts, *Spiritual Emotions*, 78–93.

he was a Son, he learned obedience through what he suffered," we might say that Jesus also learned humility through what surprised him on difficult days like the one back home in Nazareth.

Jesus's Amazement at Unexpected Belief (Matt. 8:5–13; Luke 7:1–10)

As noted above, Matthew drops Mark's attribution of "amazement" to Jesus over his hometown's unbelief, opting simply to identify their lack of faith/ trust as the reason Jesus did not perform "many" miracles there (Matt. 13:58). But Matthew does allow for Jesus's "amazement" (*thaumazō*) in another scene that is not found in Mark but is shared with Luke (Matt. 8:5–13 // Luke 7:1–10). Here, however, quite the opposite of not displaying many acts of power, Jesus demonstrates one of his most extraordinary feats, a most amazing act, we could truly say (though Matthew and Luke don't call it such): healing a severely ill man on the brink of death from long distance, without ever meeting the patient! And far from miring in stubborn unbelief, the one who solicits Jesus's aid for a household member exhibits nonpareil faith and elicits Jesus's "amazement" (Matt. 8:10 // Luke 7:9). Against the backdrop of such an incredible miracle by Jesus, his amazement/surprise takes on a more positive, expansive emotional tenor amid the humbling effect of discovering an unprecedented level of faith/trust in his restorative power.

We again seek to understand Jesus's response of surprise within its overall affective-relational context, focusing primarily on Luke's lengthier account. Emotional attitudes and social codes figure prominently in the narrative. Before revealing Jesus's amazement, the story surprises the reader in three related ways. First, a character other than Jesus dominates the discourse. Second, that figure is not one we expect to engage with Jesus, like a disciple or a religious author-ity; it is a Roman officer-soldier of middling "centurion" rank in Capernaum. The only thing we've heard about soldiers thus far is John the Baptist's demand that they "not extort money from anyone by threats or false accusation" (Luke 3:14)—which leads to the third, and most dramatic, surprise: this Roman mili-tary officer is a good guy, a "worthy" (*axios*) man in the opinion of the city's Jewish elders, defying stereotypes of malevolent, money-grubbing soldiers (7:4).[34]

Such worthiness implies the centurion's trustworthiness, reliability, and faithfulness, which in turn commend Jesus's belief in him as a trustworthy recipient of Jesus's aid. (He's not laying a trap for Jesus, as some scribes and Pharisees have tried to do [Luke 6:7–11].) All this is evidenced in the officer's

34. See Brink, *Soldiers in Luke-Acts*.

exemplary emotional-relational character. Notice three more surprising features from this perspective:

1. The fact that the centurion had "a slave" (*doulos*) is not surprising at all; in fact, we might expect he owned several slaves (cf. Luke 7:8) and would not be shocked if he treated them badly. But Luke focuses on the centurion's sincere concern for a particular slave "he valued highly [*entimos*], . . . who was ill and close to death" (7:2). The notion of "high value/worth" in Greek and English can connote economic status with or without a deep emotional attachment. The officer may want Jesus to heal this slave because he is a skilled, responsible, "valuable" manager of the household or estate.[35] It would be bad for business if the centurion lost this profitable slave. Yet the "high-value" term (*entimos*) does not preclude feelings of "precious" endearment,[36] and the lengths the centurion goes to secure Jesus's aid for the slave through local elders and "friends" suggests a personal emotional connection more than a merely transactional employment arrangement. Moreover, when the centurion delivers his request to Jesus through brokers, he refers, in his own voice, to this slave (*doulos* [7:2–3, 8]) as "my servant" or "my child" (*pais* can mean either [7:7]).

2. The goodwill the Roman officer has built with the city's Jewish leaders derives, as they inform Jesus, from his construction of a new synagogue in town (Luke 7:5). Of course, such benefaction could be purely strategic on the centurion's part, making him look generous, getting his name on a plaque, and above all, securing the elders' loyal clientage.[37] But in their pitch to Jesus about the centurion's "worthiness" to be granted healing for his slave, the elders commend his love for "our people/nation" (*ethnos*), using the same verb (*agapaō*) that Luke's Jesus employs to enjoin "love for enemies" (6:27, 32, 35) and that drives the Torah's double-commandment to "love God" and "love neighbor" (10:26–28). As I will unpack more fully in the next two chapters, the emotion of agapic love prompts selfless action on behalf of the beloved. Spurred by some degree of affection for the Jewish people toward constructive enhancement of their community, the Roman centurion models edifying love and breaks down ethnic barriers.

3. While Jesus responds favorably to the elders' message, certain devoted "friends" (*philoi*) of the centurion supply more information about his wishes. No need, they tell Jesus, to come all the way to the house, since the centurion believes that Jesus must "only speak the word" to effect healing (Luke 7:6–8). Or, more apropos of the officer's mindset, Jesus has only to "give the order"

35. See the managerial roles of slaves in Jesus's parables (Matt. 18:23–35; 21:33–41; 24:45–51; 25:14–30; Luke 12:42–48; 19:12–27; 20:9–18) discussed in Glancy, *Slavery*, 110–15.
36. BDAG 340.
37. See Moxnes, "Patron-Client Relations"; Danker, *Luke*, 12, cf. 6–17.

as a supreme authority figure to make things happen, as the military man knows from his career of taking orders from superiors and giving them to subordinates. Although we might suppose that he schemes to avoid a direct encounter with Jesus so as not to appear beholden to this upstart folk healer from Nazareth, officers more typically prefer those who serve them to perform their ministrations with all due deference. In an earlier biblical incident, for example, the Syrian general Naaman, who traveled to Elisha's home in Israel seeking a cure for his leprosy, became incensed when the prophet refused to come outside and attend personally to this foreign commander, choosing rather to prescribe a humiliating treatment plan—via a messenger, no less—of seven dips in the dirty Jordan River. Eventually, Naaman followed Elisha's word and was healed, but he did so in a huff (2 Kings 5:9–14).

Generals are not accustomed to taking orders from anyone, least of all cocky, eccentric civilians from another country. Lower-ranking officers, like centurions, would not normally submit themselves to such figures either, especially in an imperial context of occupying the foreigner's territory. Of course, Jesus does not snub the centurion as Elisha does Naaman; Jesus is perfectly willing to enter the soldier's house. Nonetheless, the centurion's willingness to let small-town Jesus have the dynamic, dominant word (which is guaranteed to spread like wildfire throughout Capernaum; the Jewish elders and man's friends are sure to gossip) marks an extraordinary demonstration of humble submission to Jesus's authority and trustful affirmation of his power.

The Roman officer's love and esteem for his slave and for the Jewish people, together with his humility and trust before the itinerant Jewish prophet Jesus, have a profound emotional impact on Jesus. Indeed, upon hearing the friends' message, the "amazed" Jesus literally turns (*strapheis*) to a large company of followers, captures their solemn attention ("I tell you [all]"), and announces the wondrous relational-emotional significance of this moment: "Not even in Israel have I found such faith" (Luke 7:9). This is the first of seven strategic *strephō*-moments, turning points in Luke's narrative, when Jesus's physical turnaround signals a critical plot development within an emotional episode (7:9, 44; 9:55; 10:23; 14:25; 22:61; 23:28).[38] In the first three, Jesus turns against or overturns conventional social and moral prejudices fueled by skewed emotional judgments about three groups:

- *Roman soldiers*: Jesus overturns popular Jewish distrust (for good reason!) of the Roman military via a centurion in Capernaum who evidences extraordinary humility and faith (7:2–10).

38. See Spencer, *Luke*, 374–75, 574.

- *Sinners*: Jesus overturns religious teachers' all-too-common animus against sinful persons in the case of a woman in Simon the Pharisee's home who evinces extraordinary love and faith (7:44–50).
- *Samaritans*: Jesus overturns James and John's violent opposition to ethnocentric Samaritans who refuse to receive the Jewish Jesus en route to Jerusalem (9:51–55). This time Jesus appeals to no counter-example (though he will showcase a merciful Samaritan in a parable [10:33–37] and commend a grateful Samaritan he meets [17:15–19]); nonetheless, he still "turned and rebuked" his disciples' overwrought retaliatory scheme to incinerate the inhospitable Samaritan village with heavenly fire (9:54–55). Hostile emotions ran high on both Samaritan and Jewish sides of the border, but here two emissaries of Jesus blaze out of control.

While in all three scenes Jesus turns to break social stereotypes and correct emotional misjudgments, only in the centurion incident does Luke indicate some attitudinal adjustment on Jesus's part as well. Only here is Jesus himself said to be "amazed." Only here does he experience an affective-relational shift in perspective.

For both Luke and Matthew, the surprising issue is not that Jesus suddenly realizes that the God of Israel cares for Gentiles and includes them in the plan of salvation. This embracive project has already been plainly revealed in the covenant with Abraham and prophecies of Isaiah highlighted in Luke's infancy narratives (1:55, 72–73; 2:29–32). It has been supplemented by Jesus's ancestral connection with Rahab, Ruth, and other Gentile women in Matthew's genealogy (Matt. 1:2–6) and his exhortation to "love your enemies," which doubtless includes foreigners, in his Sermon on the Mount/Plain (Matt 5:43–48 // Luke 6:27–36) preceding the centurion episode. Accordingly, while Jesus's commendation of the centurion's faith certainly disabuses his followers of virulent anti-Roman or anti-Gentile feelings they might harbor, the effect on Jesus himself is less corrective than *expansive*.

Until this experience with this extraordinary man, Jesus does not realize the extent to which non-Jews, in particular a presumed Roman enemy of Israel, could show such incredible humility and trust, even beyond what Jesus's own people have shown thus far during his ministry. This receptive Roman officer stationed in Capernaum thoroughly outshines his recalcitrant hometown synagogue in Nazareth. Yet again, Jesus's thrust appears more positive than negative, aiming less at lambasting his followers and other Jews for their sluggish faith (it corrupts the point to twist Jesus's pro-Gentile approval into an anti-Jewish invective) than at enlarging both their limited concepts of faith in God's (re)creative word and their constricted circles of faithful (trustworthy) fellowship.

While we may say again that the amazed Jesus learns and grows by this experience, here the tone (flavor) of his surprise abounds with elevated wonder and awe at this remarkable centurion's trust in Jesus's divine power, which ultimately redounds to the capacious grace and glory of God who seeks the healing, restoration, and salvation of all people—slave and master, Jew and Roman, friend and enemy. We find ourselves, not for the first time, in the dynamic realm of love, arguably the most elevated—and elusive—emotion of all, to which we will devote more attention in the next two chapters.

8

What's Love Got to Do with It?

The Compassionate Jesus and Pastoral Ministry

J esus loves me, this I know, for the Bible tells me so." So Karl Barth summarized his entire theological project in a single line from the song his mother taught him.[1] This song has been the anthem of Sunday schools for generations, encapsulating what Christians believe—and feel!—to be Jesus's main, if not sole, emotion. Any reluctance to attribute other emotions to God and God's Son, for fear of compromising divine stability, vanishes when it comes to love. The many vacillations of human love in various contexts— romance, marriage, parenting, friendship, work, food, and drink (I honestly love coffee)—do not apply to the *steadfast love* that defines the divine nature: "God *is* love" (1 John 4:8).

While this study has sought to flesh out Jesus's emotional repertoire in the Gospel narratives beyond love, it's not surprising that other emotions we've considered have been entangled with love. The banner example of Jesus's dealings with Martha, Mary, and Lazarus—whom he's explicitly said to love throughout the ordeal of Lazarus's illness, death, and resuscitation (John 11:3, 5, 36)—entwines these loving feelings with pangs of anger, grief, and disgust, as we explored in chapters 3–6. We also sought in chapter 7 to understand Jesus's amazement/surprise in the orbit of common sentiments of love toward

---

1. Late in his life, during his only visit to America in 1962, Barth offered this statement in response to a student's question at the University of Chicago. See R. Clson, *Journey of Modern Theology*, 309.

kinfolk and his uncommon teaching of love toward enemies, such as Roman military men, although the narratives do not say he "loved" them or indicate any relational emotion other than amazement at their level of faith/belief.

Oddly enough, the Synoptic Gospels seldom balance Jesus's teaching about love with explicit uses of typical "love" language, *agap-* and *phil-*, to describe Jesus's benevolent actions. Matthew and Luke report Jesus's growing reputation as a "friend [*philos*] of tax collectors and sinners" (Matt. 11:19 // Luke 7:34). Yet while both Gospels *show* Jesus actively loving and befriending such questionable folk, the "friend" label is a slur affixed by Jesus's antagonists. While we may infer some aspects of how Jesus feels about these "friends," the accounts are not brimming with emotional detail.

Perhaps most surprising is that the only time the Synoptic Gospels state that "Jesus loved" anyone occurs in Mark's version of Jesus's encounter with a rich man who inquires about the path to eternal life. In response, Jesus lays down a demanding condition, which he knows the man will find hard to swallow; nonetheless, Jesus issues his injunction in love: "Jesus, looking at him, *loved* [*ēgapēsen*] him, and said, 'You lack one thing: go, sell what you own, and give the money to the poor'" (Mark 10:21). In fact, this proves more than the rich man can handle, leaving him "shocked" and "grieving" (10:22). The emotional freight of this scene is not lost on Jesus's disciples, who become "perplexed" at Jesus's stringent words (10:24). Here, in this unique Markan account, Jesus's *agapē* pulses within a dynamic affective network, which we will turn to study in the next chapter.

Although *agap-* and *phil-* are primary words for "love," another pair of love-related terms, *splanchnon* and *eleos*, variously rendered as "compassion," "mercy," and "pity," motivate multiple acts of the Synoptic Jesus's ministry, especially feeding and healing (Matt. 14:13–21; 15:32–39; Mark 6:30–44; 8:1–10; Luke 9:10–17), and also two of his most compelling parable figures: the good Samaritan who ministers to an assaulted traveler (Luke 10:33–37) and the gracious father who welcomes home his wastrel son (15:20–32). Though such actions are potentially laden with motivational feelings, "moving" Jesus and the parable characters "with compassion," they are not necessarily so. A person may perform a good work of loving-kindness or mercy perfunctorily, randomly, or obediently, with little or no feeling attached. We shall see to what extent Jesus becomes emotionally involved in his charitable deeds.

By any reckoning, love is a complex emotion, a "many-splendored thing," as the popular song from a 1955 movie attests. But there's a flip side, too, complicating the splendiferous tones, more aptly captured in another hit tune, this one sung by Tina Turner in her inimitable raw-edged style: "What's love got to do, got to do with it / What's love but a secondhand emotion."[2] Though trying to discount love as a cheap "secondhand emotion" that only leads to heartache, she scarcely convinces herself. She knows that love cannot be captured in simple sound bites. Though leaving her "confused," "dazed," and "scared," it "means more than" anything one can calculate by purely "logical" means. The question keeps coming, keeps pressing, never fully answered: What's love got to do with it?

What's love got to do with Jesus's ministry beyond the Sunday school ditty, as sweet as it is? What's love got to do with any of us, with life in all its complexity? To provide yardsticks for assessing the emotional dimensions of Jesus's love, I will survey some relevant scripts and patterns presented in the Bible and by various philosophers and psychologists.

Scripts and Patterns of Love and Compassion

From ancient Greek plays and novels to modern Hollywood movies and Harlequin paperbacks, romantic love has been scripted ad nauseam. The Hebrew Bible even chimes in at points, as in Jacob and Rachel's love story (see Gen. 29:20) and the Song of Songs's erotic poetry. The Gospels, however, have little interest in romantic affairs. That's not to say they're prudish—but their prime love interest fits the larger Torah vision, encompassing the God of love, all "neighbors," and "one another," near and far. Titillating theories of Jesus's romantic involvement with Mary Magdalene find no basis in the Gospel narratives, and not because they're engaged in some priggish, misogynist cover-up. However we might distinguish the so-called historical Jesus from the Gospels' literary portraits, Jesus's identity as a celibate, apocalyptic prophet of God's in-breaking reign on earth best fits the available evidence.[3] This urgent, world-changing mission allowed Jesus no time or space for normal marital and social entanglements.

The "scripts" I have in mind to help us understand Jesus's love align with the broader "script theory" of psychologist Silvan Tomkins. In this view, core "affects" like anger, disgust, surprise, and fear, while including "feelings" and "emotions" that bear the same names, operate within more "scripted" scenarios of cultural experience. We both act out "innate scripts" through the physical body and absorb "learned scripts" from the social environment.

2. Tina Turner, "What's Love Got to Do with It?," recorded May 1, 1984, track 2 on *Private Dancer*, Capitol.

3. See Allison, *Jesus of Nazareth*, 172–216; Ehrman, *Jesus*, 103–245; Spencer, *What Did Jesus Do?*, 105–6, 175–76, 256–59.

These scripted plots, however, allow for considerable improvisation and interpretation, for "freedoms of affects in time, in intensity, in density of investment, in choice of objects, and in . . . various degrees of urgency," amplifying "psychological processes, such as perception, cognition, and action, within the scene itself."[4]

The Torah's and the Prophets' Scripts of Love

We should remain alert to bodily manifestations of the intensity, density, object-focus, and urgency of Jesus's love disclosed in the Gospel narratives. Of the learned scripts affecting, shaping, and motivating Jesus's love, the literal script of the Torah is the most formative. Far from a formulaic program, however, the Torah provides a living, dynamic script (*Scrip*ture) suffused with the memory, tradition, education, worship, and fellowship of faithful Jews, like Jesus. And at the heart of this scriptural environment throbs the loving relationship between God and God's people rooted in covenant.

Resonant with ancient political treaties between lord (suzerain) and subject (vassals) and more diffuse social contracts between "the protector and his protégé, the patron and his client," the Torah scripts a legal drama of the Lord God's covenantal bond with Israel cemented by love.[5] Salient in this pact is Israel's duty to love God through faithful service and obedience to God's commandments delivered through Moses. The Shema credo from Deuteronomy 6 establishes the fundamental covenantal link between lordship, loyalty, love, and obedience: "Hear [*Shema*], O Israel: The LORD is our God, the LORD alone. You shall love the LORD your God. . . . Keep these words that I am commanding you today" (Deut. 6:4–6). Aptly, this core divine love mandate extends to the entire community: "You shall love your neighbor as yourself: I am the LORD" (Lev. 19:18). Together these Torah texts constitute the dual "greatest commandments" endorsed by Jesus and other Jewish teachers (see Matt. 22:34–40; Mark 12:28–34; Luke 10:25–28).

This legal-contractual assessment of the Torah's covenantal love script is accurate, as far as it goes. But it doesn't go far enough emotionally or theologically. While one might mechanically discharge a duty to help a superior (a divine or human overlord) or a subject (a child, an employee) under an official banner of "love," *without* accompanying loving feelings, emotional stimulation is certainly not antithetical to loving action and indeed can positively motivate it. Notice the extended Shema passage: "You shall love the LORD

---

4. Mosher and Tomkins, "Scripting the Macho Man," 61.
5. Levenson, *Love of God*, 38. I'm indebted in this section to Levenson's entire chapter, "A Covenantal Love," 1–58.

your God with all your heart, and with all your soul, and with all your might. Keep these words that I am commanding you today in your heart. Recite them to your children and talk about them when you are at home and when you are away, when you lie down and when you rise. Bind them as a sign on your hand, fix them as an emblem on your forehead, and write them on the doorposts of your house and on your gates" (Deut. 6:5–9).

On the basis of this key covenantal text embedding the legal duty to love God in recitative practice and interior processing, Jon Levenson argues "that the language of love in the covenantal context has resonances of both service and feeling. It would be extreme to imagine that such internalization would not involve the emotions, and centrally so."[6] I would add that the imaginative multimedia presentations of the love command (recite, bind, write) in multiple venues—somatic (heart, hand, head), social (home, away), and material (bed, doorposts, gates)—heighten and broaden the *felt experience* of covenantal love, while modulating tendencies to "over-intellectualize" such experience.[7] Internal, heartfelt sentiment also motivates the command to love other people: "You shall not hate in your heart anyone of your kin . . . or bear a grudge against any of your people, but you shall love your neighbor as yourself: I am the LORD" (Lev. 19:17–18).

In addition to appreciating the emotional tenor of the Torah's love script, we should take full measure of the theological strain, including God as loving agent as well as object of others' love. If honorably engaged in a covenantal pact with their subjects and servants, then the overlords, masters, and patrons assume benevolent obligations of love. As Levenson states, "Where the servant owes his lord obedience, the lord owes his servant protection, succor, and if called for, rescue from enemies. Nevertheless, the relationship is still explicitly one of love; though it is not marked by equality, it is still marked by profound reciprocity."[8] Again, of course, affectionate feelings may or may not attend oversight responsibilities; indeed, we might presume that the more august the lord (think Caesar Augustus), the less inclined he would be to become emotionally involved with lowly subjects.

More than obligation and diplomacy, however, fuel God's love for Israel— something akin to affection and intimacy. In the chapter of Deuteronomy that follows the command to love God wholeheartedly, we learn of God's first love for Israel, not born out of self-gain—what Israel could do for God—but

---

6. Levenson, *Love of God*, 29.

7. On the "felt character" of emotions, not least love, see Deonna and Teroni, *Emotions*, 1–13; Deonna and Teroni, "Emotional Experience"; Pugmire, *Sound Sentiments*, 61–64. On the tendency to "over-intellectualize" emotions like love, see Goldie, *Emotions*, 41 (cf. 39–43).

8. Levenson, *Love of God*, 37.

out of gracious choice and jealous desire: "It was not because you were more numerous than any other people that the LORD set his heart [ḥašaq] on you and chose you—for you were the fewest of all peoples. It was because the LORD loved ['ahabat] you and . . . redeemed you from the house of slavery. . . . Know therefore that the LORD your God is God, the faithful God who maintains covenant loyalty with those who love him and keep his commandments" (7:7–9).

The term rendered "set [his] heart" (ḥašaq) here and in Deuteronomy 10:15 is associated with ardent feelings of being "smitten with love"[9] or "fall[ing] in love,"[10] like those consuming a young man longing to marry a beautiful woman (21:11; cf. Gen. 34:8). The passionate tenor aligns with possessive, jealous feelings—not wanting to share the lover with anyone else—even becoming "angry" with the lover should they desire someone else (see Deut. 7:4).

Related emotions of "mercy," "steadfast love," "compassion," "kindness," and "graciousness" emerge in a dramatic, seminal moment of divine self-revelation to Moses on Mount Sinai (Exod. 34:6–7):

> The LORD, the LORD, a God merciful and gracious, slow to anger, and abounding in steadfast love and faithfulness, keeping steadfast love for the thousandth generation, forgiving iniquity and transgression and sin, yet by no means clearing the guilty. (NRSV)

> The LORD! The LORD! A God compassionate [raḥum] and gracious, slow to anger, abounding in kindness and faithfulness, extending kindness to the thousandth generation, forgiving iniquity, transgression, and sin; yet He does not remit all punishment. (NJPS)

This significant theological disclosure reverberates across the Hebrew Bible.[11]

The principal outcome of God's mercy and compassion in this tradition is a slowness to punish sinful behavior in a fit of pique and, indeed, an eagerness to forgive iniquitous acts (though not forever if the guilty persist in being unrepentant). A critical issue with forgiveness, divine or human, is, again, whether one must *feel* kindly or sympathetically toward offenders in order to offer genuine forgiveness—whether individuals must "find it in their hearts," as we say, to forgive. A similar problem obtains on the other side: How much, if any, remorse must one feel to evidence repentance and receive forgiveness?

---

9. McBride, "Deuteronomy," 268–69.
10. Levenson, *Love of God*, 42.
11. See Num. 14:18–19; Neh. 9:17; Pss. 86:15; 103:8–10; 145:8–9; Jer. 32:18; Joel 2:13; Jon. 4:2; Nah. 1:3; see also Trible, *God and the Rhetoric of Sexuality*, 1–5, 38–39.

A ritual-legal system can establish precepts and policies governing performed acts of repentance and remission but cannot legislate, regulate, or arbitrate internal feelings. How many tears must one cry, how fervently must one say "sorry," to prove regret and a desire to reform? Nevertheless, however difficult they are to calibrate, processes of seeking, receiving, and granting forgiveness are never purely clinical operations but involve all affected parties in a tangled web of emotional motivations and repercussions, conscious and unconscious. The compassionate, merciful God of Israel, for one, seems to find pathos "in his heart" toward his flawed, beloved people, motivating divine forgiveness.[12]

In the Gospels, Jesus assumes the divine prerogative of directly pronouncing forgiveness on two individuals: a paralyzed man lowered through the roof in the home where Jesus is teaching (Matt. 9:2–6 // Mark 2:5–10 // Luke 5:20–24) and a sinful woman who washes Jesus's feet in the home of Simon the Pharisee, where Jesus is dining (Luke 7:48). In Luke's story, from the cross Jesus also asks his Father to forgive his executioners (23:34).[13] In each of these three cases, however, Jesus delivers his forgiveness judgment or petition straightforwardly, without emotional display (no loud voice, tender touch, or flowing tears) or mention of his love or compassion. To be sure, the encounter with the "sinful woman" positively oozes with loving feelings and actions—tears, kisses, caresses, and tresses—on *her* part, demonstrating *her* "much love" toward Jesus (7:37–39, 44–46). But while Jesus happily accepts her loving ministrations and chides his host for demeaning her hospitality, Jesus's subjective love for this woman is not accentuated. His forgiveness is cast more in transactional terms of canceled debt (7:40–43) than emotional terms of compassionate pity.

Although the Gospels do not explicitly regard Jesus's acts of forgiveness as expressions of his compassion or mercy, they do report his acts of healing and feeding as products of "being moved with compassion" (*splanchnizomai*) toward and "having mercy" (*eleeō*) upon needy persons (see discussion of these emotion-driven acts below). Such good works not only satisfy covenantal-legal demands of divine compassion but also evidence God's passionate creational-parental care for Israel. Having "observed the misery" of the people enslaved in Egypt (Exod. 3:7), God moves to deliver them as a desperate parent springs to save his or her endangered child. Through Moses, God the Father voices his impassioned demand to Pharaoh: "Thus says the

---

12. See the thoughtful, nuanced debate of the emotional aspects of forgiveness in the Bible in Lambert, "Mourning over Sin/Affliction"; and D. Olson, "Emotion."
13. See discussion of this text, including the question of its authenticity, in Spencer, *Luke*, 593–601.

LORD: *Israel is my firstborn son*. I said to you, 'Let *my son* go that he may worship me'" (4:22–23).

The prophet Hosea later recalls this divine parental rescue mission motivated by love: "When Israel was a child, I loved him, and out of Egypt I called my son" (Hosea 11:1). In his eighth-century BCE context, however, Hosea proceeds to mediate God's emotional struggle with Israel/Ephraim's rebellious, wayward behavior, despite God's persistent, nurturing love manifested in healing and feeding—precisely what the compassionate Jesus will do for his people.

> The more I called them,
>   the more they went from me;
> . . . .
> Yet it was I who taught Ephraim to walk,
>   I took them up in my arms;
>   but they did not know that I *healed* them.
> I led them with cords of human kindness,
>   with bands of love.
> I was to them like those
>   who lift infants to their cheeks.
> I bent down to them and *fed* them. (11:2–4)

Tragically, however, God's unfaithful "son" pushed God's patience and risked abandonment in exile to Egypt (again) and Assyria (Hosea 11:5), to the great distress of the offended God, but not enough to overcome God's fierce and fiery compassion:

> How can I give you up, Ephraim?
>   How can I hand you over, O Israel?
> . . . .
> My heart recoils within me;
>   My compassion grows warm and tender.
> I will not execute my fierce anger;
>   I will not again destroy Ephraim. (11:8–9)

Although the parental image of God in this text is not gender specific, James Luther Mays implies a correlation with the father's compassion toward his runaway son in Jesus's parable:

A shift in the style of the divine saying [in Hosea 11:8] marks a transition from the narrative about Israel's past and present to an impassioned self-questioning by Yahweh. Now the elect people are addressed directly as though the beloved *prodigal son* stood in the presence of his father to hear what he shall say about his failure. The complaint against him (vv. 1–7) has been spoken; the word of complete punishment is expected. But instead the father pours out mingled sorrow and love in rhetorical questions which deny just punishment.[14]

Yet, the absence of gender identity also allows for maternal resonances,[15] especially since the verb (*kamar*) rendered "grows warm and tender" in Hosea 11:8 (NRSV, CEB; "kindled" in NASB, KJV) designates a birth mother's compassion for her infant son's survival in the famous case of the two prostitute-mothers adjudicated by Solomon: "The woman whose son was alive said to the king—because compassion for her son *burned within* [*kamar*] her—'Please, my lord, give her the living boy; certainly do not kill him!'" (1 Kings 3:26). Further, the word for "compassion" in this text, *rahamim* ("loving feeling/compassion"),[16] relates to the singular noun *rehem* ("womb/uterus"), the adjective *rahum* ("compassionate/ merciful"), and the verb *riham* ("show love for/show mercy/have compassion on").[17] The woman's physical womb becomes an apt metaphor for warm, compassionate care of needy persons. While fathers like God (Ps. 103:13) and brothers like Joseph (Gen. 43:30) also demonstrate such deep-seated compassion, the maternal-natal model remains primary.[18]

Luke's Jesus casts himself as a mother hen longing to gather her brood (the people of Jerusalem) under her protective wings; but lamentably, despite his best intentions and efforts, the obstinate "chicks" go their own disastrous way (Luke 13:34–35). Although Luke uses no love/compassion language in this text, the passage clearly reflects a mother's passionate care instincts and marks a companion vignette to the father's compassionate (*splanchnizomai* [15:20]), open-armed welcome of his wayward son. These examples suggest the possibility of finding other traces of parental compassion underlying Jesus's acts of healing and feeding.

14. Mays, *Hosea*, 156 (emphasis added).

15. See Yee, "Book of Hosea," 279: "Hosea 11 does not call God 'mother,' but it does not call God 'father' either. The chapter highlights a parental love that stresses other dimensions of the God/Israel relationship vis-à-vis the marital love described in Hosea 1–3. Such a love is creative . . . instructive . . . tolerant and patient . . . unconditional . . . corrective . . . and a healing love that helps bring a wayward child to wholeness."

16. Holladay, *Concise Hebrew and Aramaic Lexicon*, 337.

17. Holladay, *Concise Hebrew and Aramaic Lexicon*, 337. See the groundbreaking study "Journey of a Metaphor" in Trible, *God and the Rhetoric of Sexuality*, 31–59.

18. See also Jer. 31:20, an important parallel to Hosea 11:8, discussed fully in Trible, *God and the Rhetoric of Sexuality*, 40–50. Note Trible's translation: "Is Ephraim my dear son? my darling child? / For the more I speak of him, the more I do remember him. / Therefore, my womb trembles for him; I will truly show motherly-compassion upon him" (45, 50).

But what about the *feelings* factor, we ask again, this time concerning compassion, mercy, and related notions? In English usage, the word "compassion" closely correlates with "sympathy" and "empathy": *feeling with* ("com-"/"sym-") and *within* ("em-") others. The Stanford professor of biology and neurology Robert Sapolsky pithily defines "compassion" in terms of "where your resonance with someone's distress leads you to actually help"—a nice amalgam of emotion and action, what we might call synergistic sympathy.[19] But the matter becomes more complicated with respect to empathy. The Yale psychologist and philosopher Paul Bloom presses key distinctions between sympathy and empathy. Whereas sympathy, in Bloom's view, reflects considered relational feelings *with* a fellow sufferer stimulating benevolent outreach, he regards empathy as a more objective diagnosis of *what* or *how* someone feels based on personal experience. Consequently, it proves more variable as an altruistic spur;[20] simply knowing how it feels to walk in someone's shoddy shoes does not automatically move you to buy the poor pedestrian new footwear, still less, to give them your shoes! Having walked in such shoes may evoke a kind of empathetic horror to never go that way again, indeed, to run away from the shoeless as fast as possible. Of course, empathy can warm the heart as well as chill it, and it can prompt helpful action. In any case, lending a helping hand does not *require* empathy: one can meet another's need, with or without tender affection, without having experienced the need oneself. Jesus knew times of hunger (Matt. 4:1–2 // Luke 4:1–2; see also Mark 11:12), which may have helped fuel his feeding ministry. But, as we will see, he was also moved with compassion to aid blind persons and a bereft widow, though he himself was never so afflicted.[21]

The professor of psychology and neuroscience Abigail Marsh is more sanguine about empathy's salutary potential to "internally re-create another person's emotion" of being "frightened or distressed, and wanting to make the

19. Sapolsky, *Behave*, 523.

20. Bloom, *Against Empathy*; Bloom, *Just Babies*, 33–37. See also the careful discussion in Sapolsky, *Behave*, 521–52.

21. Concerned that overreliance on sympathetic feeling blunts the moral imperative to care actively for *all* persons, the philosopher-theologian Nicholas Wolterstorff (*Justice: Rights and Wrongs*, 392–93) stresses the significance of "conviction" over compassion: "The affective side of the self cannot, all by itself, expand or even sustain human rights culture. Conviction must also be engaged—conviction of the right sort, of course, conviction that this human being has great worth"; cf. Wolterstorff, *Justice in Love*, 116–18, 131–33. While I take his point, I would argue for a more robust and interactive affective-cognitive-volitive process of ethical decision-making and practice. Compassion is not some squishy sentiment that may or may not bubble up within sensitive souls but rather a sober sympathy born of considered engagement with hurting humanity. Spiritual "conviction" that convinces and motivates reflects passionate commitment to God's law of love.

person feel better."[22] From her extensive research and interviews—including with extreme psychopathic individuals, on the one end, and sacrificial altruists, on the other end (willing, even eager, to donate a kidney to a stranger)—Marsh discovered an apparent causal connection between a person's "empathic responsiveness to others' fear" and a correspondent motivation to allay that fear. Psychopaths demonstrate severely limited capacity to "read" fear in others' faces and "register" it in their brains. By contrast, hyper-altruists display "extra sensitivity" to others' fearful expressions, which stimulates "extra activity . . . to move them past ordinary levels of compassion into something extraordinary." Even more garden-variety altruists seem "to be more strongly affected by the 'field of force' that promotes compassion because the sight of someone suffering affects them more strongly than it affects the average person."[23]

This "strong empathic response to distress cues" could prove counterproductive for would-be helpers and healers by paralyzing them in a web of fear. Taking on too much of others' fear can be overwhelming. Marsh observed, however, that committed caretakers tend to maintain a remarkable equilibrium "to *feel* scared but not *act* scared," to be "both sensitive to fear *and* brave in the face of others' distress."[24]

The connection Marsh observes between love and fear, between the capacity to be moved with compassion and empathic sensitivity to others' alarm, raises a curious issue concerning Jesus's emotional life. As noted before, the Gospels never explicitly attribute fear to Jesus, even though he urges others, "Do not be afraid," and moves to calm their hearts and environments (Matt. 14:24–27; Mark 6:48–52; Luke 12:32; John 6:18–21). While Jesus acknowledges others' fear, he doesn't internalize that fear within himself. While stirred by some distressing emotions, Jesus doesn't operate out of fear, even empathetic fear. Nonetheless, given his extraordinary, compassionate ministry to vulnerable and debilitated persons, we remain attentive to implicit signals of Jesus's emotional attunement to these persons' precarious, frightening situations.

Aristotle's Rhetoric of Mercy and Ethic of Love

Unlike in previous chapters, which I began with Aristotle's seminal treatment of a particular emotion, here I've given primary attention to the Hebrew

22. Marsh, *Fear Factor*, 136.
23. Marsh, *Fear Factor*, 152–53.
24. Marsh, *Fear Factor*, 197, 199 (emphasis original). In terms of neurochemistry, Marsh associates altruists' heightened capacity to feel and fix other's fear with dense concentrations in the amygdala of oxytocin, the hormone necessary for birthing, nursing, and nurturing babies.

Bible—always foundational for Jesus and the Gospels but especially so with
the core emotional virtue of love and its correlates, compassion and mercy.
But Aristotle's insights on these emotions remain worthy of our attention.

Aristotle includes *eleos* in his *Rhetoric* catalog of passions as the umbrella
term for mercy, pity, compassion, sympathy, and associated feelings of "pain
at an apparently destructive or painful event happening to one who does not
deserve it and which a person might expect himself or one of his own to suffer, and this when it seems close to hand" (*Rhet.* 2.8.1 [1385b]). This succinct
definition underscores four elements of someone's misfortune likely to elicit
others' compassion:

- *Intensity*: a notably "destructive or painful" affliction
- *Unfairness*: an arbitrary misfortune not caused or deserved by the
  sufferer
- *Commonality*: a calamity that sparks others' ominous sense of vulnerability to the same experience
- *Proximity*: a pressing crisis that others sense could also engulf them
  soon ("close to hand")[25]

These elements correspond with some of those discussed above: "intensity"
recalls the initial component of Tomkins's script theory; and the last two
points, which stress the felt vulnerability of the sympathizer or empathizer,
relate to Marsh's "fear factor" motivating compassionate action. Aristotle's
point about unfairness raises the key issue of justice, which both complements
and complicates sentiments and judgments of love and mercy. The Torah's
"rule of law" within a covenantal love story relentlessly pursues the dynamic
bonds between justice and love, righteousness and compassion; or, to cite
that immortal prophetic capsule of Torah ethics, enjoining God's people
"to do justice, and to love kindness [mercy], and to walk humbly with your
God" (Mic. 6:8).[26]

Across the Gospel tradition, Jesus blazes a dual-track path of God's love
and justice, which he feels other religious teachers have not adequately pur-
sued. Witness his impassioned critique of certain legal experts: "But woe to
you Pharisees! For you tithe mint and rue and herbs of all kinds, and neglect
justice and the love of God; it is these you ought to have practiced, without

25. I draw here on material in Spencer, *Luke*, 184. See fuller discussion of Aristotle's view in
Nussbaum, *Upheavals of Thought*, 306–15; Konstan, *Emotions*, 210–15; Konstan, *Pity Transformed*, 34–35, 49–51, 128–36.
26. See also Exod. 23:6; Lev. 19:15; Deut. 10:18; 16:19; 24:17; 27:19; 32:4.

neglecting the others" (Luke 11:42). We will see below how concerns about justice intermingle with love and compassion to drive his acts of feeding and healing.

In *Nicomachean Ethics*, Aristotle breaks down three "kinds of friendly love," all involving some form of "reciprocal love" whereby "those who love each other wish for the good things for each other" (8.3 [1156a.5–9]). For the most part, Aristotle uses *phileō* for "love" in this discussion but not exclusively. He also uses *agapaō*, more or less synonymously, as well as *stergō* (a verb commonly used for familial love in classical Greek) and a form of *erōs* for "erotic love." Aristotle envisions a three-dimensional framework of loving relationships.[27]

- *Utilitarian*: "Those who love [*philousin*] on account of utility feel affection [*stergousi*] for the sake of their own good" (8.3 [1156a.14–16]). Here transactional pragmatism prevails. Both lover and loved, friend and befriended, benefit from each other, though not necessarily in mutual proportion and not because of who they are as persons but merely because of what they offer. They receive benefit from, but do not *take advantage* of, the other.
- *Hedonic*: "Those who love [*philousin*] on account of pleasure [*hēdonēn*], for people are fond of [*agapōsi*] those who are witty, not because they are of a certain sort, but because they are pleasant to them" (8.3 [1156a.12–14]). The "young" fit this category because of their propensity to "passion" (*pathos*), not least that directed toward "erotic love" (*erotikoi*) (8.3 [1156a.332–1156b.3]). Aristotle has no problem with pursuing friends and lovers for pleasure (in moderation) but underscores again that such love should be more object (pleasure) than subject (person) oriented.
- *Complete*: "Complete [*teleia*] friendship [*philia*] is the friendship of those who are good and alike in point of virtue. . . . Each person involved is good simply and for the friend" (8.3 [1156b.7–14]). Unlike with utilitarian and hedonic relationships, complete love matches do not depend on goods the couple provide to one another but on the inherent goodness of each individual: "The lover [*erastēs*] is pleased by seeing the beloved [*erōmenos*], the beloved by being attended to by his lover . . . on account of who they themselves are" (8.4 [1157a.5–8, 18–19]). Such ties prove stronger than those based purely on usefulness or pleasure. "Complete" friendships include useful and pleasant benefits but are not determined by them.

27. See Solomon, *Love*, 11–15.

Aristotle affirms loving passion in terms of pleasant feelings as a periodic part of complete love but not as the permanent whole. Apart from John 15:9–11, where Jesus connects his "joy" with love for his disciples, the Gospels say nothing about the pleasure Jesus derives from his compassionate acts toward others. And only the Fourth Gospel portrays Jesus's close, loving bond of friendship with his disciples "to the end [*telos*]" (John 13:1; cf. 15:13–15). The Synoptic examples of Jesus's loving acts are episodic, not telic or "complete," with needy persons he never encounters again. Nevertheless, even absent hedonic and telic language, we should scan these loving scenes for traces of what Jesus himself may receive emotionally and what "ends" he promotes. Are his compassionate, "agapic" ministrations wholly self-denying, dispassionate acts of service unaffected by fickle feelings? Or is Jesus "moved with compassion" in a more emotive-active process?

In this chapter, I focus on a sizeable group of texts from the Synoptic Gospels featuring Jesus's compassion and mercy, flagged by *splanchnizomai* ("move with compassion") and/or *eleeō* ("have mercy") language. In the next chapter, I will turn to examine the singular case of Jesus's "love" (*agapaō*) for a wealthy inquirer in Mark and the sequence of Jesus's loving treatment of his beloved disciple(s) "to the end" of the Fourth Gospel.

Loving from the Gut: Explaining *Splanchna* and Elucidating *Eleos*

We continue to negotiate the semantic tension between not loading excessive emotional freight onto single words and yet recognizing that word study can enhance emotional intelligence,[28] providing that emotion words are interpreted in their narrative and social-cultural contexts. We sketched above a background portrait of love-related notions of "compassion" and "mercy" in the Hebrew Bible and Aristotle's classical Greek writings. As we now seek to understand the emotional force behind Jesus's acts of compassion (*splanchna*) and mercy (*eleos*) in our Greek Gospels, we foreground the more immediate literary milieu of these terms in common (*koinē*) Hellenistic-Jewish usage.

The plural noun *splanchna* refers anatomically to "inner parts of the body, especially the intestines,"[29] or "the viscera, inward parts, entrails,"[30] "bowels," or "guts." The Maccabean literature reflects this usage in the grisly context

28. See the emphasis on "affective labeling" or "labeling emotions with a nuanced vocabulary" in the work of the director of the Yale Center for Emotional Intelligence, Marc Brackett, *Permission to Feel*, 19, 55, 104–20.

29. L&N 1:101.

30. BDAG 938.

of the Greek-Syrian ruler Antiochus IV's torturous execution of devout Jews, which justified a retributive gut-punch:

> As soon as [Antiochus] stopped speaking he was seized with a pain in his bowels [*splanchnōn*], for which there was no relief, and with sharp internal tortures— and that very justly, for he had tortured the bowels [*splanchna*] of others with many and strange afflictions. . . . And so it came about that he fell out of his chariot as it was rushing along, and the fall was so hard as to torture every limb of his body. . . . And so the ungodly man's body swarmed with worms, and while he was still living in anguish and pain, his flesh rotted away, and because of the stench the whole army felt revulsion at his decay. (2 Macc. 9:5–9)

The book of Acts reports the fate of Jesus's betrayer Judas in similar terms of severe intestinal distress: "Now this man acquired a field with the reward of his wickedness; and falling headlong, he burst open in the middle and all his bowels [*splanchna*] gushed out" (1:18).

For their part, those martyrs whom Antiochus subjected to the rack and fire valiantly sacrificed their bodies and bowels out of faithfulness to God's law. As Eleazar defied Antiochus, "Nor will I transgress the sacred oaths of my ancestors concerning the keeping of the law, not even if you gouge out my eyes and burn my entrails [*splanchna*]" (4 Macc. 5:29–30). Which is exactly what Antiochus did to two of seven martyr-brothers during his reign of terror: "They immediately brought him [brother #3] to the wheel, and while his vertebrae were being dislocated by this, he saw his own flesh torn all around and drops of blood flowing from his entrails [*splanchnōn*]" (10:8); "they led him [brother #6] to the wheel. . . . His back was broken, and he was roasted from underneath. To his back they applied sharp spits that had been heated in the fire, and pierced his ribs so that his entrails [*splanchna*] were burned through" (11:17–19).

With all this lurid language, one might associate *splanchna* more readily with the emotion of disgust than with compassion. But as vital organs of the gastrointestinal system, bowels, when functioning properly (not ruptured or roasted!), are as emotionally neutral as they are physically necessary. Any bowel discomfort we feel after a spicy meal might make us cranky but should not send us into an emotional tailspin. Yet, where the science of gastroenterology offers scant emotional insight, the art of metaphor and metonymy, whereby a bodily organ may evoke associated ideas or states of being, has a long history of serving emotional interests: think of "heart" representing the seat of emotions, especially love.[31] Everyone

31. See Mol, "*Head* and *Heart*."

understands that saying "I love you with all my heart" has nothing to do with pumping blood and everything to do with feeling affection. As strange as it may sound to our ears, in the Greek biblical world, "bowels," like "heart," functioned as a metonym of emotions, something akin to our "gut feelings."[32] And ironically, given the torturous treatment of literal bowels just discussed, these organs could still be viewed as figurative reservoirs of love and compassion.

A remarkable double twist in the Maccabean story features the emotional response of the seven martyred brothers' *mother*, forced to witness each son's horrific death before facing her own torture and execution. The first twist shifts from the sons' physically wracked bowels to a mother's emotionally wrenched "bowels" in response to her children's suffering: "Observe how complex [*polyplokos*[33]] is a mother's love for her children [*philosteknias storgē*], which draws everything toward an emotion [of sympathy] felt in her inmost parts [*splanchnōn sympatheian*]" (4 Macc. 14:13). Such intense, instinctive maternal feeling is rooted in nature: "Even unreasoning animals, as well as human beings, have a sympathy [*sympatheian*] and parental love [*storgēn*] for their offspring" (14:14). While fathers could share in this emotional bond, they could not do so at the gut level of mothers, "who because of their birth pangs have a deeper sympathy [*sympathesteras*] toward their offspring than do the fathers" (15:4). Accordingly, we expect the bereft Maccabean mother to be an emotional wreck, deserving of our greatest sympathy, since "in seven pregnancies she had implanted in herself tender love [*philostorgian*] toward [her sons], and because of the many pains she suffered with each of them she had sympathy [*sympatheian*] for them" (15:6–7).

In the second twist, however, the Maccabean mother defies such natural emotional-maternal "logic" in favor of virile, rational logic (*logismos*): "The mother showed her greater love [*ēgapēsan*] for piety [*eusebeian*] that . . . preserves [her sons] to everlasting life," greater than natural maternal affection in this life (4 Macc. 15:3 NETS). Further, "How great and how many torments the mother then suffered as her sons were tortured on the wheel and with the hot irons! But devout reason [*eusebēs logismos*], giving her heart a man's courage in the very midst of her emotions [*splanchna*], strengthened her to disregard, for the time, her parental love [*philoteknian*]" (15:22–23 NRSV). By resisting "the flood of [her] emotions [*pathōn*]" (15:32), she boldly

32. See BDAG 938 on *splanchnon*: "As often in the ancient world, inner body parts served as referents for psychological aspects: of the seat of emotions."

33. The term connotes "much-twisting, complex, intricate," according to Liddell and Scott, *Liddell and Scott's Greek-English Lexicon, Abridged*, 574.

caps off her sons' sacrifices with her own violent martyrdom, becoming an exceptional model of stalwart loyalty to God and country, the "mother of the nation, vindicator of the law, champion of piety" (15:29 NETS) (think Mother Russia, Lady Liberty, Lady Justice).

This exemplary role, however, as "vindicator of the law," emphasizing dispassionate, dutiful obedience to God's precepts at all costs, including the ultimate sacrifice of a mother's life and her sons' lives, severely saps the holistic, heartfelt energy pulsing throughout the Torah's covenantal law of love that was sketched above. Moreover, by effectively disemboweling the mother's natural affections (*splanchna*) for her sons to serve a supposedly higher, more rational rule of law and love, the Maccabean-Stoic model all but severs the creational-parental cords of love, compassion, and mercy binding together Father/Mother God and his/her children in the Bible.

Consonant with the Hebrew Bible's visceral, maternal metaphor of compassion as fervent, womb-like childcare, in classical Greek *splanchna* could refer to a woman's actual womb: for example, "from her womb [*splanchnōn*] and her sweet birth-pangs Iamus came right away into the light" (Pindar, *Ol.* 6.43).[34] Yet the conceptual transfer of *splanchna* from internal organs to maternal loving feelings and compassionate care doesn't occur until the Hellenistic period, and by then the physical vehicle of the metaphor seems less focused on the womb than on gastrointestinal innards.[35] Even so, as we've seen, the Hellenistic Jewish Maccabean literature closely connects the mother's deep affection (*splanchna*) for her seven sons with her carrying and birthing them (4 Macc. 15:6–7).[36] (This is by no means to deny the profound love that adoptive mothers, caregivers, and other women [and men] have for their children.) Contemporary Catholic theology has seized on uterine imagery to illuminate God's core nature of compassion and mercy, epitomized in Pope Francis's *The Name of God Is Mercy*, coordinated with the Holy Year of Mercy (2015–16): "The Greek verb that indicates this compassion is *splanchnizomai*, which derives from the word that indicates internal organs or the mother's womb. It is similar to the love of a father and mother who

---

34. All Pindar quotations are from Pindar, *Odes*. See also Pindar, *Nem.* 1.35: "When the son of Zeus suddenly came out of his mother's womb [*splanchnōn*] into the brilliant light, escaping her birth"; cf. Sophocles, *Antigone*, lines 1065–66; Mirguet, *Early History of Compassion*, 34–36; Koester, "σπλάγχνον," 548–49.

35. Koester, "σπλάγχνον," 549.

36. Cf. other LXX texts that associate passionate, parental feelings with inner parts: "When one cherishes a son, one will bind up his wounds, and with every cry one's insides [*splanchna*] will be troubled" (Sir. 30:7 NETS). "She [Wisdom] also . . . recognized the righteous man and preserved him blameless with God and kept him strong in the face of compassion [*splanchnois*] for his child" (Wis. 10:5 NETS).

are profoundly moved by their own son; it is a visceral love. God loves us in this way, with compassion and mercy."[37]

With or without uterine associations, "compassion" (*splanchna*) and "mercy/pity" (*eleos*) closely affiliate in Greek scriptural usage.

A just person takes pity on the lives of his cattle, but the feelings [*splanchna*] of the impious are without mercy [*aneleēmona*]. (Prov. 12:10 NETS)

He who laughs at the poor provokes his maker. . . . But he who has compassion will find mercy [*episplanchnizomenos elēthēsetai*]. (Prov. 17:5 NETS)

By the tender mercy [*splanchna eleous*] of our God, the dawn from on high will break upon us. (Luke 1:78)

They [two blind men] shouted even more loudly, "Have mercy on [*Eleēson*] us, Lord, Son of David!" . . . Moved with compassion [*splanchnistheis*], Jesus touched their eyes. (Matt. 20:31, 34)

When [a Samaritan] saw [the robbed man], he was moved with pity [*esplanchnisthē*]. He went to him . . . and took care of him. . . . "Which, . . . do you think, was a neighbor to the man who fell into the hands of the robbers?" He [the lawyer Jesus addressed] said, "The one who showed him mercy [*eleos*]." (Luke 10:33–37)

While, as noted above, one can theoretically perform compassionate and merciful acts with little to no emotional involvement, these examples reinforce a strong emotive component behind such beneficent service.

A work of Hellenistic-Jewish biblical interpretation, the *Testament of Zebulun*, part of the pseudonymous *Testaments of the Twelve Patriarchs*, also develops related themes of compassion and mercy in vivid language. Indeed, some manuscripts of this *Testament* title the piece "On Good-Compassion and Mercy" (*Peri eusplanchnias kai eleous*).[38] The writing stages Zebulun's poignant deathbed reflections on that heinous family tragedy when Zebulun and nine brothers sell their younger sibling Joseph into slavery and scheme to inform their father, Jacob, that his beloved boy has been killed by a wild beast. Embellishing the Genesis narrative, the testamentary Zebulun aims to distance himself from his malicious brothers on emotional grounds. Although

---

37. Pope Francis, *Name of God Is Mercy*, 92 (cf. 113); see also the noted theologian Cardinal Walter Kasper, *Mercy*, 41–44.

38. Mirguet, *Early History of Compassion*, 51; see 49–57 for fuller discussion of compassion and mercy in the *Testament of Zebulun*; cf. Mirguet, "Emotional Responses," 848–57, and responses to that article by Konstan, "Varieties of Pity"; Lateiner, "Pain and Pity."

ultimately complicit in Joseph's ill-treatment, Zebulun claims he acted "in ignorance." Even as he weeps "much in secret," he keeps silent for fear of his brothers' reprisal (*T. Zeb.* 1.5–7).[39] In the heat of the moment, as Joseph pleads for mercy and for consideration of their father's "deep feelings" (*splanchna*) (2.2), Zebulun confesses, "I was moved to pity and began to weep; my courage grew weak and all the substance of my inner being [*splanchnōn*] became faint within my soul. Joseph wept, and I with him; my heart pounded, the joints of my body shook and I could not stand. And when he saw me crying with him, while the others were coming to kill him, he rushed behind me beseeching them" (2.4–6). Being so "moved with compassion [*splanchnizomenos*] for Joseph," Zebulun refuses to eat anything for two days, while Joseph languishes in a pit before being sold to traders (4.1–5).

For his good intentions and emotions, though not accompanied by sufficient action, Zebulun claims "the Lord blessed me," granting him and his children good health and success, even as his brothers and their children became ill and died "because they did not act in mercy [*eleos*] out of their inner compassion [*splanchnois*]" (*T. Zeb.* 5.1–5). But Zebulun's emotional virtue, what we might call his "good heart," was not just a source of reward for him, but also a spur to benevolence. Emotional attitude mobilizes ethical action. Zebulun became a pioneering boat-builder and fisherman, supplying fish for his and his father's family. He also "tended the flock of my brothers" in winter, when fishing slowed down. Moreover, "being compassionate" (*splanchnizomenos*) spilled over to outsiders, as he extended "some of my catch to every stranger" and provided clothing and other goods for "each person according to need" (6.1–7.1).

The dying Zebulun thus exhorts his children to emulate his compassionate and merciful passions and practices, in faithful consonance with the Lord's character, obedience to the Lord's command, and in assurance of receiving the Lord's compassion and mercy in return: "You also, my children, have compassion [*esplanchnian*] toward every person with mercy [*eleei*], in order that the Lord may be compassionate [*splanchnistheis*] and merciful [*eleēsē*] to you. . . . Whenever [God] finds compassionate mercy [*splanchna eleous*], in that person he will dwell. To the extent that a man has compassion [*splanchnizetai*] on his neighbor, to that extent the Lord has mercy on him" (*T. Zeb.* 8.1–3).

Zebulun finally stresses, to his own advantage, the element of forgiveness, which the Hebrew Bible closely connects with divine compassion and mercy (see discussion above on Exod. 34:6–7). As if clearing his conscience one last

39. Quotations of the *Testament of Zebulun* are from Kee, "Testaments of the Twelve Patriarchs," 805–7.

time, Zebulun holds up Joseph as the exemplar of God's gracious mercy—especially toward Zebulun! "For when we went down to Egypt, Joseph did not hold a grudge against us. *When he saw me*, he was *moved with compassion* [*esplanchnisthē*]. Whomever you see, do not harbor resentment, my children: love [*agapate*] one another, and do not calculate the wrong done by each to his brothers. . . . He who recalls evil receives neither compassion nor mercy [*splanchna eleous*]" (*T. Zeb.* 8.4–6).

The Maccabean mother and *Testament* patriarch Zebulun take emotional stances that are polar opposites: the former stanching her maternal gut feelings of compassion/mercy to remain faithful to God's law; the latter venting his fraternal gut feelings of compassion/mercy in an attempt to rescue the beloved Joseph—an attempt which fails miserably but which Zebulun smugly touts on later reflection. Yet both cases attest to "bowels of mercy" (*splanchna eleous*) as a deep-seated image of fellow feeling and passionate concern, especially motherly and brotherly love. We now turn to see how Jesus manages such feelings toward vulnerable persons.

Feeding the Sheep (Matt. 14:13–16; 15:32; Mark 6:34–37; 8:1–3)

Matthew 14–15 and Mark 6:1–8:10 share a sequence of events running from the beheading of John the Baptist to the feeding of the four thousand, flanking an earlier mass feeding of five thousand people. The feeding theme pervades this unit, both positively in the two major feedings and more peculiarly in the Herodian banquet scene (which serves up John's severed head on a platter [Matt. 14:1–12 // Mark 6:14–29]) and in the Canaanite/Syrophoenician woman's tense debate with Jesus over the care and "feeding" of children (Matt. 15:21–28 // Mark 7:24–30). Also, these two stories happen to be highly emotive episodes involving passionate, purposeful mothers of daughters, albeit in quite different ways.[40] On the one hand, Herodias—the wife Herod (Antipas) had taken from his brother (Herod) Philip illicitly, according to John (who denounced the marriage)—uses her dancing daughter to manipulate her husband into executing John. In the other incident, the Canaanite/Syrophoenician woman persuades Jesus, despite his initial resistance, that her daughter needs to be "fed" too, which in this case means delivering the daughter from her demon-tormented state.

Amid this emotional section in the first two Gospels, a section related to families and feedings, mothers and multitudes, Jesus "has compassion"

40. See Spencer, *Dancing Girls*, 47–75.

(*splanchnizomai*) on two hungry crowds (Matt. 14:14 // Mark 6:34; Matt. 15:32 // Mark 8:2). In the first episode, five thousand seekers pursue Jesus across a lake to a deserted area where he seeks rest and privacy with his disciples. So intent is the crowd on seeing Jesus that, even though he travels by boat and they by foot, they're waiting for Jesus when he steps ashore. How will he respond to this frustration of his retreat plans? Rather than putting the people off, even temporarily while he recuperates, his "compassion" kicks in immediately. No deliberation or negotiation, just instinctual, gut-level compassion, as if Jesus could respond in no other way.

And, as we should expect by now, emotion drives action. In Matthew's version, his compassion first motivates him to *healing* ministry (he "cured their sick" [Matt. 14:14]); in Mark's account, "he began to *teach* them many things" (Mark 6:34). As the day wears on toward evening, however, the people's nutritional need becomes apparent and problematic, given that they haven't packed any food and now find themselves in a remote location. Not matching their Lord's compassion, Jesus's disciples urge him to "send them away so that they may . . . buy something for themselves to eat" (6:36). Enough is enough: their alone time with Jesus has been curtailed by his daylong service to these masses; time to dismiss them to fend for themselves. But Jesus will have none of it. His compassionate care is not merely impulsive but durative (see discussion of Tomkins's script theory above in this chapter); and it is not selective but comprehensive, nurturing the whole person through teaching, healing, and now feeding.

More than natural instinct, however, fuels Jesus's compassion. Mark explains the rationale for Jesus's emotion: "As he went ashore, he saw a great crowd; and he had compassion for them, *because they were like sheep without a shepherd*" (Mark 6:34).[41] Combined with the desert setting, the poignant pastoral picture is one of vulnerable, wandering animals in a barren, perilous environment with no one to provide for and protect them. Hence, reprising God's and Moses's roles in Israel's wilderness trek, Jesus guides and feeds the needy multitude as their loving shepherd (recall also Hosea 11:1–4). Without the burden of abandoning a loved one on his heart, as the testamentary Zebulun carried for Joseph, Jesus still affiliates with Zebulun's compassionate sheep-tending of his brothers' flocks and fish-providing for the hungry (Mark 6:38–42), though Jesus needs no boat, as Zebulun did, to catch them. Moreover, the use of sympathetic zoomorphic language for people echoes

41. Matthew places this reference in an earlier context related to Jesus's overall ministry of proclamation and healing (Matt. 9:36). He also adds that the shepherd-less crowds were "harassed and helpless" ("troubled and abandoned" NAB; "distressed and downcast" NASB).

Zebulun's direct call for compassionate treatment of humans and animals alike, in service to all God's creation: "Now, my children, I tell you to keep the Lord's commands; show mercy [*eleos*] to your neighbor, have compassion [*eusplanchnian*] on all, not only human beings but to dumb animals" (*T. Zeb.* 5:1).

As loving, pastoral nurture overlaps with familial and neighborly care in the Hebrew Bible and *Testament of Zebulun*, so too in the New Testament Gospels, if we bring Luke into the picture. The good Samaritan's merciful tending to the health and well-being of the beaten traveler, motivated by his compassion (*esplanchnisthē*) and mercy (*eleos*) toward the victim (Luke 10:33, 37), models the love toward neighbor demanded by the Torah (10:25–37). And the father's embrace and feeding of his distant, destitute son, again spurred by deep-level compassion (*esplanchnisthē*) (15:20–24), parallels a shepherd's care for one wayward sheep in the wilderness (15:3–7). While Jesus's pastoral care for the desert throng in Mark is not directly linked to parental feelings, his passionate nurturing instincts and actions in the face of resistance (his disciples want to "send them away" [Mark 6:36]) correlate with the Syrophoenician mother's dogged commitment to meeting her daughter's physical needs (healing and "feeding") in the face—ironically—of Jesus's initial brush-off (7:27) (in Matthew's version, it's his disciples again who urge him to "send her away" [Matt. 15:23; cf. 14:15]).

In the second incident involving a hungry crowd, four thousand people come to Jesus, again in the desert. Here both Mark and Matthew focus exclusively on Jesus's feeding ministry (without prior teaching or healing), motivated by his compassion for their prolonged hunger (extending over three days rather than one) and concern for their long journey back home. Moreover, the Gospel accounts now present Jesus's feelings in his own words: "I have compassion [*splanchnizomai*] for the crowd, because they have been with me now for three days and have nothing to eat. If I send them away hungry to their homes, they will faint on the way—and some of them have come from a great distance [*makrothen*]" (Mark 8:2–3 // Matt. 15:32). The datum in Mark (dropped by Matthew) that some people had traveled a long way resonates with the father's compassionate longing (*splanchnizomai*) for his destitute son "while he was still a long way off [*makran apechontos*]" (Luke 15:20 NIV, CEB; cf. 15:13).

Mark splices Jesus's second compassionate feeding between two emotional episodes in which Jesus "sighs," the only times he does so throughout the Gospels. In the preceding story in which Jesus heals a deaf man with a speech impediment, Jesus lifts his eyes to heaven and "sighs" (*estenaxen*) before ordering the man's ears to "be opened" (Mark 7:34); in the ensuing incident, Jesus sighs (*anastenaxas*) "deeply in his spirit" at some Pharisees' insolent request for a heavenly sign (8:11–12)—right after he miraculously fed four thousand people! While the English word "sigh" can convey a range of emotions from pleasure and relief ("ahh"), on one side, to frustration and pain ("aargh"), on the other, the Greek root *stenaz*-, related to *stenos* ("narrow"), slots on the second side, carrying a sense of gut-clenching "groaning" in response to one's own or others' suffering. The compound *anastenazō* used for Jesus's frustration with the Pharisees (8:12) suggests an intensified "groaning sound from within," particularly when combined here with "in his spirit" to connote a "sigh from the depths of one's being."[42]

Thus, Jesus's compassion (*splanch*-) for the hungry correlates with his lament to God about the deaf man's disability and his complaint to the Pharisees about their failure to regard his feeding miracle as a bona fide sign of God's saving realm. Jesus's gracious feelings and actions toward hungry travelers far from home coalesce with his groaning sympathies toward sufferers. On a gut level, Jesus feels others' pain, moving him to provide necessary aid. To what degree this compassion flows from his *personal* sense of suffering and vulnerability, his empathetic identification with the afflicted, is not clear and probably beside the point (recall the discussion of empathy above).

Jesus himself has no hearing problem or speech defect, any more than he has serious nutritional deficiencies, though he knew hunger pangs from time to time, as mentioned above. But once he embarks on his public ministry, he lives as an itinerant with no permanent "place to lay his head" (Matt. 8:20 CEB // Luke 9:58 CEB; cf. Mark 6:7–11), dependent on others' hospitality. He thus has solidarity—indeed, we might assume, sympathy or fellow-feeling—with the plight of desperate people roaming (like "sheep") from village to village and into wilderness areas seeking help to survive. He hears the "groaning" of his beloved, beleaguered people, as God did during Israel's enslavement in Egypt (see *stenagmos* in Acts 7:34), groans with them, and moves to provide critical material aid.

More than honor and duty drive Jesus's feeding ministry. He's no philanthropist boosting his social reputation by generous almsgiving. Still less is he a palace-dweller and party-thrower like Herod and Caesar, currying favor with cronies and keeping the rabble in line with periodic gluts of "bread and circuses." Moreover, he's no functional social worker or religious administrator

---

42. Danker with Krug, *Concise Greek-English Lexicon*, 29. Closely connecting groaning with a "narrow," constricting experience, see Theodotion's version of Sus. 1:22: "And Sousanna groaned [*anestenaxen*] and said, 'Things are narrow [*stena*] for me on all sides. For if I do this, it is death for me; if I do not, I will not escape your hands'" (NETS). On connecting sighing/groaning with suffering, see Rom. 8:18–26; 2 Cor. 5:2–4.

manning a food bank (no disrespect to such needful work). Torah commandments to love neighbor and stranger root deep in Jesus's heart and mind,
innards and intellect, springing up from his *splanchna*, as it were, gushing
out from his guts into a feast of belly-filling sustenance for myriads: "And
all ate and were filled; and they took up twelve baskets full of broken pieces
and of the fish" (Mark 6:42–43); "They ate and were filled; and they took up
the broken pieces left over, seven baskets full (8:8–9).

Healing the Blind (Matt. 9:27–31; 20:29–34; Mark 10:46–52)

Giving sight to the blind is a characteristic demonstration of Jesus's messianic
mission (Matt.11:2–5; Luke 4:18; 7:18–22). All four Gospels feature memo-
rable incidents. Mark and John feature unique stories: the former reports a
snippet involving Jesus's two-stage healing of a blind man in Bethsaida (Mark
8:22–26); the latter relates a lengthy account of Jesus providing sight to a
blind man on the Sabbath, which led to the man's expulsion from the synagogue (John 9:1–41). Both involve the therapeutic application of Jesus's saliva
(Mark 8:23; John 9:6). Any dramatic eye-opening of the blind is inherently an
emotional event for the newly sighted person and for witnesses of the miracle,
but these two Gospel accounts do not accentuate the emotional effects.

The most emotional episodes surrounding Jesus's treatment of blind persons are the Synoptic cases where one or two blind men cry out to Jesus
"Have mercy [*eleēson*] on me/us, Son of David!" Mark has the most vivid
version involving a man named Bartimaeus (Mark 10:46–52). In Luke, the
blind man remains anonymous, setting the stage for the more prominent tax
collector named Zacchaeus, who overcomes his sight-challenged condition
(shortness, not blindness) to "see" Jesus and experience his "salvation" (Luke
18:35–19:10). Matthew, interestingly, creates what amounts to a double dou-
bling of the incident, featuring *two* (anonymous) blind men in *two* parallel
accounts: one at the same juncture as Mark's, immediately preceding Jesus's
final entry into Jerusalem (Matt. 20:29–34) and the other much earlier in the
narrative (9:27–31).

Mark's Bartimaeus story bursts with affective energy exhibited by the
blind man but curiously *not by Jesus*. Whereas we expect Mark to present
Jesus with more raw emotion than we find in the other Gospels, this episode
bucks that trend. For his part, Bartimaeus twice shouts out loudly, pleading
for Jesus's mercy over the "stern" objections of the large retinue around
Jesus. In response, Jesus stops and simply announces, "Call him," prompting
the crowd to urge Bartimaeus, "Take courage" (*tharsei*) (Mark 10:49 NAB,

NASB)—precisely what Jesus himself said to his terrified, storm-threatened disciples in 6:50. Excitedly, Bartimaeus sheds his outer garment and springs up to meet the sound of Jesus's summons. Then Jesus rather coolly asks, "What do you want me to do for you?" (10:51)—exactly the same question he just posed to James and John, in response to their impudent assertion, "We want you to do for us whatever we ask of you" (10:35). Unlike with these sons of Zebedee, however, where Jesus puts off their request for privileged seats in God's realm, he grants Bartimaeus's supplication, "Let me see again," though with little flair or fanfare (no spit, mudpack, laying on of hands). Jesus straightforwardly states, "Go; your faith has made you well" (10:52).

Though he commends the blind man's faith/trust and heals him, Jesus seems more interested in dispatching this ministerial duty and proceeding on his way into Jerusalem. In fact, the newly sighted Bartimaeus does not "go" away but rather follows Jesus "on the way" (Mark 10:52). Although Jesus doesn't discourage him from tagging along, as he did the Gerasene demoniac (5:18–19), neither does he welcome him on the journey or appear to think any more about him. This portrayal of the healing Jesus is oddly clinical: he does what's necessary to help the blind man but no more than that, in no way matching the man's intense feelings or being particularly moved by his condition.

So what? Must Jesus be touchy-feely in all his merciful, compassionate acts? Must he always be graded on his bedside (or in this case, roadside) manner? We're back to that issue of emotion's *necessary* connection to ethics. Feelings might be nice but are hardly necessary to a salutary outcome. Since Jesus performs the act of mercy the blind beggar desires, isn't that all that matters? Amen and amen. Now that he sees again, does he wish Jesus would put a little sugar on top to sweeten the experience? To even ask the question seems silly. If a programmed robot could successfully perform the life-saving heart surgery I needed, why should I quibble about such a cold mechanical procedure? (Of course, a lot of post-op TLC would still be helpful.) If we must make excuses for Jesus's more functional, less emotional treatment of Bartimaeus, the stress of his own impending brutal death by week's end seems sufficient (see 10:32–34, 38–39, 45).

Mark uncharacteristically portrays a non-emotional Jesus, and Matthew also surprises by adding emotional touches to Jesus's healing operation reported in Mark. Both Matthean scenes depict Jesus touching the eyes of the blind men to restore their sight (Matt. 9:29; 20:34). While Jesus often heals via some form of tactile contact, touching someone's eyes is particularly unusual and personal. Even without an object, the Greek verb for "touch" (*haptō*) can refer to intimate contact, including sexual engagement (1 Cor. 7:1; cf. Gen.

20:4, 6; Ruth 2:9 NASB; Prov. 6:29 LXX). And as the body's principal external *feeling* organ, the *hand* connects closely with internal emotions in an affective energy circuit, not least in matters of love and concern.

If I am stirred by your attractiveness or, alternatively, your affliction, a natural response may be to reach out (if socially appropriate) to hold your hand, thereby communicating affection or sympathy, which you will feel in some manner (hopefully positive) in your "heart" or "gut" as well as on your skin. Recall that the Shema passage links "heart" and "hand" as prime sites of inscribing God's commandments, sealing the covenant of love with Israel (Deut. 6:5–6, 8).[43] Recent psychological research confirms our intuitive sense of connection between tactile and emotional feeling.[44] Common English metaphors like "That song really touched my heart," "Her voice is silky smooth," "He rubbed me the wrong way," and "Don't be so touchy," trade on this dual sense of feeling. Or in more elegant terms, as Finland's national poet Johan Ludwig Runeberg imagines, "All the emotions that spring up in our bosom" may display as "pantomimic expressions of the hands."[45]

Still, it's possible that, like an ophthalmologist, Jesus touches the eyes of his blind "patients" as part of his medical duty, simply performing the job "at hand." Yet Matthew concludes the latter blind men's story with an explicit statement of Jesus's compassionate motivation: "Moved with compassion [*splanchnistheis*], Jesus touched their eyes. Immediately they regained their sight and followed him" (Matt. 20:34).

Although Jesus is never visually impaired himself, he is deeply pierced by the two blind men's double "Have mercy on us" cry, and his gut emotional response flows out through his hands. *Eleos* ("mercy") and *splanchna* ("compassion") flow together to form, as it were, a powerful, sight-restoring eye salve. Though these words suggest an intense sympathetic experience for Jesus, as much as for the blind men—an intensely "destructive or painful" experience that Aristotle associated with mercy/pity—it would be stretching Matthew's brief report to stress that Jesus senses this pair's blindness as an unfair (undeserved) condition or one that Jesus anticipated was proximate for himself, in conformity with Aristotle's additional judgments about mercy/pity (see *Rhet.* 2.8.1 [1385b]). No judicial calculus affects this merciful healing

43. On the hand-heart nexus in biblical literature, see also Job 31:7; Pss. 28:2–7; 78:72; Prov. 6:16–18; 16:5; Eccles. 7:26; Lam. 2:19; 3:41; Sir. 2:12; 48:19–20.

44. See Hertenstein, Keltner, et al., "Touch Communicates"; Hertenstein and Keltner, "Gender"; Hertenstein, Holmes, et al., "Communication of Emotion"; Linden, *Touch*; Spencer, "Woman's Touch," 79–84.

45. Quoted in Tallis, *Hand*, 72.

scene.⁴⁶ Jesus freely and fervently provides healing with no discussion of forgiveness. As for his own vulnerability, however, we again note that, though not anxious about being literally blinded, Matthew's Jesus is acutely aware of his imminent demise as he nears Jerusalem (Matt. 20:17–19)—a death, as it happens, that will shroud him and "the whole land" in sudden darkness (blindness) (27:45).

Releasing the Seized (Mark 9:14–29)

In the poignant Synoptic story of Jesus granting a desperate father's plea for help with his spirit-seized, convulsive son, each of the first three Gospels provides its own special affective touch. Matthew presents it as another case of Jesus granting an impassioned petition for mercy, like that lodged by the pairs of blind men. In this case, the distraught father kneels before Jesus and implores: "Lord, have mercy [*eleēson*] on my son, for he is an epileptic [*selēniazetai*] and he suffers terribly [*kakōs paschei*]; he often falls into the fire and often into the water" (Matt. 17:15). Only Matthew reinforces the boy's vulnerability by attributing his condition not only to demonic assault (17:18) but also to cosmic-celestial attack, as the term for "epileptic," following the medical mythology of the day, relates to the "moon" (*selēnē*), being "moonstruck," "experienc[ing] epileptic seizures . . . associated with transcendent powers of the moon" (see 4:24).⁴⁷ Luke adds the boy's terrible manifestations of shrieking and foaming at the mouth when in the throes of a seizure. But perhaps the most heartrending part of Luke's report is the father's "shouting" to Jesus from the crowd: "Teacher, I beg you to look at my son; he is *my only child* [*monogenēs moi*]" (Luke 9:38; cf. 7:12; 8:42).

As moving as Matthew's and Luke's accounts are, however, Mark's longer version raises the scene's emotional temperature with more awful effects of the boy's epileptic fits described by the father (Mark 9:17–18, 22) and exhibited by a grand mal seizure the boy has right then and there, at Jesus's feet (9:20). Moreover, Mark recounts Jesus's emotional reactions in much more detail (though without using typical emotion terms) as he engages with four parties, all caught up in the heat of the crisis surrounding the afflicted son: disputative *scribes*, an awestruck *crowd*, the distressed *father*, and befuddled *disciples*

---

46. See the explicit statement of the Johannine Jesus in a comparable scenario: "Neither this [blind] man nor his parents sinned; he was born blind so that God's works might be revealed in him" (John 9:3).

47. BDAG 919.

(nine of the twelve).[48] Further, Jesus and his three closest disciples (Peter, James, and John) encounter this tense scene already in progress, following their own head-spinning ordeal on a mountaintop where Jesus's appearance was brilliantly transfigured, Moses and Elijah materialized and spoke with Jesus, and Peter and partners were understandably "terrified" (*ekphoboi*) and mystified (9:6; see 9:2–13).

Jesus first notices a group of scribes "arguing" (*syzētountas*) with the disciples (not involved in the mountain experience) in the middle of a "great crowd" (Mark 9:14). Though it's no doubt a "contentious" debate,[49] Jesus initially stays calm and simply asks for information: "What are you arguing about?" Before introducing the case of the epileptic boy causing the present stir, however, Mark notes that upon seeing Jesus, the "whole crowd" is instantly "overcome with awe" (*exethambēthēsan*) and dashes to greet him (9:15). It's possible that some residual aura from Jesus's transfiguration sparks their sudden excitement. In any event, Jesus's presence clearly intensifies the emotional atmosphere.

Although Jesus doesn't receive a direct answer to his query about the heated discussion between scribes and disciples, it's not hard to connect the dots. The boy's father speaks up from the crowd, describing his son's miserable "seized" condition and how he'd sought deliverance (exorcism) from Jesus's disciples—but to no avail (Mark 9:17–18). We thus infer that the scribal professionals were taking Jesus's associates to task for their inept handling of the problem; of course, the scribes provided no help either (the boy remains desperately ill). After Jesus cures the son and leaves the scene with his disciples to enter a private home, the disciples continue to be addled by their inability to perform the requisite exorcism (as they'd previously done, under Jesus's authority, for "many" possessed people [6:7, 13]). In response to their dismay, Jesus matter-of-factly instructs them: "This kind can come out only through prayer" (9:28–29).

In dealing with these three agitated parties (scribes, crowds, disciples), Jesus keeps his cool, to a point—but not altogether and certainly not as the encounter between Jesus, the father, and his son unfolds. In Mark's account, Jesus speaks more and interrogates the supplicant more than in any other Synoptic healing story, and except for one clinical query, his speech crackles with emotion. The tense dialogue unfolds in four stages.

1. After the father apprises Jesus of his son's hazardous condition and the disciples' futile attempt to expel his tormenting spirit, Jesus accepts the

48. See Spencer, "Faith on Edge."
49. Danker with Krug, *Concise Greek-English Lexicon*, 332.

case but only after erupting in a mini-tirade: "You faithless generation, how much longer must I be among you? How much longer must I put up with you? Bring him [the boy] to me" (Mark 9:19). Jesus does not address the father alone. All the "you" words are plural in Greek, including the implied subject of the imperative verb ("[You all] bring [*pherete*] him to me"). Jesus thunders at this entire "faithless generation," encompassing the scribes, crowd, disciples, father, and pretty much everyone on earth—the whole sorry lot of "you." He hyperbolizes and catastrophizes, as passionate people often do, to punctuate a serious point. His beef is with the current generation's faithlessness (*apistos*)—their lack of trust in God's restorative purpose and power, especially on behalf of the weakest and most vulnerable, like this poor child assaulted by evil forces. Though not stated, Jesus's compassion for this and other little ones (cf. 10:13–16) seeps through amid the torrent of blame he assesses. He does not blame the victim by any means but lambasts multiple sectors of society—legal (scribes), popular (crowds), messianic (disciples), and familial (father)—for not doing their faithful part to help the victim. And Jesus takes all this ineffectuality personally and impatiently, as if to say, "How much longer must *I* deal with you, work with you, teach you to no avail. I've had it with you all!"[50]

We don't need a narrator's emotional evaluation or a soundtrack to gauge Jesus's feelings here. The tone comes through loud and clear in the printed text of Jesus's speech. Pick your label(s) where Mark provides none: Jesus is frustrated, disappointed, annoyed, angry, fed up with this callous generation, despondent, pessimistic, cynical, skeptical, incredulous about getting through to them and advancing God's right-making realm.[51]

Quite an emotional turn from the transfiguration! How different things can seem at the foot of the mountain! The juxtaposition of the gleaming epiphany in the clouds with Moses and Elijah and the gut-wrenching paroxysm on the ground over the epileptic boy's case is more than Jesus can take—for the moment. But fortunately, as we've seen before, though he honestly experiences negative emotions in trying situations, he does not indulge them for long or

50. The verb *anechomai* rendered "put up with" in Mark 9:19 more fully connotes "put up with when faced with someth[ing] disagreeable, annoying, or difficult . . . the opp[osite of the] Engl[ish] expression 'I have had it'" (Danker with Krug, *Concise Greek-English Lexicon*, 32). But by twice wondering "how much longer" Jesus can put up with these people, he hews close to the edge of "I've had it [enough]!"

51. Brackett (*Permission to Feel*, 74–77 [and endpapers]) identifies one hundred emotions (or "mood meter" terms), twenty-five each in four quadrants on axes of low-to-high pleasantness and low-to-high energy. In suggesting what Jesus *might* have felt here, I borrow a number of Brackett's terms, in this case all on the low-pleasant scale and divided between low and high energy.

allow them to cut the nerve of his therapeutic impulse. Just as he cured the leper who triggered his anger (see the discussion in chap. 3 of Mark 1:40–45), so he will deliver the boy from his "seized" affliction.

2. Jesus's second question, which follows a major seizure the boy has on the spot, reflects a calmer, more focused demeanor. Jesus asks the father about his son's medical history: "How long has this been happening to him?" Jesus's initial concern with "how long" he must continue his frustrating ministry shifts to "how long" this boy has been suffering this malady. The father answers, "From childhood," adding to the pathos of the case: effectively, this boy's *whole life* has been marred by violent convulsions (Mark 9:20–21). At this point, the father reinforces both the severity of his son's demonic ailment—informing Jesus that it "often" (*pollakis*) propels him into fire and water hazards—and the intensity of his plea for Jesus's aid: "But if you are able to do anything, have pity [or compassion (*splanchnistheis*)] on us and help us" (9:22). Whether or not one is a parent, it's not hard to sympathize with the father's extreme desperation: from the emotional depths of his being, he appeals to the *splanchna*-depths of Jesus, evoking the fervent divine-parental feeling of such language discussed above.

3. Surely, we expect, Jesus will move promptly to cast out the vicious spirit and lift up the stricken boy. Yet, if we blanched when Mark's Jesus put off the Syrophoenician mother (pleading for her demon-assaulted daughter) longer than compassion might warrant, we might faint dead away at his retort to this father. Notice Jesus's third response, echoing the father's first words but turning them into a pejorative interjection: "If you are able!" (Mark 9:23). His use of the neuter article before repeating verbatim the father's "if you are able" (*to ei dynē*) "has the effect of emphasizing that part of the father's request in 9:22 so as then to hold it up to criticism."[52]

Apparently Jesus has not exhausted all his frustration yet over these "faithless" (*apistos*) people. He takes the father's conditional plea, surely against its primary intention, as a statement of doubt (faithlessness) concerning Jesus's ability to overcome the nefarious spirit, an expression of low expectations based perhaps on the fact that his disciples, and no doubt many others before them, had failed to help. "How dare you question my power publicly!"[53] Jesus seems to bellow, before adding a crisp faith lesson: "All things can be done for the one who believes [or has faith (*pisteuonti*)]" (Mark 9:23). A good, challenging point, we might affirm—but this may not be the best time to

---

52. Donahue and Harrington, *Gospel of Mark*, 278; cf. Wallace, *Greek Grammar*, 238.
53. Recall, by contrast, that the leper in Mark 1:40 positively affirms Jesus's ability to heal him ("You can make me clean"), while leaving open Jesus's willingness to do so ("If you choose").

make the point to the beleaguered father with his demon-battered son lying on the ground. Pastoral Care 101 admonishes caregivers not to exacerbate a sick person's suffering by suggesting that their or their family's insufficient faith keeps them from getting well. It's hard to muster more faith when you're already at the end of your rope, to say nothing of worrying about offending God, Jesus, a doctor, or a minister by expressing a little doubt after a long run of disappointing debilitation.

4. Before reflecting further on Jesus's stunning "If you are able!" retort, we register his critical *fourth* utterance: a dramatic speech-act, as the crowd comes "running together,"[54] following the father's impassioned rejoinder to Jesus's rebuke of his paltry faith ("I [do] believe [*Pisteuō*]; help my unbelief [*apistia*]!" [Mark 9:24]).[55] Here Jesus speaks with adamant authority to the vile perpetrator of this mess: "You spirit that keeps this boy from speaking and hearing, I command you, come out of him, and never enter him again!" (9:25). The vicious demon obeys and exits the boy and the scene, but it does so with a final cacophonous, convulsive outburst, leaving the child to rest in a peace that strikes most observers, however, as the peace of *death*—a comatose, terminal peace! No more words from Jesus now, as he moves to take the corpse-like boy "by the hand" and raise him up (9:26–27), a resuscitation reminiscent of that performed on Jairus's (actually) deceased daughter (5:39–42).[56] After such a boisterous, tensioned-filled episode, Jesus's final physical-emotional touch brings true peace and wholeness. We might wish that Jesus had applied this compassionate touch from the start.

But however we might wish to finesse one of the most emotionally charged Gospel scenes, we must deal with the narrative at hand in all of its raw richness. "All's well that ends well" doesn't cut the interpretive mustard here. Matthew and Luke's efforts to trim and tame Mark's tumultuous narrative—not least Jesus's cascade of frustrated feelings—are understandable but not altogether acceptable for those daring, with Mark, to let Jesus be Jesus, however uncomfortable he might make us.

54. Observing the crowd "running" toward this scene here in Mark 9:25 and earlier in 9:15 reinforces the high kinetic energy of the entire incident.

55. The father's remarkable emotional resilience compares with the persistence of the Syrophoenician mother.

56. In this previous episode, some friends bring Jairus the bad news—"Your daughter is dead" (Mark 5:35)—only to have Jesus soon contradict them: "The child is not dead but sleeping" (5:39). There could be a fine line in the ancient world between prolonged sleep and death. Sleep ("rest in peace") became a common metaphor for death, anticipating a future awakening or resurrection. While we cannot be sure of the precise medical diagnoses, it seems that Jairus's daughter was actually dead for a time (though Jesus aims to "awaken" her to new life), and the father's son was in a deep epileptic coma. In any case, the stories are closely related in Mark's narrative.

Yet maybe this remarkable account is not as uncomfortable as all that. Indeed, I suggest it can bring a certain "emotional refuge,"[57] as well as challenge, to practitioners of compassion and mercy. Admittedly, I cannot speak for Mark's intentions, certainly not while I slap a "pastor" or "hospital chaplain" badge on my exegetical-scholar hat and thereby speak as a fool, though, I trust, a well-meaning and genuinely concerned fool. In any case, I refuse to ignore or apologize for Jesus's intense feelings of frustration, or whatever we want to call them, in Mark's presentation. The hands-on, on-the-ground work of compassion toward hurting bodies and souls, the actual work of loving neighbors as oneself, as Mark's Jesus affirms from the Torah (Mark 12:28–34), is as demanding and draining—taking "all your strength" (12:30)—as it is worthwhile and wonderful.

Burnout in caregiving professions is common knowledge, amply supported by scientific research and anecdotal report. And it's hardly a new phenomenon in human history—even for "Jesus Christ, the Son of God" (Mark 1:1), who incarnates God's loving, compassionate, merciful realm on earth and *in the process* needs moments of prayerful recharging away from the madding crowd (see 1:35; 3:13; 6:31–32, 45–46; 7:24; 9:2–8; 14:32–42). Yet this "self-care" process is problematic for Jesus, partly because he's rarely left alone for long and his gut compassionate drive overwhelms his contemplative desires (as we saw in the "sheep"-feeding incident in 6:34–44) and partly because his own personal distress keeps mounting toward the breaking point. Right before he encounters the tumultuous scene surrounding the epileptic boy, as he descends from the transfiguration summit with Peter, James, and John, his thoughts turn downward from his glorious previewed "Beloved Son of God" destiny to his immediate inscribed path as Suffering Son of Man, who must "go through many sufferings [*polla pathē*] and be treated with contempt" (9:12). In other words, he must go through terrible physical and emotional turmoil. And right after the episode involving the spirit-seized son, Jesus tries for the second time to get his disciples to realize he's about to be betrayed and killed before rising from the dead after three days (9:30–31). Thus Jesus deals with the demon-seized boy at the same time that he himself is being seized in the vise of suffering unto death.

On a gut level, Jesus knows and feels the pressure of mending a broken world riddled with distress and distrust (faithlessness), including distress and

---

57. See the definition of "emotional refuge" in Reddy, *Navigation of Feeling*, 129: "A relationship, ritual, or organization (whether informal or formal) that provides safe release from prevailing emotional norms and allows relaxation of emotional effort . . . , which may shore up or threaten the existing emotional regime" (see fuller discussion, 128–29, 145–54); cf. Spencer, "Song of Songs."

distrust directed against him and his therapeutic efforts. In some measure, mysteriously unique to him in his full-fledged union with God and humanity in the fellowship of suffering, Jesus is vulnerable to proximate,[58] painful injury and infirmity. And he operates out of this vulnerability with raw passion, including periodic frustration and weariness as well as persistent compassion and mercy—marks of a wounded healer who truly "sympathizes with our weaknesses," to borrow the language of Hebrews, and welcomes our "bold" supplication, with whatever faith we have, "so that we may receive mercy and find grace to help in time of need" (Heb. 4:15–16).[59]

Supporting the Widow (Luke 7:11–17)

The final Gospel story demonstrating Jesus's compassion in action is found only in Luke 7:11–17. It represents a companion case to the story of the spirit-seized boy: both are about Jesus's ministry to a parent's debilitated "only" son before a large assembly that ultimately praises God for the miracle they witness (cf. 9:37–43). Luke sets the present scene on the outskirts of the village of Nain, about five miles southeast of Nazareth. As Jesus nears the town's gate, accompanied by "his disciples and a large crowd," he meets another "large crowd" heading out, a funeral procession bearing the deceased body of a "young man," a widow's "only son" (7:12, 14). Amid this jam-packed environment, Jesus "saw her [autēn] . . . had compassion [esplanchnisthē] for her [autē] and said to her [autē], 'Do not weep'" (7:13). This doubly bereft and especially vulnerable woman, having lost her husband and only son, receives Jesus's full sympathetic attention; he feels deeply with her, as much as possible, in her grievous loss, even though he has no direct marital or maternal experience.

Jesus's imperative exhortation, "Do not weep" (mē klaie), should not be interpreted as rebuking the mother's teary display of emotion, as we might expect from a rigorous Stoic sage. What's the point of disrupting your tranquility and making a bad situation worse by excessive grieving? No use crying over spilt milk or a dead son. This is not to say that a good Stoic would not reach out and help the suffering widow, but such charitable action would ideally stem from a calm, clear-headed decision, not from an impulsive churning of the "bowels" or burning of the heart. Luke's Jesus, however, uses rather than

58. Recall Aristotle's (Rhet. 2.8.1) association of compassion with painful events "close at hand."

59. On the "wounded healer," see Nouwen, Wounded Healer, R. Williams, Wound of Knowledge.

squelches his emotional energy in his therapeutic work. Though operating with poise and purpose to support this distressed woman, he does so within the coursing stream of compassionate feeling rather than stanching its flow. Emotion moves Jesus to act. His gut-stirring love stimulates his remedial ministry, impelling him to touch the "stretcher on which the dead man was being carried" (7:14 CEB), command the widow's son to "rise" to new life, and restore "him to his mother" (7:14–15). To the end, this episode focuses on Jesus's compassionate care for this woman.

This is the first use of *splanch*- language in Luke since 1:78 (noted above), fusing *splanchna* and *eleos* in extolling God's "compassions/bowels of mercy." While that text (which is part of Zechariah's song following the birth of his son, John) closely associates God's compassion/mercy with "forgiveness of . . . sins" (Luke 1:77) to be mediated through (grown-up) John's baptismal mission, Jesus's outreach to the widow at Nain has nothing to do with remitting her sins or her son's sins. Rather, this sympathetic ministry is all about restoration and provision, physically, relationally, emotionally, and materially: restoring bodily life to the young man, restoring an only son to his widowed mother, and thereby providing her with vital emotional and material support from male kin in a patriarchal society.[60] Deliberately giving the young man to his mother suggests his responsibility to care for her as she has cared for him.

This complex, affective, life-and-death episode fueled by Jesus's compassion aptly sets the stage for his two parables featuring *splanchnizomai* in action: upon seeing the "half dead" (*hēmithanē*) victim on the roadside, the Samaritan "was moved with pity [or compassion]" (*esplanchnisthē*) to bind up his wounds, take care of him, and pay for his convalescence (Luke 10:30–35); and upon seeing his bedraggled, runaway son, the father "was filled with compassion" (*esplanchnisthē*), rushed toward him, embraced him, ignored his confession of sin, and ordered for him a fresh set of clothes and a celebratory feast, "for this son of mine was dead and is alive again!" (15:20–24).

While, again, Jesus cannot tap into personal feelings of losing a spouse or a child, he can relate to the threat of death, which he will soon admit in Luke 9:22. Luke's narrative closely connects the incident at Nain with the volatile prior proceedings at Nazareth around the theme of Jesus's prophetic vocation and vulnerability. In Luke's seminal account of the Nazareth event launching Jesus's public mission, Jesus presents himself to his hometown people as God's consummate Spirit-anointed prophet scripted by Isaiah (4:16–24) and typified by Elijah and Elisha (4:25–27). His family and neighbors respond first with general "amazement" but ultimately with full-on "rage," inflaming

60. See Spencer, "Neglected Widows," 718–21, 723–24.

them to haul Jesus to the cliff at the edge of town with intent to hurl him off (4:28–30). Although he somehow escapes their clutches, his experience of vehement rejection and of facing violent demise in this programmatic episode sticks close to Luke's Jesus throughout his prophetic journey.

In response to Jesus raising the widow's son from the dead, reminiscent of Elijah's and Elisha's similar feats (1 Kings 17:17–24; 2 Kings 4:8–37),[61] the crowd in Nain recognizes Jesus's prophetic display and becomes "seized" with "fear" (*phobos*) (Luke 7:16). Emotions run high again, and we naturally wonder what this stunned assembly might do to Jesus. Remember that fear, like amazement or surprise, can prompt a range of reactions, bad and good, constricting and elevating. In this case, unlike at Nazareth, shock and awe modulate into glorification of God and jubilant exclamation: "'A great prophet has risen among us!' and 'God has looked favorably on his people!'" (7:16). Perhaps here at Nain, Jesus's sympathy with hurting humanity breaks out more strongly, more viscerally, more *splanchna*-like, than in Nazareth, although he clearly identifies there with scriptural prophetic paradigms of support for the poor, infirm, and bound (4:18–19). Perhaps Jesus's passion for ministry has become more intensely compassionate. That will not prevent his crucifixion down the line, but maybe this emotional connection makes the difference with the present company surrounding the widow at Nain.

61. See Brodie, "Towards Unraveling"; Evans, "Function of the Elijah/Elisha Narratives," 76–79.

9

What's Love Got to Do with It?

The Compassionate Jesus and Discipleship

Two very different people, two very remarkable cases, illuminate the love connection motivating Jesus's leadership and call to discipleship. One is an attractive would-be disciple, the only person Jesus is explicitly said to love in the Synoptic Gospels—who sadly, however, fails to meet Jesus's requirement. The other is the model disciple in the Fourth Gospel, who is repeatedly characterized as "the one whom Jesus loved," as Jesus loved all his followers "to the end."

Loving at a Cost (Mark 10:17–27)

The "rich young ruler," as he is popularly known, is a composite Gospel figure who asks Jesus, "What must I do to inherit eternal life?" but ultimately leaves disappointed because he's not willing to "do" what Jesus demands (which is, to be sure, incredibly demanding). Each Synoptic Evangelist stresses the character's wealth; only Matthew, however, calls him a "young man" (Matt. 19:20) and only Luke labels him a "ruler" (Luke 18:18). In the absence of distinguishing the man's age and position, Mark focuses on his representative status as a rich person with "many possessions" (Mark 10:22–25).

Mark also, again, supplies a wider array of emotion terms describing three figures: Jesus, the rich man, and the disciples.

Jesus. Only Mark notes that Jesus "loved" (*ēgapēsen*) the rich man (10:21); and remarkably, this is the only individual designated as the object of Jesus's *agapē* in the Synoptic Gospels. Unpacking the meaning and motivation of this love is our main concern in this section. But as always, Jesus's emotion must be understood in the affective web of the entire event.

Rich Man. Only Mark sets the scene in motion with energetic physical action, as the rich man "ran up" to Jesus,[1] who himself was "setting out on a journey [or way (*hodon*)]," and "knelt before him" (10:17). The rich man appears both excited (running) to engage Jesus and devoted (kneeling) to his teaching. Such fervent attraction helps to explain his emotional deflation upon hearing Jesus's demand for total divestment of all his resources on behalf of the poor (10:21). Unwilling to rise to that extreme level of discipleship, the man turns away both "shocked" (*stygnasas*) and "grieving" (*lypoumenos*) (10:22; Matt. 19:22 // Luke 18:23 retain only the "grieving/sad" response).

Disciples. After the rich man leaves, Jesus addresses his disciples with a stunning commentary on what they've just witnessed: "How hard it will be for those who have wealth to enter the kingdom of God!" (Mark 10:23). In turn both Mark 10:26 and Matthew 19:25 report that the disciples "were greatly astounded" (*exeplēssonto*) by this "hard" saying, seemingly antithetical to God's saving purpose. Again, however, Mark doubles down on the emotional reaction, adding that the disciples were also "perplexed [*ethambounto*] by these words" (Mark 10:24).

Jesus's love for this inquiring rich man thus embeds in the rich—and thorny—emotional soil of attraction, devotion, shock, grief, perplexity, and astonishment. It is by any measure a tough love, a costly love, costing Jesus a promising disciple-recruit who proves unwilling, even unable, to pay the "impossible" (Mark 10:27) price of giving over all his resources to the poor (10:21).

This dense emotional context of Jesus's love interweaves with the scriptural thread running through the exchange between Jesus and the rich man, focused on Torah observance. Here the foundational covenantal law of love we discussed above comes to life in a moving "real world" encounter. The rich man rushes to Jesus not to dally with him, not to test him or bog him down in trivialities but to ask in all sincerity and with all due respect a literally life-and-

---

1. Compare the crowd that "ran forward" (*prostrechō*) to Jesus in the scene just discussed surrounding the spirit-seized boy (Mark 9:15; see also 9:25 [*episyntrechō*]).

death question: "Good Teacher, what must I do to inherit eternal life?" (Mark 10:17). In response, Jesus promptly—and humbly—grounds this critical life matter in God's Torah: "Why do you call me good? No one is good but God alone" (10:18). Jesus both humbles his eager inquirer, upbraiding him for his flattering address of Jesus as "Good," and humbles *himself* as servant of the only good and holy God. Of course, "No one is good but God alone" echoes the Shema (see Deut. 6:4), which invokes the covenantal demand to love this exclusive Lord "with all your heart, and with all your soul, and with all your might" and "to keep these words that I am commanding you today in your heart" (6:5–6) as the basis for flourishing life (cf. 5:33; 6:2–3; 30:6, 15–20).

Right on cue with Deuteronomy, Jesus follows his "God alone" affirmation with, "You know the commandments" (Mark 10:19). In addition to reinforcing the vital principle of God's Torah as the way of life, Jesus also affirms his inquirer as one who "knows" the law and walks in God's "way" (*hodos*).[2] Moreover, by proceeding to enumerate only the latter commandments from the Decalogue (10:19), Jesus seems to assume the rich man's commitment to the one true God of Israel enjoined in the first four commandments, his little slip in calling Jesus "Good" notwithstanding. The last six commandments, which comprise five prohibitions (no murder, adultery, stealing, lying, or coveting) plus the mandate to honor one's parents (Exod. 20:12–17; Deut. 5:16–21), all exemplify love for others, the second overarching "great commandment" in tandem with the priority duty to love God (see Mark 12:28–34). In Jesus's list of the latter Ten Commandments, all the Synoptic writers drop the "no coveting" stipulation, while only Mark's Jesus adds, "You shall not defraud," which effectively duplicates "You shall not steal" (*mē aposterēsēs*) (10:19).[3] We suspect that Jesus suspects some financial malfeasance in this wealthy man's background, as is all too common for those who accumulate great riches.

The man briskly and boldly answers: "Teacher, I have kept all these since my youth" (Mark 10:20). But does he answer truthfully? Pride, the desire to impress, and a willingness to fudge the books in one's favor are also tell-tale signs of many opulent people. Yet, while Jesus is about to share some hard truth with this rich man, he does not question the man's love for God and neighbor evidenced in his longtime faithfulness to Torah commandments. Although Jesus delimited ascribing "goodness" to God alone, in a more general

2. Walking in the "way of God" constitutes a major theme in Mark and across the Bible. The common Greek word for "way," "road," or "journey" (*hodos*), used sixteen times in Mark (including in 10:17), stretches beyond its pedestrian meaning to symbolize a "way of life." See Marcus, *Way of the Lord*.

3. BDAG 121 defines *apostereō*: "to cause another to suffer loss by taking away through illicit means, rob, *steal, despoil, defraud*" (emphasis original).

sense he appears willing to accept this seeker as a genuinely "good man" devoted to performing "good deeds." And it's this implied "good" evaluation that may partly account for Jesus's emotional response at this juncture, right before he drops the bombshell about the "one thing you lack," which seems impossible to achieve.

Perception and emotion, seeing and feeling, closely intertwine again in Jesus's dealings with others, as in normal human experience.[4] Here a particularly keen look motivates deep love: "Jesus, *looking at* [*emblepsas*] him, *loved* [*ēgapēsen*] him and said, 'You lack one thing'" (Mark 10:21). The first verb, *emblepō* (an intensified form of a basic word for "see, look" [*blepō*]), connotes looking "straight at" someone,[5] looking "carefully" (10:21 CEB) with rapt attention and clear focus (cf. 8:25). Jesus maintains this same laser-like perceptual mode when explaining to his befuddled disciples how this or any rich person enters God's saving realm: "Jesus *looked at* [*emblepsas*] them and said, 'For mortals it is impossible, but not for God; for God all things are possible'" (10:27). Jesus is intensely engaged with his interlocutors throughout this scene.

And his intense focus, preoccupied from the start, as we have seen, with the Torah-sealed covenantal bond of love with God and all God's people, merges with an intimate feeling of (agapic) love toward this one particular well-meaning seeker who nevertheless falls short. Although Jesus doesn't touch the man with his hands to effect some miraculous transformation, he is personally touched within by this man's situation.

Adapting Aristotle's perspective, Martha Nussbaum identifies a key cognitive component of compassion toward someone under stress: understanding that this suffering "person, or creature, is a significant element in my scheme of goals and projects, an end whose good is to be promoted." In other (Aristotelian) words, the loving (compassionate, merciful) person makes a "eudaimonistic judgment" that feeling and acting sympathetically forges a mutually dignified and beneficial relationship with a struggling individual, treated both as an *end* in himself, worthy of a flourishing life, and as a *means* to realizing the lover's own life goals.[6] In Mark's story, Jesus thoughtfully, perceptively, passionately seeks this rich man's well-being, fulfilling the man's particular life story intertwined with "following" (Mark 10:21) Jesus's own life mission

4. With reference to perceiving others' suffering, Jean-Jacques Rousseau writes, "To see it without feeling it is not to know it" (*Émile*, 222; quoted in Nussbaum, *Upheavals of Thought*, 323). For helpful philosophical discussions of the link between emotions and perceptions, particularly sensory perceptions, see Brady, *Emotional Insight*, 45–117; Price, *Emotion*, 81–104.

5. Newman, *Concise Greek-English Dictionary*, 60.

6. Nussbaum, *Upheavals of Thought*, 321 (see also 304–27).

and God-guided way of salvation. Jesus is no armchair advisor, still less a distant and flippant critic, of this rich man. This man matters to Jesus.

That makes what Jesus has to say to this rich man all the more difficult. He lays out the stark conditions of discipleship he and his followers have exemplified: leaving *everything* behind in service to God and needy humanity (Mark 10:28; cf. 1:16–20; 6:7–13; 8:34–37). He pulls no punches and cuts no deals with this rich man, "good" though he is and however beneficial he might be to Jesus's movement. Jesus knows "how hard," even "impossible," it will be for this rich man to comply with this mandate to surrender all. He no doubt anticipates the man's "shocked" and "grieving" departure.

But he does so with no "gotcha" glee that would expose the rich man's Achilles' heel and embarrass him in front of truly "dedicated" disciples (as if to say, "So this rich guy—who's probably exploited the poor to pad his portfolio—thinks he can waltz right in and get some extra eternal life insurance without paying the cost!"). In other Gospel stories, Jesus levels harsh criticism against the wealthy and powerful (Mark 12:41–44; Luke 6:24–25; 12:13–21; 16:19–31) and coolly turns away serious would-be followers unwilling to meet his stringent standards (Matt. 8:18–22 // Luke 9:57–62)—but not in this case. Here he speaks the hard truth about the all-encompassing demand to love God and others with everything one has, and he speaks that truth *in love*, knowing the man is not (yet) up to it. It's not so much that Jesus forgives the man for his shortcoming; sin and forgiveness don't come into this picture. But Jesus understands how hard it will be for the rich man to divest himself of all his possessions and, we might also surmise, how bad the man will feel when he turns away.

Further, we can reasonably posit that Jesus sympathizes to some degree with the rich man's situation. Although Jesus does not come from a privileged background and has no abundant personal material resources to give, he nonetheless leaves behind his family and carpentry vocation (see Mark 6:3) to pursue a hand-to-mouth itinerant mission thoroughly dependent on God's provision through others' hospitality. And if, for the moment, we broaden our christological horizon to include Jesus's pre-incarnate existence, as imaged by the apostle Paul, we discover an even closer affinity with the rich man: "You know the generous act of our Lord Jesus Christ, that though he was rich, yet for your sakes he became poor, so that by his poverty you might become rich" (2 Cor. 8:9; cf. Phil. 2:5–11).

My aim here is not to cast the loving Jesus in Mark as some bleeding-heart softie, sensitive to others' feelings to such a degree as to relieve them of all guilt and responsibility. Again, in his love for this rich man, Jesus cuts him no slack in meeting the rigorous requirements of God's kingdom. (Not incidentally, this comports with the Torah's ethical demands for those who love God and neighbor: "If there is anyone among you in need . . . within the land the LORD your God is giving you, do not be hard-hearted or tight-fisted toward your needy neighbor. You should rather open your hand, willingly lending enough to meet the need, whatever it may be. . . . I therefore command you, 'Open your hand to the poor and needy neighbor in your land'" [Deut. 15:7–8, 11].) Jesus does not hesitate to issue the hard command. But in making an emotional connection with the rich man, in expressing the hard command with compassion rather than harsh condemnation, I suggest Jesus leaves the way open for the man's possible reconsideration and return.

Of course, other than being stunned and saddened, we're not told how the man processes Jesus's injunction. Does he feel Jesus's love here? Who knows? But Jesus's subsequent affirmation that "for God *all things are possible*" (Mark 10:27) intimates that Jesus has by no means closed the door on the rich man's salvation.

Loving to the End (John 13–21)

No strand of the New Testament stresses the interpenetrating love between Father and Son, God's love for the world, and Jesus's love for his people more than the Johannine Gospel and letters. Previewed in John 11, Jesus's love especially manifests in John 13–21, mostly in private sessions with his closest followers. This unit of the Fourth Gospel commences and concludes with passages emphasizing Jesus's love for "his own" generally and for a "beloved disciple" more specifically.

> Having loved [*agapēsas*] his own who were in the world, he loved [*ēgapēsen*] them to the end. . . . One of his disciples—the one whom Jesus loved [*ēgapa*]— was reclining next to him. (John 13:1, 23)

> Peter turned and saw the disciple whom Jesus loved [*ēgapa*] following them; he was the one who had reclined next to Jesus at the supper. . . . This is the disciple who is testifying to these things and has written them. (21:20, 24)

While these framing passages only use *agap*- language, there's nothing magical about this wording in comparison with the equally common *phil*- terms for "love." Both verb forms, for example, identify the special disciple "whom Jesus loved" (*ephilei* in John 20:2; *ēgapa* in 13:23; 21:20). Moreover, both terms characterize the consummate bond between Father and Son (*agapa* in 3:35; *philei* in 5:20), as well as God's love for Jesus's followers (*agapa/agapēsei* in

14:23; *philei/pephilēkate* in 16:27) or Peter's love for Jesus (multiple, inter-changeable uses of both terms in 21:15–17). No significant semantic differ-ence obtains between these love terms, certainly not enough to distinguish *philos* "as devotion based in the emotions" from *agapē* as "devotion based in the will [meaning] *like, feel affection for.*"[7] Apart from the tight connection between emotion, motivation, and volition is the problem of determining a word's emotional tenor apart from contextual usage. Meaning inheres in word sequences and scenarios, not in dictionary entries.[8]

Consonant with the "festival of the Passover [*pascha*]" setting (John 13:1) and Jesus's impending Passion ("suffering" [*paschō*]), his love for "his own" is not merely formal and clinical but fervent and (com)passionate. In the analysis that follows, I will investigate key stations of John's Passion narrative to uncover a more granular emotive picture of Jesus's mature love for his fol-lowers. To this end, since John 13–17 provides a kind of farewell "testament" that Jesus leaves his closest associates,[9] the compassion-soaked *Testament of Zebulun* may offer valuable points of comparison.

I organize this survey of Jesus's endless love "to the end" around four im-ages of his "beloved" disciples as (1) servants, (2) children, (3) friends, and (4) a model disciple.

Beloved Served Servants *(John 13:1–30)*

Along with the Passover setting, the Fourth Gospel stages Jesus's loving farewell instructions against two other emotive backdrops: one, the ominous specter of *betrayal* by one of his disciples, Judas Iscariot, a tool of "the devil" (John 13:2); and two, the focal place of *communion* with his disciples around the dinner table—still including Judas, whose nefarious plot remains unknown to his colleagues.

Around this table Jesus undertakes an extraordinary demonstration of love. Removing his outer garment, wrapping a towel around his waist, and filling a basin with water, he performs the servant duty of washing the feet of each disciple (John 13:4–5), including the feet of the man he knows will hand him over to the authorities. Although such duty hardly need be carried out with loving sentiment—and normally would not be by household attendants—it

---

7. B. Friberg, T. Friberg, and Miller, *Analytical Lexicon*, 399 (emphasis original).

8. See Kagan, *What Is Emotion?*, 216: "Let us agree to a moratorium of the use of single words, such as *fear, anger, joy,* and *sad,* and write about emotional process with full sentences rather than ambiguous naked concepts that burden readers with the task of deciding who, whom, why, and especially what" (emphasis original).

9. See Kurz, *Farewell Addresses*, 71–120.

takes on a dramatically different character in the hands of this foot-washing Teacher, Lord, and Master; it provides his subordinate servants with a moving, table-turning model of their humble responsibility to "wash one another's feet" (13:12–17). Though Jesus does not overly emote in this ministration (like the effusive woman in Luke 7 who drenches Jesus's feet with perfume and tears and dries them with her hair), the basic gesture requires a certain intimacy of touch and massage. Moreover, Jesus stresses to Peter that this "cleansing" act goes beyond perfunctory performance of hospitable duty, signaling a thorough, holistic (*holos*) sharing "with me" (*met' emou*)—participating, partnering, having a full part (*meros*) in Jesus's embodied life and work (John 13:8–10). Such "cleansing" here focuses not on pardoning the disciples' sins but on preparing them, setting them apart, for sacred service to God and Christ.

With this vivid enactment of love for his disciples and assurance of their close-knit relationship with him, Jesus begins his farewell message on a positive note. He also makes instructive use of the occasion, providing a striking object lesson for the loving service to each other he expects from them. But he offers this challenge constructively, without rebuke.

Suddenly, however, Jesus's mood changes, as he becomes "troubled in spirit" (*etarachthē tō pneumati*) (John 13:21), matching the inner turmoil he recently experienced at Lazarus's gravesite (11:33). Now his consternation roils over the impending betrayal by one of his own: "Very truly, I tell you, one of you will betray me" (13:21). This is not new information for Jesus: as he washed the disciples' feet, "he knew [already] who was to betray him" (13:11). But now this datum hits him hard, not because of the physical pain and suffering of death it will cause for Jesus but because of the present emotional wrench and upheaval it brings to the loving bond with his disciples. "*One of you* [*heis ex hymōn*] will betray me" (13:21). That's the rub. One of this tightly knit circle of twelve servants, one whom Jesus had specially chosen (6:70–71) to nurture, teach, equip, and love "to the end [*telos*]" (13:1), will soon choose to end this relationship in a treacherous way.[10] Such a "complete [*teleia*] friendship . . . of those who are good and alike in point of virtue," as Aristotle puts it (*Eth. nic.* 8.3 [1156b.7–8]), will be shattered in pieces by this one diabolical disciple, as Jesus (and we readers) know. And that tragic betrayal of love affects Jesus deeply.

We might assume that Jesus would now expose Judas to the group in hopes of spurring Judas's change of heart or cuing the other eleven to thwart the

10. Along with indicating Jesus's choice of the Twelve, including Judas, John 6:70–71 provides an ominous preview of Judas's treachery: "'Did I not choose you, the twelve? Yet one of you is a devil.' He was speaking of Judas son of Simon Iscariot, for he, though one of the twelve, was to betray him."

plot. In fact, however, Jesus leaves the identity of this "one of you" open, allowing Judas to exit the dinner and execute his plan without obstruction. (Some think Jesus dispatches Judas to purchase food for Passover or give alms to the poor [John 13:29].) Of course, Jesus's announcement stirs up the anxiety of the whole company. The disciples begin eyeing one another before one pipes up and asks the question on everyone's mind: "Lord, who is it?" (13:22, 25). Jesus thus shares his emotional turmoil with his confidants, but he does so in a cryptic way that fosters distrust among them, seemingly making a bad situation worse.

Why Jesus takes this tack is difficult to discern. Partly, he wants his deathly "hour" to proceed apace rather than to be "saved" from it. He's already accepted this "troubling" fate as his God-ordained purpose for coming into the world (John 12:27). But also, I suggest, Jesus deliberately creates emotional tension in order to press all his associates to reassess their love for and loyalty to him as his departure draws near, to renew their commitment to keep walking in his "light" as the "darkness" grows thicker (see 12:35–36). Will they love *him* to the end, as he loves them? Will they remain faithful to him or by cowardice, apathy, or self-interest effectively wind up joining the betrayer?

As it happens, the "one" (*heis*) disciple who poses the "Who is it?" question to Jesus is dramatically juxtaposed to the "one [*heis*] of you" Jesus says will betray him. Singularly identified as "the one whom Jesus loved [*ēgapa*]" (John 13:23), this spokesman represents all of Jesus's disciples, all of "his own," whom he loves. We will consider this special "beloved disciple" more fully below. For now, we simply observe his station at the table, "reclining next to" Jesus, or more literally, "reclining" (*anakeimenos*), in the customary dining position, on Jesus's "chest" (*kolpos*) in 13:23, alternatively described as "lying [*anapesōn*] . . . close to the breast [*stēthos*] of Jesus" in 13:25 (RSV). The scene places this disciple in close physical contact with Jesus at the most honored seat on his right side.

The "chest" (*kolpos*) reference further evokes figuratively the relational image of being "closely and intimately associated, with the implication of strong affection for—'to be closely involved with, to be close beside.'"[11] In Johannine terms, it conjoins the bond between Jesus and this "beloved disciple" with that between Jesus and his divine Father from the "beginning" of

---

11. L&N 1:448 (cf. 219); see meaning of *kolpos* (κόλπος) in Danker with Krug, *Concise Greek-English Lexicon*, 204: "'front of the (human) chest', chest, bosom, breast, in NT always in ref[erence] to special social recognition and status through personal contact" (Luke 16:22–23; John 1:18; 13:23). See further Moloney, *Gospel of John*, 387: "The physical position of the Beloved Disciple is described twice [*kolpos* in 13:23; *stēthos* in 13:25]. This close physical proximity is a symbol of both affection and commitment."

the world: "No one has ever seen God. It is God the only Son, who is close to the Father's heart [or bosom (*eis ton kolpon*)], who has made him known" (John 1:18). It is this sacred bond of love among Father, Son, and disciple that the satanically influenced Judas is about to breach. Stretched between the polarities of diabolical betrayal and beloved loyalty are the hearts, minds, and wills of the eleven other disciples, and indeed all other present—and future (see 17:20; 20:31)—believers in Jesus. Will they faithfully trust and love Christ to the end?

Filling out the wider background for Judas's betrayal of Jesus's love, we may recall the example of Israel's twelve patriarch-brothers (prototypical of the twelve apostles), when the ten oldest "conspired to kill" the second youngest, Joseph (Gen. 37:19–20), but settled for selling him to slave-traders and convincing their father, Jacob, that his special, beloved son (see 37:3–4) had been mauled to death by a wild beast (37:31–34). As we've seen, the patriarch Zebulun, in the later testament bearing his name, claims he provided compassionate, merciful support to Joseph throughout this ordeal, although he still acquiesces to his brothers' malicious schemes. At best, Zebulun is a flawed model of loyal love, particularly in terms of channeling sympathetic feeling toward Joseph into strategic action. But he does at least sound an alarm against betraying one's "own," even as he embodies an emotional tension akin to that Jesus creates among his twelve disciples regarding their loving commitment to him. "Lord, who is it?" ("Who among us won't stick with you to the end, no matter the consequences? Is our group not as faithful as we think? How can we honestly 'serve one another,' as you've just demonstrated, if we can't fully trust one another?")

Beloved Obedient Children *(John 13:33–35; 14:18–31; 15:9–12)*

After the Servant-Lord Jesus has disturbed the group with his talk of betrayal and dismissed Judas to do the dirty business he's "going to do," Jesus shifts to a loving, parental mode with the eleven remaining disciples, offering both emotional support and further upheaval. In a characteristic Johannine term of address, Jesus tenderly calls them his "little children" (*teknia*) (John 13:33; cf. 1 John 2:1, 12, 28; 3:18; 4:4; 5:21) as he informs them that he has only a "little longer" to be with them in this world and that where he's heading they "cannot come" for a while (13:33, 36). Naturally, such an ominous announcement further stokes the disciples' anxiety; indeed, they become emotionally "troubled" (*tarassō*), as Jesus did in 13:21 when disclosing the presence of a betrayer among them. Accordingly, out of his empathy with their "troubled" state and sense of peace regarding his fate, Jesus comforts his beloved children: "Do not let your hearts be troubled [*tarassesthō*]" (14:1); "Peace I leave with you; my peace I give to you. . . . Do not let your hearts be troubled [*tarassesthō*], and do not let them be afraid" (14:27).

In chapter 14, Jesus unpacks for his followers the rationale undergirding his legacy of emotional refuge. Though his counsel is richly textured, it boils down to reassuring his "children" of his future return and reunion with them after his resurrection—and in the interim, his continuing residence with them through his Spirit. In short, "I will not leave you orphaned [*orphanous*]" (John 14:18). In light of his imminent "going away . . . to the Father" (14:28), Jesus's thoughts and feelings concentrate now on his own parental care for his beloved disciples, whom he's about to leave behind. Yet they will by no means be left abandoned and alone. They "will know" with blessed assurance their ongoing familial fellowship with the Father and Son, "that I am in my Father, and you in me, and I in you" (14:20) and that the Father and Son "will come to [you] and make our home [*monēn*] with [you]" (14:23).[12]

Far from an abstract, metaphysical concept, this circle of divine communion enveloping the children-disciples will become palpable and pervasive through the presence of the Holy Spirit, "another Advocate" like Jesus (NRSV), "another Comforter" (KJV), "another Helper" (NASB), "another Companion" (CEB), whom Jesus will petition the Father to "call alongside" (*paraklētos*) them to teach, guide, and nurture them (John 14:16 AT; cf. 14:25–26; 15:26–27; 16:5–14). More than that, more in fact than the earthly Jesus could provide, the Spirit not only "abides *with/beside* you [all] [*par' hymin*]" but will also be "*in/among* you [all] [*en hymin*]" at all times and in all places (14:17). In this Farewell Discourse, Jesus intimates that his beloved children will continue to feel his parental care for them through the indwelling, accompanying Spirit.

In particular, Jesus wants the disciples to share his positive, affective experience in this dire "hour," to share his love, peace, and joy (John 15:10; 14:27; 15:11). (We will examine Jesus's joy in the next chapter.) Consistent with what we've seen in the Torah and the Synoptic Gospels, the Johannine Jesus grounds his and his follower's love for God and one another in obedience to God's commandments. But the Fourth Gospel distinctively characterizes such loving obedience as the appropriate response of children to the loving Father. Jesus the Son again sets the example: "I do as the Father has commanded me,

---

12. The word for "home" (*monē*) is a place where one *stays*—a "dwelling place" or "abode" (related to the verb *menō*, "stay/abide"); see BDAG 658. It appears only twice in the New Testament: here in John 14:23 and earlier in 14:2. Together these verses stress the close, mutual inter-dwelling between Father/Son and "children": the Son Jesus prepares residences (*monai*) with the Father, to which he "will take you [all] to myself" (14:2–3), even as the Father and Son "come *to them* and make our home [*monēn*] *with them*" (14:23).

so that the world may know that I love the Father" (14:31; cf. 8:27–28). Such filial submission by Jesus derives not from a mere functional sense of duty to the Heavenly Patriarch but from a strong emotional echo of the Father's love for the Son. And in turn, as Lord Jesus mediates Father God's commandments to his disciples—chiefly the commandment to "love one another"—he does so from his own experience of mutual love with the Father extended to his twelve "children": "As the Father has loved me, so I have loved you; abide in my love. If you keep my commandments, you will abide in my love, just as I have kept my Father's commandments and abide in his love. . . . This is my commandment, that you love one another, as I have loved you" (15:9–12).

Love fuels and fills all life in the divine-human family in accordance with the Father's will. Love is the sustaining environment—the air, the water, the ground—in which family members must "abide." "Abiding" not in passive repose or lax indolence but in active, love-inspired and love-directed obedience, what the Torah conveys as covenantal, holistic love that animates heart, hands, head, and home (Deut. 6:4–9).

Following his foot-washing demonstration and prediction of betrayal, Jesus delivers to his stunned disciples a "new commandment, that you love one another . . . as I have loved you" (John 13:34). On the one hand, there's really nothing "new" about this directive: it's as "old" as the Torah. On the other hand, Jesus adds a new standard for fulfilling it: "as I have loved you." Jesus has just presented a new, "touching" drama (foot washing) of what mutual love involves. It is love in action: hands-on, feet grounded, serving each family member—even the extra dirty, disloyal ones. But such love in motion is also love in *emotion*, not necessarily with hyper-expressive energy but with tender, touching care, physically and emotionally. Although John does not use a great deal of emotive language, the scene pulses with poignant affect. Remember that scene: that's what it looks and feels like to love one another in God's household.

Beloved Intimate Friends (John 15:12–17)

Thus far the Johannine Jesus has imaged his relationship with his beloved followers in common master-servant and parent-child hierarchies—with a notable deconstructive twist. The loving Jesus assumes all the positions, the lower servant/child as well as the higher master/parent, encompassing in and around himself the divine-human communion, knitted together in fidelity to God's love commandments. In John 15, Jesus makes another rhetorical shift, reconfiguring his association with the disciples (now minus Judas) as friendship: "I do not call you servants any longer, . . . but I have called you friends [*philous*]" (John 15:15). Jesus now upgrades them, as it were, from subordinate household servants/slaves (*douloi*) and children (beloved, yes, but still below him in status) to more collaborative friends.

We should not think, however, that in antiquity the notion of friendship necessarily entailed equality. In the pervasive patronage system, elite patrons cultivated "friends" among grateful clients who in turn could serve as brokers or middlemen between patrons and future clients. We see this arrangement in Luke 7 when the centurion in Capernaum dispatches "friends" (*philoi*) to Jesus to mediate his healing of the officer's slave (Luke 7:6–8). Later in John's Gospel, the Jerusalem mob urges Pontius Pilate to crucify Jesus by appealing to Pilate's loyalty to Caesar: "If you release this man [Jesus], you are no *friend* [*philos*] of the emperor" (John 19:12).[13] Above all, Governor Pilate wanted to maintain "friendly" relations with Caesar, not as bosom buddies but as a trusted client-ruler. Similarly, in the Maccabean literature, emissaries of the Greek-Syrian ruler Antiochus IV attempted (unsuccessfully) to persuade Mattathias the priest to offer sacrifices to the ruler and thus become a "friend of the king," with accompanying material benefits and political duties but hardly intimate camaraderie (1 Macc. 2:17–18).

By calling the eleven disciples his "friends," Jesus is not abdicating his lordship over them or his position as commander-in-chief. Indeed, the friendship text in John 15:12–17 is framed by "This is my commandment" (15:12) and "I am giving you these commands" (15:17)—commands he expects his disciple-friends to obey (see also 15:14: "You are my friends if you do what I command you"). But again, Lord Jesus is not lording his commanding authority over them but rather laying down the law of *mutual love*—"love [for] one another as I have loved you" (15:12; cf. 15:17). Although valuing loyalty, a bedrock element of friendship (which is why Judas no longer merits "friend" status), Jesus does not demand obsequious adoration or servile action to boost his own reputation and resources. He is not that kind of friend or lord. Caesar wouldn't be caught dead stooping down to tend to anyone, certainly not to wash underlings' filthy feet.

Beyond his remarkable foot-washing service, Jesus adds two equally, if not more, dramatic proofs of close friendship with his followers: death and disclosure; laying down his life for them and letting them in on everything he knows.

First, Jesus presents the supreme evidence of love (*agapē*) as offering "one's life for one's friends [*philōn*]" (John 15:13), as he has done and will do "to

---

13. See Meeks, *Origins of Christian Morality*, 39–41; Ringe, *Wisdom's Friends*, 65; Spencer, *What Did Jesus Do?*, 53, 82n5.

the end," like a good shepherd giving his life to save cherished sheep he knows by name (10:3, 14–18). Though most English versions render the transitive verb *tithēmi* as "lay down (one's life)," with the principal connotation of laying down one's life in *death*, it also has a broader meaning of "placing, putting, presenting, offering" some object or part of one's life. Sharon Ringe interprets Jesus's usage in John as "*appointing*" or committing his entire life for the well-being of his sheep- and friend-disciples; while death marks the ultimate consequence of this assignment, it does not constitute the whole purpose of what the Father sent the Son to do.[14] More simply, we may take Jesus's understanding of friendship as giving himself entirely to his beloved ones in life as well as in death, embodying the mission of God who "so loved the world that he gave his only Son" to provide "eternal life," the very life of God, for those who trust in God's love (3:16). In Aristotelian terms, this represents a consummate, perfected *philia*, far beyond mere utilitarian or hedonic interests, committed to what "is good simply and for the friend," whatever it takes (*Eth. nic.* 8.3 [1156b.13–14]).

Second, a major part of Jesus's total life-sharing entails full disclosure of everything he knows about God and the world: "I have called you friends, because I have made known to you everything [*panta*] that I have heard from my Father" (John 15:15). True friends tell each other everything; they don't keep secrets from one another. This is not to suggest that the Johannine Jesus establishes a covert society with his closest followers, a kind of Gnostic sect. He has remained open to the wider world, trying to persuade unbelievers of the truth, though with limited success: "I have much to say about you and much to condemn; but the one who sent me is true, and I declare to the world what I have heard from him" (8:26). To be sure, Jesus's disciples don't always grasp his wisdom either, but their trusting hearts (save Judas's) are (mostly) in the right place.

The Fourth Gospel's portrayal of Jesus as the consummate Revealer of God on earth, "the only Son, who is close to the Father's heart [or bosom (*kolpon*)], who has *made him known* [*exēgēsato*]" (John 1:18)—has "revealed" (NAB) the Father, "explained" (NASB) the Father, "exegeted" the Father[15]—closely associates Jesus with *personified Wisdom* in biblical literature.[16] The

14. Ringe, *Wisdom's Friends*, 67, 80–83. See John 15:16, where Jesus "appoints" his friends, in turn, to fulfill their active purpose in the relationship: "You did not choose me but I chose you. And I *appointed* [*ethēka* (from *tithēmi*)] you to go and bear fruit."

15. The verb *exēgeomai*, literally "lead out," means "to set forth in great detail, expound" (BDAG 349). Seminarians and biblical scholars commonly speak of doing biblical *exegesis*, seeking to "bring out" the full meaning(s) of the text.

16. On Wisdom Christology in the Fourth Gospel, see Scott, *Sophia and the Johannine Jesus*; Witherington, *Jesus the Sage*, 370–80.

Hellenistic Jewish book Wisdom of Solomon particularly accentuates Wisdom's role as the intelligent, inspired manifestation of God who forges dynamic, loving friendships with human "souls" in a fashion strongly resonant with John's depiction of Jesus's relationship with his disciples:

> And all things, both what is secret and what is manifest, I learned,
> for she that is the fashioner of all things taught me, namely wisdom
>   [*sophia*].
>
> For there is in her [*Sophia*-Wisdom] a spirit [*pneuma*] that is
>   intelligent, holy,
> unique, of many parts, subtle,
> free-moving, lucid, unpolluted,
> distinct, invulnerable, loving the good [*philagathon*], sharp,
> unhindered, beneficent, loving towards humanity [*philanthrōpon*],
> firm, unfailing, free from care,
> all-powerful, all-surveying
> and penetrating all spirits [*pneumatōn*]
> that are intelligent, pure, most subtle.
> . . . .
> Although she is one, she can do all things,
> and while remaining in herself, she renews all things,
> and in every generation she passes into holy souls [*psychas*]
> and makes them friends of God [*philas theou*] and prophets;
> for God loves [*agapa*] nothing except the person who lives with
>   wisdom [*sophia*]. (Wis. 7:21–23, 27–28 NETS)[17]

This friend-making Wisdom, like the Johannine Christ, is not setting up a transactional network (LinkedIn) to further God's business or accumulating casual contacts (Facebook "friends") for publicity or amusement. These are true, intimate *(S)spirit*ual friends bound together by a strong, "perfect" twenty-one-strand cord of Divine Wisdom-Spirit (*Sophia-Pneuma*) composed "of many parts [manifold (*polymeres*)]" spanning the breadth of cognitive (intelligent) and affective (loving) experience.[18]

While neither the book of Wisdom nor the Fourth Gospel characterizes divine-human friendship in superficial, sentimental terms, both envision a substantial, emotional relationship that sustains friends with felt support during times of suffering. Such camaraderie was highly valued by sages in the ancient world, as exemplified in the evocative notion of a friend as a "second

17. See E. Johnson, *Friends and Prophets*, 40–45; Ringe, *Wisdom's Friends*, 40–42.
18. Not by accident, Wis. 7:22–23 enumerates twenty-one characteristics of Wisdom—a multiple of the "perfect" three and seven in biblical numerology.

self." The Roman statesman and philosopher Cicero regards this concept as friendship's most significant blessing.

> And great and numerous as are the blessings of friendship, this certainly is the sovereign one, that it gives us bright hopes for the future and forbids weakness and despair. In the face of a true friend a man sees as it were a *second self*. So that where his friend is he is; if his friend be rich, he is not poor; though he be weak, his friend's strength is his; and in his friend's life he enjoys a *second life* after his own is finished. This last is perhaps the most difficult to conceive. But such is the effect of the respect, the loving remembrance, and the regret of friends which follow us to the grave. While they take the sting out of death, they add a glory to the life of the survivors. (Cicero, *Lael. Amic.* 23)[19]

The Hellenistic Jewish sage Jesus Ben Sira makes the same point from a negative standpoint, warning against opportunists who feign friendship and "second self" partnership during good times but who "will not stand by you in time of trouble."

> When you gain friends, gain them through testing,
>   and do not trust them hastily.
> For there are friends who are such when it suits them,
>   but they will not stand by you in time of trouble.
> . . . .
> And there are friends who sit at your table,
>   but they will not stand by you in time of trouble.
> When you are prosperous, they become your *second self*,
>   and lord it over your servants;
> but if you are brought low, they turn against you,
>   and hide themselves from you. (Sir. 6:7–12)

Judas fits the bill of the faux friend who sits at table with Jesus and receives his loving ministrations, only to go out and betray him to the authorities. Beyond exposing Judas's basic greedy, larcenous character (John 12:6), the Fourth Gospel provides no particular motive for his abandoning Jesus. But we might reasonably assume that, since Judas knows the terrible ordeal facing Jesus (the plot has already been hatched [11:45–57; 12:9–11]), he wants nothing more to do with Jesus as he is "brought low."

19. See Falconer's translation "a sort of image of himself" (instead of "second self") in Cicero, *De senectute, De amicitia, De divinatione.* See also Cicero, *How to Be a Friend*, 139: "For every person loves himself, not for any kind of profit he can make from this love but because he is dear to himself on his own account. Unless we can transfer this kind of feeling to friendship, we will never find true friendship. A friend is, quite simply, another self."

By contrast, amidst his own suffering, Jesus faithfully sticks with the eleven "chosen" friends (John 13:18) to the end of his life (and beyond!) in the course of their "troubles" and insecurities, even though they will not always stick with him. Except for the singular Beloved Disciple, none will follow him to the cross (19:25–27). Peter will flatly deny he knows Jesus (13:36–38; 18:15–18, 25–27), and the others, Jesus foresees, "will be scattered, each one to his home, and you will leave me alone" (16:32). Jesus's love for his fickle friends—a love as intense, intimate, and permanent as that interpenetrating him and his Father—amounts to treating them as a second self or loving them as he loves himself. Moreover, in Ciceronian terms, Jesus may take solace in the fact these close friends will carry on his memory and mission after his death, giving him a kind of second life. Yet, because Jesus will himself rise again to new life and infuse his disciple-friends with the Holy Spirit, he will impart, along with much-needed peace, a *divine* "glory to the life of [his] survivors" (beyond what Cicero envisioned) as his authorized deputies: "Peace be with you. As the Father has sent me, so I send you" (20:21–22). By any reckoning, the Johannine Jesus loves his friends with an ardent, abiding passion stronger than death (cf. Song 8:6).

Beloved Model Disciple *(John 13:23–25; 19:26–27; 21:1–23)*

But there's this one special disciple who is never identified by proper name but simply as "the one whom Jesus loved." The first appearance of this anonymous "Beloved Disciple" (BD, for short), as he is commonly called ("he" is male, evidenced by masculine pronouns), comes at the table scene in John 13:23–25 (RSV), discussed above, where he reclines on Jesus's chest and asks Jesus, at Peter's behest, to identify the traitor in their midst.[20] Although from the start BD is clearly distinguished from the betrayer Judas (13:2, 18–30) and the denier Peter (13:23–26, 36–38), I do not think this gives "the impression that he was an outsider to the group of best-known disciples."[21] Rather, BD appears as the best example among them of true discipleship—a model, representative, loyal figure. This idealized, "beloved" portraiture, however, does not blur his individual character in action: he eats, reclines, stands, runs, fishes—all in connection with other close associates of Jesus, including Mary Magdalene and Jesus's mother. Though exemplary, he is not some

20. Some think that BD makes a brief, early entrance into the Fourth Gospel at 1:35–40 as the unnamed party of the "two disciples" of John the Baptist (the named one is Andrew), who, at the Baptist's direction, begin to follow Jesus. Nothing more is said here, however, about Andrew's companion, including no hint of his being "beloved" by Jesus.

21. Brown, *Community of the Beloved Disciple*, 34.

mystical, collective icon. As Adele Reinhartz states, "Although there is clearly an idealizing element in the [Beloved] Disciple's presentation in this Gospel, as suggested by his anonymity, his narrative role leads us to picture him as a 'real' individual, an intimate friend of Jesus, and the implied author of this Gospel [see 19:35; 21:20–24]."[22]

Our concern with this fascinating, mysterious figure has to do with his special beloved status: why Jesus loved him in particular and what we discover about Jesus's love in relation to *this* disciple in specific emotional situations. Beyond the pre-Passover table setting, two sites stand out: at the cross on The Place of the Skull/Golgotha (John 19:16–17) and on the beach of the Sea of Tiberias/Galilee (21:1; cf. 6:1).

Jesus and the Beloved Disciple at the Cross. With his named male disciples nowhere in sight as he hangs from the cross, the dying Jesus is attended by some female followers—"his mother, and his mother's sister, Mary the wife of Clopas, and Mary Magdalene" (John 19:25)—and the anonymous BD. In one of the most moving scenes in all Gospel literature, Jesus focuses on "his mother and the disciple whom he loved standing beside her" (19:26). Like BD, Jesus's mother is not named here or anywhere else in John's Gospel, which accords this pair's relationship to each other and to Jesus a representative function in the narrative—again complementing, not erasing, their individual identities.

In the first of his three sayings from the cross, the Johannine Jesus triangulates with his mother and BD, forging an expanded familial circle appropriate to his imminent physical demise and absence. His words are short, sweet, and stunning. First, "Woman, here is your son" would most naturally draw his mother's attention to Jesus one last time ("Here I am, Mother. This is it, the last time we'll see each other in this life"). But then Jesus speaks to BD, directing BD's attention away from Jesus to the woman by his side: "Here is your mother." BD takes the cue, knowing precisely what Jesus means: "And from that hour the [beloved] disciple took her into his own home" (John 19:26–27). The dying Jesus effectively transfers his filial role to BD. BD now receives the mantle of sonship, assuming Jesus's elder-son responsibility for caring for his mother.

In any reckoning, the Fourth Gospel fashions a breathtaking, loving scene and does so without a surfeit of emotional language. Indeed, the parsimony of words allows their emotional power to strike with full, unimpeded force. "To

---

22. Reinhartz, *Befriending the Beloved Disciple*, 23. The speculative question of BD's historical identity is not our main concern here. Raymond Brown (*Community of the Beloved Disciple*, 31) believes he was a "historical person" and the "hero of the [Johannine] community," while still granting that "the [Beloved] Disciple was idealized, of course."

the end" Jesus thinks of meeting others' needs, not least the one who bore and raised him, though this Gospel glosses over that period in favor of highlighting his mother's role in catalyzing his first public "sign," which "revealed his glory" and sparked his disciples' belief in his messianic mission (John 2:11; see 2:1–5). The supporting role of Jesus's mother spans this Gospel from the first to the final "hour" (see 2:4; 19:27), a role Jesus aims to see sustained and nurtured after his death via BD whom Jesus dubs his "second self," as it were. BD will live on in Jesus's stead alongside his mother, perpetuating his love for "his own" as one who most keenly knows Jesus's love.

The report that "the disciple took her into his own home," which is found in most English versions, supplies the word "home," which is absent in the Greek text. In the immediate context, this gloss makes good sense: BD supports Jesus's bereft mother by incorporating her into his "own" household. However, the plural substantive neuter adjective *ta idia* used here carries a broader sense of "one's own kin, people, country, things, surroundings"—the whole orbit of one's life. And the *idios* adjective arcs back not only to the beginning of Jesus's Farewell Discourse in 13:1 but also to the prologue and key points in between. Notice the thread:

He came to what was his own [*ta idia*], and his own people [*hoi idioi*] did not accept him. (John 1:11)

Jesus himself had testified that a prophet has no honor in the prophet's own country [*tē idia patridi*]. (4:44)

The Jews were seeking all the more to kill him, because he was . . . also calling God his own Father [*patera idion*], thereby making himself equal to God. (5:18)

He calls his own sheep [*ta idia probate*] by name and leads them out. When he has driven out all his own [*ta idia*], he walks ahead of them, and the sheep follow him. . . . I am the good shepherd. A good shepherd lays down his life for the sheep. A hired man, who is not a shepherd and whose sheep are not his own [*ta probata idia*], sees a wolf coming and leaves the sheep and runs away. (10:3, 4, 11–12 NAB)

Having loved his own [*tous idious*] who were in the world, he loved them to the end. (13:1)

If you belonged to the world, the world would love you as its own [*to idion*] . . . but I have chosen you out of the world—therefore the world hates you. (15:19)

The hour is coming, indeed it has come, when you will be scattered, each one
to his [own] home [*eis ta idia*], and you will leave me alone. Yet I am not alone
because the Father is with me. (16:32)

And from that hour, the [beloved] disciple took her into his own home [*eis ta
idia*]. (19:27)

As these references reveal, through the *idios* idiom the Fourth Gospel charts
Jesus's complex web of love-relations with his Father, fellow Jews generally,
disciples (sheep), and the world. The dynamic bond of love between Jesus
and his "own" Father is eternal and unbreakable, as is their loving care for the
world and everyone and everything in it, which "came into being" through
the divine creative Word (John 1:3, 10). Yet groups of Jesus's "own" variously
dishonor, abandon, hate, and seek to kill him, betraying his love one way or
another. Judas proves not so singular in his villainy after all. But Jesus remains
stalwart in his loving purpose, ensuring that his faithful BD will continue to
extend Jesus's love to all "his own" throughout the community.

The Risen Jesus and the Beloved Disciple on the Beach. From the cross,
BD's story moves to Jesus's empty tomb, to which he runs (at Mary Magdalene's prompting) ahead of Peter, looks in, and "believes," though *what*
he believes is not specified (John 20:1–9). At some later point, BD and some
other disciples, including Peter, encounter the risen Jesus on the beach of the
Galilean sea. Not that they recognize him right away. They've just concluded
an unsuccessful night of fishing, when he—though they don't know it's *him*
yet—comes to the shore at daybreak, calls them "children," and advises them
to shift their net to the "right side of the boat," where they "will find some
[fish]." "Some" turns out to be a massive haul of large fish (153, to be exact),
requiring all hands on deck to drag it ashore (21:4–6, 8, 11). BD again proves
to be Jesus's most perceptive disciple, blurting out to Peter, "It is the Lord!"
(21:7). Poor Peter had stripped down to his birthday suit after the night's work
and doesn't want Jesus to see him in such a state (especially after his recent
shameful denials); so he throws his clothes back on and jumps into the sea
(21:7). BD one-ups (outstrips!) Peter again.[23]

Soon, however, the whole company has breakfast with the risen Jesus on
the beach. As it happens, Jesus already has fish broiling over a charcoal fire,
along with some bread (John 21:9–14). It's like the feeding of the multitude
all over again (6:1–14) but now with just this close group of disciples—an
act of loving fellowship and hospitality al fresco, counterpointing the indoor

23. On BD's "one-upmanship" of Peter, see Brown, *Community of the Beloved Disciple*,
31–32, 84–87; Spencer, *What Did Jesus Do?*, 69–71.

foot-washing and banquet scene. But in both cases, it's BD, the one *defined* by Jesus's love (13:23–25; 21:7), who most intimately and insightfully senses Jesus's nurturing love in action.

The love theme intensifies after breakfast, as Jesus zeroes in on Peter's relationship with him. Three times, Jesus asks "Simon son of John, do you love me?" (twice using *agapaō*, once *phileō*); each time Simon Peter answers, "Lord, you know I love you [*philō se*]"; and in return each time Jesus commissions him for pastoral ministry ("tend my sheep"; "feed my sheep") (John 21:15–17). The emotional force of this exchange accelerates with each repetition, such that "Peter *felt hurt* [*elypēthē*]" when Jesus questioned his love "the third time" (21:17). We recall this *lyp-* term from chapter 5 on Jesus's anguish, describing the Synoptic Jesus's soul-crushing grief and sadness during his final trials. Elsewhere in the Fourth Gospel, this language appears only in John 16 where Jesus speaks to his distraught disciples of the "sorrow [or pain (*lypē*)] [that] has filled your hearts" (16:6) at present—but will soon "turn into joy" when they see him again after his death (16:20–22). It is precisely that restorative, joyful dimension of Jesus's love that Peter misevaluates emotionally with his hurt feelings. By getting Peter to affirm his love for Jesus three times near a charcoal fire and each time reinforcing Peter's pastoral ministry—effectively anointing him as a "second shepherd" in Jesus's stead—Jesus evokes Peter's threefold denial of Jesus by the same kind of firelight (*anthrakia* [18:18; 21:9]). He does so not to rub Peter's nose in that hour of failure but to restore him fully within the beloved community.

Jesus goes on to forecast the way Peter will die, with bound hands stretched out by some forceful authority who will drive Peter "where you do not wish to go" (John 21:18–19). Jesus presents such a fate to Peter not as a form of punishment but rather as a sign of partnership with Jesus to the end, a fellowship in his crucifixion, as the final means "by which he would glorify God" (21:19; cf. 13:36).[24]

Peter does not seem altogether reassured by Jesus's questions and comments. Or maybe he just gets distracted by BD, whom Peter sees "following them" (not outracing him this time). In any case, Peter wants to know BD's fate: "Lord, what about him?" (John 21:21) (which seems to mean, "So I'm going to be a pastor and martyr, fine. But how does that stack up with BD's mission and death?"). Peter stays mired in competition with BD—even jealous or envious, perhaps, of BD's perceived higher ranking in the community. Whatever Peter's feelings here, Jesus brushes them off as irrelevant to

24. Early tradition reports that Peter was crucified upside down in Rome; see *Acts Pet.* 37/ *Mart. Pet.* 8; Origen, *Commentary on Genesis*, vol. 3 (cited in Eusebius, *Hist. eccl.* 3.1).

Peter's—and all disciples'—priority duty to *follow Jesus*: "If it is my will that [BD] remain until I come, what is that to you? Follow me!" (21:22). While comfortable in his emotional skin and sensitive to others' emotions, Jesus does not indulge petty, distractive emotions.

With his brusque "what's it to you" rebuke of Peter, Jesus by no means rescinds his restoration of Peter or relegates his pastoral work to a trivial, subordinate level under BD. Jesus purposes to establish and extend an inclusive, beloved community suffused with mutual, dynamic love for "one another," as the Father and Son love each other and love all God's people, represented—not replaced—by the Beloved Disciple. As Jesus thrice compels Peter's love, so the Father and Son woo the love of each child of God.[25] Such all-encompassing love is obedient to divine commands, compliant with divine aims, and heartfelt in the divine bosom.

---

25. Bauckham (*Testimony of the Beloved Disciple*, 86) distinguishes between Peter's *active* role and BD's *receptive* role in relation to Jesus's love: "It is worth noticing that, whereas in Peter's case the Gospel emphasizes his love for Jesus, in the beloved disciple's case it emphasizes Jesus' love for him." While I grant this individualized distinction between Peter and BD, I think Bauckham goes too far in discounting BD as an "ideal" and "model" figure in the Fourth Gospel.

10

That's Good!

The Joyous Jesus

Did Jesus feel good about himself and his career? Did he have a good time and know how to enjoy himself? Did he smile and laugh? Was he a pleasant, happy guy to be around? If these questions seem odd to ask about the Gospel portraits of Jesus, they should! They are much more appropriate to modern psychological analyses and personality inventories than to ancient Gospel biographies, not because the Gospels are sacred writings (unless one equates sacred with sour and dour) but because they are *serious* writings about the life and death of God's Son confronting the most critical matters of life and death on earth. And they are theological biographies about a *selfless* hero who gives himself wholly for others' salvation and restoration. He's no party animal (despite his frequent table-fellowship)[1] or happy-go-lucky wanderer (despite his bare-bones itinerant mission). He's no self-preoccupied navel-gazer, constantly monitoring his feelings, moods, and vital signs (no Fitbit). He's never described as smiling or laughing (but neither is anyone else). His defining "hour" is not "happy hour" (despite his munificent wine provision in John 2) but the hour of trial, suffering, and death on behalf of a broken world.[2]

---

1. Contra Funk, *Honest to Jesus*, 208: "[Jesus] is the proverbial party animal, as one of our colleagues in the Jesus Seminar has put it." While often dining as a guest in others' homes, Jesus regularly uses these occasions to instruct the diners and critique the host! See Spencer, *What Did Jesus Do?*, 97–105.

2. See John 2:4; 4:21, 23; 7:30; 8:20; 12:23, 27; 13:1; 16:21, 25, 32; 17:1.

Nevertheless, while Jesus scarcely exemplifies a frivolous, fun-loving, or sunny disposition, he is by no means joyless. Of course, it all depends on how we interpret the emotion of "joy" (Greek *chara*; Latin *gaudium*) in distinction from other pleasant feelings. Generally speaking, "joy" represents something more substantial, elevated, and specifically motivated than "happiness," which applies to most any type and level of good sensation. As the Roman sage Seneca maintained, "Real joy [*gaudium*] is a serious matter" (*Let.* 23.4). Anticipating fuller analysis below of Seneca's and other ancient philosophers' views on joy, we may affirm from the outset that, far from being outside the scope of the Gospels' sober presentation of Jesus's character and mission, his experience of joy would be expected by serious thinkers to feature prominently in his exemplary life of wisdom and virtue. Also, as we will see, discussions of joy in the ancient world, like other emotions, anchor in social-relational contexts, rather than in personal assessments of "subjective well-being."[3] Accordingly, reports of Jesus's joy in the Gospels focus on his joyous relationship with the divine Father and Spirit and with his disciples.

There is not, we must admit, an abundance of evidence of Jesus's joy. But two Gospel cases explicitly evince his joy. The first, reported in Luke 10:17–24, involves Jesus's experience of joy "in the Holy Spirit" in response to his disciples' joy upon returning from their exorcising mission in his name. Instead of simply mirroring and affirming their joy, however, Jesus critiques it and identifies what motivates his joy in relation to them and his Father. The second case comes from the Farewell Discourse in the Fourth Gospel, where Jesus refers to "my joy" intertwined with "my love" for his disciple-friends (see chap. 9 of this study). Jesus desires that his joy might be channeled to his beloved ones and "complete" or "made full" (*plērōthē*) within them (John 15:11; 17:13 NASB), displacing their present and future "sorrow/pain" (*lypē*) over Jesus's looming death and departure (16:6, 20–24).

As we unpack these two joy texts below, we will seek to discover the nature of Jesus's joy, what motivates this emotion, and how he feels and expresses it in comparison with ancient and modern appraisals of joy. First, however, to provide a benchmark for understanding Jesus's joy, we attend to what he teaches about joy and how the Gospels depict others' joy in relation to him.

As attested in the Beatitudes from the Sermon on the Mount/Plain in Matthew/Luke and from other statements, Jesus shows particular interest

3. "Subjective well-being" is the stock in trade of modern surveys of happiness, as subjects report how they feel when prompted at random moments. While these studies can yield useful information, they remain limited. Unless prompted in close proximity to receiving extraordinary good news from a friend or loved one, it would be rare for someone to report, "I feel joyful" about a certain relationship.

in helping people lead "blessed" or "happy" lives. The term *makarios*, heading each Beatitude, means "blessed, fortunate, happy, privileged," especially applied to "recipient[s] of divine favor."[4] Such blessedness or happiness denotes more a graced state of well-being than an uplifting sensation or feeling, though emotions constitute an integral part of one's "state" or "condition," and Jesus's Beatitudes include emotional elements, though not in conventional terms. For example, the benediction "Blessed [or happy] are those who mourn, for they will be comforted" (Matt. 5:4; cf. Luke 6:21b, 25b) conjoins blessedness with sadness in anticipation of future comfort. The last Beatitude associates blessedness with persecution as the pathway *to* joy: "Blessed are you when people revile you and persecute you and utter all kinds of evil against you falsely on my account. Rejoice [*chairete*] and be glad [*agalliasthe*], for your reward is great in heaven, for in the same way they persecuted the prophets who were before you" (Matt. 5:11–12). Luke's version enhances the joyful outcome of such assault: "Rejoice [*charēte*] in that day [of revilement] and leap for joy [*skirtēsate*]" (Luke 6:23; cf. 1:41).[5] Joy is thus conceived not so much in antithesis to suffering as in process with it, moving in, through, out of, and beyond suffering in solidarity with God's suffering servants and prophets, culminating in Jesus Messiah.

In her wide-ranging and well-argued work *God and the Art of Happiness*, theologian Ellen Charry investigates what she calls the "asherist perspective" in the biblical and ecclesial tradition, based on the Hebrew word for "blessed/happy" ('*ašre* = Greek *makarios*). '*Ašre* is common in poetic and wisdom beatitudes. Its initial, eponymous usage appears in Genesis 30:13, as Jacob's less-favored wife, Leah, rejoices in God's blessing her with another son: "'Happy am I! For the women will call me happy'; so she named him Asher ['*ašer*]." Centuries later, the prophet Anna comes from this tribal line of Asher and aptly proceeds in Luke's Gospel "to praise God and to speak about the child [Jesus] to all who were looking for the redemption of Jerusalem" (Luke 2:36, 38).[6] Anna's joy caps the celebratory spirit in Luke 1–2 focused on the birth of Jesus, the "Savior, who is the Messiah, the Lord" (2:11) and his prophetic forerunner, John (1:14, 47, 58; 2:10).[7]

4. BDAG 610–11.
5. See the interpretation of *skirtaō*, as used in Luke 6:23, in L&N 1:303–4: "to be extremely happy, possibly implying . . . actually leaping or dancing for joy—'to be extremely joyful, to dance for joy.' . . . The phrase 'for joy' clearly expresses 'reason,' and therefore it may be useful to translate 'dance for joy' as 'dance because I am so joyful' or '. . . so happy.'"
6. Charry, *God and the Art of Happiness*, xi, 157–277.
7. See Green, "'We Had to Celebrate!,'" 171–76.

Charry places redemption at the heart of God's asheristic purpose. God graciously saves so that God's people might flourish to the fullest. But the people have their part to play in this blessed drama of salvation: "God and humanity work as a team, with God leading and humanity following"— particularly following in faithful obedience to God's benevolent commands.[8] As Charry summarizes, "Salvation is the healing of love that one may rest in God. Asherism works out that healing process in a life of reverent obedience to divine commands that shape character and bring moral-psychological flourishing and enhance societal well-being. . . . The biblical foundation of asherism [is] enjoyment of life through dynamic obedience to edifying commands that enable us to flourish that God may enjoy us and we enjoy God."[9] This nexus of love-obedience-joy fits closely with our treatment of Jesus's love in chapters 8–9, especially in the Fourth Gospel.[10] The emphasis on the joyous "healing of love" and "societal well-being" also fits the communal, celebratory finales of recovering the lost sheep, coin, and son in the Lukan Jesus's triad of parables, including "joy in heaven" as well as on earth (Luke 15:6–7, 9–10, 24–25, 32).

Jesus not only promotes joy through his teaching but also inspires "great joy" through his birth (Matt. 2:10 [Magi]; Luke 1:47 [Mary]; 2:10 [shepherds]), ministry (Luke 13:17; 19:6, 37), resurrection (Matt. 28:8; John 20:20), and ascension (Luke 24:52). Yet joy does not always have a perfectly rosy hue in relation to Jesus. In the post-resurrection scenes, responses of joy sometimes mix with less sanguine emotions. In Matthew, the women who first discover Jesus's empty tomb leave the scene "quickly with fear [*phobou*] and great joy [*charas*]" (Matt. 28:8); and in Luke, the disciples to whom Jesus appears and shows his nail-scarred hands and feet experience doubt and shock in the midst of their joy: "They were still incredulous [*apistountōn*] for joy [*charas*] and were amazed [*thaumazontōn*]" (Luke 24:41 NAB).

In his foundational parable of the soils delineating different responses to his message, Jesus identifies one type of hearers with "rocky" hearts who first receive the word "with joy [*charas*]" but easily "fall away" in time of hardship for lack of deep roots (Mark 4:16–17 // Matt. 13:20–21 // Luke 8:13); in this context, joy proves shallow and superficial, much like "amazement." Two more pejorative examples of joy emerge in Jesus's last days from shady characters with sinister interests against him. First, the chief priests are "greatly pleased" (or "rejoice" [*echarēsan*]) to learn of Judas's betrayal scheme, displaying a "joy

8. Charry, *God and the Art of Happiness*, 173.
9. Charry, *God and the Art of Happiness*, xi; see also Spencer, *Luke*, 170–71.
10. On happiness in the Fourth Gospel, see Charry, *God and the Art of Happiness*, 230–50.

[that is] vicious on a grand scale,"[11] which they happily back up with payment to Judas (Mark 14:10–11; Luke 22:3–5). Second, Herod Antipas is "very glad [or rejoices] exceedingly" (echarē lian) to weigh in on Pontius Pilate's trial of Jesus (Luke 23:8)—not to serve the cause of justice but to satisfy his longstanding curiosity about this putative miracle-worker. And when Jesus refuses to perform for Herod or respond in any way, Herod dispatches him back to Pilate after "treat[ing] him with contempt and mock[ing] him" (23:6–11). So joy can be a moral emotion with an "ethical register,"[12] serving good or bad aims. Evil people can derive great pleasure from evil plots. Virtue—or the lack thereof—matters in the experience of joy, as ancient and modern thinkers confirm.

Joy in Wisdom and Virtue: Ancient and Modern Perspectives

Greek and Roman Perspectives

In Aristotle's great work of moral philosophy, Nicomachean Ethics, he roots the experience of joy (chara) in good, noble, liberal, virtuous actions that characterize a flourishing life-state of "happiness" (eudaimonia) and produce positive feelings (passions) of "pleasure" (hēdonē): "The man who does not rejoice [chairōn] in noble actions is not even good; since no one would call a man just who did not enjoy [chaironta] acting justly, nor any man liberal who did not enjoy [chaironta] liberal actions; and similarly in other cases. If this is so, virtuous actions must be in themselves pleasant [hēdeiai]. . . . Happiness [eudaimonia] then is the best, noblest, and most pleasant [hēdiston] thing in the world" (Eth. nic.1.8 [1099a.17–25]).[13] This correlation of joy with ethical action (virtue), experiential condition (happiness), and emotional reaction (pleasure) sets the stage for many of the subsequent philosophical and psychological appraisals of joy, both religious and secular, not all of which prove as holistic as Aristotle's.[14] Some thinkers, that is, take more pains to distinguish joy from happiness and pleasure, particularly elevating joy as a super-virtuous attitude, disposition, or "spiritual" emotion beyond more mundane levels of happiness and pleasure.

11. Roberts, Spiritual Emotions, 118.
12. McMahon, "Joy in the History of Emotions," 109.
13. Aristotle, "Ethica Nicomachea," in Basic Works, 945.
14. See Frazzetto, Joy, Guilt, Anger, Love, 206: "In truth, hedonism and eudaimonia are not mutually exclusive. You can shape your character and develop admirable virtues while exercising the ability to enjoy pleasure. Pleasure does not always equate to selfish fleeting satisfaction and can be nurtured by higher goals. It is possible to have hedonistic motivations, achieve momentary happiness, while still keeping an eye on your long-term plans. Fleeting rewards don't come in the way of self-improvement. In short, you can at once be hedonistic and embrace eudaimonia" (cf. discussion 204–8).

The Hellenistic-Jewish philosopher Philo of Alexandria also stresses the wise person's "feeling of joy" associated with virtue. Yet he links this experience more closely with a rational, self-disciplined "soul" or "mind" than with pleasurable, other-directed acts: "Since then it is only in the virtues of the soul that genuine and unadulterated joy is found, and since every wise man rejoices, he rejoices in himself, and not in his surrounding circumstances; for the things that are in himself are the virtues of the mind on which it is worthy for a man to provide himself" (Philo, *Worse* 137; cf. 135–40).[15] Among the circumstances Philo discounts in relation to joy are material wealth, social status, and physical prowess (*Worse* 136). He does, however, allow for Aaron's joyful reunion with his brother, Moses, as they join up to carry out God's saving mission (*Worse* 135; see Exod. 4:14—"when [Aaron] sees you [Moses] his heart will be glad" [NRSV]; "when he sees you, he will be glad [*charēsetai*] in himself" [NETS]).

Philo also closely conjoins joy with hope, particularly viewing hope as a prelude to joy. Although regarding hope primarily as an intellectual attitude, a "rational part of the soul," he also characterizes hope as a "*propatheia* of joy," a "pre-emotion/passion" of joy, an instinctive "anticipation of good" (*QG* 1.79; cf. *Worse* 138–39).[16] For example, when Sarah laughs at the prospect of bearing Abraham a son in their old age (Gen. 18:11–12), she is evincing, in Philo's reading, not joy but rather hope in anticipation of possible future joy (*QG* 4.15–16). As Margaret Graver comments, "Sarah is still uncertain; she has 'begun to rejoice' but is not actually rejoicing." Granting the Stoic view that joy ranks chief among the *eupatheiai* ("good passions/emotions"), Philo strictly delimits true joy "to God and to the virtuous in contemplation of God," a "state of knowledge" that Sarah has not yet realized. At least, Graver continues, Sarah has potential for reaching this holy, joyous goal, since she has ceased to experience the "manner of women" (Gen. 18:11), which Philo interprets not as the capacity to bear children but as the proclivity to feel inferior, "ordinary emotions of fear, sorrow, pleasure, and desire."[17] Apparently, only by sterilizing her base emotional (female) nature can Sarah hope to attain the passionate virtue of joy.

Although Stoic thinkers took joy to be a "serious matter" of ethical import, they did not take all the joyous feeling out of the subject.[18] Note the nuanced

15. In Philo, *Works of Philo*, 127; unless otherwise noted, all Philo references in this section are from *Works*.

16. Quoted in Graver, *Stoicism and Emotion*, 104; and see discussion of *propatheia* in chap. 1 above.

17. Graver, *Stoicism and Emotion*, 104.

18. Contra the sweeping assessment in Green, "Joy," 448: "Neither set [of 'joy' or 'happiness' terms] refers in the first instance to emotions as these are popularly understood today. In Greco-Roman antiquity emotions generally were understood as irrational impulses to be

summary of the Stoic view of joy by Diogenes Laertius: "They [Stoics] say that there are three emotional states which are good [*eupatheias*], namely, joy [*charan*], caution, and wishing. Joy, the counterpart of pleasure [*hēdonē*], is rational elation. . . . And accordingly, as under the primary passions [*pathē*] are classed certain others subordinate to them, so too is it with . . . good emotional states . . . ; under joy [they bring] delight, mirth, cheerfulness" (*Lives* 7.116). Though wary of wild passion (*pathos*) unbridled by careful reason (*logos*), the Stoics did affirm, we underscore again, the estimable value of good passions (*eupatheiai*) *as* passions, with joy as the primary example. To be sure, unlike Aristotle, the Stoics strictly demarcated "rational" (*eulogon*) joy from pleasure (*hēdonē*); as a "good passion," joy derives from "good reason" (*eulogos*), from a virtuous mentality. Yet joy is not "pure reason" or cold rationality but rather "rational *elation*" or, better, "elevation" or "uplift" (*eparsis*), bringing us back into the elevated realm of awe and wonder, which cannot help but also be the realm of feeling, of felt emotions. Graver pulls together the emotional and ethical aspects of this assessment of Stoic joy: "Joy is 'well-reasoned elevation' [per Diogenes Laertius] corresponding on a feeling level to the happy excitement the ordinary person experiences on winning a raffle or leaving on vacation. But joy differs from those feelings in being directed at genuine good: a generous action, for instance would be an occasion for joy, and the proper object of the feeling would be the generosity itself, as exercised on that occasion."[19]

This perspective on joy is further developed by the prominent Roman sages and statesmen Cicero and Seneca, both of whom were heavily influenced by Stoic philosophy. Cicero distinguishes "two ways we may be moved as by the presence of something good. When the mind is moved quietly and consistently, in accordance with reason, this is termed 'joy' [*gaudium*]; but when it pours forth with a hollow sort of uplift [*exultat*], that is called 'wild or excessive gladness [*laetitia*],' which they define as 'an unreasoning elevation [*elationem*] of mind'" (*Tusc.* 4.13; cf. 4.66).[20] Notice that while Cicero morally differentiates joy from gladness on various grounds, he does not deny their common motivation—the result of being *moved*, being excited physically and emotionally—by "something good." Joy and gladness share a fellow feeling.

---

controlled by a rational person. 'Joy' and 'happiness' refer instead to the complex of proclivities and behaviors associated with human flourishing." A more balanced perspective acknowledges the "complex" of emotions/feelings along with inclinations and actions in ancient and modern perspectives on joy. See, for example, D. Robertson, *How to Think*, 122: "For Stoics, feelings of pleasure in themselves are neither good nor bad. Rather, whether our state of mind is good or bad, healthy or unhealthy, depends on the things we take enjoyment *in*" (emphasis original).

19. Graver, *Stoicism and Emotion*, 52.
20. Graver, *Cicero on the Emotions*, 44.

But they vary in degree of emotional expression and rational foundation. Whereas joy moves "quietly and consistently, in accordance with reason," gladness can manifest in irrational ways both "hollow" and "wild," superficial and superfluous. Although Cicero mentions "uplift" and "elevation" only in relation to gladness, he does so in order to indicate that such experiences may lack solid substance and sound reason. By implication, however, one can alternatively experience substantial uplift and rational elevation; in other words, one can experience true, joyous elation.

In his *Letters on Ethics*, Seneca counsels one Lucilius to "learn how to be joyful" and to "learn where [joy] is to be found" (*Let.* 23.3–4). Joy thus inheres in philosophy, in investigative, educative, and contemplative study, the life of the mind.[21] Because joy is so serious and substantive, so highly valued and elevated, it is, to reverse the directional metaphor, worth digging down for in hidden recesses.

> Shallow mines yield but a little; the most precious lodes are hidden deep in the earth, and it is these that will repay with digging ever greater abundance. The pleasure that is in the amusements of the many is slight and superficial. And any joy lacks foundation when it has been imported from elsewhere. The joy of which I am speaking, to which I seek to direct you, is solid through and through, and has its widest scope within. (*Let.* 23.5)

Again, however, while Seneca distances joy from "slight and superficial" pleasures and "trivial feelings," he does not dissociate joy from genuinely pleasant feelings in the "heart" as well as in the "energetic" mind:

> Do you now suppose [Lucilius] that . . . I am taking away many pleasures? Not at all: what I want is that gladness [*laetitiam*] should never be absent from you. I want it to be born in your own home—and . . . inside of you. Other delights [*hilaritates*] do not fill the heart; they are trivial feelings that merely smooth the brow. Surely you don't think that every person who smiles is rejoicing [*gaudere*]! The mind must be energetic [*alacer*][22] and confident; it must be upright, superior to every trial. (*Let.* 23.3)

In another letter, answering a prior correspondence from Lucilius, Seneca admits to normal feelings of pleasure not strictly permitted by Stoic dogma but hardly ruinous to one's mental health: "From your letter I derived great pleasure—for you must allow me to use common parlance; you mustn't recall

21. See Graver, "Anatomies of Joy"; Solomon, *Joy of Philosophy*, 3–16.
22. In classical usage, *alacer* means "lively, brisk, quick, eager, active; glad, happy, cheerful," according to Lewis and Short, *Latin Dictionary*, s.v. ālăcer.

my words to their Stoic meanings. It is our doctrine that pleasure is a fault. Be that as it may, 'pleasure' [*voluptatem*] is the word we generally use to refer to a glad feeling of the mind [*animi hilarem adfectionem*]. . . . [And] in our ordinary speech we often say that we are overjoyed [*magnum gaudium*]." Yet, while granting some flexibility in popular conversation, Seneca still insists on ennobling the virtue of "joy" (*gaudium*) above ordinary pleasure or hilarity. Echoing Cicero, he affirms that "joy pertains only to the wise person, for it is the elevation of a mind [*animi elatio*] toward goods that are real and its own." Moreover, events that people commonly report as joyous, like winning a high office or bearing a child, "far from causes for joy [*gaudium*], are frequently the beginnings of sorrow. For it is an attribute of joy that it never ceases or turns into its opposite" (*Let.* 59.1–2). In the Fourth Gospel, Jesus will also reflect on the image of childbirth in the context of joy and sorrow, though differently than Seneca does, as we will see below.

Spinozan and Protestant Perspectives

The sixteenth and seventeenth centuries ushered in the early modern period of radical new thinking in theology and ethics—in large measure a renewing (Renaissance) and reforming (Reformation) of classical and scriptural values—with fresh reflection on the primacy of joyful faith and practice. As we discussed Spinoza's treatment of wonder in chapter 7, so we now consider his incisive analysis of joy. In the third part of his *Ethics*, titled "On the Nature and Origin of Affects," Spinoza defines "affect" as a nexus of physical, mental, and behavioral processes, thus anticipating much scientific analysis of the subject today: "By affect I understand affections of the body by which the body's power of acting is increased or diminished, aided or restrained, and at the same time, the ideas of these affections" (*Ethics*, pt. 3, D3). In his eleventh postulate expounding this affect-driven body-mind-action dynamic, he concentrates on the prime "passions" or "affects of joy [*laetitae*] and sadness." "By joy, therefore, I . . . understand . . . that *passion by which the mind passes to a greater perfection. And by sadness, that passion which it passes to a lesser perfection. The affect of joy which is related to the mind and body at once I call pleasure or cheerfulness, and that of sadness, pain or melancholy*" (pt. 3, P11; emphasis original).

Spinoza's "idea" of joy is not some abstract concept but rather a fully embodied, pleasurable or cheerful feeling-state, pulsing with the "power of acting" (see *Ethics*, pt. 3, P37), of moving one to "perfection," to perfective actions, to flourishing wholeness. Of course, joyous passions must again accord with rigorous reason and virtuous character. Yet Spinoza allows joy a wide scope for generating "good" outcomes: "By good . . . I understand every kind of joy, and whatever leads to it, and especially what satisfies any kind of longing, whatever that might be" (pt. 3, P39). Even so, not everything joy stimulates proves virtuous; Spinoza defines "pride" as "a species of madness" attending excessive self-exultation or "*joy born of the fact that a man thinks more highly of himself than is just*" (pt. 3, P26; cf. P29, P30; emphasis original).

However, where pride betrays joy's good intentions by fixating inward on the self and backward on the past, love fuels true joy's outward, object-directed focus, and hope furthers joy's forward, open-ended vision.[23] Regarding love, that "*which usually affects the mind with joy or sadness, we love it or hate it*" (*Ethics*, pt. 3, P16; emphasis original) and that "which usually affects us with an equally great affect of joy, we shall love it with an equally great striving of joy" (pt. 3, P17)—for "love is a joy, accompanied by the idea of an external cause" (pt. 3, "Definitions of the Affects" VI). As for hope, "*hope is nothing but an inconstant joy which has arisen from the image of a future or past thing whose outcome we doubt.*" Conversely, "*fear . . . is an inconstant sadness, which has also arisen from the image of a doubtful thing.*" Once, however, "the doubt involved in these affects is removed" and the outcome clarified, "hope becomes *confidence*, and fear, *despair*—namely, *a joy or sadness which has arisen from the image of a thing we feared or hoped for*" (pt. 3, P18; emphasis original).

This interacting and inter-affecting cluster of joy, love, and hope in counteracting and counter-affecting relation to sadness, hate, and despair typifies Spinoza's principle that "*an affect cannot be restrained or taken away except by an affect opposite to, and stronger than, the affect to be restrained*" (*Ethics*, pt. 4, P7; emphasis original). Spinoza thus accords more salutary potential to emotions than the Stoics allowed. As the neuroscientist Antonio Damasio comments, in thoughtful engagement with Spinoza's ideas, "Spinoza recommended that we fight a negative emotion with an even stronger but positive emotion brought about by reasoning and intellectual effort. Central to his thinking was the notion that the subduing of the passions should be accomplished by reason-induced emotion and not by pure reason alone."[24] And the strongest, most beneficial, most reasonable of all emotions is joy, interlaced with love and hope.

Such touting of the high virtues of joy, love, and hope, with or without accompanying feelings, sounds very religious, very spiritual, very Christian

---

23. See Philo's linkage of joy and hope in *QG* 4.15–16 (discussed earlier in this chapter).
24. Damasio, *Looking for Spinoza*, 12.

even, as Paul's famous love chapter in 1 Corinthians 13 and list of Spirit-generated fruits in Galatians 5 attest (see also Rom. 5:2–5). Though hardly an orthodox Christian, Spinoza still anchored his understanding of human affective experience in "the idea of God," a highly philosophical notion, to be sure, but one still mediated through the passions,[25] especially joy and love. Not that the perfect God personally has passions[26] but that we know God via our reason-grounded passions: "He who understands himself and his affects clearly and distinctly rejoices, and this joy is accompanied by the idea of God. Hence, he loves God, and (by the same reasoning) does so the more, the more he understands himself and his affects" (*Ethics*, pt. 5, P15). And again, for all its intellectual grounding, Spinoza's idea of God is no cold, calculated concept but rather the source of the most pleasurable, joyous experience one can imagine: "*We take pleasure in, and our pleasure is accompanied by the idea of God as a cause.* From this kind of knowledge there arises the greatest satisfaction of mind there can be, that is, joy" (pt. 5, P32; emphasis original). Spinoza was part mystic and contemplative, it seems.

And so is Damasio, partly because of his engagement with Spinoza but mostly because of his groundbreaking research in the neurobiology of human feelings and emotions in conjunction with reason: "Reason lets us see, while feeling is the enforcer of our determination to see. What I find attractive in Spinoza . . . is the recognition of the advantages of joy and the rejection of sorrow and fear, and the determination to seek the former and obliterate the latter. Spinoza affirms life and turns emotion and feeling into the means for its nourishing, a nice mixture of wisdom and forethought."[27] Nevertheless, Damasio finds Spinoza too rationalistic, passive, and Spartan for his tastes, closer to Stoics (and Vulcans like Spock) and further from more balanced and vivacious Aristotelian and Christian ways of life.

> Spinoza does not go as far as the Greek and Roman Stoics in his divestiture of life's trappings, but he gets awfully close. . . . Why should Aristotle's wisdom not prevail here? Aristotle insisted that the contented life is a virtuous and happy life, but that health, wealth, love, and friendship are part of the contentment. . . . Spinoza's God is an idea, rather than the flesh and blood that, for example,

25. See further: "*The mind can bring it about that all the body's affections, or images of things, are related to the idea of God*" (*Ethics*, pt. 5, P14; emphasis original).

26. "*God is without passions, and is not affected with any affect of joy or sadness*" (*Ethics*, pt. 5, P17; emphasis original).

27. Damasio, *Looking for Spinoza*, 277; note also: "Central to [Spinoza's] thinking was the notion that the subduing of the passions should be accomplished by reason-induced emotion and not by pure reason alone" (12).

the Christian narrative has created. Spinoza might have drunk with God, as Novalis[28] said of him, but his God is rather dry.[29]

Clearly, the Gospel narratives, with their lively portraits of the table-fellowshipping, wine-supplying Son of God and "Word made flesh," do not trade in mere "ideas" of God (drunk or dry). Although Jesus is not explicitly said to experience joy or happiness at dinner tables or wedding feasts, and while he uses these settings to challenge others' restrictive viewpoints and habits, he fully participates in these joyous events—physically, socially, emotionally, as much as intellectually (ideationally). And he doesn't need Aristotle or Seneca to expand his vision of joy. Jesus's Jewish scriptural tradition sets the table for enjoying all of God's good creational gifts, material and spiritual, secular and religious. As Beyreuther and Finkenrath summarize, "In the OT there is no apology for joy in the good things of life, such as health (Sir. 30:16), wise children (Prov. 23:25), eating and drinking (Ps.104:14–15), peace in the land (1 Macc. 14:11)."[30]

In the previous century, the pioneering Protestant Reformers Martin Luther and John Calvin touted joy as a core concomitant of Christian faith—a vibrant joy full of feeling gripping heart, mind, and will, and grounded in God's gracious gifts, earthly and heavenly. In a remarkable letter (May 23, 1534) to Joachim von Anhalt, a young German prince prone to bouts of depression, Luther offers pastoral counsel, encouraging the pursuit of everyday joyous activities in gratitude to God:

> I should like to encourage Your Grace, who are a young man, always to be joyful [fröhlich], to engage in riding and hunting, and to seek the company of others who may be able to rejoice with Your Grace in a godly and honorable way. . . . Accordingly God has commanded us to rejoice in his presence. . . . No one realizes how much harm it does a young person to avoid pleasure [Freude] and cultivate solitude and sadness. . . . For gladness and good cheer,

28. Novalis was the pen name of Georg Philipp Friedrich Freiherr von Hardenberg, a German Romantic poet and philosopher (1772–1801).

29. Damasio, *Looking for Spinoza*, 278; see his entire final chapter ("Who's There?," 265–89) for a thoughtful reflection on the nature of God. For a brief discussion of Spinoza's view of joy and God, see Potkay, *Story of Joy*, 14, 132.

30. Beyreuther and Finkenrath, "Joy, Rejoice," 2:357. McMahon ("Joy in the History of Emotions," 112) frames his quotation of Beyreuther and Finkenrath with this appraisal: "God, as the giver of all joy, had sanctified joy, making many of its earthly varieties holy and just. . . . Joy may be had happily, healthily, in the fruits of the table and the fruits of one's loins. And though it is also true that such joys are transitory, as the author of Proverbs cautions—for 'even in laughter the heart may ache, and joy may end in grief' (Prov. 14:13)—they are not to be disdained or dismissed in and of themselves."

when decent and proper, are the best medicine for a young person, indeed, for all people.[31]

Luther does not dash off this prescription in perfunctory fashion; rather, it comes from his own experience of guilt-ridden depression and what we might call *theological cognitive therapy* derived from his reformative thinking about God's joyous grace: "I myself, who have spent a good part of my life in sorrow and gloom, *now* seek and find pleasure wherever I can. Praise God, we *now have sufficient understanding* [of the Word of God] to be able to rejoice with a good conscience and to use God's gifts with thanksgiving, for he created them for this purpose and is pleased when we use them."[32]

Luther's translation of the Bible into vernacular German and his biblical commentaries reinforce his (re)discovery of heartfelt joy in Christ. Luther scholar Birgit Stolt observes that overall "Luther dedicated great care to the emotional side of the text. As far as feelings went, he was richly endowed and possessed a genial capacity to give expression to his emotions."[33] Although more affirming and less suspicious of feelings than his more sober co-religionists, Luther was far from anti-intellectual. He took seriously the full-fledged biblical image of the "heart" as the integrated seat of thoughts, feelings, and desires, the dynamic junction of intellect and affect. As Stolt describes Luther's viewpoint, "The heart was wise and the understanding warm."[34]

And wise hearts and warm minds, attuned to God's word and will, generate jubilant, joyous responses: "Whoever reads Luther today should consider that the word *fröhlich* [in Luther's time] denotes 'an exultant [*jubelnde*] joy,' often about help from God. This takes a central place in Luther's theology and language."[35] For example, in commenting on the Magnificat, Luther states that "God becomes so dearly loved that the heart overflows with happiness, skips and jumps for joy" (as Elizabeth's child leaps in utero in the presence of the pregnant Mary [Luke 1:41, 44]).[36] Mary's humility is no abject, stringent self-debasement but rather an exultant, expansive (magnifying) spur to her rejoicing in God's marvelous uplifting grace and power.[37]

31. Luther, *Luther: Letters*, 93.
32. Luther, *Luther: Letters*, 93 (emphasis added); cf. McMahon, *Happiness*, 164–67.
33. Stolt, "Luther's Translation," 388.
34. Stolt, "Luther's Translation," 375.
35. Stolt, "Luther's Translation," 392; see 390–92 for fuller discussion of Luther's usage of *fröhlich*.
36. Quoted in Stolt, "Luther's Translation," 390–91.
37. See Just, "My Soul Magnifies the Lord."

In the section of his Galatians lectures commenting on the fruit of the Spirit (Gal. 5:22–23), Luther roots joy (the second "fruit" after love) in the person and work of Christ, operative in the believer both inwardly, in Spirit-inspired thoughts and feelings, and outwardly, in faithful speech and activity. Joy "is the voice of the Bridegroom and the bride [alluding to John 3:29]; it means joyful thoughts about Christ, wholesome exhortations, happy songs, praise, and thanksgiving, with which godly people exhort, arouse, and refresh one another. . . . When this is a joy of the Spirit, not of the flesh, the heart rejoices inwardly through faith in Christ . . . and outwardly it demonstrates this joy in its words and actions."[38] Again, a very balanced, holistic, and salutary assessment of Christian joy.

At the same time, however, Luther the biblical exegete has a less generous view of joy's counterpart, sorrow or sadness, than Luther the pastoral counselor (to young Prince Joachim). Luther feels just as passionately about sorrow's negative valence as he does about joy's positive one; or rather, he claims to speak for how strongly, how *militantly* even, *God feels* about these matters as royal commander-in-chief of God's people: "God is repelled by sorrow of spirit; He hates sorrowful teaching and sorrowful thoughts and words, and He takes pleasure in happiness. For he came to refresh us, not to sadden us. Hence the prophets, apostles, and Christ himself always urge, indeed command, that we rejoice and exult." Luther cites Zechariah 9:9 for his prophetic example, Philippians 4:4 as his apostolic example, and Luke 10:20 (one of the key texts discussed below) for his Christ case: "Rejoice that your names are written in heaven."[39] Luther's impassioned, imperative stance on ebullient joy all but vilifies any melancholic lapses for any reason. He even goes so far as to demonize depression. As McMahon writes, "'Tristitia omnis a Sathana,' Luther affirmed on numerous occasions. 'All sadness is from Satan.' We should flee it like the Devil."[40]

John Calvin shows similar high esteem for the emotion of "spiritual joy," thus disabusing some later "Calvinist" purveyors of dour dogma and austere ethics. But he also views such joy as evidence (fruit) of authentic Christian faith, limited only to those chosen ones God has redeemed in Christ. For those outside Christ, Calvin offers scant joy and hope: "Those upon whom the curse of God rests taste not even the least particle of happiness" (*Institutes* 3.7.8). For the faithful in Christ, however, Calvin offers much emotional encouragement, not only prospects of abundant joy and hope but sympathies for those

38. Luther, *Lectures on Galatians*, 93; cf. Potkay, *Story of Joy*, 76–77.
39. Luther, *Lectures on Galatians*, 93.
40. McMahon, *Happiness*, 173.

suffering sorrow and sadness. Here Calvin parts ways with Luther's harsh "satanic" view of sadness. Calvin has no truck with the "iron philosophy" of "new Stoics, who count it depraved not only to groan and weep but also to be sad and care ridden." He notes that Jesus himself "groaned and wept both over his own and others' misfortunes"—a dimension of Jesus's emotional life we examined at length in chapters 4–5. Calvin goes on to stress that Jesus predicted his disciples would share similar distress as a mark of blessing, per the Beatitude "Blessed are those who mourn" (Matt. 5:4) and his farewell teaching in the Fourth Gospel, "The world . . . will rejoice; but you will be sorrowful and will weep (John 16:20 [examined below])" (*Institutes* 3.8.9).

By no means, however, does Calvin advocate sorrowful suffering as a virtuous end in itself; rather he views it as an opportunity for compassionate ministry and faithful endurance tethered to vigorous joy: "For Scripture praises the saints for their forbearance when, so afflicted with harsh misfortune, they do not break or fall; so stabbed with bitterness they are at the same time flooded with spiritual joy" (*Institutes* 3.8.10). Of course, these "saints" follow in Christ's cross-bearing footsteps and complex feelings of pain and pleasure: "However much in bearing the cross our minds are constrained by the natural feeling of bitterness, they are as much diffused with spiritual joy. From this, thanksgiving also follows, which cannot exist without joy; but if the praise of the Lord and thanksgiving can come forth only from a cheerful and happy heart—and there is nothing that ought to interrupt this in us—it is clear how necessary it is that the bitterness of the cross be tempered with spiritual joy" (3.3.11).

Although there is much to celebrate in these leading Reformers' advocacy of spiritual joy, a nagging pastoral concern complicates the matter, particularly from Luther's side but also from Calvin's.[41] Characterizing joy as a Christian duty, a matter of obedience to Christ's command (Rejoice!), need not be any more onerous than the command to love God and others (closely tied with joy in John 15–16). But it can become downright oppressive the more that *lack of joy* (that is, sorrow/sadness) is taken as a sign of sinfulness, accursedness, separation from God, and alliance with Satan. Branding the depressed person as sinner *because* of their depression only compounds the problem, blames the victim, and dilutes God's compassion. Job's three "comforters" proved to be more fiends than friends. The matter can become worse under some rigid systems of Evangelical and Reformed theology that hammer home the utter

---

41. I'm indebted here to McMahon, *Happiness*, 164–75, and Potkay, *Story of Joy*, 73–78, though McMahon ignores Calvin's more balanced view of suffering/joy I just presented, and Potkay focuses on Luther, with no treatment of Calvin.

helplessness of anyone to save themselves, leaving them in a state of total dependence on God to provide joyous relief, *if* God wills. At its most extreme, such thinking discourages depressed people, believers and unbelievers, from seeking medical and/or practical help as if it were somehow ungodly. Luther and Calvin were better pastors and friends than that, as Jesus the compassionate shepherd-friend certainly was, which sadly has not prevented some of their followers from straining their teachings through a very tight sieve. That really is depressing.

Recent "Spiritual" Perspectives

I focus here on a "spiritual" assessment of the emotion of joy by two senior academics writing in the first decade of the new millennium. Robert Roberts, a philosopher and ethicist at Baylor University, has written extensively on emotion theory;[42] in *Spiritual Emotions: A Psychology of Christian Virtues* (2007), a more practical work from an avowed Christian perspective, Roberts reflects on "spiritual emotions," including the emotion of joy.[43] George Vaillant, a research psychiatrist and professor at Harvard Medical School who is best known for directing the Harvard Study of Adult Development over five decades,[44] explores the scientific underpinnings of religious experience in *Spiritual Evolution: How We Are Wired for Faith, Hope, and Love* (2008), which includes a substantive chapter on joy.[45] I draw on these works as I highlight themes of potential relevance to our examination of Jesus's joy in Luke and John.

Of a piece with Roberts's cognitive-evaluative approach to emotions is his focus on *perception*: how we *see* someone or a situation determines to a large measure how we *feel* about them.[46] Regarding joy and sadness, Roberts offers the apt example of the Judahites' different feelings about constructing the second temple in Jerusalem, reported in Ezra: "And all the people responded with a great shout when they praised the LORD, because the foundation of the house of the LORD was laid. But many of the priests and Levites and heads of families, old people who had *seen the first house* on its foundations, *wept* with a loud voice . . . though many *shouted aloud for joy*, so that the people could not distinguish the sound of the joyful shout from the sound of the people's weeping" (Ezra 3:11–13). Here we see mixed feelings about the same

42. See, for example, Roberts, *Emotions: An Essay*; Roberts, "Emotions and the Canons."
43. Roberts, *Spiritual Emotions*, 114–29 (chap. 8).
44. Vaillant, *Aging Well*; Vaillant, *Triumphs of Experience*.
45. Vaillant, *Spiritual Evolution*, 119–34 (chap. 9).
46. On the connection between emotions and perceptions, see chap. 9n4.

event based on mixed perceptions: one group sees Solomon's glorious temple superimposed on this inferior reconstruction; the other group sees fresh steps toward restoration out of the rubble of destruction and exile; the former group weeps woefully with an eye to the past; the latter shouts joyfully with an eye to the future. Both responses reflect serious, meaningful concerns about the people's very existence in relation to their God (this is not about the temple structure per se), and they are not mutually exclusive.

Roberts sees a "unity of mind among the celebrants. However opposite the pain of the one group is to the pleasure of the other, the two groups agree in the fundamental orientation of their hearts"—toward loving and worshiping God. And emotions of sadness and joy not only can coexist but can even work together toward such a goal: "The possibility of sadness is tightly bound to the capacity for joy. A godly sadness is as precious in the eyes of the Lord as the joy that corresponds to it."[47] Further, sorrow and gladness, like all emotions, represent "concern-based construals," in Roberts's view, targeted at what most concerns us, what we care most about.[48] On the positive side, "joy is a kind of *satisfaction*. You care about something—your baby, the temple [as in Ezra]—and you *see the situation as satisfying your care*, as being very good from the standpoint of your care."[49] Strengthening such happy satisfaction of care are related "joyful emotions" of "gratitude, hope, and peace."[50]

As a physician and scientist concerned about positively promoting health and well-being, not just managing illness and ill-temper, Vaillant seeks to remedy the lack of attention therapists and researchers have paid to joy.[51] Some of this neglect stems from joy's close association with spiritual experience, best left to religious professionals. For his part, however, Dr. Vaillant has no qualms about stepping in where other medical experts fear to tread. He opens his chapter on joy by noting that the Jesuit philosopher and paleontologist Pierre Teilhard de Chardin "considered joy the most infallible sign of the presence of God" and that "cross-culturally, spiritual joy is widely valued. Joy is a common accompaniment of all 'white light,' 'near-death,' and mystical experience."[52] Moreover, in distinguishing joy from happiness, he flatly declares, "Joy is spiritual; happiness is secular."[53] But Vaillant concentrates mostly on *connection*—primarily connection among human beings and the

47. Roberts, *Spiritual Emotions*, 115.
48. Roberts, *Spiritual Emotions*, 11, 14; Roberts, *Emotions: An Essay*, 60–179.
49. Roberts, *Spiritual Emotions*, 116 (emphasis original).
50. Roberts, *Spiritual Emotions*, 120.
51. Vaillant, *Spiritual Evolution*, 119: "Of all primary human emotions, joy is the one least studied."
52. Vaillant, *Spiritual Evolution*, 119–20.
53. Vaillant, *Spiritual Evolution*, 124.

universe but also connection with God as the lifeblood of joy circulating through and around suffering, not bypassing it: "Joy is all about connection with others; happiness is all about drive reduction for the self. Happiness allows us to run from pain, while joy . . . allows us to acknowledge suffering. . . . Happiness is tame. In contrast joy is a primary emotion. Joy is perceived subjectively in our viscera. Joy is connection to the universe. . . . Joy is laughing from the gut, and we often weep with joy. Happiness displaces pain. Joy encompasses pain."[54]

This connective drive of joy is notably manifest in contexts of reunion and return: "Joy includes recognition of longing, of both coming and going, of weeping followed by reunion." To illustrate this point, Vaillant quotes the farewell scene between the risen Jesus and his disciples (following their recent reunion after Jesus's death) in the last two verses of Luke: "And it came to pass while he blessed them, He was parted from them and carried up into heaven. And they worshiped him, and returned to Jerusalem with great joy – Luke 24:51–52."[55] Vaillant could have easily closed the reunion loop by also quoting the conclusion of the departure scene at the beginning of Luke's second volume, in which divine messengers promise the disciples that "this Jesus . . . will come [back] in the same way as you saw him go into heaven" (Acts 1:11).

The desire for the return of absent or distant loved ones is a particularly deep-seated, hardwired component of parental childcare. "Since children will wander off, a powerful reward system is needed to retrieve them from freeways and from tigers—especially if it takes ten to twenty years for them to grow up." Vaillant credits joy as that reward or "motivational system that reinforces return."[56] Surprisingly, he does not cite Luke again, which provides the perfect example of joyous parental embrace of a returning child after a long, far, and fraught absence. As the father in Jesus's parable declares to his elder son regarding his prodigal younger sibling, "We had to celebrate [euphranthēnai] and rejoice [charēnai], because this brother of yours was dead and has come to life; he was lost and has been found" (Luke 15:32; cf. 15:6–7, 9–10).

Joy in Spirit and Insight: Jesus's Mission (Luke 10:17–24)

Another case of joyful return in Luke merits attention, involving another encounter between Jesus and his associates. It occurs in the middle of his ministry rather than at the end and this time directly connects with Jesus's own

54. Vaillant, *Spiritual Evolution*, 124
55. Vaillant, *Spiritual Evolution*, 126.
56. Vaillant, *Spiritual Evolution*, 127.

experience of joy rather than implying it through a parable. Yet this is not a time of "pure joy," as Jesus challenges his followers' misguided motivation before revealing his reasons for true joy. Like the philosophers, ethicists, and psychologists discussed above, Luke's Jesus regards joy as "serious" business, worth careful, thoughtful understanding as well as enlivening, uplifting feeling.

Jesus dispatches an advance group of seventy paired delegates (thirty-five teams)[57] to all the places he plans to visit, with a mission of promoting God's realm of peace (Luke 10:5–6) and health (10:9) to those who will receive it. He sends them out in full solidarity and authority with himself and with God: "Whoever listens to you listens to me, and whoever rejects you rejects me, and whoever rejects me rejects the one [God] who sent me" (10:16). Upon completing this mission, "the seventy *returned with joy* [*charas*]" (10:17), obviously regarding their work as a great success, worthy of celebrating. Yet the primary reason for their joy concerns a surprising (to them) accomplishment, not covered in Jesus's original commission: "Lord, in your name even [*kai*] the demons submit to us!" This victory marks a notable improvement over their failure to expel an evil spirit (9:39–40), compounded by their resisting a maverick exorcist outside their circle (9:49–50). Of course, liberating people from demonic oppression is a good thing, one means of bringing God's peaceful, healthful realm to earth, as Jesus himself demonstrates (11:20; cf. 9:1–2). But the disciples seem a tad too excited about their demon-conquering exploits for Jesus's taste. Rather than echoing their joy or applauding their success ("Way to go, guys. I'm proud of you!"), he launches into a mini-lesson on demonology, culminating in a rebuke—"Nevertheless, *do not rejoice* [*mē chairete*] at this"—and a redirection of their joyous energy (10:18–20).

What is Jesus's point here? He's not aiming to tamp down the seventy missionaries' enthusiasm; he's no spoilsport. And, again, he's certainly not suggesting that they shouldn't have bothered helping those afflicted by demons. Indeed, he reinforces his opposition to Satan and his evil minions. Throughout Jesus's ministry, he has sought to fell these evil forces on earth (Luke 4:1–13, 31–37, 41; 8:26–39; 9:37–43; 11:14–23; 13:10–17), extending their deserved "fall from heaven" (cf. Isa. 14:3–22; Rev. 12:9–12). And he has enlisted his disciples in the fight, equipping them with authority "over all the power of the enemy" (10:18–19). But "this" militant spiritual power, as necessary as it is to exercise in dire situations ("just war"), does not rate as a prime reason for joy in Jesus's book. War is hell any way you slice it. Calling it "spiritual" war against evil "spirits" does not make it less hellish, and

---

57. A well-known textual variant numbers the missionaries at seventy-*two* rather than seventy. The exact number does not bear on my argument here; for simplicity's sake, I stick with seventy.

euphoric victory songs over violently vanquished foes (such as Moses's Song in Exod. 15:1–18 or "The Battle Hymn of the Republic") express more than a little *Schadenfreude* ("joy in harm") at others' expense.[58] And the more joy aligns with power conflicts of any kind, the more it risks being corrupted by corruptible power.

To be sure, Mary rejoices in song over Almighty God's toppling "the powerful from their thrones" and divesting the rich of their resources, but such jubilation is embedded in the context of her continuing humility as God's lowly servant and God's purpose of "lifting the lowly" and "filling the hungry," not making them the new power brokers and wealth managers (Luke 1:46–49, 52–53). Although observers respond with praise and amazement over Jesus's miracles, including his exorcisms, he himself does no victory shouting, dancing, preening, or chest-thumping. That's the stuff of glory-glutted rulers, pretenders to godlike, heavenly stature, like the "fallen" Satan and his avatars, such as the ancient king of Babylon (Isa. 14:12) or Herod Agrippa I (Acts 12:20–23; Josephus, *Ant.* 19.343–52). From the start, Jesus staunchly resists self-adulating, self-advancing, Satan-tempting triumphalism (Luke 4:5–8). True joy avoids even the appearance of evil association and exploitation. As Seneca further states in *Letter 59* (discussed above): "When our poet Virgil says 'and evil joys of mind [*mala gaudia*],' he speaks elegantly, but not properly, for no joy is evil. He merely applied that term to pleasures, and expressed his meaning in that way, for the people referred to are happy with what is bad for them" (*Let.* 59.3).

The seventy tip off their self-absorbed distortion of joy with the language of their report. Although they acknowledge their dependence on Lord Jesus's "name," they put themselves in the center of the picture; note the word order following the Greek text: "Lord [*Kyrie*], even the demons are subject to us [*hēmin*] in the name of you [*sou*]" (Luke 10:17 AT). The Lord and his name frame the spotlighted missionaries: "Look, Lord, at what *we* have done! (. . . with your help, of course)." They're finally starting to make a name for themselves in this world. Three cheers for them!

But Jesus has a different perspective on the name game related to joy, honor, power, and service. He grants their successful employment of his name to resist demonic opposition and relieve sufferers from oppression but takes no particular pleasure in this work for himself or for his followers (presumably, if there's any joy to be had, it should be reserved for those healed and freed). Jesus's name is not to be trifled with or used to boost one's own name. Just ask the seven sons of Sceva, itinerant exorcists who dallied with Jesus's (and

58. Potkay, *Story of Joy,* 9.

Paul's) name in Acts, to their utter humiliation (Acts 19:13–17). What Jesus does encourage, nevertheless (*plēn*),[59] as a reasonable and virtuous source of their name-related joy is the fact that "your names are written in heaven" (Luke 10:20). Fine, but what does that piece of information mean here? Until now, Luke's Jesus has said nothing about a heavenly registry. The reference seems to come out of the blue.

On closer examination, however, this statement makes good sense and begins to fill out Jesus's understanding of joy just before he experiences his own joy "at that same hour" (Luke 10:21). Along with using the keyword "name" again, he reiterates the realm of "heaven," thus shifting the seventy's attention to the secure enrollment they enjoy in the very sphere from which Satan and his demons have fallen! Rather than rejoicing in who's under them, subject to their control, in worldly power terms (even if it's hellish spirit-powers they're subduing) they should celebrate their sacred, graced place *with God*—Father, Son, and Spirit (all "three" are mentioned in the two ensuing verses [10:21–22])[60]—and *under God* in the divine "heavenly" realm. Of course, apart from faithful communion with God through Christ in the power of the Spirit, they would have no capacity whatsoever to overcome evil forces. They would remain stuck right where some of them recently were, totally "faithless" and inept to cast out the convulsive spirit tormenting a father's only child (9:37–41).

The joy Jesus enjoins derives from *connection*, as Vaillant emphasizes—in this case, loving connection with all children and friends of God and Christ signed or "booked" (by "name"!) into "heaven," the dynamic divine realm of peace and justice.[61] But joy also abounds in this realm for God's people in their *subjection* to God's gracious will—not forced subjugation but freely offered obedience to God's love-commands. In this sense the Reformers were right to see joy, like love, as a *felt duty* owed to a gracious Lord (without Luther's demonization of grief and depression) in concert with faithful following of the Lord's directive will.

An illuminating text from the LXX combines the call to be subject to God with keynotes of "book" and "name": "And the Lord . . . wrote a *book of*

59. Fifteen of thirty-one New Testament uses of the adversative conjunction *plēn* ("however, nevertheless, except") occur in Luke's Gospel; four additional references appear in Luke's second volume, Acts.

60. The term "Trinity" never appears in the New Testament; likewise, the New Testament contains no formal exposition of the doctrine of the Trinity. But passages such as Luke 10:21–22 certainly hint at "triune" fellowship among Father-Son-Spirit. See the "Trinitarian Theology" section in Spencer, *Luke*, 649–59.

61. To be clear, "heaven" in biblical theology represents not so much a bounded celestial location as a dynamic realm penetrating the entire universe of God's creation; see Wright, *Surprised by Hope*.

remembrance before him for those who fear the Lord and *reverence his name.* And they shall be mine, says the Lord Almighty . . . , and I will choose them as a person chooses his son *who is subject* to him. And you shall turn and discern between the just and between the lawless and between the one *who is subject to God* and the one who is not subject" (Mal. 3:16–18 NETS). The prophet writes these words in a context in which many of God's people "are not keeping a distance from the injustices of [their] fathers" (3:7 NETS)—that is, not being faithful to God's just way or true to God's holy name. Indeed, they "swear by [God's] name falsely and against those who defraud the hired worker of his wages and those who oppress the widow and those who buffet orphans and those who turn aside justice from the guest" (3:5 NETS). But those who do "reverence his name" and actively submit to God's demand for justice, especially for the most vulnerable persons, God etches in the divine memory book, in the family album, as it were, where a father (or mother) holds a beloved son (or daughter) in mind and heart for all time and eternity. The name-registering "book of remembrance" certifies connection, affiliation, loyalty, and honor—all solid reasons for joy! Accordingly, peoples all around "will call you happy [*makariousin*]" (3:12 NETS).

As we've already underscored, Luke's Jesus does not just expound on principles of joy to his excited disciples; he himself also experiences joy "in the Holy Spirit" (Luke 10:21). Luke uses a different verb for Jesus's "rejoicing," *agalliaō*, rather than the more typical *chairō* that marks the seventy's joyful response. Perhaps with this word shift, Luke subtly reinforces the qualitative distinction between Jesus and his delegates' joy on this occasion. Yet the two terms closely align in meaning, as in Matthew 5:12, where Jesus doubly urges his audience, "Rejoice [*chairete*] and be glad [*agalliasthe*]" (synonymous parallelism). If we press for some semantic variation, *agalliaō* tends to carry more emotive force: to "be exceedingly joyful, exult."[62] Thus, Luke 10:21 might be better rendered thus: he "was overjoyed in the Holy Spirit,"[63] or he "overflowed with joy from the Holy Spirit" (CEB). Moreover, some solid ancient textual witnesses omit "holy,"[64] linking Jesus's joy with the single word "spirit" (*pneumati*), which could refer either to the divine Spirit or to Jesus's human spirit—or more likely both, concerning the divine-human Christ. In any case, it would not unduly stretch Luke's meaning to stress Jesus's intense personal experience of ebullient joy within his embodied "spirit" in intimate fellowship with God's Spirit. Again, Jesus

62. BDAG 4.
63. Culy, Parsons, and Stigall, *Luke*, 352.
64. See Omanson, *Textual Guide*, 128.

has no desire to sap the seventy's joy or his own. Indeed, his joy appears to exceed their joy because of his greater insight into the joyous heartbeat of the cosmos created and cohabited by God. Luckily for his followers then and now, Luke's Jesus shares what he knows that brings him—and should bring them and us—such joy.

What Jesus knows about joy he communicates in prayer (Luke 10:21–22) to his "Father, Lord of heaven and earth" in the hearing, it seems, of a public audience before "turning [and speaking] to the disciples . . . *privately*" (10:23). In his opening, "I thank [or praise (*exomologoumai*)] you, Father" (according to most English versions), Jesus uses a verb usually rendered "confess/acknowledge." Literally meaning "speak out [*ex*] the same word/thing," it becomes associated with "mak[ing] a public statement or response indicating agreement/acknowledgement."[65] In early church communities, it designated core public rituals, both negative and affirmative: confessing sins (Matt. 3:6; Mark 1:5; Acts 19:18; James 5:16; cf. 1 John 1:9) and confessing Jesus as Lord and Christ (Phil. 2:11; cf. Luke 12:8; John 9:22; Rom. 10:9–10; 1 John 4:2–3). By offering up in joyful spirit his own public confession of his Father's lordship over heaven and earth, Jesus happily submits to God's supreme authority and responsibility, thus exercising his own lordly vocation with humility (following Mary's Magnificat) and not exploiting his "heavenly" status or lording it over the world, as Satan had tempted him to do and as his disciples wish he would do! (See Luke 4:5–7; 9:46–48; 22:24–27.) Jesus fundamentally roots his joy in mutual connection with and subjection to all creation under the rule of God the Father, Lord of heaven and earth, a rule as graciously involved and inclusive as it is powerful and sovereign.

As Jesus's prayer joins with the heavenly chorus of "great joy for all the people" that attended his birth on earth (Luke 2:10; see 2:10–14), a celebration of good news for all creatures great and small, it is primarily the "small" ones, those of lesser note and status in conventional assessments, who bring him the greatest joy. And they make Jesus happy because they make the Father happy: "Indeed, Father, this brings you happiness" (10:21 CEB) or "good pleasure" (*eudokia*).[66] What particularly elates the Father and Son is "this": the choice

---

65. Danker with Krug, *Concise Greek-English Lexicon*, 135; cf. Culy, Parsons, and Stigall, *Luke*, 352: "I acknowledge to you, Father" (Luke 10:21).

66. BDAG 404–5. In biblical contexts, *eudokia* (εὐδοκία) often carries a prime *volitional* force, as in NRSV's "gracious will" rendering in Luke 10:21. See also Shrenk, "εὐδοκέω, εὐδοκία," 2:750: "The evidence in relation to εὐδοκία points . . . overwhelmingly to the sense of the sovereign will of God. . . . We thus have to understand by εὐδοκία the unfathomably gracious and sovereign good-pleasure of God"; Peppard, *Son of God*, 111: "The word εὐδοκία expresses God's sovereign will to elect and to save" (cf. 106–12). Given the integration, however, among feeling, desiring, willing, and decision-making, the volitional component of *eudokia* by no means

of the Father through the Son to disclose "these things" to *little children*, even "*infants*," before revealing them to presumed sophisticates and scholastics, the so-called wise and intelligent. "These things" (*tauta* [10:21]) quickly becomes "all things" (*panta* [10:22]) Jesus has received from the Father in their intimate communion with each other, their knowing "all" about each other, which they choose to share, welcoming others into the joyous fellowship—especially the littlest and lowliest ones most poised to receive good news and spiritual knowledge with joy.

By no means anti-wisdom or anti-intellectual, Jesus appreciates the "rational" and "logical" bases of joy. Knowledge, insight, and discovery of the universe (the heavens and the earth), rightly perceived, stir the heart and mind with that joyous sense of elevation and expansion, akin to wonder, to which open-minded—and openhearted—philosophers and scientists happily attest. But too often, self-styled gurus and experts fall in love with their own genius and lock into their own formulas and dogmas. Pride prevails over humility, as Spinoza understood—and Luke's Mary much earlier: "the proud in the thoughts of their hearts [*dianoia kardias*]" are destined for dissolution and downfall, while those of lowly mind and heart (like little children) will be "lifted up" in joy (Luke 1:51–52).

Further, the knowing that bears the fruit of joy is as relational as it is rational, as experiential as it is expert. Again, it's the knowledge of infants, who delight in discovering the wonderful new world they have entered, mediated through intimate relations with parents, caregivers, and other children.[67] And it's also the pleasing personal and participatory knowledge that binds together Father, Son, and Spirit in joyous communion and draws in humble persons receptive to divine revelation or, we could say, draws them up into the "heavenly" fellowship.[68] Though teeming with fresh new ideas and insights about God and God's creation, this joy extends far beyond and deeper than any metaphysical "Idea(s)" of God, as Spinoza tilted toward. This is relational joy through and through, all the way up and down.

Its connection with children also evokes a serious sense of play. Children take their play very seriously indeed, and the more intently they play, the more joy they experience—and the more they learn in the process. Vaillant's evolutionary approach to joy, which focuses on connection and reunion, also incorporates the element of play.

precludes a concomitant emotional element: a good choice that the Father happily makes out of a good heart—with feeling!

67. See chap. 4, "Emotions and Infancy," in Nussbaum, *Upheavals of Thought*, 174–237; Potkay, *Story of Joy*, 14–15; McMahon, "Joy," 109–10.

68. On "participation" as a core trinitarian theme, see Fiddes, *Participating in God*.

> Another reason . . . that natural selection supported the emotion of joy . . . is to reinforce play. . . . Limbic, rough-and-tumble play, characteristic of children in every culture, elicits both joy and happiness. . . . Play . . . is also about survival. If procreation is rewarded with the fleeting feeling of orgasm, so play is rewarded by the more enduring emotion of joy. Play teaches us to tolerate risk. The infant plays peekaboo: Mother is gone, and then she returns—joy. . . . The joy of risky play is the child's reward for taking all those chances.[69]

Though not stressing the joy of child's play in his present prayer, in an earlier chapter, Luke's Jesus does use images of children playing games to illustrate human nature leading up to his main point regarding true *Wisdom* personified—namely that She (*Sophia*) "is vindicated by all her children," of whom Jesus himself and John the Baptist are prime examples (Luke 7:31–35). Neither the folk-teacher Jesus from Nazareth nor the rough-hewn John in the desert fit conventional models of intelligentsia, any more than playful tots do.

But true Wisdom delights in gleeful, childlike celebration with God and all creation. As Wisdom caps her soaring testimonial song in the Hebrew Bible,

> And I was daily his *delight*,
> *rejoicing* before him always,
> *rejoicing* in his inhabited world
> and *delighting* in the human race. (Prov. 8:30b–31)

Thus the NRSV (along with most English versions) captures the emphatic parallelism (chiasm) of the Hebrew, where double "delight" frames double "rejoicing." The CEB opts for more stylistic freedom, with greater accent on playful dimensions of joy ("fun/frolicking").

> I was having fun,
> smiling before him all the time,
> frolicking with his inhabited earth
> and delighting in the human race. (Prov. 8:30b–31 CEB)

As it happens, the verb for "rejoicing" (*śāḥaq*) is used elsewhere in the Hebrew Bible, as Richard Clifford notes, meaning "'to play with,' 'to entertain,' 'to play'"—including the bustling play of "boys and girls" in city streets (Zech. 8:5).[70]

---

69. Vaillant, *Spiritual Evolution*, 128.
70. Clifford, *Proverbs*, 97. The verb also applies to the play of wild animals (Job 40:20; Ps. 104:26).

Moreover, the term for "delight" (ša'ăšu'îm) can apply to a child, specifically, the Lord's "child in whom I delight," referring to the collective Ephraim/Israel (Jer. 31:20 NIV).[71]

Although the delightful, joyful image in Proverbs 8 likens Wisdom to a "master worker" or "artisan" ('āmôn) rather than a child (8:30a), she is a craftswoman who enjoys her creative work with God and with the world and the people fashioned by God. Heaven and earth are her playgrounds and human beings her playmates. In Proverbs 8:32–34, Woman Wisdom goes on to address her children, encouraging them to be "happy" and "wise," more specifically to find happiness *through* wisdom, through following the wise, instructive path she's laid out for them. And, again, such truly happy wisdom or wise joy is intensely relational. As Clifford writes, "The relationship between Wisdom and her disciples on earth in vv. 32–34 mirrors the relationship between Wisdom and Yahweh in heaven."[72]

In the same way, the relationship between Jesus—the child and prophet of Wisdom (Luke 2:40, 52; 7:33–35; 11:49)—and his disciples on earth mirrors the joyous relationship in the Spirit between Jesus the Son and his Father, "Lord of heaven and earth" (10:21–22). Jesus stands at the hub of this Wisdom family as both *receiver* and *revealer* of inspiring and uplifting divine knowledge. In his faithful, filial subjection to God, Jesus receives the fullness of God's revelation, from which he then guides his children/disciple-subjects to know, love, and follow God's way in a spirit of joy. Turning to share a private word with his disciples, Jesus declares those especially "blessed" (or happy [*makarioi*]) who "see what you see" concerning the true wisdom of God in Christ through the Spirit (10:23). This joyous feeling attends keen *perception* of divine wisdom and purpose (see Roberts above), not mere observation of ephemeral phenomena or militant subjugation of alien forces. Bloated pretentions to wisdom and power, fostering specious pride rather than genuine joy, are the stuff not only of ivory tower sophists and scholars but also of "many prophets and kings" (10:24), many head-in-the-clouds visionaries and gilded-throne rulers absorbed in their own schemes and obsessed with their own conquests. Such ersatz authorities create their own reality, see what they want to see. But they don't see God, they don't find truth, and they don't feel joy—not true joy, at least. Such is the provenance of honest and humble, teachable and reachable, perceptive and playful children and disciples.

---

71. This term also appears multiple times in Ps. 119, "with the meaning of delight in God's word or teaching (Ps. 119:24, 77, 92, 143, 174)." Clifford, *Proverbs*, 97.

72. Clifford, *Proverbs*, 97.

Joy in Pain and Suffering: Jesus's Farewell (John 15:9–11; 16:4–24; 17:1–26)

Both times the Johannine Jesus mentions "my joy" in his final words before his arrest and death, he aims to share this joy with his disciples to the full: "so that my joy may be in you, and that your joy may be complete" (John 15:11); "so that they might have my joy made complete in themselves" (17:13). *Connection* (again) and *completion*: internal and communal joy inspiring and uniting Jesus and his followers, stimulating and elevating joyous "passion by which the mind passes to a greater perfection [completeness]" (Spinoza, *Ethics* pt. 3, P11). Most remarkably, Jesus testifies to such fulsome joy at his direst "hour" of betrayal and suffering, which he knows will also bring excruciating pain and sorrow for his beloved disciples.

Yet, while he expects this joy to prevail over agony and grief, he does not dismiss sad emotions and experiences as somehow shameful capitulations to Satan's will (as Luther puts it), unbefitting Christ himself or any true disciple. He ministers in his last hours with sympathy and encouragement, rather than threat and guilt. To be sure, Jesus undergoes no "Gethsemane" ordeal in the Fourth Gospel. While his "soul is troubled" at the prospect of death, he promptly talks himself out of this gloomy feeling into a glorious fulfilling of God's will: "And what should I say—'Father, save me from this hour'? No, it is for this reason that I have come to this hour" (John 12:27–28). Further, he cedes no power to the evil "ruler of this world," as he calls the devil, to bring him down: "Now the ruler of this world will be driven out" (12:31); "the ruler of this world . . . has no power over me" (14:30); "the ruler of this world has been condemned" (16:11).

But this diabolical ruler is not going down without a fight; he is wreaking as much "trouble" as he can for God's Son and other children. He worms his way into the heart of Judas Iscariot (John 13:2, 27) to betray Jesus to the death-dealing authorities, fomenting continuing "trouble in spirit" for Jesus (13:21) and his beleaguered associates. As we've seen throughout this study, for all its "high" depiction of Jesus's confident sense of purpose and control over life and death, John's Gospel does not conceal embodied emotional life, fleshed out and felt out in critical situations, like at Lazarus's grave and in the shadows of the cross. To various degrees, Jesus feels anger, grief, disgust, love—and joy—in the midst of turmoil, throughout his Passion, his intensely felt suffering for and with his "own" and the entire world.

Jesus's first self-reference to joy comes in the immediate context of his self-imaging as the "true vine," planted and cultivated by his Father "the Vine-grower" and in turn sprouting and nurturing his beloved disciples so they might "bear much fruit"—provided they "abide in my love," remaining *connected* in the Vine and he in them (John 15:1–11). Love and joy flow together within Jesus and overflow outward to his co-laborers. Moreover, these interpersonal references follow close on the heels of Jesus granting his "peace" to his disciples through the Father's gift of the Holy Spirit, who "will teach [them] everything, and remind [them] of all that [he has] said to [them]" so they might also experience peace in their hearts, free from fear and anxiety (14:25–27).

The Johannine Jesus demonstrates and communicates a dynamic emotional triad of love-joy-peace as the principal fruit of the circulating passionate trinity of the Father-Son-Spirit, drawing all creatures and creation into its loving-joyous-peaceful vortex. Paul provides the perfect caption for this dramatic picture in Galatians 5:22 (see above in discussing Luther): "The fruit of the Spirit is love, joy, peace." And Luke 10:21–22 provides apt commentary, linking Jesus's "rejoicing" in the S/spirit with the Father's revelation of intimate "things" through the Son to God's children and learner-disciples. Joyous communion nourishes mind and heart and flourishes through lifelong teaching, reminding, reviewing.

In the four Gospels, John 16:4–24 offers Jesus's fullest and most personal perspective on joy amid sorrow, swirling again around twin themes of revelation and reunion. Jesus knows that his farewell word to his closest followers, frankly disclosing his imminent departure from this life, hits them hard: "*Because* I have said these things to you, *sorrow* [or *pain* (*lypē*)] has filled your hearts" (John 16:6). Jesus precipitates as well as participates in their sorrow. Tellingly, he does not belittle or berate his friends for these bad feelings. He does not indulge them either, but rather he moves to reveal significant truth, particularly *prospective* truth to buoy their spirits in the present by disclosing a promising future. As noted above in the discussion of Philo, Spinoza, and Vaillant, joy is as tightly tethered to hope as it is to love and peace (love-joy-peace-hope: the emotive trio becomes a quartet). Jesus emphasizes ("I tell you the truth") that, in fact, "it is to [their] advantage that [he goes] away" because only then will the Spirit-Advocate come to them (16:7). This Divine Spirit will be with (and in) them permanently, patiently comforting and counseling them as they are able to receive further revelation of "all" that the Father and Son know and feel (16:13–15). In the withering heat of this present hour, Jesus understands, again without recrimination, that his beloved ones "cannot [yet] bear" the full light of truth—which especially illuminates a brighter, happier future of new life and purpose: "When the Spirit of truth comes, . . . he will declare to you the things *that are to come*" (16:13).

Beyond the future nurture of the Spirit that Jesus promises, he also forecasts that most joyous prospect of reunion: "A little while, and you will no longer see me, and again a little while, and *you will see me*" (John 16:16). The narrative drives home this hope through threefold repetition: (1) Jesus's initial statement (16:16); (2) his disciples' querying "to one another" the meaning of this statement, which they echo verbatim (16:17); and (3) Jesus's empathic, interrogative (but not interrogational) affirmation of their confusion, setting the stage for his clarification ("Jesus knew that they wanted to ask him, so he said to them, 'Are you discussing among yourselves what I meant when I said' . . . [repeating his original statement]") (16:19). Sensitive to the span of earthly time, which so acutely affects emotional attitudes (time may heal all wounds but only over an extended period), Jesus stresses that his followers can anticipate seeing him again in "a little while" (*mikron*) after his imminent death, itself set to happen in the same "micro" time frame. Jesus and his disciples stand on the brink of shocking, rapid-fire events that will spark a dizzying emotional circuit of sorrow and joy. The soon-coming joy primarily points to the *risen Lord's* earthly reunions with his distressed followers in a garden, in a house, and on a beach (20:11–21:23)—reunions of rejoicing (*chairō* [20:20]), combined with peace (20:19, 21, 26), faith/trust (20:27–29), and love (21:15–17).

Yet in his first post-resurrection appearance, which is to Mary Magdalene in the garden, Jesus indicates another departure is at hand—namely, his ascension "to my Father and your Father, to my God and your God" (John 20:17), news he wants Mary to relay to his "brother"-disciples. Neither she nor the male disciples can "hold on" to him now (20:17), as he reinforces by popping in and out of a locked house where they're meeting and popping up on a shoreline where some of them are fishing. Though not mentioned in John 15–21, the joyous hope of a final return and permanent reunion with Christ at some time after his ascension (a so-called second coming) lingers in the air from earlier in the Farewell Discourse: "Do not let your hearts be troubled. . . . I go and prepare a place for you, [and] I will come again and will take you to myself, so that where I am, there you may be also" (14:1–3). Of course, in between Jesus's post-resurrection appearances and his ultimate return, his beloved ones will still enjoy intimate fellowship with the Father and Son—"my Father and your Father, my God and your God"—through the abiding presence of the Holy Spirit (20:22).

But spiritual communion, as vibrant and vital as it is, does not fully match seen-and-felt bodily contact and connection with beloved ones, epitomized in the hugging, kissing, clothing, and feasting reunion of the longing father and his lost son (Luke 15:20–24). In another of his ethically focused letters, Seneca also extols the higher, happier joy of embodied *presence* with dear friends: "We get joy from those we love even in their absence, but it is light and fleeting. The sight of them, their presence, their conversation, has in it a kind of living pleasure, especially not only when you see the one you want, but see that one as you want him to be. Give me yourself, then: a great gift" (*Let.* 35.3). Absence may make the heart grow fonder—but only with hope of blessed reunion; otherwise the heart just gets sicker or number. As for Jesus's "friends," joyous hope abounds that they will "see again" the incarnate Christ for all eternity.

But once more Jesus candidly, yet compassionately, admits to his confidants that the prospect of future resurrection and reunion does not altogether mitigate the piercing pain of his separation from them in death, made all the more galling by their enemies' sneering *Schadenfreude*: "Very truly, I tell you, you will weep and mourn, but the world will rejoice [*charēsetai*]; you will have pain [*lypēthēsesthe*]"—though not for long, because "your pain will turn into joy" (John 16:20). It's not simply that pain will be replaced by joy but that somehow pain will *become* joy (*charan genēsetai*), will contribute to the alchemy of joy. This is not to glorify suffering for its own sake but to incorporate it into the whole affective human experience, pushing toward the consummative goal of flourishing joy.

Speaking of "pushing," Jesus draws on the visceral, life-giving experience of a birthing mother to make his point about pain and joy: "When a woman is in labor, she has pain [*lypēn*], because her hour [*hē hōra*] has come. But when her child is born, she no longer remembers the anguish because of the joy [*charan*] of having brought a human being into the world" (John 16:21). We recall that Philo's Stoic appraisal of Sarah's embryonic ("pre-emotion"/*propatheia*) joy (laughter) at the future prospect of having a child ultimately gives way to her self-controlled, non-emotional delivery of the promised son Isaac (meaning "laughter"!), since, in Philo's view, the natural "ways of women," including painful and joyful passions, had ceased for the aged Sarah. Jesus, however, has no qualms about embracing the entire reproductive process, in which women play the most labor-intensive and emotively sensitive part, sweeping from searing pain to soaring joy as the basic arc of all creative experience generated by God in and through human beings.

Notably, the Johannine Jesus links his present and pending experience of pain and joy with that of a childbearer via the synchrony of the critical "hour"—his "hour" of Passion and her "hour" of parturition—both issuing joyous new life through excruciating flows of blood and water (John 19:34; cf. 3:3–7). Accordingly, Jesus does not merely exercise parental care for his beloved adopted "children," ensuring that they will not be "orphaned" after his death (14:18) but effectively claims to be their *birth mother*, giving them life through "her" body and guiding them through the sorrows and joys of lived experience, from birth to death (and beyond) within the growing family of God. Stretching the metaphor to the breaking point (but also strengthening its emotional vitality), as Jesus the Son intimately participates "in" the Father and the Spirit (14:20), "he" also figuratively functions as Jesus the *Mother*, bringing forth God's children into the world through labor pangs pulsing with loving joy and peace (see 16:21–24, 33).

In Seneca's letter referenced above, he notes that giving birth is commonly regarded as a source of joy. But he challenges this folk wisdom as discounting the future sorrow that awaits the mother as she struggles to raise her child in a precarious world and also as diluting pure joy: "Nonetheless, in our ordinary speech we often say that we are overjoyed [*magnum gaudium*] that one person was elected consul, or that another was married or that a wife has given birth, events which, far from being causes for joy [*gaudium*], are frequently the beginnings of future sorrow [*futurae tristitiae*]. For it is an attribute of joy [*gaudio*] that it never ceases or turns into its opposite" (*Let.* 59.2). Again, Jesus is scarcely naive about continuing bouts of suffering in a fraught environment: "In the world you face persecution"; or it could read, "You all are having [*echēte*] distress" (John 16:33 AT; cf. 15:18–16:4). But he is not an emotional purist when it comes to joy. More in line, as it happens, with modern affective science, he regards joy not only as streaming together with positive emotions like love and peace but also with painful feelings of sorrow in a dynamic feedback loop coursing within, in-between, and among people in a complex world.

Jesus caps his Farewell Discourse in the Fourth Gospel with an extended prayer to his Father, offered on behalf of and in the hearing of his disciples (John 17:1–26). Although much longer than his prayer in Luke 10:21–22, this one echoes the focus on joy and related themes found in Luke. While the Johannine Jesus is not explicitly reported as praying joyously "in the Holy Spirit" (Luke 10:21), his final comments have been filled with references to the vital Spirit-Advocate. Moreover, as Luke's Jesus rejoices in his Father's "gracious will" to reveal to Jesus's disciples—and to include them in—the joyous fellowship of Father and Son (Luke 10:21–24; cf. 10:17–20), the Johannine Jesus grounds his followers' experience of spiritual joy in intimate knowledge of God, in full participation in the knowing, living, loving relationship of Father and Son.

And this is eternal life, that they *may know you*, the only true God, and Jesus Christ whom you have sent. (John 17:3)

I have *made your name known* to those whom you gave me from the world. . . . Now *they know* that everything you have given me is from you; for the words that you gave to me I have given to them, and they have received them and *know in truth* that I came from you. (17:6–8)

I speak these things in the world so that they may have *my joy made complete in themselves*. I have given them your word. (17:13–14)

Righteous Father, the world does not *know you*, but I *know you*; and *these know* that you have sent me. I *made your name known* to them, and I *will make it known*, so that the love with which you have loved me may be in them, and I in them. (17:25–26)

Finally, though the joy Jesus has and shares with his associates thrives in the "heavenly" realm of God, it is by no means some ethereal, ecstatic, escapist joy quarantined from the volatile "earthly" world. The Johannine Jesus forever remains the Word made flesh who brought all creation into being and who himself has come into the world and "lived among us" (John 1:1–14). While he is physically leaving the rough-and-tumble world for a while, he's by no means abandoning it, as is clear in his climactic prayer: "I am not asking that you [Father] take them out of the world, but I ask you to protect them from the evil one" (17:15). Yet in this world where they remain, with all its suffering, sadness, and satanic assaults—along with its grace, goodness, and godly care—they may still have abiding joy, the very joy of Christ.

EPILOGUE

Final Thoughts about
Jesus's Emotions

I make no attempt here to summarize the main facets of Jesus's emotions of anger, anguish, disgust, surprise, compassion, and joy presented in the Gospel narratives. Rather, I offer a few final reflections on the emotional life of Jesus and possibilities for future research regarding biblical characters' (including God's) experiences of "mixed feelings and vexed passions," along with evaluative judgments about emotions across biblical literature.[1]

First, I want to underscore that the Gospel evidence concerning the passions of Christ, while substantial and significant and often glossed over in commentaries and other interpretive media, remains selective and succinct. The Gospels provide nothing close to a full psychological profile of Jesus or an in-depth probe of his emotional states. They provide specific *cases* in particular *contexts* of Jesus's emotions, which I've tried to analyze within those contexts, consistent with the narrative framework of all affective experience. Accordingly, despite my chapter subtitles—"The Angry Jesus," "The Anguished Jesus," and the like—I do not suggest that Jesus had an irascible or tortured personality or that he was a severely bitter or depressed person with "emotional problems," as we carelessly say about some people, to whom Jesus, by the way, would have extended merciful aid (consider the extreme case of the Gerasene demoniac in Mark 5:1–20). If someone does struggle with

1. See the collection of seventeen essays ranging across the biblical canon in Spencer, *Mixed Feelings*.

261

an unhealthy emotional tendency—and who doesn't from time to time?—we should encourage honest admission of their challenges and therapeutic treatment from a competent, compassionate professional.

But the Gospel portraits of Jesus, while honest about Jesus's passionate human reactions and interactions, also honor Jesus as God's beloved Son, the anointed Messiah, the incarnate Christ, the consummate revelation of God's glory in and to humanity and all creation. Hence even Jesus's vehement emotions, which so easily get the best of us in harmful ways, operate in his life toward virtuous ends, for truly good ("best") purposes. As for Jesus's positive emotions of surprise/wonder, love/compassion, and joy, the love/compassion dimension virtually defines his nature (God *is* love) but not in some abstract, artificial way. Jesus grows and evolves in love, as in all aspects of his human life, remarkably expanding his horizon of love in humble fashion—for example, in his dealings with "foreigners" like the Roman officer in Capernaum concerned about his ill slave or the Syrophoenician mother of an afflicted little girl.

A second observation clarifies Jesus's working through his potentially negative emotions toward salutary ends. The Gospels do not theorize as did Stoic philosophers about natural and neutral pre-emotional impulses (*propatheia*) that must be nipped in the bud before they become problematic: no harm, no foul in having initial twinges of anger, say, at an offending person, but one mustn't give in to these initial jolts for a moment, or they will turn truly harmful to one's psychic health, to say nothing of the damage that may result from hostile backlash. However, the Gospel reports of Jesus's first emotional responses to provocative people and situations do not portray him flicking away reflexive blips of anger, grief, or any other feeling like annoying gnats or, in more spiritual terms, like temptations to sin.

His anger at the leper in Mark 1, his anguish in Gethsemane, and the swirl of these emotions together with disgust near Lazarus's tomb are not presented in any sense as extraneous attacks to fend off or evil tendencies to overcome; neither are they merely preliminary knee-jerk impulses, disjointed from Jesus's unfolding appraisals and movements. Rather, these emotions affect the entire scene as integral components of Jesus's engagement with the people, events, and environments at hand. Jesus incorporates his anger, grief, and disgust—along with his compassion and other positive emotions—into his overall experience. His incipient emotions spark other emotions and thoughts and decisions and actions, fulfilling his indomitable will to flourishing life and resolute saving purpose.

Speaking of will and purpose segues into a third point, which I stressed throughout this study but which bears repeating one more time. Simply put, emotions reflect what moves us at a gut level—not merely of impulse, again, but at a gut level of *importance*. Passions signal what we're passionate about, what matters to us most. Accordingly, we may miss aspects of Jesus's core concerns by dismissing or discounting emotional elements he displays in the Gospels, particularly the intensity and persistence with which Jesus pursues his mission from the depths of his own experiences, not least those of pain and suffering. He is moved to loving action toward the least and lowly by shared pathos, not (merely) a sense of duty; by genuine sympathy for hurting humanity, not (merely) obedience to God. Of course, we can apprehend Jesus's staunch commitment to life and salvation without attending to his emotional involvement, but in so doing we sap much of the passion from the Passion of the Christ and from our experience of faith in Christ. Theologian Paul Tillich aptly describes that experience as "participation in the subject of one's ultimate concern with one's whole being." Such faith constitutes "an act of the personality as a whole," pulsing in dynamic "tension between the cognitive function of man's personal life, on the one hand, and emotion and will, on the other hand."[2] Heartfelt trust in Christ is best nourished by appreciating the Gospel portraits of the incarnate Christ's own holistic, heartfelt engagement with the human condition in a precarious world.

Obviously, I have shifted into a pastoral mode of challenge and comfort, which leads to a fourth comment: I've offered a primarily exegetical, descriptive study of Jesus's emotional life in the Gospels, *not* a pastoral, therapeutic one. Although I regularly preach and teach in local churches and occasionally serve as interim pastor (as I'm doing at the time of this writing), I greatly exceed my brief when I drift into pastoral counseling about emotions or anything else. I would like to think that my assessments of emotion theory in general (both ancient and modern, in theology, philosophy, and psychology), and of several key emotions of Jesus in particular, have some relevance to contemporary pastoral ministry.[3] Yet in no way do I imagine some facile correspondence between Jesus's emotional life and ours today, as if we simply determine "What Did Jesus Feel" (W.D.J.F.) and then advise every Christian to feel that way too—just like Jesus. Discipleship is a demanding, lifelong journey in a thicket of challenging contexts, not a simple, formulaic, step-by-step process. It requires our own multifaceted maturing in wisdom with

2. Tillich, *Dynamics of Faith*, 5, 8 (cf. 37–38).

3. I recommend the sophisticated treatment of emotions by a professor of pastoral theology and practice, Barbara J. McClure. Based on careful historical study and theoretical analysis, McClure seeks to ascertain, "How are emotions related to the telos, or final aim, of life? How ought we to engage emotions in the pursuit of flourishing?" She astutely advocates a balanced approach to flourishing life: "Flourishing cannot be engaged without including careful attention to emotions, and an adequate understanding of flourishing cannot be separated from the desires of the Sacred for the world." McClure, *Emotions*, 187.

Jesus's vital help, but it doesn't mean following in Jesus's *exact* steps, with or without sandals.

Finally, where might we go from here to gain further understanding of emotions in the Bible? While this study has concentrated on six key emotions many regard as "basic" or near-universal to human experience across the ages (though perceived and expressed in various cultural forms), these scarcely exhaust humanity's rich emotional repertoire. Related but distinct cousins, near and far, to these basic emotions include frustration related to anger, wonder related to surprise, and compassion related to love, not to mention other separate emotion classifications. Cowen and Keltner enumerate twenty-seven emotions, Brackett a cool one hundred.[4] Neither list is set in stone. Possibilities thus abound for fruitful emotion research, including study related to biblical literature.

One category of emotions investigated by academic psychologists and philosophers seems particularly suited to biblical scholarship. "Self-conscious emotions" (SCE)[5] or, as one philosopher calls them, "moral emotions of self-givenness"[6]—such as pride, shame, and guilt—have obvious relevance to biblical theology and ethics. They figure prominently in the biblical story, starting with Adam and Eve's alienation from God, each other, and the environment, and run throughout the multigenerational drama of flawed humanity in need of reconciliation. Although the Gospels do not portray Jesus himself ever feeling pride, shame, or guilt,[7] they report his wise counsel concerning these common self-conscious emotions.

Fear typically heads any emotion list, short or long (though in his famous discussion of opposite sets of passions, Aristotle slots fear in the third position: anger/calmness, friendliness/enmity, and then fear/confidence [*Rhet.* 2.5 (1382a–83b)]). And fear is right up there with shame as the primordial human emotion in Genesis, as Adam confesses to God: "I heard the sound of you in the garden, and I was afraid, because I was naked; and I hid myself" (Gen. 3:10).[8] Fear is still going strong as ever today, in spite of—or maybe because of—our technological advances, which for all their sophistication remain woefully impotent in the face of the COVID-19 pandemic that swept the world in 2020. I use the past tense "swept" in hope for better days when

---

4. Cowen and Keltner, "Self-Report"; Brackett, *Permission to Feel.*
5. See Tangney and Fischer, *Self-Conscious Emotions*; Tracy, Robins, and Tangney, *Self-Conscious Emotions.* For an application to biblical studies, see Prakasam, "Pride of Babylon."
6. See Steinbock, *Moral Emotions*, 27; see also 28–133.
7. In chap. 4, however, I did explore Jesus's possible feelings of brokenhearted *regret* ("if only") over Jerusalem's failure to "recognize" God's "visitation" (Luke 19:41–44).
8. See Robin, *Fear*, 1, 7.

this book is published in 2021. But as I draft these words in April 2020 on the Saturday before Easter, I write with very mixed emotions: in hope of resurrection, yes; but also in not a little fear of this deadly plague that still rages strong. And, of course, such a volatile, viral vortex is ripe for exploiting people's fear to the hilt.

Although the Gospels never explicitly attribute fear to Jesus, he comes closest perhaps in his whirlwind of other distressing emotions when closely confronting death: at Lazarus's graveside, at Gethsemane on the eve of his own death, and at Golgotha on the cross. In any event, he certainly engages others' experiences of fear in perilous situations with sympathy and under-standing, though not coddling. In an earlier study, I offered one analysis of Jesus's most extensive teaching on fear in Luke 12:4–34,[9] but more work remains to be done on this complex topic throughout the Gospels and the entire Bible, ranging from the high duty to fear God ("The fear of the LORD is the beginning of wisdom" [Prov. 9:10]) to the call to *fear not* in certain crisis situations because of the Lord's powerful and gracious watch-care.

As we continue to be emotional creatures, for good and ill, we should do everything we can to understand this fascinating dimension of our lives—and the life of the Triune God, in whose image we are made—and how it impacts our biblically rooted faith and practice. May we move full steam ahead in this worthy endeavor, without fear!

9. Spencer, "To Fear and Not to Fear."

Bibliography

Adolphs, Ralph, and David J. Anderson. *The Neuroscience of Emotion: A New Synthesis*. Princeton: Princeton University Press, 2018.

Aeschylus. *Suppliant Maidens. Persians. Prometheus. Seven against Thebes*. Translated by Herbert Weir Smyth. LCL. Cambridge: Harvard University Press, 1926.

Ahmed, Sara. *The Cultural Politics of Emotion*. New York: Routledge, 2004.

Akerlof, George A., and Robert J. Shiller. *Animal Spirits: How Human Psychology Drives the Economy, and Why It Matters for Global Capitalism*. Princeton: Princeton University Press, 2009.

Allison, Dale C., Jr. "The Eye Is the Lamp of the Body (Matthew 6.22–23 = Luke 11.34–36)." *New Testament Studies* 33 (1987): 61–83.

———. *Jesus of Nazareth: Millenarian Prophet*. Minneapolis: Fortress, 1998.

Anselm. *Proslogium; Monologium; An Appendix in Behalf of the Fool by Gaunilon; and Cur Deus Homo*. Translated by Sidney Norton Deane. Chicago: Open Court, 1939.

Arendt, Hannah. *Eichmann in Jerusalem: A Report on the Banality of Evil*. Revised edition with introduction by Amos Elon. London: Penguin, 2006.

Aristotle. *De Anima*. Translated by C. D. C. Reeve. Indianapolis: Hackett, 2017.

———. "Ethica Nicomachea." In *The Basic Works of Aristotle*, translated by W. D. Ross, edited by Richard McKeon, 927–1112. New York: Modern Library, 2001.

———. *Metaphysics*. Translated by Hugh Tredennick. LCL. Cambridge, MA: Harvard University Press, 1933.

———. *Nicomachean Ethics*. Translated by Robert C. Bartlett and Susan D. Collins. Chicago: University of Chicago Press, 2011.

———. *On Rhetoric: A Theory of Civic Discourse*. Translated by George A. Kennedy. 2nd ed. New York: Oxford University Press, 2007.

267

Baden, Joel S., and Candida R. Moss. "The Origin and Interpretation of *sāraʿat* in Leviticus 13–14." *Journal of Biblical Literature* 130 (2011): 643–62.

Baier, Annette. "Feelings That Matter." In *Thinking about Feeling: Contemporary Philosophers on Emotions*, edited by Robert C. Solomon, 200–213. New York: Oxford University Press, 2004.

Bailen, Natasha, Haijing Wu Hallenbeck, and Renee Thompson. "How to Deal with Feeling Bad about Your Feelings." *Greater Good Magazine*, November 26, 2018. https://greatergood.berkeley.edu/article/item/how_to_deal_with_feeling_bad _about_your _feelings.

Barrett, C. K. *The Gospel according to St. John: An Introduction with Commentary and Notes on the Greek Text*. 2nd ed. Philadelphia: Westminster, 1978.

Barrett, Lisa Feldman. *How Emotions Are Made: The Secret Life of the Brain*. Boston: Houghton Mifflin Harcourt, 2017.

Bartsch, A., P. Vorderer, R. Mangold, and R. Viehoff. "Appraisal of Emotions in Media Use: Toward a Process Model of Metaemotion and Emotion Regulation." *Media Psychology* 11 (2008): 7–27. doi:10.1080/15213260701813447.

Bauckham, Richard. *The Testimony of the Beloved Disciple: Narrative, History, and Theology in the Gospel of John*. Grand Rapids: Baker Academic, 2007.

Baumeister, Roy F. "Emotions: How the Future Feels (and Could Feel)." In *Homo Prospectus*, by Martin E. P. Seligman, Peter Railton, Roy F. Baumeister, and Chandra Sripada, 207–23. New York: Oxford University Press, 2016.

Beavis, Mary Ann. *Mark*. Paideia: Commentaries on the New Testament. Grand Rapids: Baker Academic, 2011.

Beck, Richard. *Unclean: Meditations on Purity, Hospitality, and Mortality*. Eugene, OR: Cascade Books, 2011.

Ben Ze'ev, Aaron. *The Subtlety of Emotions*. Cambridge, MA: MIT Press, 2000.

Bertelsen, Lone, and Andrew Murphie. "An Ethics of Everyday Intensities and Powers: Félix Guatarri on Affect and the Refrain." In *The Affect Theory Reader*, edited by Melissa Gregg and Gregory J. Seigworth, 138–57. Durham, NC: Duke University Press, 2010.

Beyreuther, Erich, and Günter Finkenrath. "Joy, Rejoice." In *The New International Dictionary of New Testament Theology*, edited by Colin Brown, 2:352–61. 3 vols. Grand Rapids: Zondervan, 1976.

Bieringer, Reimund, Didier Pollefeyt, and Frederique Vandecasteele-Vanneuville, eds. *Anti-Judaism and the Fourth Gospel*. Louisville: Westminster John Knox, 2001.

Bird, Michael F. *Evangelical Theology: A Biblical and Systematic Introduction*. Grand Rapids: Zondervan, 2013.

Bloom, Paul. *Against Empathy: The Case for Rational Compassion*. New York: Ecco, 2016.

———. *Just Babies: The Origins of Good and Evil*. New York: Crown, 2013.

Bonanno, George A. "Loss, Trauma, and Human Resilience: Have We Underestimated the Human Capacity to Thrive after Extremely Aversive Events?" *American Psychologist* 59 (2004): 20–28.

———. *The Other Side of Sadness: What the New Science of Bereavement Tells Us about Life after Loss*. New York: Basic Books, 2009.

Bonanno, George A., and Nigel P. Field. "Examining the Delayed Grief Hypothesis across 5 Years of Bereavement." *American Behavioral Scientist* 44 (2001): 798–816.

Borg, Marcus J. *The Heart of Christianity: Rediscovering a Life of Faith*. New York: HarperSanFrancisco, 2003.

———. "Jesus and the Christian Life." explorefaith.org. March 16, 1999. http://www.explorefaith.org/LentenHomily03.16.99.html.

Bosworth, David A. "Faith and Resilience: King David's Reaction to the Death of Bathsheba's Firstborn." *Catholic Biblical Quarterly* 73 (2010): 691–707.

———. "Understanding Grief and Reading the Bible." In *Mixed Feelings and Vexed Passions: Exploring Emotions in Biblical Literature*, edited by F. Scott Spencer, 117–38. Resources for Biblical Study 90. Atlanta: SBL Press, 2017.

Bovon, François. "The Soul's Comeback: Immortality and Resurrection in Early Christianity." *Harvard Theological Review* 103 (2010): 387–406.

Brackett, Marc. *Permission to Feel: Unlocking the Power of Emotions to Help Our Kids, Ourselves, and Our Society Thrive*. New York: Celadon Books, 2019.

Brady, Michael S. *Emotional Insight: The Epistemic Role of Emotional Experience*. Oxford: Oxford University Press, 2013.

Brewer, Douglas J., Terence Clark, and Adrian A. Phillips. *Dogs in Antiquity, Anubis to Cerberus: The Origins of the Domestic Dog*. Aris & Phillips Classical Texts. Liverpool: Liverpool University Press, 2002.

Brink, Laurie. *Soldiers in Luke-Acts: Engaging, Contradicting, and Transcending the Stereotypes*. WUNT 2/362. Tübingen: Mohr Siebeck, 2014.

Brinkema, Eugenia. *The Forms of the Affects*. Durham, NC: Duke University Press, 2014.

Brodie, Thomas L. "Towards Unravelling Luke's Use of the Old Testament: Luke 7.11–17 as an *Imitatio* of 1 Kings 17.17–24." *New Testament Studies* 32 (1986): 247–67.

Brown, Raymond E. *The Community of the Beloved Disciple: The Life, Loves and Hates of an Individual Church in New Testament Times*. London: Geoffrey Chapman, 1979.

———. *The Death of the Messiah: From Gethsemane to the Grave; A Commentary on the Passion Narratives in the Four Gospels*. 2 vols. Anchor Bible Reference Library. New York: Doubleday, 1994.

Cairns, Douglas L. *Aidōs: The Psychology and Ethics of Honour and Shame in Ancient Greek Literature*. Oxford: Clarendon, 1993.

Calvin, John. *Calvin: Institutes of the Christian Religion*. Edited by John T. McNeill. Translated by Ford Lewis Battles. 2 vols. Library of Christian Classics. Philadelphia: Westminster, 1960.

Caputo, John D. *Cross and Cosmos: A Theology of Difficult Glory*. Bloomington: Indiana University Press, 2019.

———. *The Folly of God: A Theology of the Unconditional*. Salem, OR: Polebridge, 2016.

———. *The Weakness of God: A Theology of the Event*. Bloomington: Indiana University Press, 2006.

———. *What Would Jesus Deconstruct? The Good News of Postmodernism for the Church*. The Church and Postmodern Culture. Grand Rapids: Baker Academic, 2007.

Charry, Elaine T. *God and the Art of Happiness*. Grand Rapids: Eerdmans, 2010.

Cicero, Marcus Tullius. *Cicero on the Emotions: Tusculan Disputations 3 and 4*. Translated by Margaret R. Graver. Chicago: University of Chicago Press, 2002.

———. *How to Be a Friend: An Ancient Guide to True Friendship*. Translated by Philip Freeman. Ancient Wisdom for Modern Readers. Princeton: Princeton University Press, 2018.

———. *Laelius de Amicitia*. Translated by Evelyn S. Shuckburgh. Edited by Rhonda L. Kelley. Project Gutenberg, 2013. http://www.gutenberg.org/files/2808/2808-h/280 8-h.htm.

———. *De senectute, De amicitia, De divinatione*. Translated by William Armistead Falconer. LCL. Cambridge, MA: Harvard University Press, 1923.

Clark, Andy. *Supersizing the Mind: Embodiment, Action, and Cognitive Extension*. Oxford: Oxford University Press, 2008.

Clark, Andy, and David Chalmers. "The Extended Mind." *Analysis* 58 (1998): 7–19.

Clement of Alexandria. "The Stromata, or Miscellanies." In *Fathers of the Second Century: Hermas, Tatian, Athenagoras, Theophilus, and Clement of Alexandria (Entire)*. Vol. 2 of *Ante-Nicene Fathers*, edited by Alexander Roberts and James Donaldson, 299–568. New York: Christian Literature, 1885–96. Reprint, Grand Rapids: Eerdmans, 1950–51.

Clifford, Richard J. *Proverbs: A Commentary*. Old Testament Library. Louisville: Westminster John Knox, 1999.

Clivaz, Claire. "The Angel and the Sweat like 'Drops of Blood' (Lk 22:43–44): P^{69} and f^{13}." *Harvard Theological Review* 98 (2005): 419–40.

Cobb, John B., Jr., and David Ray Griffin. *Process Theology: An Introductory Exposition*. Philadelphia: Westminster, 1976.

Collins, Raymond F. *These Things Have Been Written: Studies on the Fourth Gospel*. Louvain Theological & Pastoral Monographs 2. Leuven, Belgium: Peeters, 1990.

Cotter, Wendy J. "The Parable of the Feisty Widow and the Threatened Judge (Luke 18.1–8)." *New Testament Studies* 51 (2005): 328–43.

Cowen, Alan S., and Dacher Keltner. "Self-Report Captures 27 Distinct Categories of Emotion Bridged by Continuous Gradients." *Proceedings of the National Academy of Sciences* 114 (2017): E7900–7909. https://doi.org/10.1073/pnas.1702247114.

Culpepper, R. Alan. *Anatomy of the Fourth Gospel: A Study in Literary Design.* Foundations & Facets: New Testament. Philadelphia: Fortress, 1983.

Culy, Martin M., Mikeal C. Parsons, and Joshua J. Stigall. *Luke: A Handbook on the Greek Text.* Waco: Baylor University Press, 2010.

Damasio, Antonio. *Descartes' Error: Emotion, Reason, and the Human Mind.* New York: Penguin, 1994.

———. *Looking for Spinoza: Joy, Sorrow, and the Feeling Brain.* Orlando, FL: Harcourt, 2003.

Danby, Herbert. *The Mishnah.* London: Oxford University Press, 1933.

Danker, Frederick W. *Jesus and the New Age: A Commentary on St. Luke's Gospel.* 2nd ed. Minneapolis: Fortress, 1988.

———. *Luke.* Proclamation Commentaries. Philadelphia: Fortress, 1976.

Danker, Frederick W., with Kathryn Krug. *The Concise Greek-English Lexicon of the New Testament.* Chicago: University of Chicago Press, 2009.

Darwin, Charles. *The Expression of the Emotions in Man and Animals.* Edited by Paul Ekman. 4th ed. Oxford: Oxford University Press, 2009 (orig. 1872).

David, Susan. *Emotional Agility: Get Unstuck, Embrace Change, and Thrive in Work and Life.* New York: Avery, 2016.

Deonna, Julien A., and Fabrice Teroni. "Emotional Experience: Affective Consciousness and Its Role in Emotion Theory." In *The Oxford Handbook of the Philosophy of Consciousness,* edited by Uriah Kriegel, 102–23. Oxford: Oxford University Press, 2020.

———. *The Emotions: A Philosophical Introduction.* London: Routledge, 2012.

Derrett, J. Duncan M. "The Evil Eye in the New Testament." In *Modelling Early Christianity: Social-Scientific Studies of the New Testament,* edited by Philip F. Esler, 65–72. London: Routledge, 1995.

Descartes, René. *The Passions of the Soul: An English Translation of "Les Passions de l'âme."* Translated by Stephen H. Voss. Indianapolis: Hackett, 1989 (orig. 1649).

DeSteno, David. *Emotional Success: The Power of Gratitude, Compassion, and Pride.* Boston: Houghton Mifflin Harcourt, 2018.

Dinkler, Michal Beth. "'The Thoughts of Many Hearts Shall Be Revealed': Listening In on the Lukan Interior Monologues." *Journal of Biblical Literature* 134 (2015): 373–99.

Diogenes Laertius. *Lives of Eminent Philosophers.* Translated by R. D. Hicks. LCL. Cambridge, MA: Harvard University Press, 1925.

Dixon, Thomas. "'Emotion': The History of a Keyword in Crisis." *Emotion Review* 4 (2012): 338–44.

Dodd, C. H. *The Interpretation of the Fourth Gospel.* Cambridge: Cambridge University Press, 1953.

———. *The Parables of the Kingdom.* Rev. ed. New York: Scribner, 1961.

Donahue, John R., and Daniel J. Harrington. *The Gospel of Mark.* Sacra Pagina 2. Collegeville, MN: Liturgical Press, 2002.

Dunn, J. D. G. *Unity and Diversity in the New Testament: An Inquiry into the Character of Earliest Christianity.* 3rd ed. London: SCM, 2006.

Ehrenreich, Barbara. *Bright-Sided: How Positive Thinking Is Undermining America.* New York: Picador, 2009.

Ehrman, Bart D. *Jesus: Apocalyptic Prophet of the New Millennium.* New York: Oxford University Press, 1999.

———. "A Leper in the Hands of an Angry Jesus." In *New Testament Greek and Exegesis: Essays in Honor of Gerald F. Hawthorne,* edited by Amy M. Donaldson and Timothy B. Sailors, 77–98. Grand Rapids: Eerdmans, 2003.

Ekman, Paul. "An Argument for Basic Emotions." *Cognition and Emotion* 6 (1992): 169–200.

———. *Emotions Revealed: Recognizing Faces and Feelings to Improve Communication and Emotional Life.* 2nd ed. New York: St. Martin's Griffin, 2007.

Ekman, Paul, and Daniel Cordaro. "What Is Meant by Calling Emotions Basic?" *Emotion Review* 3 (2011): 364–70.

Elliott, John H. "Paul, Galatians and the Evil Eye." In *The Social World of the New Testament,* edited by Jerome H. Neyrey and Eric C. Stewart, 223–34. Peabody, MA: Hendrickson, 1991.

Elliott, Matthew A. *Faithful Feelings: Rethinking Emotion in the New Testament.* Grand Rapids: Kregel, 2006.

Evans, Craig A. "The Function of the Elijah/Elisha Narratives in Luke's Ethic of Election." In *Luke and Scripture: The Function of Sacred Tradition in Luke-Acts,* by Craig A. Evans and James A. Sanders, 70–83. Eugene, OR: Wipf & Stock, 1993.

Ferris, Iain M. *Cave Canem: Animals and Roman Society.* Stroud, UK: Amberley, 2018.

———. "If You Owned a Dog in Ancient Rome, It Revealed Quite a Lot about You." *K9 Magazine.* January 30, 2018. https://www.k9magazine.com/if-you-owned-a-dog-in-ancient-rome-it-revealed-quite-a-lot-about-you/.

———. "Six Things You (Probably) Didn't Know about Animals in Ancient Rome." *HistoryExtra.* February 20, 2019. https://www.historyextra.com/period/roman/6-things-you-probably-didnt-know-about-animals-in-ancient-rome/.

Fiddes, Paul S. *Participating in God: A Pastoral Doctrine of the Trinity.* Louisville: Westminster John Knox, 2000.

Fisher, Philip. *The Vehement Passions.* Princeton: Princeton University Press, 2002.

Fisk, Bruce N. "See My Tears: A Lament for Jerusalem (Luke 13:31–35; 19:41–44)." In *The Word Leaps the Gap: Essays on Scripture and Theology in Honor of Richard B. Hays*, edited by J. Ross Wagner, C. Kavin Rowe, and A. Katherine Grieb, 147–78. Grand Rapids: Eerdmans, 2008.

Fontaine, Johnny J. R., and Klaus R. Scherer. "Emotion Is for Doing: The Action Tendency Component." In *Emotional Components of Meaning: A Sourcebook*, edited by Johnny J. R. Fontaine, Klaus R. Scherer, and Cristina Soriano, 170–85. Series in Affective Science. Oxford: Oxford University Press, 2013.

Fontaine, Johnny J. R., Klaus R. Scherer, and Cristina Soriano, eds. *Components of Emotional Meaning: A Sourcebook*. Series in Affective Science. Oxford: Oxford University Press, 2013.

Forster, E. M. *Aspects of the Novel*. Edited by Oliver Stallybrass. Harmondsworth, UK: Penguin, 1974.

Fortenbaugh, William W. *Aristotle on Emotions*. 2nd ed. London: Duckworth, 2002.

Francis (pope). *The Name of God Is Mercy: A Conversation with Andrea Tornielli*. Translated by Oonagh Stransky. New York: Random House, 2016.

Frazzetto, Giovanni. *Joy, Guilt, Anger, Love: What Neuroscience Can—and Can't—Tell Us about How We Feel*. New York: Penguin, 2013.

Frede, Dorothea. "'Mixed Feelings' in Aristotle's *Rhetoric*." In *Essays on Aristotle's Rhetoric*, edited by Amélie Oksenberg Rorty, 258–85. Berkeley: University of California Press, 1996.

Fredrickson, Barbara L. "The Broaden-and-Build Theory of Positive Emotions." *Philosophical Transactions of the Royal Society of London* 359 (2004): 1367–77. doi:10.1098/rstb.2004.1512.

———. "Cultivating Positive Emotions to Optimize Health and Well-Being." *Prevention and Treatment* 3, article 1 (2000). http://journals.apa.org/prevention/volume3/pre0030001a.html.

Fredriksen, Paula. *From Jesus to Christ*. 2nd ed. New Haven: Yale University Press, 2000.

Fretheim, Terence E. *The Suffering of God: An Old Testament Perspective*. Overtures to Biblical Theology. Philadelphia: Fortress, 1984.

Friberg, Barbara, Timothy Friberg, and Neva F. Miller. *Analytical Lexicon of the Greek New Testament*. Baker's Greek New Testament Library. Electronic edition. Grand Rapids: Baker Academic, 2000.

Friedrichsen, Timothy A. "The Temple, a Pharisee, a Tax Collector, and the Kingdom of God: Rereading a Jesus Parable (Luke 18:10–14a)." *Journal of Biblical Literature* 124 (2005): 89–119.

Frijda, Nico H. *The Emotions*. Studies in Emotion and Social Interaction. Cambridge: Cambridge University Press, 1986.

———. "Laws of Emotion." *American Psychologist* 43 (1988): 349–58.

Frijda, Nico H., and Batja Mesquita. "The Analysis of Emotions: Dimensions of Variation." In *What Develops in Emotional Development?*, edited by Michael F. Mascolo and Sharon Griffin, 273–95. New York: Plenum, 1998.

Funk, Robert W. *Honest to Jesus: Jesus for a New Millennium*. New York: Harper-Collins, 1996.

Gilbert, Daniel T., and Timothy D. Wilson. "Why the Brain Talks to Itself: Sources of Error in Emotional Prediction." *Philosophical Transactions of the Royal Society of Biological Sciences* 364 (2008): 1335–41.

Glancy, Jennifer A. *Slavery in Early Christianity*. Minneapolis: Fortress, 2006.

Goldie, Peter. *The Emotions: A Philosophical Exploration*. Oxford: Oxford University Press, 2000.

———. *The Mess Inside: Narrative, Emotion, and the Mind*. Oxford: Oxford University Press, 2012.

Goldstein, Rebecca Newberger. "Mattering Instinct." *Edge*, September 10, 2018. https://www.edge.org/conversation/rebecca_newberger_goldstein-the-mattering-instinct.

———. "Mattering Matters." *Free Inquiry* 37, February/March 2017. https://www.secularhumanism.org/index.php/articles/8609.

———. "What Really Matters? An Interview with Rebecca Goldstein." *IAI News*. September 3, 2018. https://iainews.iai.tv/articles/rebecca-goldstein-on-what-really-matters-auid-1141.

Graver, Margaret R. "Anatomies of Joy: Seneca and the *Gaudium* Tradition." In *Hope, Joy, and Affection in the Classical World*, edited by Ruth R. Caston and Robert A. Kaster, 123–42. New York: Oxford University Press, 2016.

———. *Cicero on the Emotions: Tusculan Disputations 3 and 4*. Chicago: University of Chicago Press, 2002.

———. *Stoicism and Emotion*. Chicago: University of Chicago Press, 2007.

Green, Joel B. *Body, Soul, and Human Life: The Nature of Humanity in the Bible*. Studies in Theological Interpretation. Grand Rapids: Baker Academic, 2008.

———. "Jesus on the Mount of Olives (Luke 22:39–46): Tradition and Theology." *Journal for the Study of the New Testament* 26 (1986): 29–48.

———. "Joy." In *Dictionary of Jesus and the Gospels*, edited by Joel B. Green, Jeannine K. Brown, and Nicholas Perrin, 448–50. 2nd ed. Downers Grove, IL: IVP Academic, 2013.

———. "'We Had to Celebrate and Rejoice!' Happiness in the Topsy-Turvy World of Luke-Acts." In *The Bible and the Pursuit of Happiness: What the Old and New Testaments Teach Us about the Good Life*, edited by Brent A. Strawn, 169–83. Oxford: Oxford University Press, 2012.

Gregory of Nazianzus. "Orations, Letters." Translated by Charles Gordon Browne and James Edward Swallow. In vol. 7 of *Nicene and Post-Nicene Fathers*, 2nd series, edited by Philip Schaff and Henry Wace, 185–482. Buffalo: Christian Literature,

1894. Revised and edited for New Advent by Kevin Knight. http://www.newadvent
.org/fathers/3103.htm.

Gregory of Nyssa. "Against Eunomius." Translated by H. A. Wilson. In vol. 5 of
Nicene and Post-Nicene Fathers, 2nd series, edited by Philip Schaff and Henry
Wace, 33–249. Buffalo: Christian Literature, 1893. Revised and edited for New
Advent by Kevin Knight. http://www.newadvent.org/fathers/290103.htm.

———. *Anti-Apollinarian Writings*. Translated by Robin Orton. Fathers of the
Church 131. Washington, DC: Catholic University of America Press, 2015.

Grout, James. "Dogs in Ancient Greece and Rome." *Encyclopaedia Romana*. Retrieved
February 19, 2020, from https://penelope.uchicago.edu/~grout/encyclopaedia
_romana/miscellanea/canes/canes.html.

Gruen, Erich. "Greek *pistis* and Roman *fides*." *Athenaeum* 60 (1982): 50–68.

Haidt, Jonathan. "Elevation and the Positive Psychology of Morality." In *Flourishing:
Positive Psychology and the Life Well-Lived*, edited by Corey L. M. Keyes and Jonathan Haidt, 275–89. Washington, DC: American Psychological Association, 2003.

———. "The Emotional Dog and Its Rational Tail: A Social Intuitionist Approach
to Moral Judgment." *Psychological Review* 108 (2001): 814–34.

———. *The Happiness Hypothesis: Finding Modern Truth in Ancient Wisdom*. New
York: Basic Books, 2006.

———. "The Positive Emotion of Elevation." *Prevention & Treatment* 3, article 3
(2000). https://doi.org/10.1037/1522-3736.3.1.33c.

———. *The Righteous Mind: Why Good People Are Divided by Politics and Religion*.
New York: Pantheon, 2012.

Haidt, Jonathan, Clark McCauley, and Paul Rozin. "Individual Differences in Sensitivity to Disgust: A Scale Sampling Seven Domains of Disgust Elicitors." *Personality
and Individual Differences* 16 (1994): 701–13.

Harris, William V. *Restraining Rage: The Ideology of Anger Control in Classical
Antiquity*. Cambridge, MA: Harvard University Press, 2001.

Hertenstein, Matthew J., and Dacher Keltner. "Gender and the Communication of
Emotion via Touch." *Sex Roles* 64 (2011): 70–80.

Hertenstein, Matthew J., Rachel Holmes, Margaret McCullough, and Dacher Keltner.
"The Communication of Emotion via Touch." *Emotion Review* 9 (2009): 566–73.

Hertenstein, Matthew J., Dacher Keltner, Betsy App, Brittany A. Bulleit, and Ariane R.
Jaskolka. "Touch Communicates Distinct Emotions." *Emotion* 6 (2006): 528–33.

Heschel, Abraham Joshua. *The Prophets: Two Volumes in One*. Peabody, MA: Hendrickson, 2009 (orig. 1962).

Holladay, William L. *A Concise Hebrew and Aramaic Lexicon of the Old Testament*.
Grand Rapids: Eerdmans, 1971.

Homer. *The Odyssey*. Translated by Robert Fagles. Introduction and notes by Bernard
Knox. New York: Penguin, 1997.

Hume, David. *A Treatise of Human Nature*. Edited by David Fate Norton and Mary J. Norton. Oxford Philosophical Texts. Oxford: Oxford University Press, 2000.

Hunt, Lynn. *Inventing Human Rights: A History*. New York: Norton, 2007.

Immordino-Yang, Mary Helen, and Antonio Damasio. *Emotions, Learning, and the Brain: Exploring the Educational Implications of Affective Neuroscience*. New York: Norton, 2016.

———. "We Feel, Therefore We Learn: The Relevance of Affective and Social Neuroscience to Education." *Mind, Brain, and Education* 1 (2007): 3–10.

Ivtzan, Itai, Tim Lomas, Kate Hefferon, and Piers Worth. *Second Wave Positive Psychology: Embracing the Dark Side of Life*. New York: Routledge, 2016.

Izard, Carroll E. *Human Emotions*. New York: Springer Science+Business Media, 1977.

———. "The Many Meanings/Aspects of Emotion: Definitions, Functions, Activation, and Regulation." *Emotion Review* 2 (2010): 363–70.

Jaeger, John. "Abraham Heschel and the Theology of Jürgen Moltmann." *Perspectives in Religious Studies* 24 (1997): 167–79.

Johnson, Elizabeth A. *Friends and Prophets: A Feminist Theological Reading of the Communion of Saints*. New York: Continuum, 1998.

Johnson, Luke Timothy. *The Gospel of Luke*. Sacra Pagina 3. Collegeville, MN: Liturgical Press, 1991.

Jones, Karen. "Trust as an Affective Attitude." *Ethics* 107 (1996): 4–25.

Josephus, Flavius. *The Works of Josephus*. (Includes *Ant.* and *J.W.*) Translated by William Whiston. New and updated ed. Peabody, MA: Hendrickson, 1987.

Just, Arthur A., Jr. "My Soul Magnifies the Lord: Luther's Hermeneutic of Humility." *Concordia Theological Quarterly* 81 (2017): 37–53.

Kagan, Jerome. *What Is Emotion? History, Measures, and Meanings*. New Haven: Yale University Press, 2007.

Kähler, Martin. *The So-Called Historical Jesus and the Historic, Biblical Christ*. Translated by Carl E. Braaten. Philadelphia: Augsburg Fortress, 1964.

Kahneman, Daniel. *Thinking, Fast and Slow*. New York: Farrar, Straus & Giroux, 2011.

Kashdan, Todd, and Robert Biswas-Diener. *The Upside of Your Dark Side: Why Being Your Whole Self—Not Just Your "Good" Self—Drives Success and Fulfillment*. New York: Plume, 2014.

Kasper, Walter (cardinal). *Mercy: The Essence of the Gospel and the Key to Christian Life*. Mahwah, NJ: Paulist Press, 2013.

Kaufman, Scott Barry. *Transcend: The New Science of Self-Actualization*. New York: TarcherPerigree, 2020.

Kazen, Thomas. "Disgust in Body, Mind, and Language: The Case of Impurity in the Hebrew Bible." In *Mixed Feelings and Vexed Passions: Exploring Emotions in*

Biblical Literature, edited by F. Scott Spencer, 97–115. Resources in Biblical Study 90. Atlanta: SBL Press, 2017.

Kee, Howard C. *Community of the New Age: Studies in Mark's Gospel*. New Testament Library. London: SCM Press, 1977.

———. "Testaments of the Twelve Patriarchs: A New Translation and Introduction." In *Apocalyptic Literature and Testaments*. Vol. 1 of *The Old Testament Pseudepigrapha*, edited by James H. Charlesworth, 775–828. Garden City, NY: Doubleday, 1983.

Kelly, J. N. D. *Early Christian Doctrines*. Rev. ed. New York: Harper & Row, 1978.

Keltner, Dacher, and Jonathan Haidt. "Approaching Awe, a Moral, Spiritual, and Aesthetic Emotion." *Cognition and Emotion* 17 (2003): 297–314.

Koester, Helmut. "σπλάγχνον κτλ." In *Theological Dictionary of the New Testament*, edited by Gerhard Friedrich, translated and edited by Geoffrey W. Bromiley, 7:548–59. Grand Rapids: Eerdmans, 1971.

Konstan, David. *The Emotions of the Ancient Greeks: Studies in Aristotle and Classical Literature*. Toronto: University of Toronto Press, 2006.

———. *Pity Transformed*. Classical Inter/Faces. London: Duckworth, 2001.

———. "The Varieties of Pity." *Journal of Biblical Literature* 133 (2014): 869–72.

Krause, Sharon H. *Civil Passions: Moral Sentiment and Democratic Deliberation*. Princeton: Princeton University Press, 2008.

Kübler-Ross, Elisabeth, and David Kessler. *On Grief and Grieving: Finding the Meaning of Grief through the Five Stages of Loss*. New York: Scribner, 2005.

Kuhn, Karl Allen. *The Heart of Biblical Narrative: Rediscovering Biblical Appeal to the Emotions*. Minneapolis: Fortress, 2009.

Kurz, William S. *Farewell Addresses in the New Testament*. Zacchaeus Studies: New Testament. Collegeville, MN: Liturgical Press, 1990.

Kysar, Robert. *John, the Maverick Gospel*. 3rd ed. Louisville: Westminster John Knox, 2007.

LaCugna, Catherine Mowry. *God for Us: The Trinity and Christian Life*. New York: HarperOne, 1993.

Lambert, David A. "Mourning over Sin/Affliction and the Problem of 'Emotion' as a Category in the Hebrew Bible." In *Mixed Feelings and Vexed Passions: Exploring Emotions in Biblical Literature*, edited by F. Scott Spencer, 139–60. Resources in Biblical Study 90. Atlanta: SBL Press, 2017.

Lateiner, Donald. "The Emotions of Disgust, Provoked and Expressed in Earlier Greek Literature." In *Emotions in the Classical World: Methods, Approaches, and Directions*, edited by Douglas Cairns and Damien Nelis, 31–52. Heidelberger althistorische Beiträge und epigraphische Studien 59. Stuttgart: Franz Steiner, 2017.

———. "Pain and Pity in Two Postbiblical Responses to Joseph's Power in Genesis." *Journal of Biblical Literature* 133 (2014): 863–68.

Lateiner, Donald, and Dimos Spatharas. "Introduction: Ancient and Modern Modes of Understanding and Manipulating Disgust." In *The Ancient Emotion of Disgust*, edited by Donald Lateiner and Dimos Spatharas, 1–42. Emotions of the Past. Oxford: Oxford University Press, 2016.

Lazarus, Richard S. *Emotion and Adaptation*. New York: Oxford University Press, 1991.

Lazarus, Richard S., and Bernice N. Lazarus. *Passion and Reason: Making Sense of Our Emotions*. New York: Oxford University Press, 1994.

Levenson, Jon D. *The Love of God: Divine Gift, Human Gratitude, and Mutual Faithfulness in Judaism*. Princeton: Princeton University Press, 2016.

Levine, Amy-Jill. *Short Stories by Jesus: The Enigmatic Parables of a Controversial Rabbi*. New York: HarperOne, 2014.

Levine, Lee I. A. "Judaism from the Destruction of Jerusalem to the End of the Second Jewish Revolt: 70–135 C.E." In *Christianity and Rabbinic Judaism: A Parallel History of Their Origins and Early Development*, edited by Hershel Shanks, 125–49. Washington, DC: Biblical Archaeology Society, 1992.

Lewis, Charlton T., and Charles Short. *A Latin Dictionary: Founded on Andrews' Edition of Freund's Latin Dictionary*. Revised, enlarged, and in great part rewritten by Charlton T. Lewis and Charles Short. Oxford: Clarendon, 1879. http://www.perseus.tufts.edu/hopper/text?doc=Perseus:text:1999.04.0059:entry=alacer&highlight=alacer.

Liddell, Henry George, and Robert Scott. *Liddell and Scott's Greek-English Lexicon, Abridged*. Mansfield Centre, CT: Martino, 2015 (orig. 1871).

Linden, David J. *Touch: The Science of Hand, Heart, and Mind*. New York: Viking, 2015.

Lister, Rob. *God Is Impassible and Impassioned: Toward a Theology of Divine Emotion*. Wheaton: Crossway, 2013.

Loader, William. "Challenged at the Boundaries: A Conservative Jesus in Mark's Tradition." *Journal for the Study of the New Testament* 63 (1996): 45–61.

Longenecker, Richard N. *Biblical Exegesis in the Apostolic Period*. 2nd ed. Grand Rapids: Eerdmans, 1999.

Lucian. *The Works of Lucian of Samosata*. (Includes *Men.*) Translated by H. W. Fowler and F. G. Fowler. Oxford: Clarendon, 1905.

Lukianoff, Greg, and Jonathan Haidt. *The Coddling of the American Mind: How Good Intentions and Bad Ideas Are Setting Up a Generation for Failure*. New York: Penguin, 2018.

Luna, Tania, and LeeAnn Renninger. *Surprise: Embrace the Unpredictable and Engineer the Unexpected*. New York: Perigree, 2015.

Luther, Martin. *Lectures on Galatians*. Edited by Jaroslav Pelikan and Walter A. Hansen. Vol. 27 of *Luther's Works*. St. Louis: Concordia, 1964.

———. *Luther: Letters of Spiritual Counsel*. Edited and translated by Theodore G. Tappert. Library of Christian Classics. Louisville: Westminster John Knox, 2006.

Madigan, Kevin J. "Ancient and High-Medieval Interpretations of Jesus in Gethsemane: Some Reflections on Tradition and Continuity in Christian Thought." *Harvard Theological Review* 88 (1995): 157–73.

Malina, Bruce J., and Jerome H. Neyrey. "First-Century Personality: Dyadic, Not Individual." In *The Social World of Luke-Acts: Models for Interpretation*, edited by Jerome H. Neyrey, 67–96. Peabody, MA: Hendrickson, 1991.

Malina, Bruce J., and Richard L. Rohrbaugh. *Social-Science Commentary on the Synoptic Gospels*. Minneapolis: Fortress, 1992.

Marcus Aurelius. *Meditations with Selected Correspondence*. Translated by Robin Hard. Oxford World Classics. Oxford: Oxford University Press, 2011.

Marcus, Joel. *The Way of the Lord: Christological Exegesis of the Old Testament in the Gospel of Mark*. Louisville: Westminster John Knox, 1992.

Mars, Rogier B., Franz-Xaver Neubert, MaryAnn P. Noonan, Jerome Sallet, Ivan Toni, and Matthew F. S. Rushworth. "On the Relationship between the 'Default Mode Network' and the 'Social Brain.'" *Frontiers in Human Neuroscience*, June 21, 2012. doi: 10.3389/fnhum.2012.00189.

Marsh, Abigail. *The Fear Factor: How One Emotion Connects Altruists, Psychopaths, and Everyone In-Between*. New York: Basic Books, 2017.

Massumi, Brian. *Parables of the Virtual: Movement, Affect, Sensation*. Durham, NC: Duke University Press, 2007.

Matheson, Benjamin. "More Than a Feeling: The Communicative Function of Regret." *International Journal of Philosophical Studies* 25 (2017): 664–81.

Matthews, Shelly. "The Weeping Jesus and the Daughters of Jerusalem: Gender and Conquest in Lukan Lament." In *Doing Gender—Doing Religion: Fallstudien zur Intersektionalität im frühen Judentum, Christentum und Islam*, edited by Ute E. Eisen, Christine Gerber, and Angela Standhartinger, 381–403. WUNT 2/302. Tübingen: Mohr Siebeck, 2013.

Mays, James Luther. *Hosea: A Commentary*. Old Testament Library. Philadelphia: Westminster, 1976.

McBride, S. Dean, Jr. "Deuteronomy." In *The HarperCollins Study Bible*, edited by Harold W. Attridge, 255–309. Rev. ed. New York: HarperCollins, 2006.

McClure, Barbara J. *Emotions: Problems and Promise for Human Flourishing*. Waco: Baylor University Press, 2019.

McMahon, Darrin M. *Happiness: A History*. New York: Grove Atlantic, 2006.

———. "Joy in the History of Emotions." In *Doing Emotions History*, edited by Susan J. Matt and Peter N. Stearns, 103–19. Champaign: University of Illinois Press, 2014.

Meeks, Wayne A. *The Origins of Christian Morality: The First Two Centuries*. New Haven: Yale University Press, 1993.

Mendonça, Dina. "Emotions about Emotions." *Emotion Review* 5 (2013): 390–96.

Menninghaus, Winfried. *Disgust: Theory and History of a Strong Sensation*. Translated by Howard Eiland and Joel Golb. Albany: State University of New York Press, 2003.

Meredith, Anthony. *Gregory of Nyssa*. Early Church Fathers. New York: Routledge, 1999.

Miller, William Ian. *The Anatomy of Disgust*. Cambridge, MA: Harvard University Press, 1997.

Mirguet, Françoise. *An Early History of Compassion: Emotion and Imagination in Hellenistic Judaism*. Cambridge: Cambridge University Press, 2017.

———. "Emotional Responses to the Pain of Others in Josephus's Rewritten Scriptures and the *Testament of Zebulun*." *Journal of Biblical Literature* 133 (2014): 838–57.

Mol, Susan. "*Head* and *Heart*: Metaphors and Metonymies in Cross-Linguistic Perspective." In *Translation and Corpora: Selected Papers from the Göteborg-Oslo Symposium 18–19 October 2003*, edited by Karin Aijmer and Hilde Hasselgård, 87–111. Gothenburg, Sweden: Acta Universitatis Gothoburgensis, 2004.

Moloney, Francis J. *The Gospel of John*. Sacra Pagina 4. Collegeville, MN: Liturgical Press, 1998.

Moltmann, Jürgen. *A Broad Place: An Autobiography*. Translated by Margaret Kohl. Minneapolis: Fortress, 2009.

———. *The Crucified God: The Cross of Christ as the Foundation and Criticism of Christian Theology*. Translated by R. A. Wilson, John Bowden, and Margaret Kohl. Minneapolis: Fortress, 1993.

———. "*The Crucified God* Yesterday and Today: 1972–2002." In Jürgen Moltmann and Elisabeth Moltmann-Wendel, *Passion for God: Theology in Two Voices*, translated by Margaret Kohl, 69–85. Louisville: Westminster John Knox, 2003.

———. *In the End—the Beginning*. Translated by Margaret Kohl. Minneapolis: Fortress, 2004.

———. *The Living God and the Fullness of Life*. Translated by Margaret Kohl. Louisville: Westminster John Knox, 2015.

———. "The Passibility or Impassibility of God: Answers to J. K. Mozley's 'Six Necessary Questions.'" In Jürgen Moltmann, *The Spirit of Hope: Theology for a World in Peril*. Translated by Margaret Kohl and Brian McNeil, 159–71. Louisville: Westminster John Knox, 2019.

———. *The Passion for Life: A Messianic Lifestyle*. Translated by M. Douglas Meeks. Philadelphia: Fortress, 1978.

———. *The Trinity and the Kingdom: The Doctrine of God*. Translated by Margaret Kohl. Minneapolis: Fortress, 1993.

Moore, Stephen D. "The Dog-Woman of Canaan and Other Animal Tales." In *Sound-ings in Cultural Criticism: Perspectives and Methods in Culture, Power, and Identity in the New Testament*, edited by Francisco Lozada and Greg Carey, 57–72. Min-neapolis: Fortress, 2013.

———. "Why the Johannine Jesus Weeps at the Tomb of Lazarus." In *Mixed Feelings and Vexed Passions: Exploring Emotions in Biblical Literature*, edited by F. Scott Spencer, 287–310. Resources for Biblical Study 90. Atlanta: SBL Press, 2017.

———. "Why the Risen Body Weeps." In *Gospel Jesuses and Other Nonhumans: Biblical Criticism and Post-poststructuralism*, 15–40. Semeia Studies 89. Atlanta: SBL Press, 2017.

Moore, Stephen D., and Janice Capel Anderson. "Taking It Like a Man: Masculinity in 4 Maccabees." *Journal of Biblical Literature* 117 (1998): 249–73.

Moors, Agnes. "Flavors of Appraisal Theories of Emotion." *Emotion Review* 6 (2014): 303–7.

Moors, Agnes, Phoebe C. Ellsworth, Klaus R. Scherer, and Nico H. Frijda. "Appraisal Theories of Emotions: State of the Art and Future Development." *Emotion Review* 5 (2013): 119–24.

Morgan, Teresa. *Roman Faith and Christian Faith: Pistis and Fides in the Early Roman Empire and Early Churches*. Oxford: Oxford University Press, 2015.

Mosher, Donald L., and Silvan S. Tomkins. "Scripting the Macho Man: Hypermascu-line Socialization and Enculturation." *Journal of Sex Research* 25 (1988): 60–84.

Moule, C. F. D. "The Individualism of the Fourth Gospel." *Novum Testamentum* 5 (1962): 171–90.

Moulton, James H., and George Milligan. *Vocabulary of the Greek New Testament*. London: Hodder & Stoughton, 1930.

Moxnes, Halvor. "Patron-Client Relations and the New Community in Luke-Acts." In *The Social World of Luke-Acts: Models for Interpretation*, edited by Jerome H. Neyrey, 241–68. Peabody, MA: Hendrickson, 1991.

Newman, Barclay M. *A Concise Greek-English Dictionary of the New Testament*. Rev. ed. Stuttgart: Deutsche Bibelgesellschaft, 2010.

Neyrey, Jerome H. "The Absence of Jesus' Emotions—the Lukan Redaction of Lk. 22,39–46." *Biblica* 61 (1980): 153–71.

———. *The Passion according to Luke: A Redaction Study of Luke's Soteriology*. Theological Inquiries. Mahwah, NJ: Paulist Press, 1985.

Nook, Eric C., Stephanie F. Sasse, Hilary K. Lambert, Katie A. McLaughlin, and Leah H. Somerville. "The Nonlinear Development of Emotion Differentiation: Granular Emotional Experience Is Low in Adolescence." *Psychological Science* 29 (2018): 1–12. https://doi.org/10.1177/0956797618773357.

Norman, Elisabeth, and Bjarte Furnes. "The Concept of 'Metaemotion': What Is There to Learn from Research on Metacognition?" *Emotion Review* 8 (2016): 187–93.

Nouwen, Henri. *The Wounded Healer: Ministry in Contemporary Society*. New York: Doubleday, 1972.

Nussbaum, Martha C. *Anger and Forgiveness: Resentment, Generosity, Justice*. New York: Oxford University Press, 2016.

———. *Creating Capabilities: The Human Development Approach*. Cambridge, MA: Harvard University Press, 2011.

———. *Frontiers of Justice: Disability, Nationality, and Species Membership*. Tanner Lectures on Human Values 8. Cambridge, MA: Harvard University Press, 2007.

———. *Hiding from Humanity: Disgust, Shame, and the Law*. Princeton: Princeton University Press, 2006.

———. "Living the Past Forward: The Present and Future Value of Backward-Looking Emotions." In *Aging Thoughtfully: Conversations about Retirement, Romance, Wrinkles, and Regret*, by Martha C. Nussbaum and Saul Levmore, 125–43. New York: Oxford University Press, 2017.

———. *Poetic Justice: The Literary Imagination and Public Life*. Boston: Beacon, 1995.

———. *The Therapy of Desire: Theory and Practice in Hellenistic Ethics*. Princeton: Princeton University Press, 1994.

———. *Upheavals of Thought: The Intelligence of Emotions*. Cambridge: Cambridge University Press, 2001.

Oatley, Keith. *The Passionate Muse: Exploring Emotions in Stories*. Oxford: Oxford University Press, 2012.

Olson, Dennis. "Emotion, Repentance, and the Question of the 'Inner Life' of Biblical Israelites in Hosea 6:1–3." In *Mixed Feelings and Vexed Passions: Exploring Emotions in Biblical Literature*, edited by F. Scott Spencer, 161–76. Resources in Biblical Study 90. Atlanta: SBL Press, 2017.

Olson, Roger E. *The Journey of Modern Theology: From Reconstruction to Deconstruction*. Downers Grove, IL: IVP Academic, 2013.

———. *The Mosaic of Christian Belief: Twenty Centuries of Unity and Diversity*. 2nd ed. Downers Grove, IL: InterVarsity, 2016.

Omanson, Roger L. *A Textual Guide to the Greek New Testament*. Stuttgart: Deutsche Bibelgesellschaft, 2006.

Oswald, Roy M., and Arland Jacobson. *The Emotional Intelligence of Jesus: Relational Smarts for Religious Leaders*. Lanham, MD: Rowman & Littlefield, 2015.

Parsons, Mikeal C. *Luke*. Paideia: Commentaries on the New Testament. Grand Rapids: Baker Academic, 2015.

Peppard, Michael. *The Son of God in the Roman World: Divine Sonship in Its Social and Political Context*. New York: Oxford University Press, 2011.

Petronius. "Satyricon." In *Petronius. Seneca Apocolocyntosis*, translated by Michael Heseltine, 1–324. LCL. London: Heinemann, 1913.

Phillips, Amber, and Eugene Scott. "The First Democratic Debate Night Transcript, Annotated." *Washington Post*, June 27, 2019, http://www.washingtonpost.com /politics/2019/06/27/transcript-night-one-first-democratic-debate-annotated.

Philo. *The Works of Philo: Complete and Unabridged*. Translated by C. D. Yonge. Rev. ed. Peabody, MA: Hendrickson, 1993.

Pigliucci, Massimo. *How to Be a Stoic: Using Ancient Philosophy to Live a Modern Life*. New York: Basic Books, 2017.

Pindar. *Odes*. Edited and translated by Diane Arnson Svarlien. 1990. http://www .perseus.tufts.edu/hopper/text?doc=Perseus%3Atext%3A1999.01.0162%3Abook %3DO.%3Apoem%3D1.

Plamper, Jan. *The History of Emotions: An Introduction*. Translated by Keith Tribe. Emotions in History. Oxford: Oxford University Press, 2015.

Plato. *Theaetetus*. Translated by Harold N. Fowler. LCL. Cambridge, MA: Harvard University Press, 1921.

Pokorný, Petr. "From a Puppy to the Child: Some Problems of Contemporary Biblical Exegesis Demonstrated from Mark 7.24–30/Matt 15.21–28." *New Testament Studies* 41 (1995): 321–37.

Pope, Michael. "The Downward Motion of Jesus's Sweat and Tears and the Authenticity of Luke 22:43–44." *Catholic Biblical Quarterly* 79 (2017): 261–82.

Potkay, Adam. *The Story of Joy: From the Bible to Later Romanticism*. Cambridge: Cambridge University Press, 2007.

Powery, Emerson B. "Gethsemane." *NIDB* 2:561–62.

Prakasam, Antony Dhas. "The Pride of Babylon in Isaiah 47 Revisited in Light of the Theory of Self-Conscious Emotions." In *Mixed Feelings and Vexed Passions: Exploring Emotions in Biblical Literature*, edited by F. Scott Spencer, 177–95. Resources in Biblical Study 90. Atlanta: SBL Press, 2017.

Price, Carolyn. *Emotion*. Key Concepts in Philosophy. Cambridge: Polity, 2015.

Prinz, Jesse. "Why Wonder Is the Most Human of All Emotions." *Aeon*. June 21, 2013. https://aeon.co/essays/why-wonder-is-the-most-human-of-all-emotions.

Proust, Marcel. *Remembrance of Things Past*. Translated by C. K. Scott Moncrief and Terence Kilmartin. 3 vols. New York: Vintage, 1982.

Pugmire, David. *Sound Sentiments: Integrity in the Emotions*. Oxford: Oxford University Press, 2005.

Railton, Peter. "Morality and Prospection." In *Homo Prospectus*, by Martin E. P. Seligman, Peter Railton, Roy F. Baumeister, and Chandra Sripada, 226–80. New York: Oxford University Press, 2016.

Reddy, William M. *The Navigation of Feeling: A Framework for the History of Emotions*. Cambridge: Cambridge University Press, 2001.

Reinhartz, Adele. *Befriending the Beloved Disciple: A Jewish Reading of the Gospel of John*. New York: Continuum, 2002.

————. *Cast Out of the Covenant: Jews and Anti-Judaism in the Gospel of John.* Lanham, MD: Lexington Books/Fortress Academic, 2018.

————. "The Gospel of John: How 'the Jews' Became Part of the Plot." In *Jesus, Judaism, and Christian Anti-Judaism: Reading the New Testament after the Holocaust,* edited by Paula Fredriksen and Adele Reinhartz, 99–116. Louisville: Westminster John Knox, 2002.

Resseguie, James L. *Narrative Criticism of the New Testament.* Grand Rapids: Baker Academic, 2005.

Ringe, Sharon H. "A Gentile Woman's Story." In *Feminist Interpretation of the Bible,* edited by Letty M. Russell, 65–72. Philadelphia: Westminster, 1985.

————. "A Gentile Woman's Story, Revisited: Rereading Mark 7:24–30." In *A Feminist Companion to Mark,* edited by Amy-Jill Levine and Marianne Blickenstaff, 79–100. Sheffield: Sheffield Academic, 2001.

————. *Wisdom's Friends: Community and Christology in the Fourth Gospel.* Louisville: Westminster John Knox, 1999.

Robbins, Vernon K. *Exploring the Texture of Texts: A Guide to Socio-Rhetorical Interpretation.* Valley Forge, PA: Trinity Press International, 1996.

Roberts, Robert C. *Emotions: An Essay in Aid of Moral Psychology.* Cambridge: Cambridge University Press, 2003.

————. "Emotions and the Canons of Evaluation." In *The Oxford Handbook of Philosophy of Emotion,* edited by Peter Goldie, 561–83. Oxford: Oxford University Press, 2010.

————. *Spiritual Emotions: A Psychology of Christian Virtues.* Grand Rapids: Eerdmans, 2007.

Robertson, A. T. *A Grammar of the Greek New Testament in Light of Historical Research.* London: Hodder & Stoughton, 1923.

Robertson, Donald. *How to Think Like a Roman Emperor: The Stoic Philosophy of Marcus Aurelius.* New York: St. Martin's Press, 2019.

Robin, Corey. *Fear: The History of a Political Idea.* New York: Oxford University Press, 2004.

Rorty, Amélie Oksenberg. "Agent Regret." In *Explaining Emotions,* edited by Amélie Oksenberg Rorty, 489–506. Berkeley: University of California Press, 1980.

Rosfort, René, and Giovanni Stanghelini. "In the Mood for Thought: Feeling and Thinking in Philosophy." *New Literary History* 43 (2012): 395–417.

Rousseau, Jean-Jacques. *Émile, or On Education.* Translated by Allan Bloom. New York: Basic Books, 1979.

Rousseau, John J., and Rami Arav. *Jesus and His World: An Archaeological Dictionary.* Minneapolis: Fortress, 1995.

Rowe, Stephen C. "Beginning in Wonder: On Socrates and the Practice of Philosophy." *Grand Valley Review* 7 (1992): 28–36.

Rozin, Paul, and April E. Fallon. "A Perspective on Disgust." *Psychological Review* 94 (1987): 23–41.

Rozin, Paul, Jonathan Haidt, and Clark R. McCauley. "Disgust." In *Handbook of Emotions*, edited by Lisa Feldman Barrett, Michael Lewis, and Jeannette M. Haviland-Jones, 815–24. 4th ed. New York: Guilford, 2016.

Rozin, Paul, Laura Lowery, and Rhonda Ebert. "Varieties of Disgust Faces and the Structure of Disgust." *Journal of Personality and Social Psychology* 66 (1994): 870–81.

Rozin, Paul, Laura Lowery, Sumio Imada, and Jonathan Haidt. "The CAD Triad Hypothesis: A Mapping between Three Moral Emotions (Contempt, Anger, Disgust) and Three Moral Codes (Community, Autonomy, Divinity)." *Journal of Personality and Social Psychology* 76 (1999): 574–86.

Sanders, E. P. *The Historical Figure of Jesus.* London: Penguin, 1993.

———. *Jesus and Judaism.* London: SCM, 1985.

———. *Judaism: Practice & Belief, 63 BCE–66 CE.* London: SCM, 1992.

Sanders, J. N. *The Gospel according to St John.* Edited and completed by B. A. Mastin. Black's New Testament Commentaries. London: Adam & Charles Black, 1968.

Sapolsky, Robert M. *Behave: The Biology of Humans at Our Best and Worst.* New York: Penguin, 2017.

Schlimm, Matthew R. "Different Perspectives on Divine Pathos: An Examination of Hermeneutics in Biblical Theology." *Catholic Biblical Quarterly* 69 (2007): 673–94.

Schottroff, Luise. *The Parables of Jesus.* Translated by Linda M. Maloney. Minneapolis: Fortress, 2006.

Schultz, Brian. "Jesus as Archelaus in the Parable of the Pounds (Luke 19.11–27)." *Novum Testamentum* 49 (2007): 105–27.

Schüssler Fiorenza, Elisabeth. *But She Said: Feminist Practices of Biblical Interpretation.* Boston: Beacon, 1992.

Scott, Martin. *Sophia and the Johannine Jesus.* Journal for the Study of the New Testament Supplement Series 71. Sheffield: Sheffield Academic, 1992.

Scrutton, Anastasia. "Emotion in Augustine of Hippo and Thomas Aquinas: A Way Forward for the Im/passibility Debate?" *International Journal of Systematic Theology* 7 (2005): 169–77.

———. *Thinking through Feeling: God, Emotion, and Passibility.* New York: Bloomsbury Academic, 2011.

Seligman, Martin E. P. *Authentic Happiness: Using the New Positive Psychology to Realize Your Potential for Lasting Fulfillment.* New York: Free Press, 2002.

———. "Building Human Strength: Psychology's Forgotten Mission." *APA Monitor* (January 1998): 2.

Seligman, Martin E. P., Peter Railton, Roy F. Baumeister, and Chandra Sripada. *Homo Prospectus.* New York: Oxford University Press, 2016.

Seneca, Lucius Annaeus. *Anger, Mercy, Revenge.* Translated by Robert A. Kaster and Martha C. Nussbaum. Chicago: University of Chicago Press, 2010.

———. *Letters on Ethics: To Lucilius.* Translated by Margaret Graver and A. A. Long. Chicago: University of Chicago Press, 2015.

Shakespeare, William. *Hamlet.* In *The Complete Works of William Shakespeare.* http://shakespeare.mit.edu/hamlet/full.html.

Shrenk, Gottlob. "εὐδοκέω, εὐδοκία." In *Theological Dictionary of the New Testament,* edited by Gerhard Friedrich, translated and edited by Geoffrey W. Bromiley, 2:738–51. Grand Rapids: Eerdmans, 1971.

Siegel, Daniel J. *Mind: A Journey to the Heart of Being Human.* New York: Norton, 2017.

Skinner, Matthew L. *A Companion to the New Testament: The Gospels and Acts.* Waco: Baylor University Press, 2017.

Snyder, C. R., Shane J. Lopez, and Jennifer Teramoto Pedrotti. *Positive Psychology: The Scientific and Practical Explorations of Human Strength.* 2nd ed. Thousand Oaks, CA: Sage, 2011.

Solomon, Robert C. *The Joy of Philosophy: Thinking Thin versus the Passionate Life.* New York: Oxford University Press, 1999.

———. *Love: Emotion, Myth, and Metaphor.* Amherst, NY: Prometheus Books, 1990.

———. *The Passions: Emotions and the Meaning of Life.* 2nd ed. Indianapolis: Hackett, 1993.

Sophocles. *The Oedipus Tyrannus of Sophocles.* Edited with introduction and notes by Richard Jebb. Cambridge: Cambridge University Press, 1887.

Soriano, Cristina, Johnny J. R. Fontaine, Anna Ogarkova, Claudia Mejía Quijano, Yana Volkova, Svetlana Ionova, and Viktor Shakhovskyy. "Types of Anger in Spanish and Russian." In *Components of Emotional Meaning: A Sourcebook,* edited by Johnny J. R. Fontaine, Klaus R. Scherer, and Cristina Soriano, 339–52. Series in Affective Science. Oxford: Oxford University Press, 2013.

Spencer, F. Scott. *Dancing Girls, "Loose" Ladies, and Women of "the Cloth": The Women in Jesus' Life.* New York: Continuum, 2004.

———. "Faith on Edge: The Difficult Case of the Spirit-Seized Boy in Mark 9:14–29." *Review & Expositor* 107 (2010): 419–24.

———. "Getting a Feel for the 'Mixed' and 'Vexed' Study of Emotions in Biblical Literature." In *Mixed Feelings and Vexed Passions: Exploring Emotions in Biblical Literature,* edited by F. Scott Spencer, 1–41. Resources for Biblical Study 90. Atlanta: SBL Press, 2017.

———. *Luke.* Two Horizons New Testament Commentary. Grand Rapids: Eerdmans, 2019.

———, ed. *Mixed Feelings and Vexed Passions: Exploring Emotions in Biblical Literature.* Resources for Biblical Study 90. Atlanta: SBL Press, 2017.

———. "Neglected Widows in Acts 6:1–7." *Catholic Biblical Quarterly* 56 (1994): 715–33.

_____. Review of *The Heart of Biblical Narrative: Rediscovering Biblical Appeal to the Emotions*, by Karl Allen Kuhn. *Review & Expositor* 107, no. 1 (2010): 91–92, https:// doi.org/10.1177/003463731010700114.

_____. Review of *Jesus' Emotions in the Gospels*, by Stephen Voorwinde. *Interpretation* 67, no. 1 (2013): 78.

———. *Salty Wives, Spirited Mothers, and Savvy Widows: Capable Women of Purpose and Persistence in Luke's Gospel*. Grand Rapids: Eerdmans, 2012.

———. "Son of God." In *The Oxford Encyclopedia of Bible and Theology*, edited by Samuel E. Balentine, 1:308–16. 2 vols. Oxford: Oxford University Press, 2015.

———. "Song of Songs as Political Satire and Emotional Refuge: Subverting Solomon's Gilded Regime." *Journal for the Study of the Old Testament* 44 (2020): 667–92.

———. "To Fear and Not to Fear the Creator God: A Theological and Therapeutic Interpretation of Luke 12:4–34." *Journal of Theological Interpretation* 8 (2014): 229–49.

———. *What Did Jesus Do? Gospel Profiles of Jesus' Personal Conduct*. Harrisburg, PA: Trinity Press International, 2003.

———. "Why Did the 'Leper' Get under Jesus' Skin? Emotion Theory and Angry Reaction in Mark 1:40–45." *Horizons in Biblical Theology* 36 (2014): 107–28.

———. "A Withered Hand, Hardened Hearts, and a Distressed Jesus: Getting a Feel for the Sabbath Scene in Mark 3:1–6." *Review & Expositor* 114 (2017): 292–97.

———. "A Woman's Touch: Manual and Emotional Dynamics of Female Characters in Luke's Gospel." In *Characters and Characterization in Luke-Acts*, edited by Frank Dicken and Julia Snyder, 73–94. Library of New Testament Studies 548. London: Bloomsbury T&T Clark, 2016.

———. "'Your Faith Has Made You Well' (Mark 5:34; 10:52): Emotional Dynamics of Trustful Engagement with Jesus in Mark's Gospel." In *Mixed Feelings and Vexed Passions: Exploring Emotions in Biblical Literature*, edited by F. Scott Spencer, 217–41. Resources in Biblical Study 90. Atlanta: SBL Press, 2017.

Spinoza, Benedict de. *Ethics*. Edited and translated by Edwin Curley. London: Penguin, 1996.

Sripada, Chandra. "Free Will and the Construction of Options." In *Homo Prospectus*, by Martin E. P. Seligman, Peter Railton, Roy F. Baumeister, and Chandra Sripada, 191–206. New York: Oxford University Press, 2016.

Stagg, Frank. *The Book of Acts: The Early Struggle for an Unhindered Gospel*. Nashville: Broadman, 1955.

Steinbock, Anthony J. *Moral Emotions: Reclaiming the Evidence of the Heart*. Evanston, IL: Northwestern University Press, 2014.

Stolt, Birgit. "Luther's Translation of the Bible." *Lutheran Quarterly* 28 (2014): 373–400.

Stump, Eleonore. "The Non-Aristotelian Character of Aquinas's Ethics: Aquinas on the Passions." In *Faith, Rationality, and the Passions*, edited by Sarah Coakley, 91–106. Directions in Modern Theology. Malden, MA: Wiley-Blackwell, 2012.

Tallis, Raymond. *The Hand: A Philosophical Inquiry into Human Being.* Edinburgh: Edinburgh University Press, 2003.

Tangney, June Price, and Kurt W. Fischer, eds. *Self-Conscious Emotions: The Psychology of Shame, Guilt, Embarrassment, and Pride.* New York: Guilford, 1995.

Tannehill, Robert C. *The Gospel according to Luke.* Vol. 1 of *The Narrative Unity of Luke-Acts.* Foundations & Facets: New Testament. Philadelphia: Fortress, 1986.

———. "Israel in Luke-Acts: A Tragic Story." In *The Shape of Luke's Story: Essays on Luke-Acts*, 105–24. Eugene, OR: Cascade Books, 2005.

———. *Luke.* Abingdon New Testament Commentaries. Nashville: Abingdon, 1996.

Theissen, Gerd. *The Gospels in Context: Social and Political History in the Synoptic Tradition.* Edinburgh: T&T Clark, 1992.

Thomas, D. Winton. "*Kelebh* 'Dog': Its Origin and Some Uses of It in the Old Testament." *Vetus Testamentum* 10 (1960): 410–27.

Thorsen, Donald A. D. "Gethsemane." *ABD* 2:997–98.

Tiede, David L. *Prophecy and History in Luke-Acts.* Philadelphia: Fortress, 1980.

Tillich, Paul. *Dynamics of Faith.* New York: Harper, 1957.

Torrance, T. F. *Space, Time, and Incarnation.* Edinburgh: T&T Clark, 1997.

Tracy, Jessica L., and Richard W. Robins. "Self-Conscious Emotions: Where Self and Emotion Meet." In *Frontiers in Social Psychology: The Self*, edited by Constantine Sedikides and Stephen J. Spencer, 187–210. New York: Psychology Press, 2007.

Tracy, Jessica L., Richard W. Robins, and June Price Tangney, eds. *The Self-Conscious Emotions: Theory and Research.* New York: Guilford, 2007.

Trible, Phyllis. *God and the Rhetoric of Sexuality.* Overtures to Biblical Theology. Philadelphia: Fortress, 1978.

Tuckett, Christopher M. "Luke 22,43–44: The 'Agony' in the Garden in Luke's Gospel." In *New Testament Textual Criticism and Exegesis*, edited by Albert Denaux, 133–44. Leuven, Belgium: Leuven University Press, 2002.

Tugade, Michele M., Barbara L. Fredrickson, and Lisa Feldman Barrett. "Psychological Resilience and Positive Emotional Granularity: Examining the Benefits of Positive Emotions on Coping and Health." *Journal of Personality* 72 (2004): 1161–90.

Tybur, Joshua M., Debra Lieberman, and Vladas Griskevicius. "Microbes, Mating, and Morality: Individual Differences in Three Functional Domains of Disgust." *Journal of Personality and Social Psychology* 97 (2009): 103–22.

Vaillant, George E. *Aging Well: Surprising Guideposts to a Happier Life from the Landmark Harvard Study of Adult Development.* Boston: Little, Brown, 2002.

———. *Spiritual Evolution: How We Are Wired for Faith, Hope, and Love.* New York: Broadway Books, 2008.

———. *Triumphs of Experience: The Men of the Harvard Grant Study.* Cambridge, MA: Belknap, 2012.

Van Eck, Ernest. "Social Memory and Identity: Luke 19:12b–24 and 27." *Biblical Theology Bulletin* 41 (2011): 201–12.

Vinson, Richard B. "The Minas Touch: Anti-kingship Rhetoric in the Gospel of Luke." *Perspectives in Religious Studies* 35 (2008): 69–86.

Voorwinde, Stephen. *Jesus' Emotions in the Fourth Gospel.* Library of New Testament Studies 284. London: T&T Clark International, 2005.

———. *Jesus' Emotions in the Gospels.* London: T&T Clark, 2011.

Wallace, Daniel B. *Greek Grammar beyond the Basics: An Exegetical Syntax of the New Testament.* Grand Rapids: Zondervan, 1996.

Watts, Rikk E. "Mark." In *Commentary on the New Testament Use of the Old Testament,* edited by G. K. Beale and D. A. Carson, 111–249. Grand Rapids: Baker Academic, 2007.

Whitman, Walt. "I Sing the Body Electric." Poetry Foundation, https://www.poetry foundation.org/poems/45472/i-sing-the-body-electric.

Williams, Bernard. *Moral Luck.* Cambridge: Cambridge University Press, 1981.

Williams, Rowan. *The Wound of Knowledge: Christian Spirituality from the New Testament to St. John of the Cross.* London: Darton, Longman & Todd, 1990.

Wilson, Brittany E. *Unmanly Men: Refigurations of Masculinity in Luke-Acts.* Oxford: Oxford University Press, 2015.

Witherington, Ben, III. *Jesus the Sage: The Pilgrimage of Wisdom.* Minneapolis: Fortress, 1994.

Wolterstorff, Nicholas. *Justice: Rights and Wrongs.* Princeton: Princeton University Press, 2008.

———. *Justice in Love.* Grand Rapids: Eerdmans, 2011.

Wright, N. T. *Surprised by Hope: Rethinking Heaven, the Resurrection, and the Mission of the Church.* New York: HarperOne, 2008.

Yee, Gale A. "The Book of Hosea: Introduction, Commentary, and Reflections." In *The New Interpreter's Bible,* edited by Leander E. Keck, 7:195–297. Nashville: Abingdon, 1996.

Zerwick, Max. *A Grammatical Analysis of the Greek New Testament.* Translated and revised by Mary Grosvenor. 4th ed. Rome: Pontifical Biblical Institute, 1993.

Author Index

Scripture and Ancient Writings Index